W9-BEL-517

Food Science and You

Food Science and You

Kay Yockey Mehas
Home Economics Teacher
Henry D. Sheldon High School
Eugene, Oregon

Sharon Lesley Rodgers
Chemistry Teacher
Henry D. Sheldon High School
Eugene, Oregon

GLENCOE
Macmillan/McGraw-Hill

Send all inquiries to:
GLENCOE DIVISION
Macmillan/McGraw-Hill
3008 W. Willow Knolls Drive
Peoria, IL 61614-1083

ISBN 0-02-677090-3

Printed in the United States of America.

5 6 7 8 9 10 VHJ 99 98 97 96 95 94 93 92

Reviewers:

Dr. Margy Woodburn
College of Home Economics
Oregon State University

Eunice L. Hartman
Penfield Central School District
Penfield, New York

ACKNOWLEDGMENTS

In writing this textbook, we have been encouraged and assisted by many people. Elton Sorensen, Principal of Sheldon High School at the time food science was introduced into the curriculum, and Dan Barnum, Curriculum Vice Principal, gave invaluable support to the interdisciplinary concept that is critical to this text. John Garrett, physics teacher, devoted many hours to helping us determine the content of the course.

We received enthusiastic support for our project from faculty members at Oregon State University. Professors from the College of Home Economics and the College of Agriculture promoted our efforts to introduce food science at the high school level. Dr. Kinsey Green, Dean of the College of Home Economics, assisted by supporting the development of a statewide curriculum guide and offering summer classes in food science.

We particularly appreciate the assistance of Dr. Marge Woodburn, Head of Foods and Nutrition, College of Home Economics, Oregon State University, and Eunice Hartman of New York, who reviewed our original manuscript.

We wish to acknowledge the many students at Sheldon High School who tested the experiments and read and commented on the rough drafts of each chapter, thus providing the input needed to make this a text suitable for high school students.

Finally, I, Kay Mehas, would like to thank my husband, Art, and children, Gustavo and Marina, for their support and understanding during the hours I spent doing research and working at the computer. I, Sharon Rodgers, would like to thank my friend, the Rev. Linda Harrell, for giving me the courage to undertake a project like this, and my mother, Mildred, and brother, Ken Rodgers, for encouraging me every step of the way.

Kay Yockey Mehas
Sharon Lesley Rodgers

TABLE OF CONTENTS

UNIT 1

Introduction to Food Science 12

UNIT 3

UNIT 1

Introduction to Food Science

Food science is a course that has a variety of applications to your everyday life. By applying what you learn about food and how it affects your body, you may develop a healthier lifestyle than you have had in the past. At the same time, you may find an area of this many–faceted field that you will choose to study further after you leave high school.

In Chapter 1, you will be introduced to food science and nutrition. You will become acquainted with the equipment used in the food science laboratory, as well as with safe techniques for carrying out food science experiments.

Next, you will learn some of the factors that are important in the scientific evaluation of food. In Chapter 2, you will discover that appearance, odor, sound, and how food feels in your mouth are just as important as taste in determining whether or not you find a food appealing.

In Chapter 3, you will learn about the materials with which you will work as you study food science. Before you can understand the changes that take place in food as it is processed, preserved, prepared, and then digested by your body, you need to learn the basic scientific information in this chapter.

Chapter 4 contains fundamental information on energy, which is given off or absorbed when changes occur in food. In this chapter, you will learn some of the ways energy is transferred, how energy changes are measured, and what units are used in describing energy changes.

You will learn about the characteristics of acids and bases in Chapter 5. You will study how acids and bases affect health and how important they are in food preparation and preservation.

CHAPTERS

What Is Food Science?

This chapter will help you . . .

- Define the study of food science and describe the main goal of food scientists.
- Explain the interrelationship of food science and nutrition.
- List the six main nutrients and food sources of each.
- Identify scientific equipment found in the laboratory and use it properly.
- Conduct food science experiments safely.
- Write accurate and complete reports on food science experiments.

Terms to Remember

balance
beaker
buret
calibrate
carbohydrates
data
enzymes
Erlenmeyer flask
fat
food science
graduated cylinder
insoluble
meniscus
minerals
nutrient
nutrition
protein
Recommended Dietary Allowances
vitamins

You want to look and feel your best. When you do, you feel good about yourself, have energy and enthusiasm, and can look forward to the challenge of each day. What you eat, how much you eat, and how food is processed, prepared, and preserved play an important part in how you look and feel and how healthy you are.

Studying food science is one way to learn how to have and maintain a healthy body throughout life.

This course will help you be a healthier person throughout your life. You will learn about various ways food is preserved, processed, and prepared. In addition, you will learn what makes food nutritious and how that nutritional value can be maintained.

You will also learn what makes food appealing to people, a crucial factor if they are going to eat it. Of course, what is appetizing to one person may not be to someone else. You may like raw carrots best, while a friend of yours prefers them stir–fried. Both of you may prefer peas to be green rather than olive–brown.

In the study of food, it is important to realize that changes in food can be controlled. Food is made up of chemicals that obey physical and chemical laws. If you find studying and controlling the changes in food interesting, you may decide to pursue one of the many careers in this field.

Food preferences are very personal. Which do you prefer—a fresh apple or applesauce?

INTRODUCTION TO FOOD SCIENCE

Food science is the study of the production, processing, preparation, evaluation, and utilization of food. It is based on many other areas of science such as chemistry, biology, physics, and psychology. Food science uses scientific methods in laboratory experiments to help understand food.

• THE HISTORY OF FOOD SCIENCE

While food science has only recently become a high school course, human beings have been concerned with the chemistry of food since ancient times. However, the most important discoveries relating to food have occurred in the last 200 years. Many of the world's foremost scientists of the late 1700s used food in experiments that led to major scientific advances.

In the early 1800s, increased knowledge of food led to the recognition of a major problem. Scientists realized that harmful substances were being substituted in foods. For example, in England, black pepper sold at that time commonly contained gravel, leaves, twigs, stalks, pepper dust, linseed meal, and ground parts of plants other than pepper. The problem became even more serious when food processing developed into a major industry. Unsafe ingredients or methods used at just one processing plant could harm thousands of people.

Food purity remained a problem until the early 1900s. Then effective methods for detecting harmful substances in foods were developed. These methods, along with new laws,

The production of food is one part of the study of food science.

Food purity is not as great a problem today as it was in the 1800s and early 1900s.

greatly improved food safety. Today even tiny amounts of harmful substances can be detected in food.

● FOOD SCIENCE TODAY

Today we find that food science has many branches, including research to:

- Develop new and better food products.
- Improve processing and storage techniques.
- Determine properties important in safe, high-quality food.

Consequently, food scientists play an important role in today's world. Through their work, they have the opportunity to improve the quality of food available to human beings everywhere.

A Metric Dictionary

This text uses the metric system because it is the standard system of measurement used by scientists all over the world. The metric system is based on the decimal system of numbers and involves multiples of ten.

Instead of such familiar units of measurement as ounces, quarts, and pounds, the metric system uses the units shown below. When measuring, metric symbols are used instead of the words. These symbols are not followed by a period.

Metric Units

Unit	Symbol	Measures
gram	g	mass
liter (LEET–ur)	L	volume
meter (MEET–ur)	m	length
degrees Celsius (SELL–see–us)	°C	temperature

The metric units shown below are combined with prefixes to show how much of a unit is being measured. Kilo (KEY–low) is the prefix for 1000 units. Its symbol is k. For example, 1000 meters would be a kilometer (km) while 1000 grams would be a kilogram (kg).

The prefix centi means one–hundredth or 0.01 of a unit, and its symbol is c. One–hundredth of a gram would be a centigram (cg), while one–hundredth of a meter would be a centimeter (cm).

Milli is the prefix for one–thousandth of a unit or 0.001. Its symbol is m. One–thousandth of a liter would be a milliliter (mL), while one–thousandth of a meter would be a millimeter (mm).

The following list will give you some idea of how metric measures compare with the common measures used in the United States.

- 1 gram = 1/28 ounce
- 1 kilogram = 2.2 pounds
- 1 liter = 1.057 quarts
- 1 meter = 1.1 yards
- 1 centimeter = 0.39 inch

FOOD SCIENCE AND NUTRITION

The study of food science goes hand in hand with the study of **nutrition.** Nutrition is the scientific understanding of how food is used by the body. Many of the current areas of research in food science grew out of a desire to provide food that has the highest nutritional value to as many people as possible. More efficient harvesting methods, new ways of processing food, and improved packaging have been developed. These procedures make it easier to feed and maintain the health of people throughout the world.

What metric units would you use to measure these food products?

• NUTRIENTS YOU NEED

A **nutrient** is a substance found in food which is needed for life and growth. Nutrients can be used by the body to function, grow, repair itself, and produce energy. There are six main nutrients needed by the human body to remain healthy.

Today food scientists conduct research to improve the quality of food.

Water is an essential nutrient. Lack of water can cause death more quickly than lack of any other nutrient. This is because the chemical reactions that occur in the body take place in water. It is suggested that each person drink six to eight glasses of water each day. Other fluids consumed would be in addition to the water.

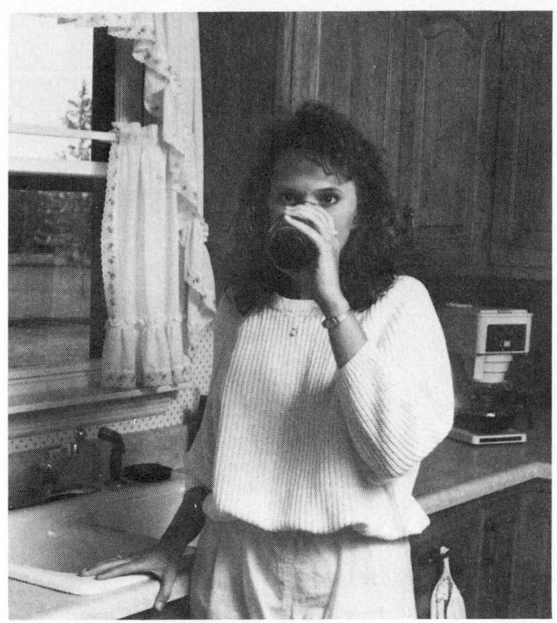

Drinking six to eight glasses of water a day helps maintain a healthy body.

Carbohydrates (kar–bo–HY–drayts) are nutrients that provide the body with energy. Sugars are carbohydrates that provide quick energy but have almost no other nutritional value. Other kinds of carbohydrates are cereals, grains like rice and oats, and legumes such as beans and peas. These carbohydrates release energy more slowly and also supply the body with other nutrients.

Fats are also nutrients needed by the body. They are a concentrated source of energy. Many people in the United States eat too much fat. Sources of fat include butter, margarine, and nuts. Food that is deep–fat fried, such as potato chips or French fries, add fat to the diet.

Proteins are nutrients that allow the body to grow and to heal after injury. Because of their role in the body, proteins are often called the body's building blocks. In addition, proteins serve other specialized purposes in the body. For example, **enzymes** (EN–zimes) are proteins that control chemical activity in living organisms. Sources of protein include meat, eggs, poultry, fish, rice, beans, and legumes such as peanuts.

Foods rich in protein are needed so the body can build and repair tissues.

Vitamins and **minerals** are nutrients needed in only small amounts in the body. However, they are critical to life. Vitamins are involved in the chemical reactions in the body. Minerals become part of the body's bones, tissues, and fluids. Fruits, vegetables, grains, and dairy products are good sources of vitamins and minerals.

• RDA FOR NUTRIENTS

To help people know how much of each nutrient they need for good nutrition, the United States government has developed **Recommended Dietary Allowances,** or RDA. RDA have been established for protein, ten vitamins, and six minerals. The RDA are reconsidered every five years by scientists from the Food and Nutrition Board of the National Academy of Sciences–National Research Council. Sometimes, the RDA for a particular nutrient will be revised if research shows that more or less of the nutrient is needed for good health. RDA include a margin of safety. Generally, they are about 30 percent higher than the average requirement.

Specific RDA are available for 17 groupings based on age, sex, pregnancy, and lactation. The RDA are only recommended, not required amounts. Specific conditions may alter the nutritional needs of a given person. For example, medical problems can change a person's needs. A physician would then recommend revised amounts of certain nutrients. Some people have a condition which causes the body to store too much of the mineral iron. These people need to limit their iron intake to remain healthy.

The U.S. government has established RDA for various groups of people based on age, sex, pregnancy, and lactation.

Computer programs can help you discover whether you are meeting the RDA for your sex and age group.

RDA are mostly used by people who work in food science, nutrition, or health care. The United States Food and Drug Administration has developed a simpler version of the RDA for consumers. These dietary guidelines are known as the United States Recommended Daily Allowances (U.S. RDA). They are average amounts of nutrients that will generally meet the needs of all people in a given age group. U.S. RDA are used in nutrition labeling of food products.

Many computer programs now exist which you can use to find out whether what you eat provides your body with the RDA for your age and sex. If such programs are available at your school, you may want to use them to see if your diet is a healthy one. You can also use data tables to find out whether or not your diet meets the RDA.

NUTRITION AND HEALTH

What you eat is important in how you feel. Your eating habits will also play a role in how healthy you are many years from now. Developing good eating habits may help you avoid being overweight or having heart disease or diabetes later in life.

Because habits can be hard to change, it is important to be aware of what you eat now. For example, do you eat an orange or potato chips for an after-school snack? If you need some-

Habits established at a young age can have a lifelong effect on nutrition and health.

NUTRITION AND YOU

Personalizing Diets

People have different dietary needs at different stages of life. Therefore tables for the Recommended Dietary Allowances (RDA) are divided into categories for infants, children, males, females, pregnant women, and lactating (milk-producing) women. In some cases, these categories are further divided by age. The values listed in the tables are specific for each category of person.

For example, infants and children generally need smaller amounts of the nutrients than mature adults do. However, they require more nutrients per unit of body weight because of their rapid growth. Adolescent males require more of some vitamins than teenage females. After growth stops, males need less iron than females. Women generally need more calcium throughout their lives than men do. Females who are pregnant or lactating must consume more of virtually all nutrients to remain healthy.

Older people often are not as active as they were when younger. As a result, they need to eat food that does not provide as much energy, yet is high in nutritional value. This is why older people are encourage to eat fruits and vegetables and to avoid fat, sugar, and excess protein.

It is important that athletes eat well-balanced diets. Eating properly enables them to develop greater endurance, lose excess body weight, and strengthen muscles. Frequently athletes eat food high in carbohydrate because it provides the energy needed to perform well.

Strenuous workouts may cause athletes to lose large quantities of water as well as minerals dissolved in the water. This is particularly true when athletes train or compete in hot weather. The water lost helps maintain body temperature. Therefore athletes need to drink extra fluid to keep their bodies functioning effectively.

thing at midmorning, do you eat an apple or a doughnut? You may be active enough to burn off the extra energy from the doughnut or the fat from the potato chips. However, these same foods may cause problems in 20–30 years if you are still eating them on a regular basis.

Just as teenagers often eat food the body does not need, they also often omit nutrients that are crucial to good health. For example, growing people need larger amounts of iron than those who are not growing. However, many teens do not eat enough iron–rich food. Many teen diets also lack specific vitamins.

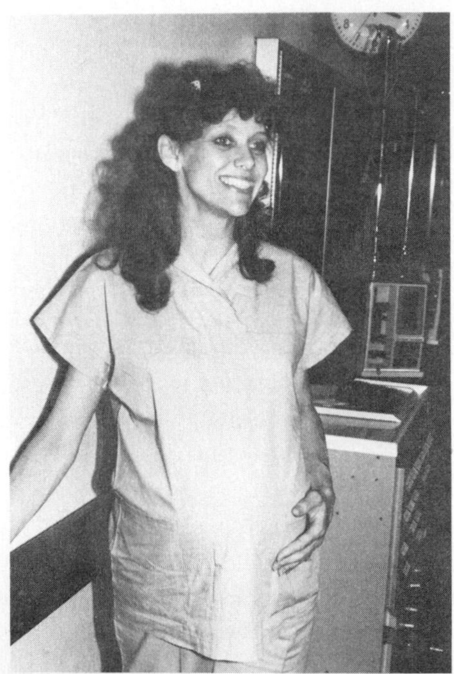

Specific RDAs for pregnant women have been developed because the nutritional health of the baby depends on the nutritional health of the mother.

LABORATORY EQUIPMENT

While studying food science, you will use some equipment usually found in any foods laboratory, such as the stove, the food dehydrator, the food processor or blender, and kitchen utensils. You will also use equipment normally found in chemistry or biology laboratories. Some of the most important pieces of laboratory equipment are pictured on page 23.

• LABORATORY CONTAINERS

A **beaker** is a container with a wide mouth and is used for holding solids or liquids. The markings on a beaker are not very accurate, so you should not use it for measuring unless only approximate amounts are needed.

A **graduated cylinder** is a tall cylindrical container used for measuring the volume of a liquid. The markings on it are accurate, so you

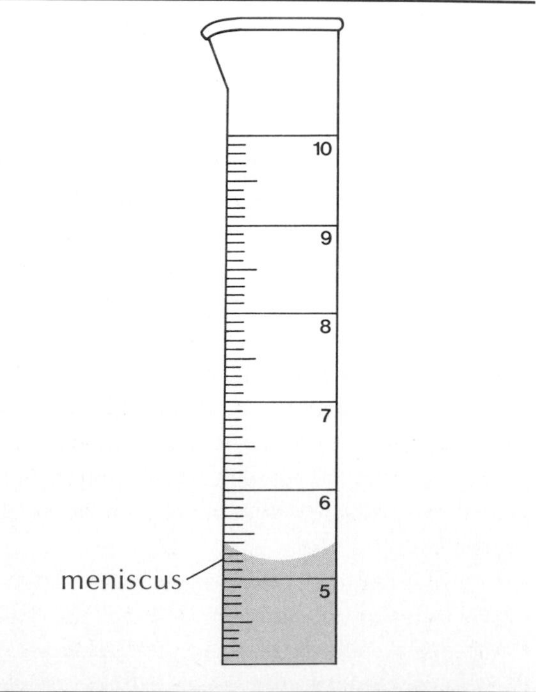

How much liquid is in this graduated cylinder?

This laboratory equipment is used in food science experiments.

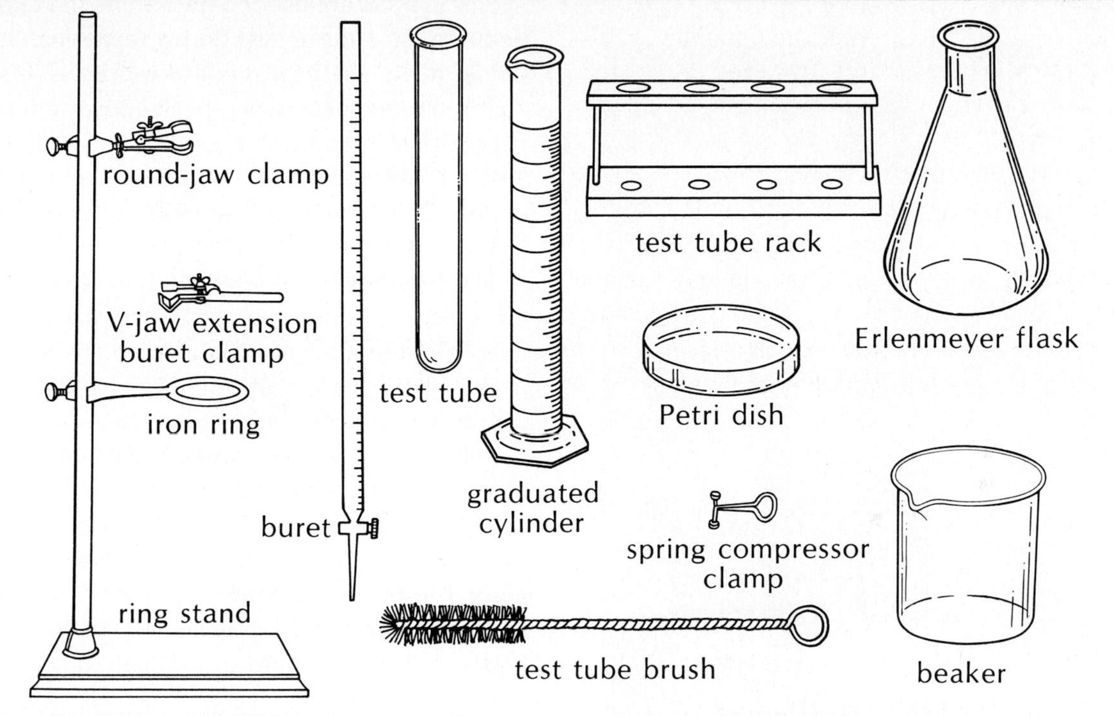

would use a graduated cylinder for making precise measurements. When you use a graduated cylinder, read the amount of liquid in it from eye level. The volume is read from the **meniscus** (muh–NIS–kus), which is the bottom of the curve the liquid forms in the cylinder. Sometimes the meniscus is not exactly at a marking line. Then the volume is estimated to tenths of the smallest units on the scale. For example, if the cylinder is marked in milliliters, you would estimate the volume of the liquid to tenths of a milliliter.

A test tube is a container used to hold a small quantity of solid or liquid. Test tube brushes are used for washing out test tubes or other narrow pieces of equipment. A test tube rack will hold several test tubes at once.

An **Erlenmeyer flask** (UR–lun–my–ur) is a cone–shaped container with a narrow neck and a broad, flat bottom. It can be used to swirl liquid without spilling it.

A **buret** (byur–ET) is a long thin glass cylinder calibrated to 0.1 mL. It is used to transfer very precise amounts of liquid in experiments.

A Petri dish (PEA–tree) is a shallow glass or plastic dish with a loose–fitting cover. You will use a Petri dish later in this course when you are growing bacteria.

Ring stands, iron rings, and clamps are devices used to hold equipment. A ring stand is a metal pole mounted in a base to which a clamp or an iron ring can be attached. Iron rings often hold beakers or flasks, while clamps support test tubes, thermometers, or burets.

A ring stand is used to hold equipment during experiments.

• THERMOMETERS

Thermometers are used to determine the temperature of substances during experiments. Unlike those used for medical purposes, laboratory thermometers are not shaken down. To get accurate readings, you must be careful to always have the bulb of the thermometer completely immersed in the substance being tested.

Since scientists throughout the world use the Celsius temperature scale, the laboratory thermometers that you will use are calibrated in Celsius degrees. In addition, Celsius degrees will be used in this textbook. However, most appliances produced in the United States are marked only in degrees Fahrenheit. Candy thermometers, which are produced primarily for home use, also usually use the Fahrenheit scale. Therefore Fahrenheit equivalents will be given in parentheses when needed so you will know what temperature to use.

Calibrating Measuring Equipment

In food science, you will use a variety of equipment to measure mass, volume, and temperature. How can you be sure that your equipment is measuring precisely?

To ensure accuracy, measuring equipment or instruments are calibrated. To **calibrate** (KAL–uh–brayt) means to check, adjust, or standardize the marks on a measuring instrument. The better the calibration, the more precisely an instrument can measure. For example, a ruler that is marked in centimeters gives only a general measurement of length. One that is calibrated in millimeters can give a more precise measurement.

Sometimes equipment must be calibrated each time you use it. For example, temperature is very important in making candy. To be sure that the thermometer you are using is accurate, you need to calibrate it before you begin making the candy.

Place the thermometer in boiling water and read the temperature of the water. Water normally boils at 100°C. Determine how far above or below 100°C the reading on your thermometer is. This is the adjustment you will need to make when using the thermometer for the candy. If your thermometer shows water boils at 102°C, you will need to add two degrees to the temperature given in your candy recipe.

Celsius and Fahrenheit

The Celsius temperature scale is used in the metric system. The Fahrenheit temperature scale is the one in common use in the United States. On the Celsius scale, the freezing point of water is 0° and the boiling point of water is 100°. On the Fahrenheit scale, the freezing point of water is 32° and the boiling point of water is 212°. Therefore a Celsius degree represents more of a temperature change than a Fahrenheit degree. This is because there are only 100 Celsius degrees between the freezing point and boiling point of water, while there are 180 Fahrenheit degrees between these two points.

If you should ever need to change Celsius degrees to Fahrenheit degrees, the formula is shown below.

$$°F = \frac{9}{5} °C + 32$$

The formula for changing Fahrenheit to Celsius is shown below.

$$°C = \frac{5}{9} (°F - 32)$$

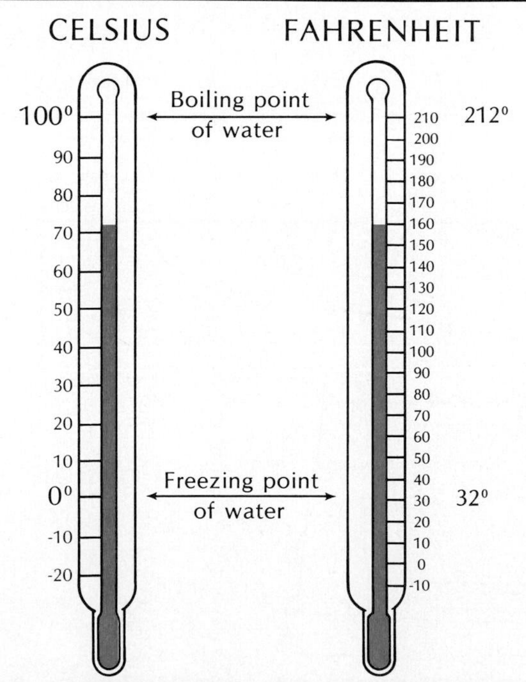

The Celsius and Fahrenheit scales use different temperature readings for the boiling and freezing points of water.

THE BALANCE

A **balance** is a scientific instrument that determines the mass of materials. Mass is a measure of the amount of matter in a sample. Technically, finding the mass of something on a balance is known as "massing" it.

The term "weighing" refers to using a spring scale to measure weight. Weight is the gravitational attraction between an object and the earth. An object's weight changes as the distance between the object and the center of the earth changes. An object becomes weightless when it gets far enough into space.

Unlike weight, mass is constant. No matter where it is measured, the same value is always determined. While you may see and hear the terms used interchangably, "mass" and "massing" will be used in this text when referring to the use of a balance.

A balance has a platform on the left, called a pan, on which the object or material to be massed is placed. To the right are three arms, or beams, that join together at a pointer. The beams hold weights, called riders, of various sizes and are calibrated beginning at zero. The pointer should be free to swing up and down in front of a scale that has a zero line in the middle. When the pan is empty and all the riders on the beams are set on zero, the pointer should come to rest on the zero line or swing an equal distance above and below the line. You will learn how to use the balance in Experiment 1–1.

Caring for the Balance

It is important to be careful with all laboratory equipment. It is especially important that you treat your balance with care because it is an expensive piece of equipment needed for your food science experiments.

You must never attempt to mass items heavier than the balance can handle. While liquids are obviously massed in a container, solids should be massed either in a container or on a piece of weighing or waxed paper. *You should never mass chemicals directly on the pan of the balance*. Should you spill any solid or liquid chemical on the balance, be sure to clean it off immediately. This will help prevent rusting or corroding of the balance pan.

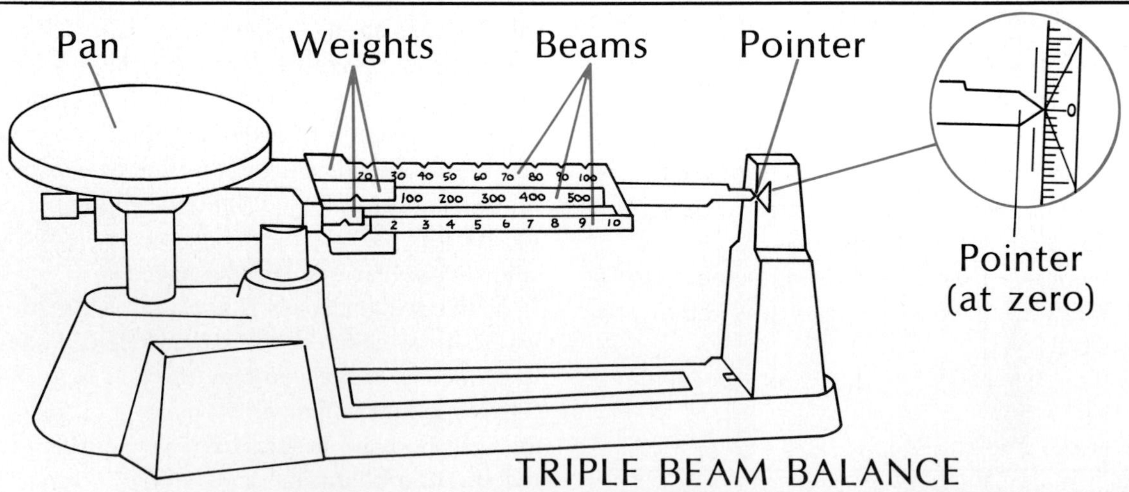

The triple beam balance is used to find the mass of substances during food science experiments.

LABORATORY SAFETY

During your study of food science, you will carry out many experiments to more fully understand the chemistry of food. Therefore it is important that you know how to work safely in a food laboratory.

● PREPARING FOR AN EXPERIMENT

When an experiment is scheduled, carefully read through the experiment *before* coming to class. If you have questions, ask them before beginning the experiment, rather than simply hoping you will be able to "figure it out" as you go along.

On the day of an experiment, dress with safety in mind. Don't wear coats, jackets, or sweaters with bulky sleeves that could knock over supplies or equipment. If your teacher instructs you to wear safety goggles or aprons, be sure you keep them on throughout the experiment.

Before you actually begin an experiment, check to see that you have all the equipment and materials you need. This will save you time later in the class period and should help you achieve better results. In addition, *wash your hands before you begin any food experiment.*

● WORKING IN THE LABORATORY

While carrying out any experiment, be sure to follow these general guidelines:

- Work in a logical, organized manner.
- Keep your work space as uncluttered as possible.
- Wash items and put them away as you finish with them.
- Dispose of any paper materials or garbage properly and promptly.
- Keep drawers and cupboard doors closed except when removing or replacing items.

Using proper procedures in the laboratory will keep you and others safe.

Beakers should not be heated directly on the stove burner.

In any experiment, careful measurements are essential for accurate results and for safety. Read and measure carefully.

If you get something on your hands, wash them immediately. Never lick your fingers. If you sneeze, cough, or touch your face or hair during an experiment, wash your hands before continuing with your work.

Be sure to do all cutting on a cutting board. This will protect your fingers from being cut. A cutting board also protects the counter or table where you are working.

It is important to pay attention and stay alert during laboratory work. For example, if your laboratory partner removes a beaker from the stove and you try to pick it up with your bare hand, you will get burned! Hot glass looks just like cold glass. Therefore you need to know where a glass has been most recently to know if it is safe to handle. Depending on the container, hot glass should be handled with tongs or a pot holder. You could also wear heat resistant gloves when handling hot glass.

Keeping pan handles away from the outer edge of the stove can help prevent accidents.

When you use the stove, you need to take special precautions. Be careful not to reach across the heated surface units or lighted gas burners. Always use a metal trivet or a special pad when you heat a beaker on the stove. Never heat an empty beaker or allow the solution in one to completely boil away. The beaker will break.

When you heat substances in a pan, turn the handle away from the outer edge of the stove. Then there will be no danger of knocking the pan to the floor as you work around the stove. If you heat something in a pan with the lid on, remove the lid by tilting it so it opens away from you. Otherwise steam may burn you. Be sure to use pot holders when handling hot pans.

• AFTER AN EXPERIMENT

When you have completed an experiment, it is important to:

- Replace all equipment in its proper place.
- Turn off all stove elements and the oven.
- Thoroughly clean the countertops, sink, and stove.
- Wash your hands well.
- Place towels and dishcloths in the designated area.

Some substances you will use in experiments are **insoluble** (in–SAHL–yuh–bul) in water. Insoluble means the material does not dissolve. Fat and egg shells are examples of materials that don't dissolve in water. Never discard any water–insoluble substance in a sink. Wrap it in paper towels and place it carefully in a wastebasket.

If you spill anything on the floor, clean it up immediately. If you drop a utensil on the floor, always wash it before reuse. Clean up any glassware you break by sweeping or brushing it into a dust pan and carefully placing it in a wastebasket. Do not handle broken glass with your hands, or you may cut yourself. Instead, if you cannot use a brush or broom, protect your hands with a paper towel.

If you have an accident, *immediately report it to your teacher*. Follow the first aid or clean up instructions you are given.

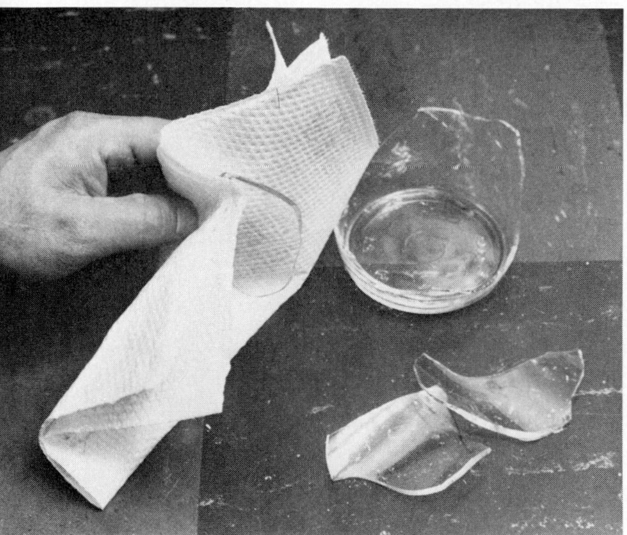

Protect yourself from cuts when cleaning up broken glass.

REPORTING EXPERIMENTAL RESULTS

Laboratory experiments are an extremely important part of a food science course. To learn as much as possible from these experiments, you should adopt an organized format for reporting your laboratory results. The format used in this book is shown on page 30.

Laboratory reports are usually kept in a notebook. Each report contains several steps or parts. Before you come to class, write the purpose and procedures portions of the report in your notebook. Completing these parts first will help you better understand what you are to do during class.

Follow the procedure to conduct the experiment. Then record your observations and findings in a data table. Do any required calculations and answer the questions. Finally, draw a conclusion about the experiment.

Writing your results and conclusions in a laboratory notebook is the final step in an experiment.

Reporting Laboratory Results

TITLE OF EXPERIMENT
PERFORMED BY (YOUR NAME)
PARTNER'S NAME
DATE

PURPOSE

State the goal of the experiment or the problem to be solved. You should learn this from reading the experiment.

PROCEDURE

It is not necessary to copy the procedure word for word. Read the experiment and write a *brief* summary. Tell the general routine of the experiment so that another student could read it and know roughly what you did.

RESULTS

Observations: These are brief descriptive statements of what you actually observe happening. They are to be made at every possible point in an experiment. They should be an honest record. This means your observations may not always agree with what the instructions say should be happening. Careful observations will make it easier to complete your report.

Data: Data (DAY–tuh) are the information you gather during the experiment. They normally are arranged most efficiently in a table or chart. Each experiment will suggest a format for a sample data table. The columns of the table and the individual number values must be properly labeled.

Calculations: Your calculations will include the solutions to any mathematical questions asked in the instructions.

Questions: Answer the questions included at the end of the instruction for each experiment.

CONCLUSION

Your conclusion may be a general statement summarizing your results. It may also be the final figure of the calculations done during the experiment.

EXPERIMENT 1–1

Using a Triple Beam Balance

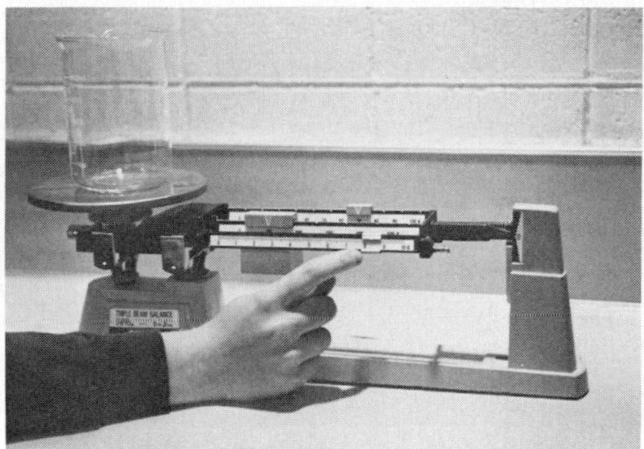

You are going to have many opportunities to mass substances in food science. Therefore one of the first skills you need to learn is how to use a balance, the instrument you will use to mass materials. This experiment is designed to teach you to use a laboratory balance.

At each laboratory station you will find either a low–form or a high–form triple beam balance. Either form is simply called a balance. If the balance does not zero properly, ask your teacher to correct the problem.

PROCEDURE

1. Obtain three objects to be massed from your teacher.
2. Place one object on the balance pan with all the riders set on zero. This will cause the pointer to point to the top of the scale.
3. Move the 100 g rider out to the first notch on its beam. If the pointer drops all the way to the bottom of the scale, 100 g is too much. You would then return this rider to zero. If the pointer does not drop, move the weight to the 200 g mark. Again, if this is too heavy, move it back to 100 g.
4. Next move the 10 g rider along its beam, one notch at a time, until the pointer drops to the bottom of the scale. When this happens, move the rider back to the previous notch.
5. Now slide the 1 g rider along its arm until the pointer settles exactly at zero.
6. You are ready to read the balance. The mass of the object on the balance is the sum of the values of the three riders. Assume the weights on your balance are arranged as follows—the first is on the 100 g notch, the second is on the 60 g notch, and the last is at what you estimate to be 2.65 g (meaning it is halfway between 2.6–2.7). The mass of the object is 162.65 grams.
7. In a data table similar to the sample data table shown below, record the name of the object and its mass.
8. Mass each of the other objects and record the information in your data table.

QUESTIONS

1. Do you think a penny would have a mass closer to 1 g, 10 g, or 100 g?
2. If you had to determine the mass of 10 mL water, how would you do it?

SAMPLE DATA TABLE

Object	Mass

EXPERIMENT 1–2

Using a Graduated Cylinder

Volume is the amount of space material occupies. It can be determined in a number of ways. For objects such as a cube or a rectangular solid, you measure the length, width, and height and multiply these values to find the volume. Liquids are even easier to work with. You simply pour the liquid into a container that has volume measurements marked on it and read the level of the liquid. In food science, you will often use a graduated cylinder for volume measurements. You will recall that it is important to read the volume from the meniscus, or the bottom of the curve the liquid forms, and to estimate the volume to one–tenth of the smallest division on the scale.

PROCEDURE

1. Fill your 100 mL beaker with water to the 20 mL line.
2. Pour this water into a 100 mL graduated cylinder. Read and record the volume of the water in your data table.
3. Repeat step 2 with 30 mL water.
4. Repeat step 2 with 25 mL water. You will need to estimate the amount you think will be 25 mL.

QUESTIONS

1. How precise were the volume readings in the beaker?
2. Which piece of equipment is calibrated more precisely, the beaker or the graduated cylinder?
3. Why do you suppose graduated cylinders cost three times as much as beakers of similar volume?

SAMPLE DATA TABLE

Beaker Reading	Graduated Cylinder Reading
20 mL	
30 mL	
25 mL	

TO SUM UP

- Food science is the study of the production, processing, preparation, evaluation, and utilization of food.
- The major advances in food science have occurred over the last 200 years.
- Today food scientists work to improve the quality of food available.
- The six main nutrients needed for life and growth are water, carbohydrates, fat, protein, vitamins, and minerals.
- The Recommended Dietary Allowances (RDA) are levels of protein, vitamins, and minerals suggested for good health.
- The study of food science involves using equipment and supplies from both the foods and science laboratories.
- Using good safety habits is important in conducting successful food science experiments.
- An organized format for reporting laboratory results helps you learn the most from the experiments you perform.

CHECK YOUR FACTS

1. Define food science.
2. What led to an increase in food purity in the early 1900s?
3. Identify the six main nutrients.
4. How often and why are the RDA revised?
5. For what purpose are graduated cylinders used?
6. What piece of equipment would you use if you wanted to be able to swirl a liquid?
7. Why is it important to clean up materials spilled on the pan of a balance?
8. On the day of an experiment, why should you read through the experiment before coming to class?
9. Why is it important to stop heating a beaker before the liquid in it boils away?
10. List three tasks you should do at the end of an experiment before leaving your laboratory station.
11. What kinds of materials can be discarded in the sink?

CRITICAL THINKING AND PROBLEM SOLVING

1. Compare and contrast food science and nutrition.
2. Why are there no RDA for carbohydrate and fat?
3. Explain the differences and similarities of RDA and U.S. RDA.
4. Explain how to read the volume of a liquid in a graduated cylinder.
5. Why should you never fill a graduated cylinder above the top line on the scale?
6. If you needed a container to hold a sample of liquid, how would you decide whether to use a beaker or an Erlenmeyer flask?
7. What would you do if a sample of liquid whose temperature you needed to determine was not deep enough to cover the thermometer bulb?
8. Explain the differences between massing and weighing an object.
9. Explain how you would mass 10 g table salt on the balance.
10. What does it mean if the pointer on your balance rests at the bottom of the scale?

CHAPTER

2

The Scientific Evaluation of Food

This chapter will help you . . .

- Define sensory evaluation.
- Identify the qualities that make up the sensory characteristics of food.
- List qualifications needed for a career in sensory evaluation.
- Explain what sensory evaluation panels do and how they are conducted.
- Describe characteristics of successful sensory testing.
- Discuss factors affecting people's food preferences.

Terms to Remember

flavor
garnishes
monosodium glutamate
mouthfeel
sensory characteristics
sensory evaluation
sensory evaluation panels
taste blind
taste buds
volatile

If you have ever cooked a meal for a group of people, you know that even the most perfectly prepared food may not appeal to everyone. People have different preferences where food is concerned, just as they do about other things. Determining what food people like and why they like it is a part of the job of those who work in **sensory evaluation.** Sensory evaluation involves scientifically testing food using the human senses of sight, smell, taste, touch, and hearing.

SENSORY EVALUATION: A SCIENTIFIC APPROACH

The qualities of a food identified by the senses are called **sensory characteristics.** These include the food's appearance, odor, taste, feel in the mouth, and sound. You use the interaction of your senses to measure food quality. Whether you judge a food acceptable depends on how the food affects your senses.

The effects of changes in ingredients, processing, or storage on food quality are reflected in its sensory characteristics. People are often able to sense such changes before chemical tests can.

• APPEARANCE

The color of food is critical in its appearance. Anyone who has read the book *Green Eggs and Ham* by Dr. Seuss knows how unappetizing such a meal sounds. Likewise, blue potatoes or purple applesauce will not appeal to most people. Even though a food may taste delicious, you have preconceived ideas about how it should look. Green vegetables should be bright green, not olive drab. Corn should be light yellow rather than mustard–colored.

The natural color of a food may indicate how ripe it is. For example, a greenish banana is not quite ripe. Color also tells if a food is past its prime. When bananas have many dark spots on their skins, they may be fine for banana bread but too ripe and soft for fruit salad.

Combinations of colors on a plate are as important as each one is individually. For example, think of broiled breast of chicken, mashed potatoes, steamed cauliflower, and canned pears. Now picture broiled breast of

The appearance, odor, taste, feel in the mouth, and sound of a food affect whether you like it or not.

The deep yellow color and brown spots on these bananas indicate they are too ripe to be the best quality for eating fresh.

chicken, a baked potato, steamed broccoli, and canned peach slices. Which meal would catch your eye in a cafeteria dinner display?

Garnishes are an easy way to add color and increase the attractiveness of food.

Color can also be added with **garnishes.** A garnish is a decorative arrangement added to food or drink. A sprig of parsley, a cinnamon apple slice, or a leaf of lettuce can add color and eye appeal to food. The use of color in food and garnishes is an important part of planning attractive, appealing meals.

Other factors also affect how appetizing food appears. A variety of textures is important. Can you imagine a plate where all the foods have the consistency of runny catsup? This would seem unappetizing no matter how attractive the colors were! The size and shape of food also affects appearance. If all the food on a plate is prepared in 1 cm cubes, it would be unappetizing to most people. A variety of sizes and shapes creates an appearance that is pleasing to the eye.

Too many foods of the same shape are not as appealing as foods with a variety of shapes.

● ODOR

After you have looked at a food and decided it is appealing enough to sample, your nose plays a crucial role. The sense of smell is an important part of food evaluation. Entering a home where bread is baking can make a person instantly hungry because the bread's aroma is so appealing. Odor can also be a safety mechanism, since a food's odor may warn that it is not safe to eat.

The smell of baking cookies adds to their appeal.

● FLAVOR

The sensory characteristic most often associated with food is its **flavor.** Flavor is the distinctive taste that comes from a food's unique blend of appearance, odor, feel, and sound. Flavor is a complicated trait that involves several senses.

Taste Buds

Once you take a food sample into your mouth, your sense of taste contributes to your perception of the food's flavor. Flavor is sensed by the **taste buds,** which are sensory organs located on various parts of the tongue. There are four types of taste buds, which register sweet, salty, bitter, or sour flavors. The tip of the tongue is sensitive to sweet and salty, the sides of the tongue respond to sour, and the back of the tongue tastes bitter flavors.

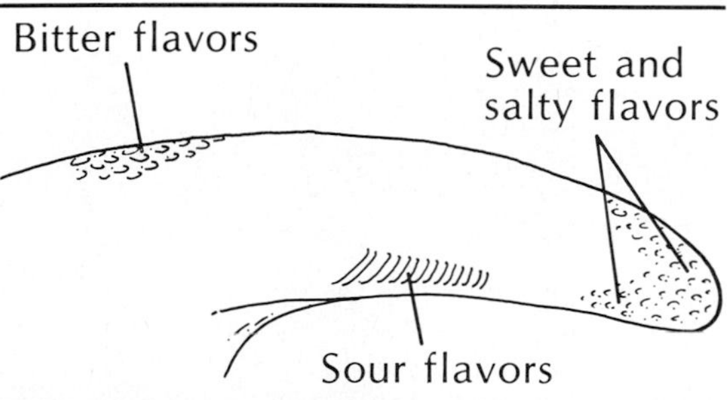

The taste buds on your tongue sense the flavor of the food you eat.

Taste Blindness

Some people are called **taste blind** because they cannot distinguish between the flavors of some foods. They may be taste blind because they suffer from certain diseases or because of treatments, such as radiation or chemotherapy for cancer. Much more common is the temporary taste blindness that results when sufferers of head colds are not able to smell and therefore, to a large extent, not able to taste.

Flavor Enhancers

Some chemicals enhance the flavors present in food. A common flavor enhancer is **monosodium glutamate** (mahn–uh–SO–dee–um GLOOT–uh–mayt), or MSG. If you check the ingredient lists on packaged food and spice blends, you will find that MSG is frequently included. The reason MSG is so widely used is that it increases the intensity of both salty and sweet flavors.

Unfortunately, MSG may cause some people to have headaches. This is sometimes known as "Chinese food syndrome" because Chinese food often contains high levels of MSG.

Mushrooms usually contain the same chemical found in MSG. That is why many food scientists feel that mushrooms enhance the total flavor of almost any dish.

TEMPERATURE

The intensity of the flavor of most food varies with its temperature. Flavors are influenced by **volatile** (VALL–uh–til) substances. Volatile means that the substance evaporates easily. In food preparation, volatile substances are usually released during heating and may affect the sense of smell.

Warm pizza has a different taste than cold pizza because heat causes the smell of the warm pizza to reach the nose.

If a food sample is too cold to cause the flavors to reach the nose, the food will not taste the way it tastes when warm. Likewise, a food that is normally served very cold may taste too strong if it is warm.

• MOUTHFEEL

Mouthfeel is a scientific term that describes how a food feels in the mouth. Mouthfeel can be illustrated by the statement, "I don't mind the taste of liver, but I hate the way it feels." Some people love peanuts yet dislike peanut butter because they don't like how it feels against the roof of the mouth.

There are many terms used to describe how something feels when touched—soft, smooth, rough, or solid. These terms can also be used to describe how food feels in the mouth. However, instead of fingers doing the feeling, it is the lips and tongue. For example, good ice cream feels smooth to the tongue, not granular. Beans in bean soup should be firm, but not tough or hard.

When food is tested, a variety of words and terms are used to describe certain aspects of mouthfeel. For example, texture can be discussed in terms of graininess, thickness, brittleness, or chewiness. Chewiness can be described as hard, tough, moderately chewy, slightly tender, or very tender.

Tenderness is an important quality in sensory evaluation. It is one characteristic that can be precisely measured by a machine. The machine measures the amount of pressure needed to cause the food to give or break.

Mouthfeel is also affected by temperature. A steak that is chewy and feels good in your mouth when hot may be undesirable when cold.

● SOUND

Finally, the sound of food affects how you feel about it. Crumbly crackers or potato chips with no snap have little appeal to most people. Cereal that seems quite tasty at first can become unappetizing if it sits in milk long enough to become soggy.

Mouthfeel is one reason some people don't like peanut butter.

The texture of a food affects its mouthfeel. What differences would there be in the mouthfeel of these foods?

WORKING IN SENSORY EVALUATION

Sensory evaluation can be a satisfying career for a person who is interested in science and food. A four–year college degree can be earned in Food Science and Technology or Foods in Business with an emphasis on sensory evaluation. This can lead to a career with unlimited personal and financial rewards. The woman who is the head of sensory evaluation for a popular United States candy company makes decisions affecting the entire company while earning a top salary.

A career in sensory evaluation involves working with people as well as with scientific principles. People are the "tools" or measuring instruments in sensory testing. Those who work in this field must know nearly as much about how the human mind works as they do about food. This helps them design sensory tests that will produce valid results. For example, people most often select items labeled "1" or "A" as the best. Therefore sensory testers use random three–digit numbers to label samples during testing. This helps prevent the labels used from affecting the results.

NUTRITION AND YOU

Sensory Characteristics and Nutrition

The sensory qualities of food can have a major effect on how well nourished people are. Food is often selected on the basis of sensory appeal rather than nutritional value. Nutritious food that does not have an appealing appearance, odor, flavor or mouthfeel is not apt to be eaten. People interested in helping others eat nutritiously use sensory qualities to increase the appeal of nutritious foods.

One of the factors sensory evaluators consider in developing new food products is texture. Most people prefer food to have a variety of textures. Few people enjoy meals that consist entirely of food that is soft and mushy. Nonetheless, there are situations in which people are forced to choose to consume only liquids.

Some people must consume liquid or semi-liquid diets because of medical conditions or injuries. One of the greatest problems they have is boredom. Eating food that is always the same consistency can become very unappealing. As a result, people may not eat enough to remain healthy. Using a variety of flavors and odors may help overcome these problems.

Frequently people on liquid diets are trying to lose weight. However, a liquid diet can be dangerous and should be undertaken only under a doctor's supervision. There are two main types of liquid formulas for dieting. One is the complete meal formula. The other is liquid protein. Most liquid proteins must carry a warning label that says that use of the product for weight reduction without medical supervision can cause serious illness or death. These products need to be used with great care.

As people age, they may have trouble with appetite because the ability to taste certain flavors declines. For some older people, most food tastes the same—it has no taste at all! For these people, the texture, color, and shape of the food on the plate is crucial. These factors may be the only ones that inspire them to eat enough to be well nourished and remain healthy.

Sensory Evaluation Panels

The results obtained during sensory testing have a tremendous impact on the development of food products. Therefore many firms use **sensory evaluation panels** to help judge new or existing food products. These panels are groups of people who evaluate food samples. Sensory evaluation panels fall into three main groups—highly trained experts, laboratory panels, and consumer panels.

Highly trained experts in sensory evaluation may work as a panel or individually. They judge the quality of a product using standards set by the food industry. They are often involved in testing during the production of wines or blends of coffee. These are very complex substances which require the skills of an expert for evaluation. For example, coffee contains over 800 substances that affect flavor.

Laboratory panels do the testing when a company is looking at the effects of certain changes in the quality of a product or when a company is working on developing a new product. These are usually small groups that work at the company's laboratory. Suppose a candy company is considering changes in a popular product. All employees who regularly eat the candy might form a panel to evaluate the proposed changes.

Large consumer panels test food items in settings other than the laboratory of the company making the item. Consumer testing can be conducted in a grocery store, a shopping mall, or at a special market research company. Several hundred people might be involved in the testing. Rather than using scientific terms and scales, testers ask consumers to tell how much they like or dislike the product.

When cereal sits in milk too long, it becomes soggy, changing both its sound and mouthfeel when eaten.

Random three-digit numbering of samples prevents the labels used from affecting experimental results.

• CONDUCTING SENSORY TESTING

There are a number of factors to be considered in planning and carrying out sensory testing in a scientific manner. The testing area needs to be as free from distractions as possible. A controlled atmosphere is best. Factors such as lighting and temperature should be kept at constant levels and outside noises and odors should be eliminated. Often individual booths are used for sensory testing to eliminate distractions.

Experts are used in the sensory evaluation of coffee because it is such a complex substance.

The temperature of all the food samples must be the same. If testing fruit juice, for example, the samples all need to be equally cold. Color differences among samples can be hidden by the use of colored lights. When the testing is a part of developing a new product, an effort is made to serve the food in the way in which it would normally be eaten.

Another factor that is considered is the contrast effect. Presenting a sample of good quality just before one of poor quality often causes panelists to rate the second sample lower than it would normally be rated. Therefore testers present samples in a random order. Usually no more than three samples are evaluated at one time.

The time of day a test is run affects the results. Late morning and midafternoon are generally considered the best times for testing. These are times when people tend to be most alert and most responsive to sensory testing.

Individual booths used in sensory evaluation help control sound, light, and temperature.

The person evaluating the food rinses the mouth with an agent, usually water, between testing the samples. When a fatty food is being tested, the water is often warm. Sometimes a bland food, such as a saltine cracker, is eaten to clear the mouth of the sample's taste.

It is important to remember that all the senses interact to create an opinion about a given food sample. When one sense is eliminated, it often is difficult to evaluate food products. Therefore members of test panels need the use of all their senses for the best results.

WHY YOU LIKE THE FOOD YOU DO

Food, even of excellent quality, still may not be liked by everyone. One factor that may influence the food you like is your cultural heritage. Every region of the world has certain food patterns and tastes that have been passed down through the centuries.

• CULTURAL HERITAGE

In ancient Greece, the diet was very simple and consisted mainly of olive oil, fish, goats' milk and cheese, wine, and bread. Certain flavorings, such as onion, garlic, parsley, oregano, honey, and cinnamon, were used in most Greek dishes. Many Greek recipes have not changed for 2500 years.

While Italians who lived in poverty ate like the Greeks did, members of the upper class of ancient Rome had a very different diet. These Romans enjoyed dairy products, such as cream, milk, cheese, curds, and whey. In addition, they used wheat to produce baked products, such as cakes, cookies, and breads. They also ate exotic foods such as sea urchins.

Meat sold in butcher shops in Rome today is very similar to what was offered in the shops of ancient Rome. Now, as then, the shops are filled with bacon, cracklings, steaks, and chops of both beef and pork. Even the vegetables and fruits enjoyed by classical Romans, such as beets, lettuce, cucumbers, peaches, grapes, and pears, are still part of the modern Italian diet. The diets of Greece and Italy illustrate how a nation's heritage influences the current food choices of its people.

The food patterns of people in the United States have been affected by the heritage of those who settled the country. As people came to the United States, they brought with them the food patterns and preparation methods of

The foods eaten by modern Italians are based on dietary patterns established hundreds of years ago.

their native countries. These have been modified by the availability of food and local customs. The pizza, tacos, and egg rolls that you enjoy today are Americanized versions of foods that came from other countries.

Advertisers try to convince consumers to buy brand names rather than products with the best sensory characteristics.

• OTHER INFLUENCES

How or whether food is enjoyed also depends upon one's level of hunger. In areas where food is very scarce, sensory evaluation is not necessary. Survival is the only concern! However, as people have enough to eat and feel safe in their surroundings, they become more concerned about the subtle differences in the food they consume.

How people evaluate food may be influenced more by the media and advertising than by true personal preferences. For example, a certain brand of mineral water that is highly advertised may be a popular drink. However, it might not win an impartial taste test.

Loyalty to a particular brand is encouraged by advertisers, even though other products may be of equally high quality. An educated consumer will test several products and will buy the one that truly tastes best, regardless of its brand name.

Salt—The Universal Flavoring

Salt is said to be the one truly universal flavoring. It has been used by people all over the world throughout recorded history. Salt gets its name from the Latin word "salarium" because, at one time, Roman soldiers were paid their salaries in salt. Scientists who study the past say most of the settlements of early civilization were in areas where salt was readily available.

In an ancient village near Kona, Hawaii, there is an area filled with stones. These were hollowed out and used as a place to evaporate salt water to provide salt for the fishing village. In ancient China, little cakes of salt were made with the Emperor's likeness stamped on each one. These were used as money.

EXPERIMENT 2–1

Odor Recognition

Normally, the senses of sight, odor, taste, touch, and, sometimes, hearing are used in evaluating food. When one sense is isolated, identification of even well-known samples can be difficult. This experiment will test your ability to identify common products by odor alone.

PROCEDURE

1. Your teacher will provide 15 samples of odorous material, both food and nonfood, in coded containers.
2. You will be blindfolded, and your partner will present each sample for your evaluation. Sniff each of the 15 samples. Your partner will record what you think each sample is on your data table. Your partner should not sniff the samples while presenting them to you.
3. After you have sniffed all 15 samples, help your partner sniff each sample while you record the results.

QUESTIONS

1. How many of the 15 substances did you identify correctly?
2. How many did your partner identify correctly? What was the highest number of correct answers by anyone in the class?
3. What does this experiment tell you about the interaction of the senses?

SAMPLE DATA TABLE

Code	Blindfolded Identification	Actual Identity of Substance

EXPERIMENT 2–2

Flavor Comparison

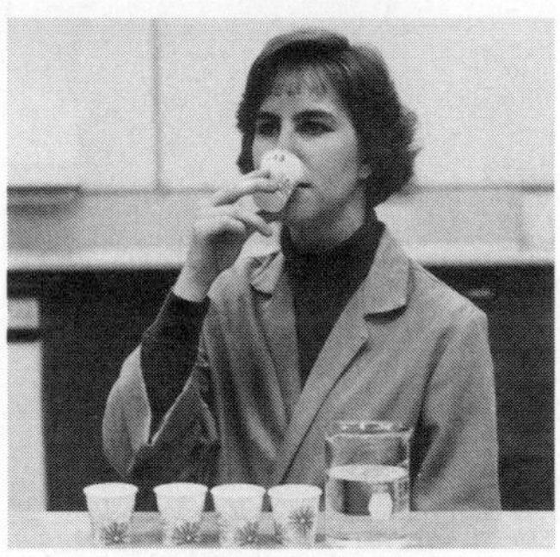

The sense of taste is divided into four categories—sweet, sour, bitter, or salty. In this experiment, you will compare the sweetness of common sugars (sugars are not all equally sweet). Then you will compare the tastes of sour and salty substances. Finally, you will compare your results with those of the class as a whole.

PROCEDURE

1. From your teacher, obtain small samples of the five sugars to be tested.
2. Taste each sample.
3. Rank each sample for sweetness. Write the name of the least sweet sample next to the 1 in your data table and the name of the most sweet sample next to the 5. Write the names of the other samples in order of sweetness next to the 2, 3, and 4.
4. Repeat steps 1–3 with the sour samples. Rank the samples from 1 (least sour) to 5 (most sour).
5. Repeat steps 1–3 with the salty samples. Rank the samples from 1 (least salty) to 5 (most salty).
6. On the chalkboard, record your rank for each substance by its name or letter.

QUESTIONS

1. How do your results on the sugar test compare with the class results? How do they compare with the sweetness of sugars as listed in food science reference books?
2. How do your results on the sour test compare with the class results? How do they compare with the actual amount of sour substances in the samples?
3. How do your results on the salty test compare with the class results? How do they compare with the actual amounts of salt in the samples?
4. In which test did you have the most trouble ranking the samples? Was this also the test in which your results differed most from the class results?
5. What are the four primary tastes?

SAMPLE DATA TABLE

Rank	Sugar Sample	Sour Sample	Salty Sample
1			
2			
3			
4			
5			

REVIEW

TO SUM UP

- Sensory evaluation involves scientifically testing the quality of food using the human senses of sight, smell, taste, touch, and hearing.
- The sensory characteristics of food are appearance, odor, flavor, mouthfeel, and sound.
- Sensory evaluation can be an exciting and satisfying career for a person interested in science and food.
- Sensory evaluation panels help evaluate new and existing food products and can be composed of trained experts or consumers.
- Conditions for successful sensory testing must be highly controlled.
- In addition to the sensory qualities of food, people's food likes and dislikes may be affected by cultural heritage, level of hunger, and advertising.

CHECK YOUR FACTS

1. Define sensory evaluation.
2. What sensory characteristics are used to judge the quality of food?
3. What does it mean to be taste blind?
4. When does food usually have the most intense flavor?
5. Explain the term mouthfeel.
6. Why do sensory testers use three-digit numbers as labels?
7. Why are individual booths generally used for sensory testing?
8. What times of day are best for doing sensory testing? Why?
9. What is the universal flavoring?
10. Name three factors other than flavor that may influence food preferences.

CRITICAL THINKING AND PROBLEM SOLVING

1. If you burn the tip of your tongue, what kinds of food are you likely to have difficulty tasting?
2. Why do people often lose their appetites when they have head colds?
3. Why do mushrooms enhance the flavor of many other foods?
4. How would the taste of a cola product served at room temperature differ from its taste when served ice cold?
5. Why are highly trained experts usually involved in testing coffee and wines?
6. Why is warm water used as a rinsing agent when fatty foods are being tested?
7. Design a taste test for comparing several brands of vanilla ice cream.

CHAPTER

3

Basic Science for Food Scientists

This chapter will help you . . .

- Compare and contrast elements and compounds.
- Describe heterogeneous mixtures and homogeneous mixtures and explain their similarities and differences.
- Identify common examples of pure substances and mixtures.
- Describe the parts of an atom.
- Recognize chemical symbols, formulas, and equations and discuss how they are used in food science.
- Explain the differences between ionic and covalent bonds and ionic and covalent compounds.
- Differentiate between chemical and physical changes in food.

Terms to Remember

atom
chemical changes
compounds
covalent bond
electrons
element
ions
ionic bond
matter
mixtures
molecule
neutrons
nucleus
physical changes
products
properties
protons
pure substances
reactants
solution

The first two chapters of this book have introduced you to:

- Food science and nutrition.
- How to safely carry out food science experiments.
- How food can be scientifically evaluated.

Now it is time to learn about the substances with which you will be working.

Anything that has mass and takes up space is known as **matter.** In this chapter, you will learn about matter and the particles of which all matter is composed. You will be introduced to the **properties** of matter. In science, a property is a feature that helps identify a substance. It is a trait or characteristic of the substance. Properties of a banana include its yellow color and long shape.

MATTER

Matter can be divided into two general categories—**pure substances** and **mixtures.** A pure substance is made up of only one kind of material and has definite properties. A mixture, on the other hand, is composed of two or more substances, which can be combined in varying amounts. Examples of pure substances and mixtures are shown in the classification of matter on page 50.

• PURE SUBSTANCES

Because a pure substance is made up of only one kind of material, it always has the same composition. It also has definite and constant properties under certain conditions. Common examples of pure substances are table salt, iron, and gold.

Elements

The simplest type of pure substance is an **element.** Elements are the substances from which all other materials are formed. They cannot be broken down into simpler substances by ordinary chemical means. There are 92 elements found in nature, each having its own properties. Examples of elements often studied in food science are oxygen, carbon, and hydrogen.

Elements are often referred to as metals or nonmetals. In general, metallic elements are shiny, conduct heat and electricity, and can be drawn into wires or pounded into thin sheets. Examples of metallic elements are aluminum,

What are the properties of the various forms of matter shown in this picture?

Salt is a pure substance while catsup is a mixture.

Which of these items is made from a metallic element and which from a nonmetallic element?

copper, and silver. Nonmetallic elements have dull surfaces, are poor conductors of heat and electricity, are brittle, and break easily. Several nonmetals are gases at room temperature. Iodine, chlorine, and carbon are nonmetallic elements.

Compounds

A second category of pure substances is **compounds.** A compound is made up of two or more elements chemically attached together. It is a substance whose properties are completely different from the properties of the elements from which it was made. In every sample of a compound, the elements are present in the same proportions. Even though compounds have their own properties, they can be broken down into the elements from which

The Classification of Matter

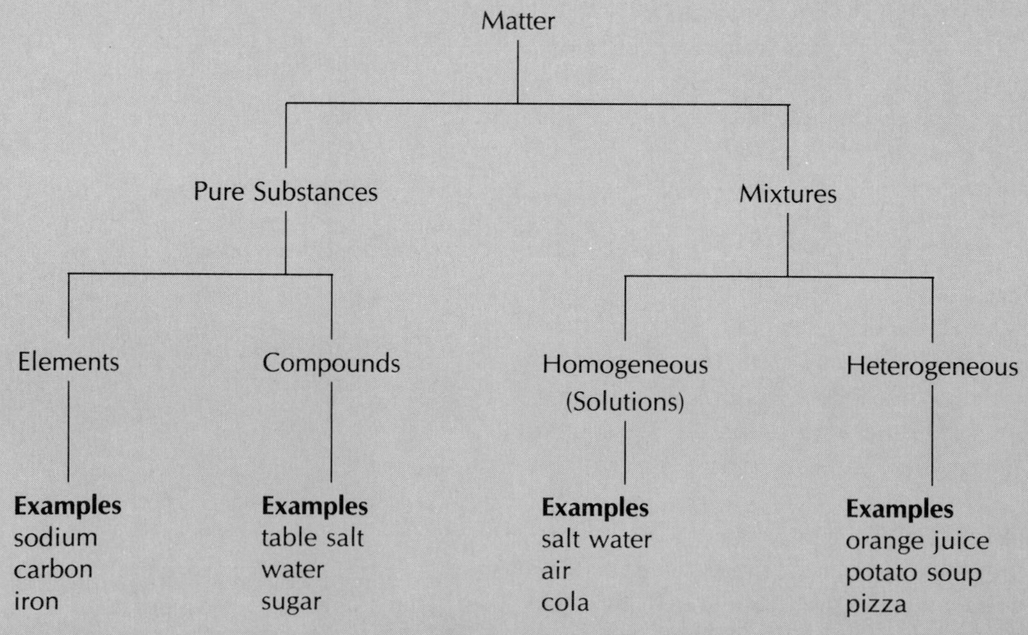

Matter

- Pure Substances
  - Elements
    - **Examples**
      sodium
      carbon
      iron
  - Compounds
    - **Examples**
      table salt
      water
      sugar
- Mixtures
  - Homogeneous (Solutions)
    - **Examples**
      salt water
      air
      cola
  - Heterogeneous
    - **Examples**
      orange juice
      potato soup
      pizza

they were formed. Water and sugar are examples of compounds.

The main compounds you will study in food science are called organic compounds. These are compounds that contain the element carbon. They also often contain hydrogen, oxygen, nitrogen, or sulfur. Some common organic compounds are wood alcohol, oil of wintergreen, and vinegar.

• MIXTURES

You will recall that mixtures contain two or more substances that have simply been combined. The substances are not chemically attached to each other, as they are in compounds. The substances making up a mixture keep at least some of their original properties. An example of a mixture found in food science is oil–and–vinegar salad dressing.

Heterogeneous Mixtures

Heterogeneous mixtures (het–uh–ruh–JEE–nee–us) are those in which the individual substances can be recognized by sight. These mixtures are not uniform in makeup or properties. Often the materials are unevenly distributed in the mixture. For example, a tossed salad is a heterogeneous mixture. When you look carefully at a bowl of salad, you can see the lettuce, carrots, celery, radishes, tomatoes, or peppers from which it is made. These ingredients can be recognized and are usually not evenly mixed in the salad.

Homogeneous Mixtures

On the other hand, a homogeneous mixture (ho–muh–JEE–nee–us) is the same in every part of a given sample. The components of a homogeneous mixture cannot be identified by sight. Salt water is an example of this type of mixture. You cannot actually see the salt when you look at a sample of salt water. However, you can taste the salt if you drink the mixture. The syrup you use with waffles or pancakes is another example of a homogeneous mixture.

A **solution** is a homogeneous mixture in which one substance is dissolved in another. Solutions play an important role in food science. They will be discussed in more detail later.

These are delicious examples of the many uses of organic compounds.

This hearty sandwich is a heterogeneous mixture in contrast to the iced tea which is a homogeneous mixture.

ATOMS

An **atom** is the smallest particle of an element that keeps the chemical properties of the element. Atoms are incredibly tiny, only about 0.000000001 (10^{-10}) meters in diameter. One gold atom is so small it takes billions of gold atoms just to make a tiny speck of gold that can be seen under a microscope.

As tiny as atoms are, they are made up of even smaller parts, called subatomic particles. The most important of these are **protons, neutrons,** and **electrons.** A proton is a particle that has a positive charge of electricity. It is present in the atom's center—the dense core of the atom called the **nucleus** (NOO–klee–us). A neutron is an uncharged particle also found in the nucleus. An electron is a negatively charged particle that moves around outside the nucleus. Electrons have almost no mass compared with protons and neutrons. The most important properties of protons, neutrons, and electrons are listed in the chart on page 53.

An atom is considered neutral when the number of negatively charged electrons equals the number of positively charged protons. When an atom reacts with other atoms, the nucleus of the atom is not involved. Rather, it is an atom's electrons that react with the other atoms.

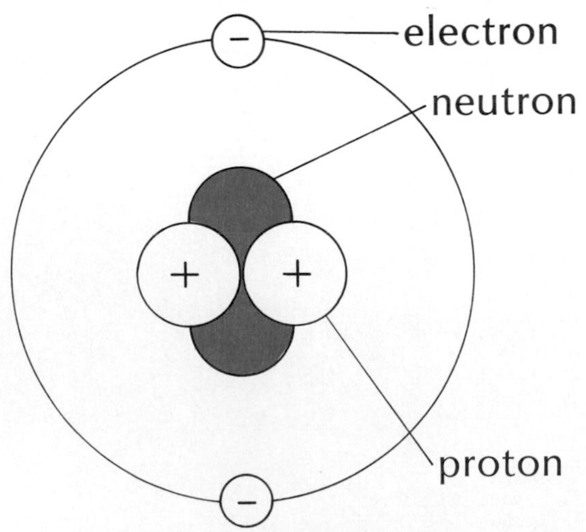

This atom has two protons and two neutrons in its nucleus and two electrons that move outside the nucleus.

Atoms and Soybeans

In trying to understand just how small and numerous atoms are, it may help to imagine what it would be like if atoms were as large as a soybean.

First, imagine a serving of soybeans on your plate. Such a serving might be a hundred (10^2) soybeans. Suppose you wanted to fill your refrigerator. It would take about a million (10^6) soybeans to fill it. A billion soybeans (10^9) would fill your whole house. A thousand houses, the number in a small town, would hold a trillion (10^{12}) soybeans. A quadrillion (10^{15}) soybeans would fill all the buildings in a large city like Baltimore or Seattle.

Now suppose there is a blizzard over North Dakota, but instead of snowing snow, it snows soybeans. North Dakota is covered with a blanket of soybeans about 1.2 m deep all the way from Minnesota to Montana and from South Dakota to Canada. To cover North Dakota this way takes about a quintillion (10^{18}) soybeans. Imagine that this blizzard of soybeans falls over the entire land of the globe so that all the continents are covered with soybeans 1.2 m deep. This global blanket would contain a sextillion (10^{21}) soybeans.

Finally, go out into the farthest reaches of the Milky Way and collect 250,000 planets, each the size of the earth. Cover each of these with a blanket of soybeans 1.2 m deep. Then, at last, you have a cotillion (10^{27}) soybeans—the number of atoms in your body!

Properties of Subatomic Particles

Protons
- Are inside the atom's nucleus.
- Have an electrical charge of +1.
- Have a mass of 1.*

Neutrons
- Are inside the atom's nucleus.
- Have no electrical charge (are neutral).
- Have a mass of 1.*

Electrons
- Are outside the atom's nucleus.
- Have an electrical charge of −1.
- Have a mass of $1/1836$.*

*Relative to the mass of a proton.

CHEMICAL SYMBOLS, FORMULAS, AND EQUATIONS

Chemists need a shorthand way to refer to the elements and compounds they use and how these materials react with each other. Chemical symbols, formulas, and equations are used to simplify the recording of chemical information.

• SYMBOLS

The names of elements used in chemistry are represented by abbreviations called symbols. Each symbol contains one or two letters. If only one letter is used in a symbol, it is always capitalized. When the symbol contains two letters, only the first is capitalized. Chemical symbols are not followed by a period. For example, **I** is the symbol for the element iodine, while **As** is the symbol for arsenic. The names and symbols of elements that are most used in food science are listed on page 54.

Formulas show the elements and the ratio of elements in a compound.

Chemical Symbols Used in Food Science

Given below are the names and symbols of the elements most often used in food science.

Elements	Symbols
hydrogen	H
carbon	C
nitrogen	N
oxygen	O
sodium	Na
aluminum	Al
phosphorus	P
sulfur	S
chlorine	Cl
potassium	K
calcium	Ca
iron	Fe

• FORMULAS

You will recall that a compound is made up of two or more elements chemically attached together. The elements and the ratio of elements in a compound are represented by a chemical formula. The formula consists of the symbols of all the elements present in the compound.

A formula represents a **molecule** (MAHL–ih–kyool) of a compound or an element. A molecule is a particle made up of two or more atoms held together by forces between the atoms. A molecule is the smallest part of a compound that can enter into chemical combinations.

When one atom of an element is present in a molecule, only the symbol of that element is written, since the symbol itself stands for one atom. For example, a molecule of carbon monoxide, a gas found in automobile exhaust, is made up of one atom of carbon and one

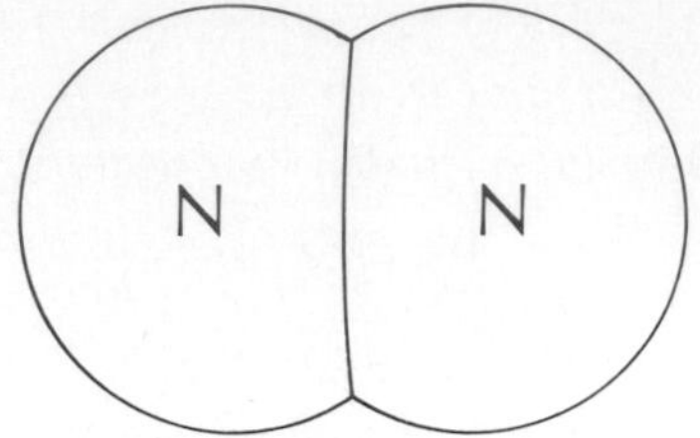

Nitrogen (N_2)

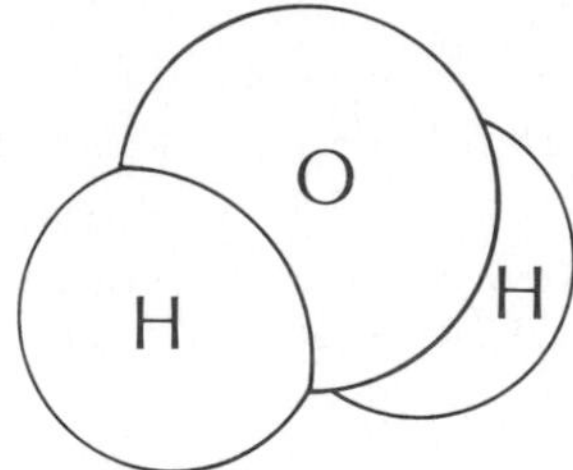

Water (H_2O)

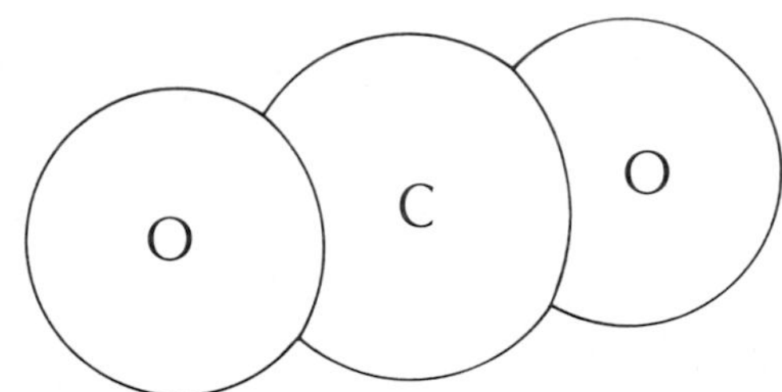

Carbon dioxide (CO_2)

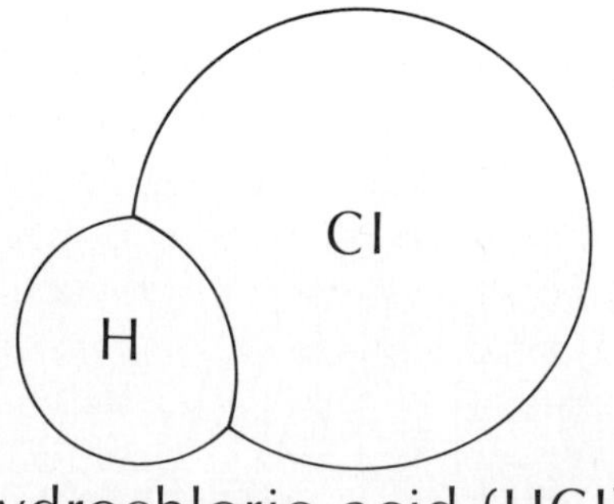

Hydrochloric acid (HCl)

These molecules are made from atoms of various elements.

atom of oxygen. Its chemical formula is written **CO.** Hydrochloric acid, the main acid found in your stomach, contains one hydrogen atom and one chlorine atom in each molecule. Its formula is written **HCl.**

Most compounds are made up of unequal numbers of atoms of the different elements. The ratio of the atoms of the elements in the compound's molecule is shown by using a subscript after the element's symbol. A subscript is a small number next to and slightly below the symbol.

For example, carbon dioxide is one of the main gases that you exhale. A carbon dioxide molecule is made up of one atom of carbon and two atoms of oxygen. Its formula is written **CO_2.** A molecule of water is composed of two atoms of hydrogen and one atom of oxygen. The formula for water is written **H_2O.** Propane, a natural gas sometimes used in camping stoves, has the formula **C_3H_8.** This means a molecule of propane contains three atoms of carbon (C_3) and eight atoms of hydrogen (H_8).

Sometimes the atoms in a molecule are alike. An oxygen molecule is made of two joined oxygen atoms. The formula for the oxygen molecule is **O_2.**

During cooking, eggs, flour, milk, and other ingredients chemically combine to make pancakes.

• EQUATIONS

You have learned that just as letters are combined to form words, chemical symbols are combined to form chemical formulas. The chemist's version of a sentence is a chemical equation. An equation is a written description of a chemical reaction using symbols and formulas.

A chemical reaction is a process in which properties of substances change as new substances with different properties are formed. The elements or compounds that are present at the start of a reaction are called **reactants** (ree–AK–tunts). The elements or compounds formed during the reaction are called **products.**

In an equation, the reactants are written first, with a plus sign between them. Then an arrow, called a yield arrow, is drawn to show that a chemical reaction takes place. The products are written on the right side of the equation after the yield arrow with a plus sign between them.

For example, glucose, a type of sugar, is "burned" in the body by being combined with oxygen. The reaction produces carbon dioxide and water. The equation describing the chemical reaction between glucose and oxygen is given below.

reactants — yield arrow — products

$$\underset{\text{Glucose}}{C_6H_{12}O_6} + \underset{\text{Oxygen}}{6O_2} \rightarrow \underset{\text{Carbon dioxide}}{6CO_2} + \underset{\text{Water}}{6H_2O}$$

This equation gives a great deal of information. First it tells what the reactants are: glucose ($C_6H_{12}O_6$) and oxygen (O_2). It also tells what the products are: carbon dioxide (CO_2) and water (H_2O). It shows how many molecules of oxygen are needed (6) to completely burn one molecule of glucose. Lastly, it shows how many molecules of carbon dioxide (6) and how many molecules of water (6) are formed.

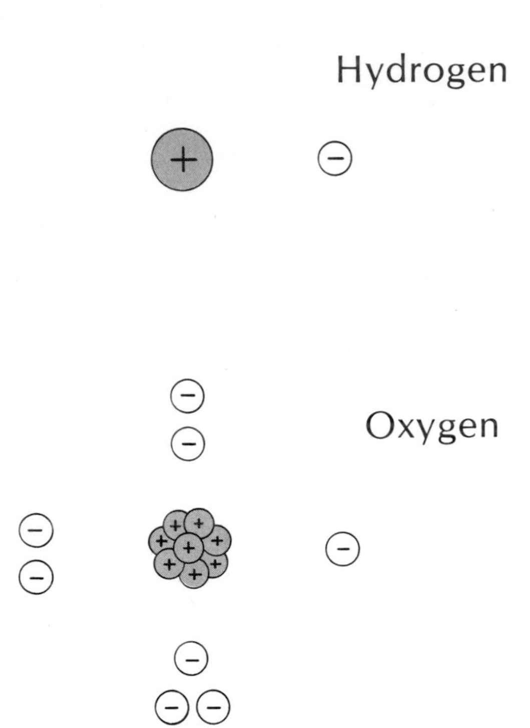

Hydrogen has only one electron in the first energy level while oxygen has two electrons in the first level and six electrons in the second energy level.

CHEMICAL BONDING

When compounds are formed, atoms of different elements are combined in a specific ratio shown by the compound's formula. The force that holds the atoms together in the molecule is a chemical bond. The number of electrons an element has affects the number and type of bonds the atom can form.

The electrons in an atom move around the nucleus in regions of space known as energy levels. The first energy level, which is closest to the nucleus, is lowest in energy. The second energy level is outside the first, so is farther from the nucleus. The electrons in the second energy level have more energy than those in the first energy level. This pattern continues with each succeeding energy level. Only a limited number of electrons are found in each energy level.

Most atoms are chemically stable when they have eight electrons in their outermost, or highest, energy level. Atoms of hydrogen and helium are exceptions because they have just one energy level. They need only two electrons to be chemically stable.

• IONIC BONDING

Sometimes an atom alters its number of electrons by transferring them to another atom. When an atom of one element transfers one or more electrons to an atom of another element, the donating atom becomes positively charged. This is because it now has more positive protons in its nucleus than negative electrons moving around it. Likewise, the atom of the element that accepts the extra electron(s) becomes negatively charged because it has more negative electrons than positive protons. These charged particles are called **ions** (EYE–ahns).

An ionic bond occurs when an electron is transferred from one atom to another.

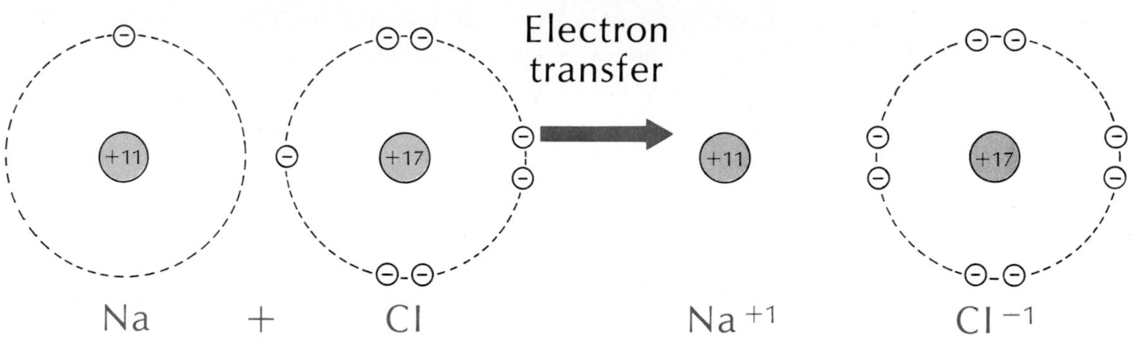

Opposite electrical charges attract. Therefore positive and negative ions are immediately attracted to each other. They are held together by what is called an **ionic bond.** An ionic bond is formed by the transfer of electrons from one atom to another. The atoms are always of different elements.

When many oppositely charged ions bond, ionic crystals form. A crystal is a solid in which the particles are arranged in a regular, repeating pattern. In ionic crystals, the positive and negative ions arrange themselves in an orderly, alternating pattern.

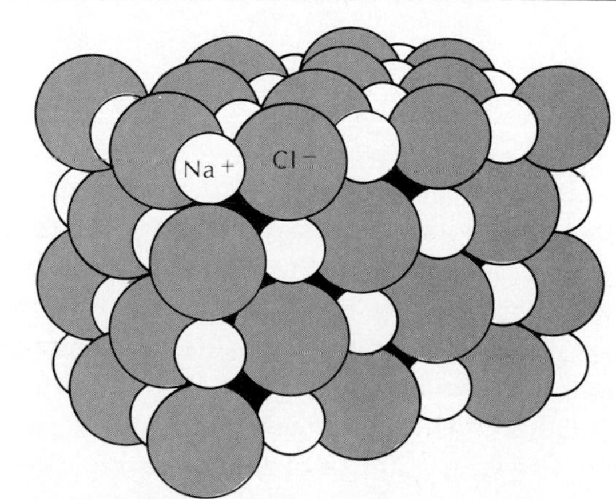

Sodium chloride forms ionic crystals in which the ions are arranged in an orderly, alternating pattern.

In general, atoms of metallic elements, such as sodium or iron, tend to form positive ions. This is because they can most easily achieve the stable condition of eight outer electrons by losing electrons. Nonmetals, like sulfur or oxygen, must gain electrons to achieve eight outer electrons. The compounds that result when metals and nonmetals bond ionically are called ionic compounds or salts. Some common ionic compounds associated with food are:

- $NaCl$—sodium chloride (table salt).
- $NaHCO_3$—sodium bicarbonate (baking soda).
- $KHC_4H_4O_6$—potassium bitartrate (cream of tartar).

• COVALENT BONDING

Ionic bonding works between metals and nonmetals. However, it does not work when two nonmetals join together. Nonmetals need to gain electrons to be stable. Therefore one nonmetallic atom cannot transfer electrons to another. Two nonmetals get the extra electrons they need to be stable by sharing electrons. When atoms share electrons with each other a **covalent bond** (ko–VAY–lunt) exists. Both elements gain electrons while neither one loses any. Compounds in which electrons are shared are called molecular compounds (muh–LEK–yuh–lur) or covalent compounds.

Water, made up of hydrogen and oxygen, is held together by covalent bonds. A hydrogen atom has one electron. It needs one more to be stable. Oxygen, on the other hand, needs two more electrons to add to its six outer electrons. Atoms of these two elements can meet each other's needs by having two hydrogen atoms each share one electron apiece with an oxygen atom. The oxygen shares one electron with each of the hydrogens. Therefore each hydrogen ends up with two electrons, while the oxygen ends up with eight outer electrons. The resulting compound, water, has a composition of two hydrogen atoms and one oxygen atom (H_2O) in each molecule of the compound.

Covalent bonds are formed when atoms share electrons with each other.

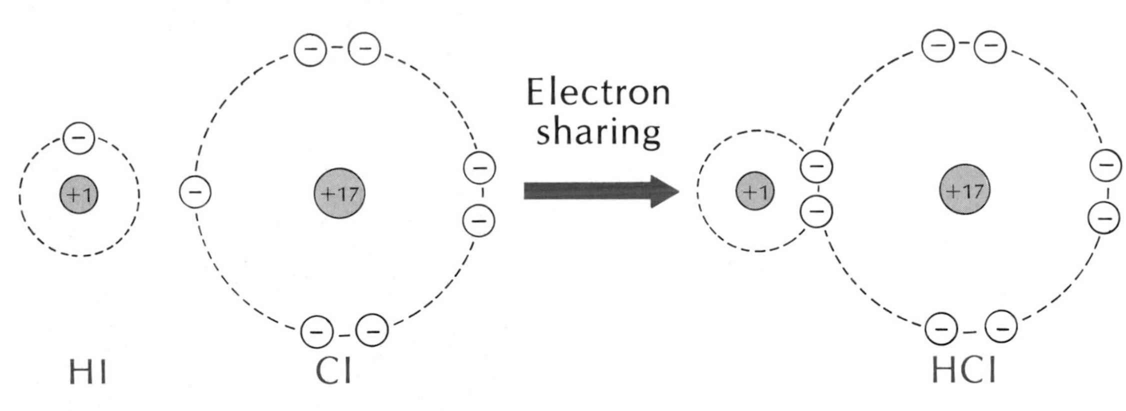

CHEMICAL AND PHYSICAL CHANGES

All the changes described so far in this chapter are examples of **chemical changes.** A chemical change is a process in which substances become new and different substances. It is possible to write an equation to describe any chemical change. The equation on page 55 reflects the chemical change that occurs when glucose reacts with oxygen. The new compounds carbon dioxide and water are formed.

Some chemical changes are reversible, like the one referred to above. In your body, glucose reacts with oxygen to form carbon dioxide, water, and energy. Plants use energy from the sun to combine carbon dioxide and water to form glucose and oxygen.

Other chemical changes cannot be reversed. Burning is an example of an irreversible chemical change. If you build a campfire to roast some hot dogs and marshmallows, the ashes, smoke, and gases produced by the wood as it burns cannot be converted back into wood.

In all chemical changes, whether they are reversible or not, the same number of atoms is present before and after the changes. For example, the equation for forming carbon dioxide is $C + O_2 \rightarrow CO_2$. One atom of carbon and two atoms of oxygen are on each side of the equation. In other words, the total mass of the reactants is the same as the total mass of the products. Because the mass stays the same, it is said to be conserved.

In **physical changes,** the basic chemical nature of matter is not changed. The properties of a substance, such as its shape, size, or physical state, are altered. However, the identity of the substance does not change.

This toast is an example of an irreversible chemical change since it cannot be changed back into untoasted bread.

Are these chemical or physical changes?

Slicing and chopping these vegetables for a salad involve a physical change in the food which has little affect on its nutritional value.

Any time a mixture is formed, a physical change takes place. Whenever a substance is dissolved in water, thus forming a solution, a physical change occurs. The substance that dissolves disappears into the water. While in solution, however, it keeps at least some of its original properties, such as taste or color. If desired, the substance can be reclaimed by simply evaporating the water. Once the water has been evaporated, the solid remaining will be exactly the same substance as was dissolved in the first place. It will have all the properties it originally had.

Mass is conserved during physical changes just as it is during chemical changes. That is, the mass of the reactants is always the same as the mass of the products.

• PHASE CHANGES

Matter can exist in three states, or phases—a solid phase, a liquid phase, or a gas phase. A solid is matter with a definite shape and a definite volume. Coal, wood, potatoes, and apricots are solids. Liquid is matter with no definite shape, but with a definite volume, such as coffee or fruit juice. Gas is matter with no definite shape or volume, such as air or oxygen.

A phase change is a physical change of matter from one state to another. Freezing is the change from a liquid phase to a solid state. Melting is the process in which a solid changes to a liquid. When ice melts, for example, the resulting product is liquid water. This has exactly the same chemical formula, $\mathbf{H_2O}$, as the ice had. The phase of the sample has changed but it is still water.

The same would be true if the liquid water were boiled and changed to steam. Vaporization (vay–pur–ih–ZAY–shun) is the process in

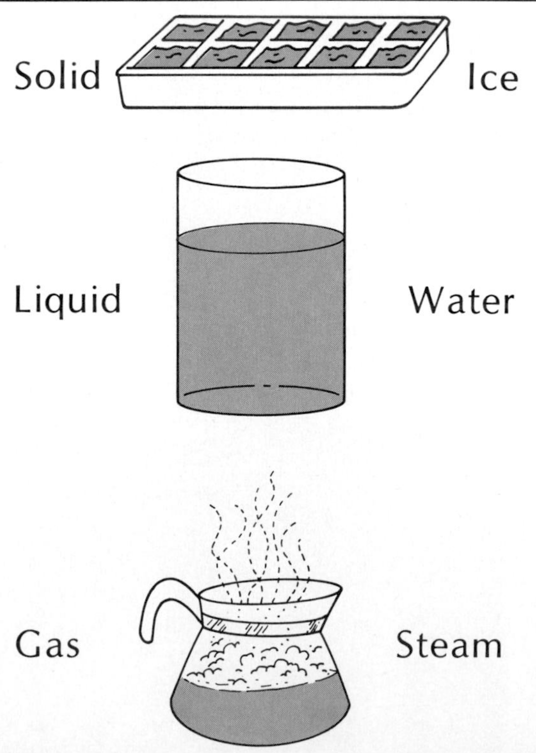

Water can exist as a solid, a liquid, and a gas.

which a liquid changes to a gas. The water vapor, or steam, would have the same chemical formula as the liquid water. Condensation (kahn–dun–SAY–shun) is the change of a gas to a liquid. When steam undergoes a phase change to liquid water, condensation occurs. Whether the phase of the water is a liquid or a gas, the compound is still water.

NUTRITION AND YOU

Chemical and Physical Changes in Food

As you have learned in this chapter, matter undergoes chemical and physical changes. Since food is matter, such changes occur in food too.

The changes that take place in food during cooking are both physical and chemical. In other words, once a potato has been cooked, it is physically and chemically different from when it was raw. Eggs are a food where cooking causes obvious visual changes. Before an egg is cooked, the egg white is an almost clear, runny liquid. After cooking, it is white and solid. Both the cooked potato and egg have been permanently changed on a molecular level.

Some of the changes made to food are distinctly physical, like slicing, chopping, or peeling. Cooking often causes chemical changes. Sometimes both kinds of changes happen at the same time. When you chew food, you grind it with your teeth, a purely physical change. At the same time, the saliva in your mouth begins to dissolve the food. This chemical change is the first step in digestion. The chemical interaction between your saliva and the food makes the physical act of chewing more effective. Both the physical and chemical changes in the mouth are needed to make the nutrients in food available for use in your body.

Some changes have no effect on nutritional value. Other changes may cause food to lose nutritional value. For example, shredding a food creates a physical change. If you shred cheese before adding it to a burrito, the shredded cheese is just as nutritious as the unshredded cheese. Even if you gently heat the cheese to melt it, its nutritional value stays the same. On the other hand, if you shred potatoes before boiling them, they will lose many nutrients that dissolve in water during cooking. Thus shredding causes no measurable loss of nutritional value in the cheese, but does in the potatoes when they are cooked.

EXPERIMENT 3–1

Mass and Volume of Beans

You are probably familiar with the fact that many substances increase in volume as they absorb water. In this experiment, you will examine the volume and mass changes of various types of dried beans allowed to soak overnight in water. You will learn to measure the volume of irregular objects, such as the beans, by finding out how much water they take the place of. This is called measuring by water displacement.

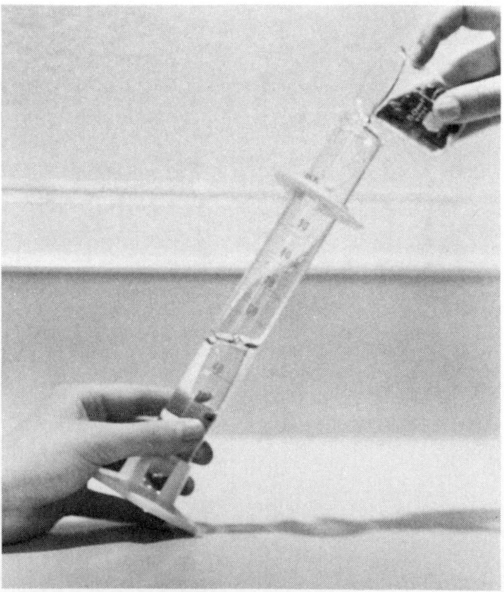

PROCEDURE

1. Count out 50 dried beans of the variety assigned to you by your teacher.
2. Determine the mass of the beans by massing them in a small beaker.
3. Pour about 40 mL water into a 100 mL graduated cylinder. In your data table, record the exact volume of water.
4. Add the beans to the water, being careful not to cause any of the water to splash out of the cylinder.
5. Read the new volume and record in your data table.
6. Transfer the beans to a 100 mL beaker half full of water. Be sure you do not leave any beans in the graduated cylinder. Label the beaker with your name and class period. Store the beaker in the location specified by your teacher.
7. The following day repeat steps 2–5 with the beans that have soaked in water overnight. Be sure to remove as much water as possible from the surface of the beans before massing them.

EXPERIMENT 3–1

QUESTIONS AND CALCULATIONS

1. Calculate the mass of one dried bean and one soaked bean, and record these values in your data table.
2. Calculate the volume of one dried bean and one soaked bean, and record these values in your data table.
3. Calculate the change in mass and the change in volume for one bean.
4. Compare the changes in mass and volume for one bean among the different varieties of beans used by different laboratory groups. Which variety of beans gained the most mass and volume? The least?
5. On the basis of class experimental results, list the factors you should consider when using beans in a recipe.

SAMPLE DATA TABLE

Measurements	Dried Beans	Soaked Beans
Mass of empty beaker		
Mass of beaker and 50 beans		
Mass of 50 beans		
Mass of one bean		
Volume of water in graduated cylinder		
Volume of water and beans		
Volume of 50 beans		
Volume of one bean	______	
Change in mass for one bean	______	
Change in volume for one bean		

EXPERIMENT 3–2

Physical and Chemical Changes

In this experiment, you will carry out two kinds of changes by dissolving substances. One change is a physical change, since the original substance can be easily reclaimed. The other is a chemical change, since the original substance is destroyed when it is dissolved.

PROCEDURE

1. Use a magnifying glass to observe crystals of sodium chloride (table salt). Describe or draw their appearance in your data table.
2. Taste a few crystals and describe the taste in your data table.
3. Repeat step 1 with sodium bicarbonate (baking soda).
4. Mass 1 g sodium chloride, and dissolve in 20 mL water in a 100 mL beaker. Stir the mixture until the solid has completely dissolved. Observe the mixture during the dissolving process.
5. Place a small amount of the mixture on a shallow glass dish called a watch glass. Carefully heat the watch glass on the stove over medium heat until the liquid just boils away. Remove the watch glass from the heat and allow to cool.
6. With the magnifying glass, observe the solid remaining on the watch glass. Taste a few of the crystals. In your data table, describe their appearance and taste.
7. Repeat steps 4–5 with 1 g sodium bicarbonate, but use 20 mL vinegar instead of water. In your data table, note the behavior of the mixture during the dissolving process.
8. Observe the solid remaining on the watch glass with the magnifying glass, and describe in your data table. Do not taste this sample.
9. To the solid remaining in step 8, add a small amount of vinegar. In your data table, describe the behavior of the mixture as the solid dissolves.

QUESTIONS

1. How did the dissolving of the sodium chloride differ from that of the sodium bicarbonate?
2. Was the substance that remained after the water evaporated sodium chloride? How do you know? What kind of change was this?
3. Was the substance remaining after the vinegar evaporated sodium bicarbonate? How do you know? What kind of change was this?

SAMPLE DATA TABLE

Samples	Original	After Evaporation
Sodium chloride Appearance		
Taste		
Sodium bicarbonate Appearance		
Behavior with vinegar		

TO SUM UP

- Matter, anything that has mass and occupies space, is divided into two categories—pure substances and mixtures.
- Elements are the simplest type of pure substance and are represented by symbols.
- A compound is made up of two or more elements chemically bonded together and is shown by a formula.
- Mixtures are composed of two or more substances combined in varying amounts.
- Atoms are the smallest particle of an element that keep the chemical properties of the element.
- Chemical bonds between atoms can be either ionic or covalent, depending on whether electrons are transferred or shared.
- A chemical change is a process where substances become new and different substances.
- Physical changes in a substance involve changes such as size, shape, or phase, but the basic identity of the substance does not change.

CHECK YOUR FACTS

1. Name and describe the two categories of matter.
2. What are substances called that cannot be broken down into simpler substances by ordinary chemical means?
3. Explain the difference between an element and a compound.
4. What is another name for a homogeneous mixture?
5. Are electrons found inside or outside the nucleus of an atom?
6. Identify the symbols for the following elements: a. sulfur b. phosphorus c. hydrogen.
7. Name the element represented by each of the following symbols: a. C b. N c. Cl d. Ca e. Na.
8. Write the formulas of the following compounds: a. sodium chloride b. water c. glucose.
9. Name the parts of a chemical equation.
10. What happens to electrons when ionic compounds are formed? When covalent compounds are formed?
11. Explain the differences between chemical and physical changes.

CRITICAL THINKING AND PROBLEM SOLVING

1. Do you think beans are pure substances or mixtures? Why?
2. Classify the following substances as homogeneous or heterogeneous mixtures: a. tomato juice b. apple juice c. mayonnaise d. pudding e. chicken soup.
3. List the names of the elements and the number of atoms of each in the following molecules:
   a. NaCl b. H_2O c. H_2SO_4 d. H_2 e. $C_6H_{12}O_6$.
4. How many molecules of water are represented in the following equation?

$$C_2H_5OH + 3O_2 \rightarrow 3H_2O + 2CO_2$$

CHAPTER

4

Energy

This chapter will help you . . .

- Describe the relationship of energy and physical and chemical reactions.
- Discuss the relationship between molecular motion and temperature.
- Explain how heat is transferred.
- Review the meaning of latent heat in phase changes.
- Compare the effect of various temperatures on rates of reaction.
- Analyze the relationship between food intake and body weight.

Terms to Remember

absolute zero
anorexia nervosa
bulimia
calories
conduction
convection
energy
joules
kilocalories
latent heat
microwaves
specific heat

All changes that take place in the universe are accompanied by a flow of **energy.** Energy is the ability to do work. It exists in many forms—as heat, chemical, electrical, mechanical, and radiant (light) energy.

Energy is involved in physical changes in which the formula or identity of a substance remains the same, such as melting ice or boiling water. Chemical changes, in which substances chemically interact to form new materials, also involve energy. For example, energy is used to create chemical changes when baking a cake. Sometimes energy is absorbed from the surroundings during these changes; sometimes energy is released.

For example, plants use the sun's energy to convert carbon dioxide and water into glucose and oxygen. When food is used by your body, energy is produced. Part of this energy is heat, but most of it is mechanical energy, or the energy of motion. You use mechanical energy when you use your muscles to breathe, lift a pencil, or run a race.

The energy from food is changed into mechanical energy during this tennis match.

The heat energy used in cooking food can come from a variety of sources.

Heat energy is the form of energy that is of the greatest interest in food science. This is because during cooking, heat energy is transferred from a heat source to the food. For example, if you were to cook an egg, you would put the egg in a pan over a heating element, which is releasing heat. The pan absorbs the heat and then transfers it to the egg. As the egg absorbs this heat energy, it undergoes chemical changes caused by the heat.

PROPERTIES OF MATTER

To understand heat transfer, it is necessary to consider some basic properties of matter. These properties affect how heat is measured and transferred.

• MOLECULAR MOTION

Absolute zero is the temperature at which all molecular motion ceases and matter has no heat energy. It is −273°C. At temperatures above absolute zero, atoms and molecules in all matter are in constant motion.

Molecules of gas travel at very high speeds in a straight line until they collide with other gas molecules or with a wall of their container. Then they bounce off in another direction. There is a great deal of empty space between molecules of gas compared with the size of the molecules.

Molecular motion in liquids is more restricted because the molecules are closer together than in gases—in fact, they touch one another. Molecules of a liquid can tumble past each other allowing the liquid to flow or move out of the way easily when an item is dropped into it. Even though liquids do not have a definite shape, they have a definite volume. This is because the forces of attraction between the molecules are strong enough to hold the liquid together.

Molecular motion in solids is more restricted than in gases or liquids. Particles are locked into a specific location in the solid. Therefore all these particles can do is vibrate and rotate.

In spite of the differences among the three states of matter, they all respond the same when heat energy is added. Heat causes the molecules to speed up. This increased molecular motion can be measured as an increase

Measuring Heat Energy

One way heat energy is measured is in units called **calories.** One calorie of heat energy is the amount of energy needed to raise the temperature of 1 g of water 1°C. Food energy is measured in **kilocalories** (kcal). These are units of 1000 calories. When referring to energy in food, most people use the term calorie. In fact, kilocalorie is the correct scientific term. Sometimes a kilocalorie is written as "Calorie," with a capital C. Usually, the calories listed in diet plans and on food packages are kilocalories.

Joules (JOOLS) are other units used to measure heat. A joule, abbreviated "J," is the metric unit of heat flow and is used in most of the world. One joule is equivalent to 0.239 cal. Conversely, 1 cal is equal to 4.18 J. The terms "calorie" and "kilocalorie" will be used in this textbook, since most Americans are more familiar with these terms.

Molecular motion decreases when a substance such as water changes from a gas to a liquid to a solid.

in temperature. Thus temperature is a measure of molecular motion.

The amount of energy required to speed up the molecules of a substance is called **specific heat.** Specific heat is the energy needed to raise the temperature of 1 g of a substance 1°C. Specific heat is measured in calories. Water has a specific heat of 1 because it takes 1 calorie to raise the temperature of 1 g of water 1°C. Glass has a specific heat of 0.20 and air has a specific heat of 0.25. Therefore both air and glass heat more quickly than water.

• HEAT TRANSFER

Heat energy always flows from a warmer material to a cooler one. One way heat is transferred is by **conduction** (kun–DUK–shun). This involves passing energy from particle to particle through molecular collisions. When two substances come in contact with each other, their molecules collide. The molecules of the warmer substance transmit some of their energy to the molecules of the cooler substance. This causes the warmer substance to cool as its molecules lose energy and slow down. Energy is transferred from the warmer substance to the cooler until the two substances are the same temperature. Only if energy is supplied continuously, as it is to a heating unit on a stove, will the warmer substance remain at a constant temperature.

Heat can also be transferred by **convection** (kun–VEK–shun), the motion of fluids or gases. When a container of liquid is heated, the fluid near the bottom becomes hot first. As the liquid heats, the molecules speed up and move farther apart, which causes the liquid to become less dense. The less dense portion of the liquid rises toward the top of the container. The cooler, heavier portion of the liquid sinks to the bottom. The cooler molecules are then heated. The process continues until all the liquid in the container is the same temperature.

HEAT AND PHASE CHANGES

In Chapter 3, you learned that a phase change is the physical change of matter from one state to another. Energy is either absorbed or released during phase changes.

When liquid water changes to ice, the liquid water gives off energy to its surroundings. The water is put into a freezer, where the air is below 0°C, to produce ice. In the freezer, the water gives off energy to the cooler surroundings. This causes its own temperature to drop until it freezes. After freezing is complete, the ice continues to cool until it reaches the temperature of the air in the freezer.

During freezing, the temperature of the water–ice mixture remains constant. At this point, the molecules are not slowing down, but rather are organizing themselves into the crystal arrangement of ice. The heat given off by the water is not lowering the temperature, but its loss allows ice crystals to form. This energy lost by the water molecules as they form ice crystals is called **latent heat.** Latent heat is the heat required to create a phase change without a change in temperature. Only when the phase change is complete will a change in energy produce a temperature change.

Latent heat is used or absorbed during the melting of ice. The temperature remains constant, since the energy gained is used to break down the ice crystal structure, rather than speed up the molecules.

A similar phenomenon occurs during vaporization. The energy that is used when water is boiled separates and spreads out the liquid water molecules. The molecules are then able to leave the body of liquid water and become steam. During this phase change, the molecules' speed, and therefore their temperature, remains constant because of latent heat.

During condensation, heat energy is released. The energy that was absorbed when the liquid became gas is released when the gas condenses back into the liquid phase.

RATES OF REACTION

The process of cooking involves the transfer of heat energy to food. However, successful cooking is more than food absorbing heat. Factors that determine whether a cooked food is actually fit to eat are:

- How much energy the food absorbs.
- How quickly the energy is absorbed.
- The rate at which the energy is transmitted.

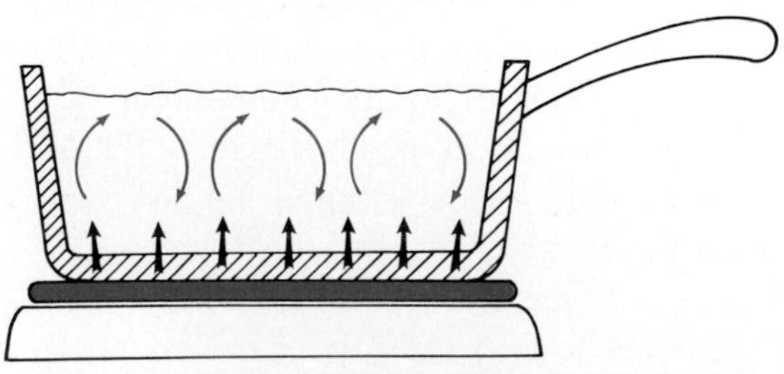

Heat is first transferred from the burner to the pan and then to the water in the bottom of the pan by conduction. Heat is then transferred within the water by convection.

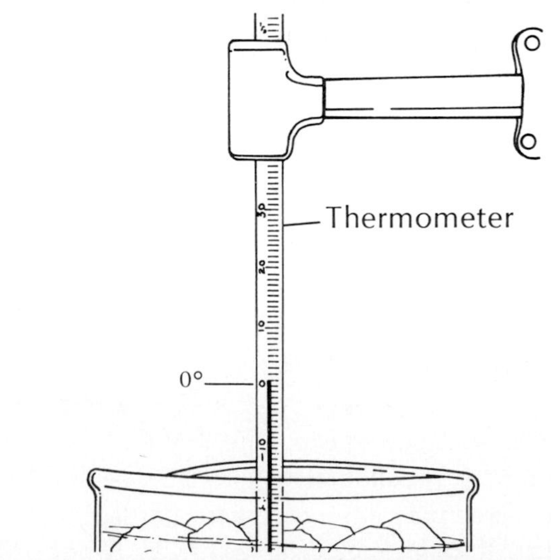

Temperature remains constant during a phase change.

For example, if a piece of meat is left in a pan over medium heat for two minutes, it may be warm but still completely raw. If the same size piece of meat is placed in an extremely hot pan for two minutes, it may char or scorch on the outside, yet still be raw on the inside.

Microwave Energy

Microwave ovens cook food by invisible waves of energy called **microwaves.** The biggest difference between microwaves and heat is that microwaves do not affect all molecules equally; heat does. Instead, microwaves have the greatest effect on water molecules.

When a sample of food is cooked in a microwave oven, the microwaves cause the water molecules in the food to vibrate very rapidly. This energy is transmitted to neighboring molecules, and the food heats.

The main advantage of microwaves over heat is that microwaves are absorbed by the food to a depth of 5–7.5 cm. Heat from traditional sources is absorbed only at the surface and then must be slowly transmitted through the food sample. Therefore microwave cooking usually takes less time.

Microwave cooking can be a time saver because microwaves penetrate food more deeply than heat.

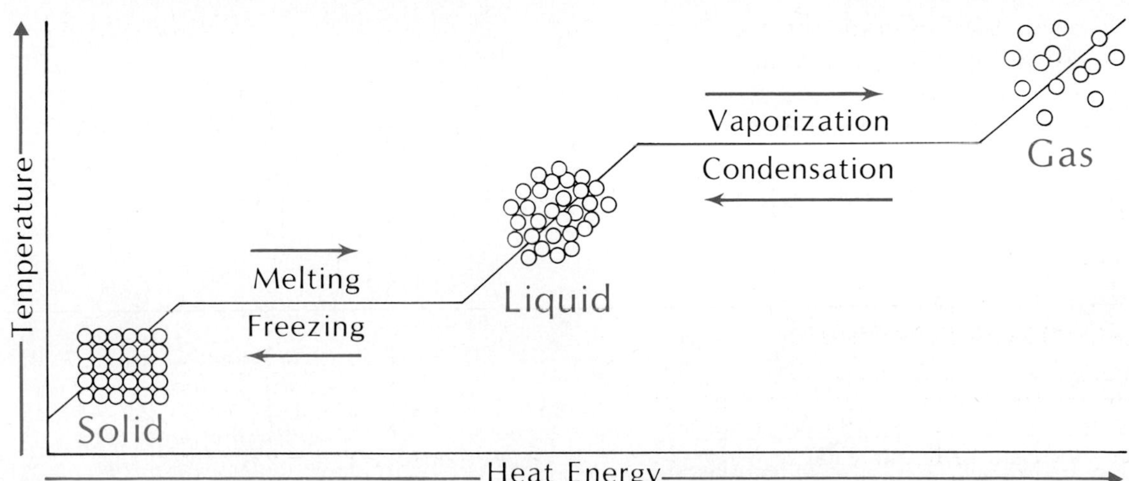

Why is the temperature line flat during the phase changes shown on this chart?

• TEMPERATURE

The temperature at which food is cooked is important. Temperature is the main factor controlling the rate of the chemical changes that take place during cooking. These chemical changes depend on the collision of molecules. Temperature affects the reaction rate in two ways.

First, higher temperatures increase the speed at which molecules move. As the molecules move more quickly, they collide with each other more often. This increases the overall rate of reaction.

In addition, higher temperatures increase the force with which the molecules collide. Since molecules must have enough energy to react when they collide, this extra force increases the chances that a reaction will actually occur.

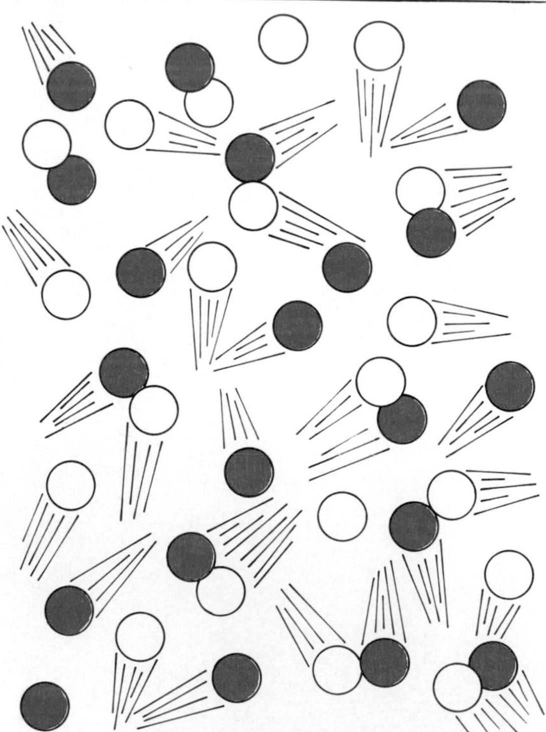

Molecules must collide with enough energy to cause a reaction.

A general rule is that the rate of a reaction doubles for every 10°C increase in temperature. By reversing the process, or lowering the temperature, the rate of reaction slows down. This is why food is stored in a refrigerator or freezer. The lower temperatures slow molecular motion. This slows the rate at which the food will spoil.

• SURFACE AREA

Another factor that affects the rate of a chemical reaction is surface area. When food is heated, the molecules in the air or water surrounding the food contain energy. When these molecules collide with the food molecules, the energy is transferred. This happens only on the surface of the food. Therefore a food with more surface area will cook faster than one with less surface area.

The temperature at the center of the food will rise eventually. This is because the molecules on the surface will collide with those next to them, transferring some energy. These molecules in turn collide with and speed up the slower molecules next to them. This process proceeds inward until the entire sample warms up.

Because the center of the thick hamburger patty is farther from the surface than the center of the thin patty, the thick patty will take much longer to cook.

Obviously, the farther the center is from the surface, the longer it will take to become hot. Therefore it will take more time for the chemical changes that take place during cooking to occur at the center of the food. You will explore the effects of temperature and surface area on the rate at which potatoes cook in the two experiments in this chapter.

The ingredients in this salad contain only a small percentage of the energy nutrients, so they are low in kilocalories.

KILOCALORIES AND YOU

All living things—from simple single-celled organisms to human beings—need energy to survive. Plants acquire energy from the sun and from nutrients in the air and the soil in which they grow. Animals get energy from the nutrients in the food they eat.

The food you consume provides you with kilocalories of energy. It would seem logical that the more you eat, the more kilocalories you would take in. However, small quantities of one food can contain more kilocalories than large quantities of another food.

Which of these servings of food contains the most kilocalories? The least?

A balance between kilocalories eaten and energy used helps maintain a constant weight.

The energy value of food varies greatly. This is because some components of food, such as water, vitamins, and minerals, do not provide any kilocalories or energy to the body. Rather, it is the fat, protein, and carbohydrate contained in food that provide energy. These energy–providing nutrients may make up as little as 4 percent of food such as lettuce. On the other hand, they can make up to 100 percent of food such as sugar, salad oil, or dry gelatin.

Since food varies in the kilocalories it contains in an average serving, it is misleading to label any one food "fattening." How much of a food you consume is what determines how many kilocalories your body receives from it.

Kilocalories in Food

The number of kilocalories varies greatly from one food to another. Listed below are the number of kilocalories in a serving of some common foods.

Food	Serving Size	Kilo-calories
Apple	1	70
Bacon, fried	2 slices	90
Banana	1	100
Biscuit	1	105
Bread, white	1 slice	70
Bread, whole wheat	1 slice	65
Broccoli	1 stalk	45
Brownie	1	95
Carrot	1	20
Celery	1 stalk	5
Cheddar cheese	2.5-cm square	70
Chicken breast, fried	94 g	155
Cocoa	250 mL	245
Cola	1 can	145
Cookie, chocolate chip	1	50
Corn	1 ear	70
Corn flakes	250 mL	100
Cottage cheese	250 mL	260
Cupcake and icing	1	130
Doughnut, cake	1	125
Egg	1	80
Frankfurter	1	170
Grape juice	250 mL	165
Grapefruit, white	½	45
Ground beef, broiled	85 g	245
Ice cream	250 mL	255
Lima beans	250 mL	190
Margarine	1 pat	35
Mayonnaise	15 mL	100
Milk, whole	250 mL	160
Orange	1	65
Orange juice, fresh	250 mL	110
Peach	1	35
Peanuts	250 mL	840
Peas	250 mL	115
Pecan halves	250 mL	740
Pickle, dill	1 large	10
Pie, apple	1/7 pie	350
Pie, pecan	1/7 pie	490
Popcorn	250 mL	25
Pork chop	98 g	260
Potato, baked	1	90
Potato, French-fried	10 pieces	155
Potato chips	10 chips	115
Pretzels, sticks	10 sticks	10
Shrimp	85 g	100
Steak, broiled	85 g	330
Tomato	1	40
Tuna, in oil	85 g	170

For some people, it may be difficult to consume exactly the number of calories the body needs to perform normal activities. A slight imbalance from day to day is not a problem. However, if a person consistently takes in more kilocalories than the body needs, the unneeded calories are stored as fat. This causes a weight gain. On the other hand, if a person consistently consumes fewer kilocalories than the body needs, protein and stored fat can be used for energy. This results in a loss of weight.

In this society, most people have access to a variety of food. Many people become heavier than they should for their height. They have consistently eaten more kilocalories than the body can use on a daily basis. Carrying extra weight is not healthy for the body. When this happens, it is necessary to limit the intake of kilocalories to lose the excess weight.

While being overweight is not healthy, neither is being underweight. Some people do not gain weight even when they eat foods rich in kilocalories. Other people may overly restrict their intake of kilocalories to maintain a desired low body weight. Consuming too few kilocalories can result in illness and even death.

Eating too much or not eating enough food can both cause health problems.

Energy—Other Times and Places

The earliest humans could not count on a constant supply of food. During the warmer months, food was plentiful. People and animals ate as much as possible so that they would survive the leaner winter months. They could survive by burning the stored energy, or fat, in the body to supplement the limited quantities of food they had to eat.

Today, members of different cultures acquire the energy they need in a variety of ways. In Ireland, the main source of energy is the potato. Rice is the main energy food in China. Due to the extensive use of cooking oil in Italy, residents gain most of their energy from fats. In the United States, people obtain energy from a greater variety of sources than do people in many other countries.

NUTRITION AND YOU

Maintaining a Healthy Weight

You can regulate your weight by controlling the amount of food and, therefore, the number of kilocalories you consume. If you want to add body fat, you would need to eat more kilocalories than your body requires for energy. On the average, every 3500 kcal of food you eat that your body does not use for energy builds up 454 g of body fat. On the other hand, for every 454 g of body fat you want to lose, you would need to eat 3500 kcal less than your body needs for energy. This would allow your body to burn stored fat, causing you to lose weight.

Your body will be healthier if you gain or lose weight gradually. One rule of thumb for losing weight suggests that you eat 500 kcal a day less than your body normally requires. This will cause you to lose 454 g of body fat a week. Eating an additional 500 kcal a day will result in a gain of 454 g in a week. Regardless of whether you want to gain or lose weight, you should eat a variety of food so you will get all the nutrients your body needs.

Maintaining your proper body weight will help you not only look your best, but will also help you be healthy. People who are extremely overweight or underweight frequently face a variety of health problems.

Many young people, especially women, become obsessed with being thin. Some of these young women, who are usually between the ages of 12–25, actually impose a starvation diet on themselves to become thinner. This behavior is an eating disorder known as **anorexia nervosa** (an–uh–REX–ee–uh ner–VO–suh). Food often becomes repulsive to anorexics. A person suffering from this disorder needs professional help. Otherwise anorexia nervosa can cause chemical abnormalities in the body that can be hazardous to health. In extreme cases, anorexia nervosa can cause death.

Bulimia (byoo–LIM–ee–uh) is another eating disorder experienced by those overly concerned with being thin. People suffering from this disorder often eat large amounts of food, sometimes even gorging themselves. Then they either make themselves vomit or take excessive quantities of laxatives. This purges the system of the food they have consumed. Repeated vomiting is hard on the body. It can cause the loss of hydrochloric acid from the stomach. This, in turn, can cause the loss of the mineral potassium. In extreme cases, lack of potassium can lead to heart failure.

At the other extreme, those who are overweight have their own health problems. People who have excessive body fat are obese. Males whose body weight is over 20 percent fat are considered obese, as are women whose body weight is over 30 percent fat. Overweight individuals have a higher incidence of high blood pressure, heart problems, circulatory problems, and problems during surgery. They also have a greater than average chance of developing diabetes and other health problems.

It is important to determine an appropriate weight for your height and build. Maintaining that weight throughout your life will help you stay healthy.

EXPERIMENT 4–1

Effect of Temperature on Cooking Rate

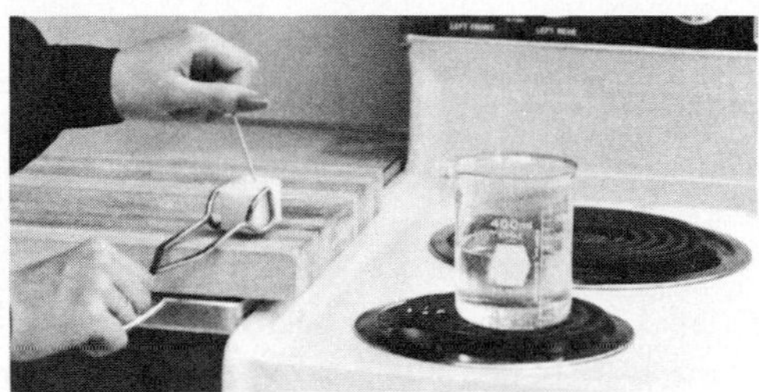

In this experiment, you will study the effect of temperature on the rate at which potatoes cook.

PROCEDURE

1. Obtain a potato from your teacher. From the potato, cut a cube 2.5 cm on each side.
2. Measure 200 mL water, using your 100 mL graduated cylinder. Pour the water into a 400 mL beaker. The water should be deep enough to completely immerse the cube of potato, although the potato is not added until later.
3. Follow the variation assigned by your teacher.
   a. **Variation 1.** Heat the water to 90°C.
   b. **Variation 2.** Heat the water to 100°C.
4. Monitor the water temperature, removing the beaker or turning down the heat as necessary to keep the temperature constant.
5. When you can keep the water temperature constant, immerse the piece of potato in the water.
6. Cook the potato, testing it every 2 minutes with a wooden toothpick. Based on how easily the toothpick punctures the potato, determine its degree of doneness, i.e., uncooked, slightly cooked, cooked. Record this information in your data table.
7. When the toothpick punctures the potato easily, note the time in your data table. Turn off the heat and remove the beaker from the stove.
8. On the chalkboard, record your variation number and the time needed to cook the potato.

CALCULATIONS AND QUESTIONS

1. List the times required to cook each of the potato cubes that were in the 90°C water. Make a similar list of the times required to cook each of the potato cubes that were in 100°C water.
2. Determine the average cooking time for the potato cubes in the 90°C water and the average cooking time for the potato cubes in the 100°C water.
3. How much difference was there between the average cooking times at the two temperatures?
4. Explain the differences in cooking time.

SAMPLE DATA TABLE

Water Temperature: °C	
Time in Minutes	**Degree of Doneness**

EXPERIMENT 4–2

Effect of Surface Area on Cooking Rate

In the last experiment, you studied the effect of temperature on the rate at which potatoes cook. In this experiment, you will use different–sized pieces of potato to study the effect of surface area on cooking rate.

PROCEDURE

1. Measure 200 mL water in your 100 mL graduated cylinder. Pour the water into a 400 mL beaker.
2. While the water is heating, obtain a potato from your teacher. From the potato, cut a cube 2.5 cm on each side.
3. Follow the variation assigned by your teacher.
   a. **Variation 1.** Use the single cube of potato.
   b. **Variation 2.** Cut the cube into eight equal–sized cubes by cutting the original cube in half in all three directions.
   c. **Variation 3.** Cut the cube into 27 equal–sized cubes by cutting the original cube in thirds in all three directions.
4. Place the piece(s) of potato in the water after it has come to a boil.
5. At 1 minute intervals, test the potato with a wooden toothpick. Based on how easily the toothpick punctures the potato, determine its degree of doneness, i.e., uncooked, slightly cooked, cooked. Record this information in your data table.
6. When the toothpick punctures the potato easily, note the time in your data table. Turn off the burner and remove the beaker from the stove.
7. On the chalkboard, record your variation number and the time needed to cook the potato.

QUESTIONS

1. Was there any difference in the total mass of potato present in each beaker?
2. Was there any relationship between the size of the potato cubes and their cooking time? What was it?
3. Explain the difference in cooking time.

SAMPLE DATA TABLE

Variation Number:	
Time in Minutes	**Degree of Doneness**

TO SUM UP

- Energy is either released or absorbed in all physical or chemical changes.
- Temperature is a measure of the molecular motion in a substance.
- Heat is transferred through conduction and convection.
- Latent heat creates a phase change without an increase in temperature.
- Heating a substance increases the rate of reaction, while cooling the substance decreases it.
- The energy needed by the body is obtained from the kilocalories in food.
- Food varies in kilocalories depending on the nutrients in the food.
- The amount of kilocalories consumed affects weight gain and loss.

CHECK YOUR FACTS

1. How is energy involved in chemical and physical changes?
2. What type of energy is most important in food science? Why?
3. What is a calorie? How does a calorie compare with a kilocalorie?
4. When temperature increases, what happens to molecular motion?
5. What is the direction of heat transfer?
6. Why does the temperature of an ice–water mixture remain constant while the ice melts?
7. State two reasons that increasing the temperature increases reaction rate.
8. Which components of food provide energy?
9. What causes people to gain weight? Lose weight?
10. What is the main source of energy in the diet of the Chinese?
11. How many kilocalories of energy must be burned to cause the loss of 454 g of body fat?

CRITICAL THINKING AND PROBLEM SOLVING

1. When an ice cube is added to water, in which direction does the energy flow?
2. Why do microwave ovens cook food faster than conventional ovens?
3. Will a cube of sugar dissolve faster in iced or hot tea? Why?
4. Which will dissolve faster—5 mL of granulated sugar, 5 mL of powdered sugar, or a sugar cube? Why?
5. Explain why fast–food restaurants generally serve thin French fries.
6. Why shouldn't a candy bar be called a fattening food?
7. Why do people in colder climates need to consume more kilocalories to maintain body weight than do people in warmer areas?
8. Explain the differences and similarities between anorexia nervosa and bulimia.

CHAPTER

5

Acids and Bases

This chapter will help you . . .

- Discuss what happens when water ionizes and how ionization relates to the formation of acids and bases.
- Identify the properties of acids and bases.
- Describe the pH scale and how it is used.
- Use indicators to measure the pH of solutions.
- Define atomic mass and mole and analyze the relationship between them.
- Explain how molarity is calculated.
- Describe the importance of pH in digestion and blood.
- Discuss ways pH is related to the properties of food, its safety, and its freshness.

Terms to Remember

acids
atomic mass
atomic number
bases
botulism
buffers
concentration
end point
equivalence point
hydroxide ions
indicators
ionization
molarity
mole
neutral
neutralization
periodic table
pH scale
titration

Many chemical reactions in food preparation, as well as reactions in the body, occur in water solution. Some of these reactions take place because water can form ions.

IONIZATION OF WATER

You have learned that certain substances form charged particles called ions. The process of forming ions is called **ionization** (eye–ahn–ih–ZAY–shun). In the formula for an ion, the symbol of the element(s) involved is written first. It is followed by a superscript showing whether the ion is positively or negatively charged. A superscript is a small letter, number, or symbol written above and to the side of another. A hydrogen ion is written as $\mathbf{H^+}$.

Scientists have found that a tiny portion of water molecules in any sample of water forms ions. When ionization occurs in water, positive hydrogen ions (H^+) are released. Negative ions, called **hydroxide ions** (hy–DRAHK–side), are formed from the remaining hydrogen and oxygen. Hydroxide ions are written $\mathbf{OH^-}$. The ionization of water is shown by the equation below.

H_2O $\longleftrightarrow$	H^+	+	OH^-
Water	Hydrogen ion		Hydroxide ion

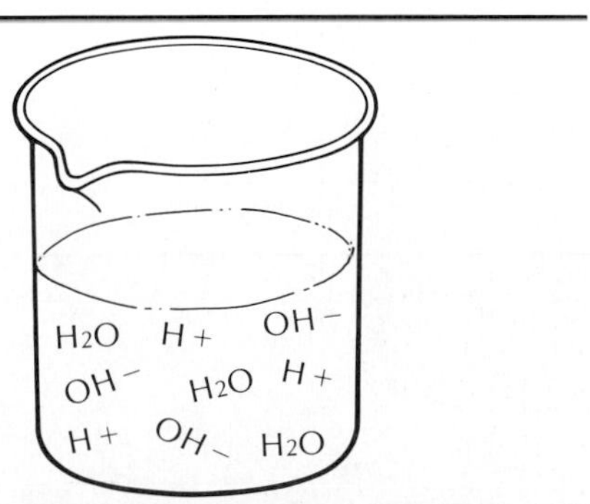

Water ionizes to form hydrogen and hydroxide ions.

The two–ended yield arrow in this equation shows that the ions can recombine to form water. All water contains some hydrogen ions and some hydroxide ions. When a water solution has an equal number of hydrogen and hydroxide ions, it is called **neutral.**

ACIDS AND BASES

There are certain substances that ionize when they dissolve in water. Some of these substances release hydrogen ions into the solution. These substances are called **acids.** Examples of acids are lemon juice and vinegar. Other substances ionize in water to produce hydroxide ions. These substances are called **bases.** Baking soda and lye are bases. When the hydrogen ions outnumber the hydroxide ions in a solution, it is called acidic. When the hydroxide ions outnumber the hydrogen ions, the solution is called basic.

• PROPERTIES OF ACIDS

All acid solutions have certain properties in common. These properties are caused by the presence of excess hydrogen ions.

Acids have a sour taste. The acetic acid in vinegar and the citric acid in citrus fruits are well–known sour–tasting acidic substances.

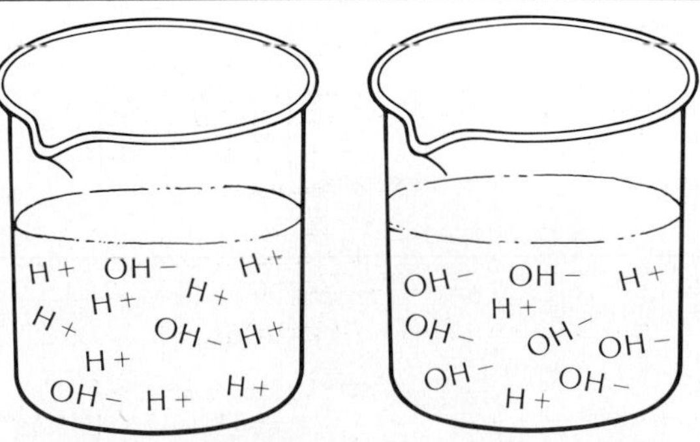

Acids release hydrogen ions in solution while bases produce hydroxide ions.

Acids change the color of certain organic dyes known as **indicators.** For example, litmus paper is an indicator that turns red in acid. Acid also changes the color of some foods such as tea and grape juice. The color of tea becomes lighter when lemon juice, an acid, is added to it. Grape juice turns reddish when acid is added. Even the color of certain flowers depends on the acidity of the soil in which they are grown. For example, hydrangeas may produce pink flowers when planted in neutral soil. Blooms can be made or kept blue by adding acidic compounds to the soil.

Acids react with bases in the process called **neutralization.** Neutralization is a chemical reaction in which hydrogen ions from an acid react with hydroxide ions from a base to produce water. The equation for neutralization is given below.

$$\underset{\text{Hydrogen ion}}{H^+} + \underset{\text{Hydroxide ion}}{OH^-} \rightarrow \underset{\text{Water}}{H_2O}$$

When neutralization occurs, acids lose their properties.

• PROPERTIES OF BASES

The chemical opposites of acids are bases, which release hydroxide ions in water solution. Bases, like acids, have certain unique properties. These traits are due in most cases to the excess hydroxide ions.

Bases taste bitter. Magnesium hydroxide, better known as milk of magnesia, has this bitter taste.

Bases feel slippery. Soaps and detergents are common household bases whose slippery feel is well–known by most people.

Bases change the color of indicators. Litmus paper turns blue in bases. Grape juice turns bluish when mixed with a base.

Bases react with acids in neutralization, producing water. During neutralization, bases lose their properties.

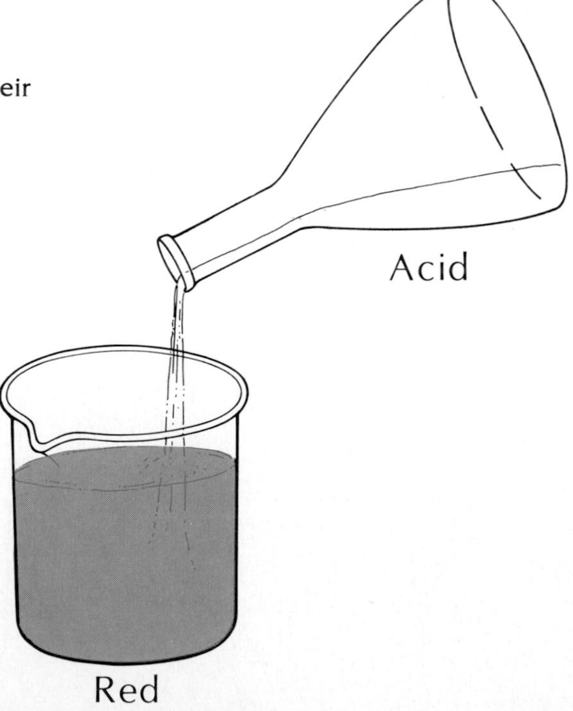

Acid changes some indicator dyes to red.

THE pH SCALE

The more free hydrogen ions there are in solution, the stronger the acid. The more free hydroxide ions, the stronger the base is. The relative number of hydrogen and hydroxide ions in a solution is measured on the **pH scale.**

The pH scale runs from 0–14. Lower numbers indicate there are more hydrogen than hydroxide ions in solution—that the solution is acidic. A 7 on the pH scale shows a solution is neutral. The numbers 8 and above show there are more hydroxide than hydrogen ions in solution. This indicates the solution is basic. Very low or very high numbers show a strong acid or base, while midrange numbers show that the acid or base is weak.

The farther away from seven the pH is, the stronger the solution. Thus, an acid solution of pH 4.2 is more acidic than an acid solution of pH 6.

The antacid tablet shown here is basic so it can be neutralized by the acid in the stomach.

Hydrogen and Hydroxide Ion Concentration

The chart below shows the relative concentrations of hydrogen and hydroxide ions in solution. The pH scale is shown on the bottom of the chart. A solution with a pH on the left side of the chart would contain nearly all hydrogen ions and would be a strong acid. As you move along the chart to the right, the concentration of hydroxide ions increases. A solution with a pH on the far right would contain nearly all hydroxide ions and would be a strong base. At the center, when the number of hydrogen and hydroxide ions is equal, the solution is neutral.

Strong Acid   Neutral   Strong Base

Hydrogen Ions   Hydroxide Ions

pH 1 2 3 4 5 6 7 8 9 10 11 12 13 14

Although many household cleaning agents are basic, few foods are.

A pH meter is used when very accurate pH measurements are needed.

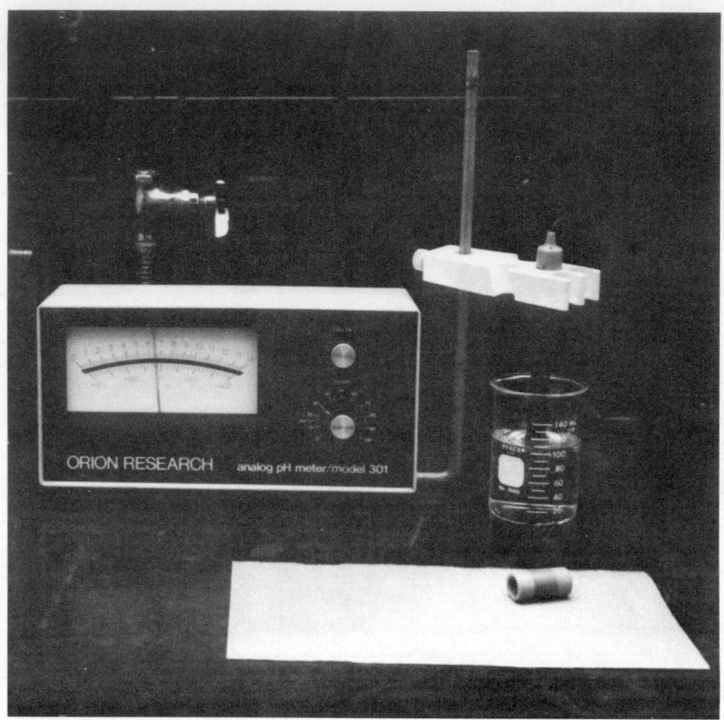

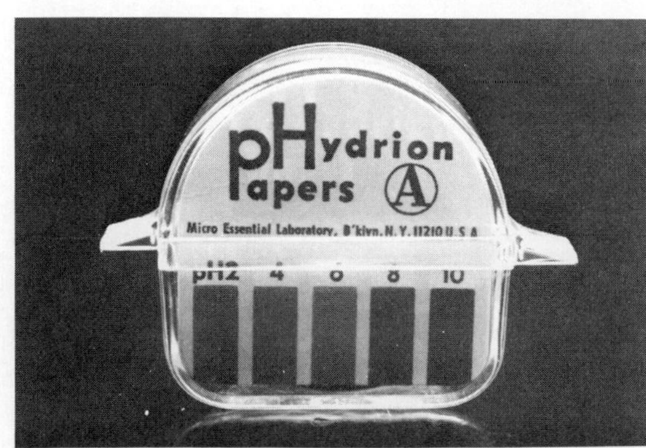

Indicator paper can show the approximate pH of a solution.

The pH of Common Solutions

Substance	pH
Gastric juice from the stomach	2.0
Vinegar	2.8
Orange juice	4.0
Coffee	5.0
Milk	6.5
Pure water	7.0
Blood	7.4
Seawater	8.5
Milk of magnesia	10.5
Ammonia	12.0
Lye	13.0

• MEASURING pH

One method of measuring the pH of a solution is to use an instrument called a pH meter. A pH meter allows a person to simply read the pH of a given solution. When precise readings are needed, a pH meter is used.

Another way to determine pH is to use indicator paper. This paper has been soaked with an indicator, a substance that changes color depending on the pH. The paper is dipped into the solution to be tested. The color of the paper is compared with a scale on which colors are matched with pH values. You will use this method in Experiment 5–1 in this chapter.

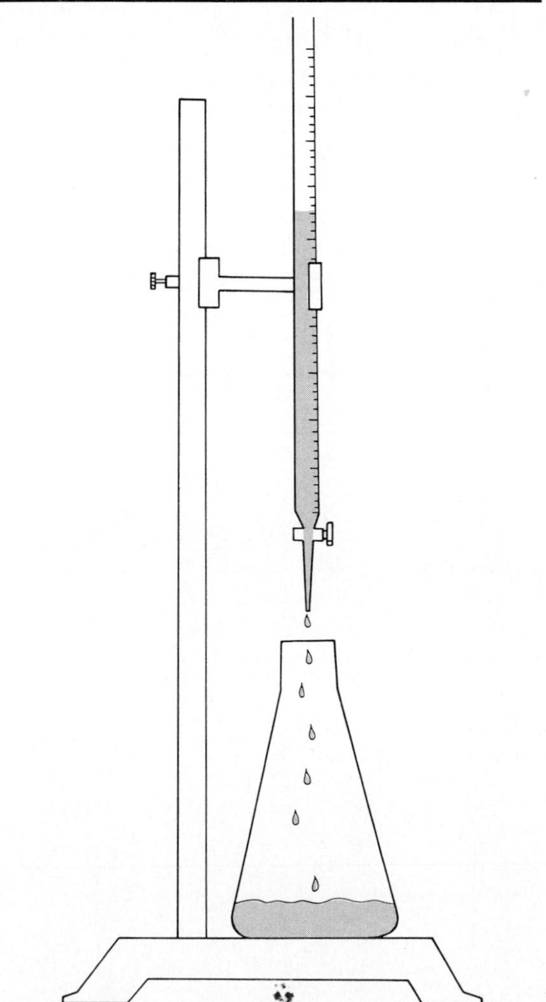

A ring stand and clamp, a buret, and an Erlenmeyer flask are basic equipment needed for titration.

A third method for finding the acidity is a procedure called **titration** (tie–TRAY–shun). Titration is a way to find the concentration of one substance by using a known volume and concentration of another substance. Therefore a known volume of an acid can be added to a known volume of a base until the solutions neutralize each other. The point at which neutralization occurs is called the **equivalence point**, or **end point.** This point is found by adding an indicator to one of the solutions before beginning the titration. The indicator will show when neutralization has occurred.

MOLES AND MOLARITY

Concentration is the measure of the amount of a substance in a given unit of volume. The concentration of an acid is the amount of hydrogen ions in a given volume of water. If the concentration of one solution used in titration

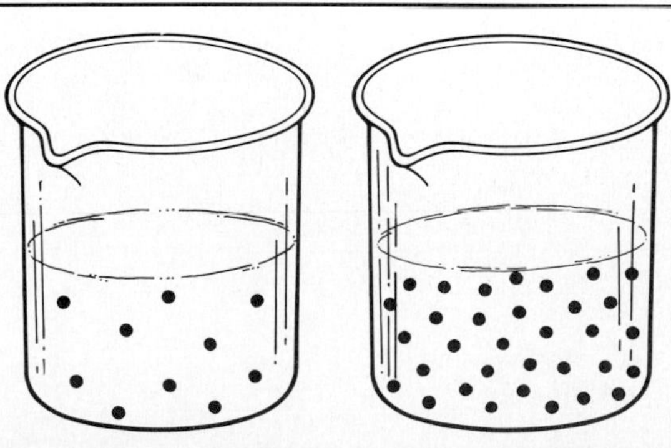

Which of these solutions is more concentrated?

is known, it is possible to figure the concentration of the other.

To carry out the calculations from titration data, a method for expressing the concentration of acids and bases is needed. Such a method involves learning more about the properties of atoms.

• ATOMIC MASS

Each element has an **atomic number** and an **atomic mass.** The atomic number is the number of protons in the nucleus of an atom. The atomic mass is the sum of the mass of the protons and neutrons in the nucleus of an atom.

The atomic mass of an atom can be found by using a **periodic table.** This is a chemical chart showing all the known elements in order of atomic number. Elements with similar properties are placed in the same vertical column in the chart.

• MOLES

Scientists often use a quantity called a **mole.** A mole is 602,000,000,000,000,000,000,000 items. It is more conveniently written 6.02×10^{23}. Just as a dozen is always 12, whether it is eggs or doughnuts, a mole is always 6.02×10^{23}. While moles would not be practical for counting eggs or doughnuts, they are useful to scientists. This is because a mole of one element always has the same number of atoms as a mole of any other element.

Scientists often want to relate the number of atoms of an element or molecules of a compound to a mass. One mole of an element is the number of grams equal to the atomic mass of the element. The atomic mass of sodium (Na) is 23, so a mole of sodium has a mass of 23 g. The atomic mass of chlorine (Cl) is 35.5, so a mole of chlorine has a mass of 35.5 g. One mole of a compound is the number of grams equal to the sum of the atomic masses of the

Atomic Mass

The atomic mass of an atom is the sum of the mass of the protons and neutrons in its nucleus. The atomic mass of an element is the average mass of a sample of atoms of that elements found in nature. Since atoms of the same element can have different masses, the atomic masses given in the Periodic Table and in this chart are often decimal numbers. These values show the relative mass of one element to another. Hydrogen has the smallest atomic mass at 1. Given below are the atomic masses for elements important in food science and nutrition.

Element	Symbol	Atomic Mass	Element	Symbol	Atomic Mass
Hydrogen	H	1.0	Sulfur	S	32.1
Carbon	C	12.0	Chlorine	Cl	35.5
Nitrogen	N	14.0	Potassium	K	39.1
Oxygen	O	16.0	Calcium	Ca	40.1
Sodium	Na	23.0	Iron	Fe	55.8
Magnesium	Mg	24.3	Zinc	Zn	65.4
Aluminum	Al	27.0	Iodine	I	126.9
Phosphorus	P	31.0			

elements in the compound. A mole of sodium chloride (NaCl) has a mass equal to the sum of the molar masses of sodium and chlorine, or 58.5 g (23 g + 35.5 g).

• CALCULATING MOLARITY

To figure the concentration of a solution, chemists often use the method called **molarity** (moe–LAR–uh–tee). Molarity is the number of moles of solute contained in a liter of solution. It is found by dividing the number of moles of solute in solution by the volume of the solution in liters.

$$\text{Molarity} = \frac{\text{Number of moles of solute}}{\text{Volume of solution in liters}}$$

A solution with a molarity of 1 would have 1 mole of solute for every liter of solution. This is called a one-molar solution and is written "1.0 M." For example, 1 mole of NaCl is 58.5 g. Therefore a one–molar (1.0 M) solution of NaCl in water contains 58.5 g NaCl for every liter of solution. A 2.0 M solution would have 2 moles of solute in each liter of solution. Therefore a 2.0 M solution of NaCl would have 117 g of NaCl for every liter of solution.

One mole of baking soda ($NaHCO_3$) contains 84 g while 1 mole of table salt (NaCl) contains 58.5 g.

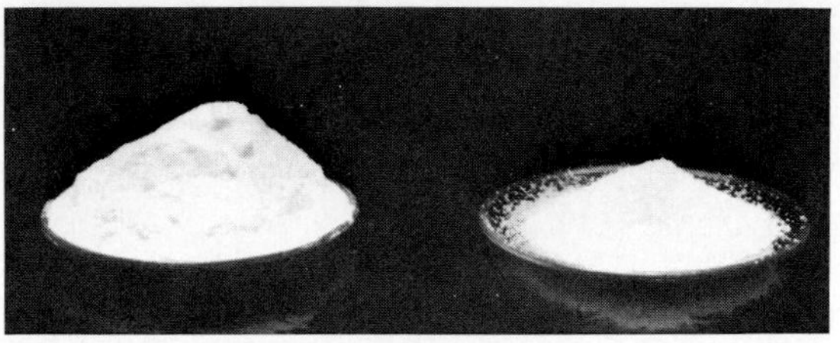

Later in this chapter, you will carry out a titration experiment using 1.0 M sodium hydroxide (NaOH) solution. This solution contains 1 mole of NaOH per liter of solution. A mole of NaOH is 40 g. To find this number, you add the number of grams in a mole of each of the elements in the compound.

Na	23 g
O	16 g
H	1 g
NaOH	40 g

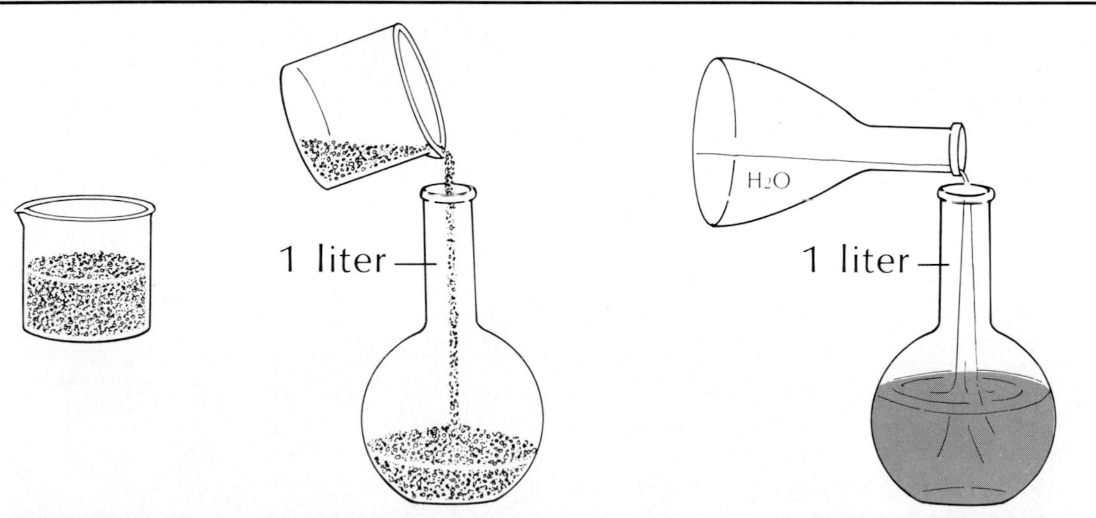

The steps in preparing a 2.0 M solution of NaCl are to mass 117 g NaCl and transfer to a 1 liter flask. Then add water filling the flask to the 1 liter mark.

Therefore a 1.0 M solution of NaOH contains 40 g of NaOH per liter of solution.

BLOOD pH

Regulation of the pH of blood is important to your health. Blood pH is about 7.4 and is held at a fairly constant level. It varies by only 0.2 in a given person. Someone whose blood pH varies much would become quite ill. If something goes wrong with the body's system of regulating blood pH, the person could develop acidosis (as–ih–DOE–sis) or alkalosis (al–kuh–LOW–sis). Acidosis is a condition in which the blood pH is 7.2 or lower. Alkalosis is the opposite condition—it involves too much base in the blood and body fluids. Both acidosis and alkalosis can cause death.

Blood pH is affected by carbon dioxide in the blood, which dissolves to form an acid. The body can adjust the amount of carbon dioxide absorbed to keep the blood from becoming too acidic. In addition, the body contains **buffers.** A buffer is a substance that helps maintain the relative balance of hydrogen and hydroxide ions in a solution. In the blood, buffers are large molecules often containing bicarbonate or phosphate ions. Blood protein also serves as a buffer. The buffers act as bases to neutralize excess acid formed by the carbon dioxide.

By keeping the dissolved carbon dioxide and the buffers in balance, the blood pH is maintained at about 7.4. If there is a large loss of bicarbonate ions or if organic acids build up, blood pH falls. The opposite conditions cause it to rise.

Food does not have an effect on the blood's pH. For example, eating large amounts of oranges or lemons does not make the blood acidic.

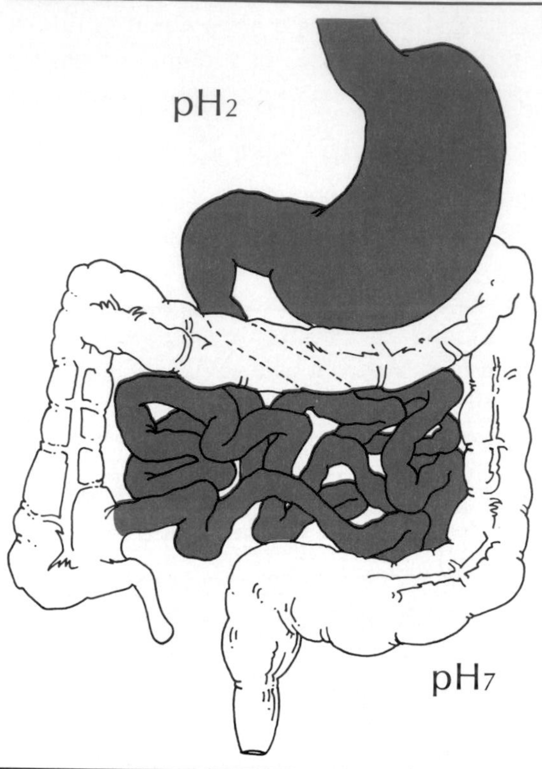

The strong acid from the stomach is neutralized in the small intestine.

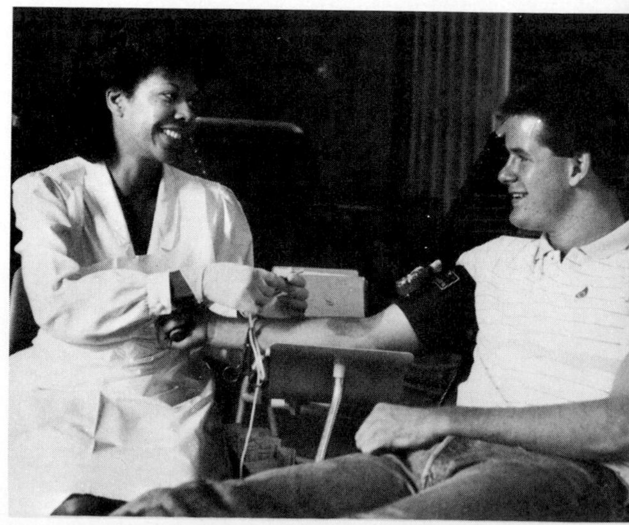

Blood taken from a healthy person will have a pH of about 7.4.

NUTRITION AND YOU

Digestion and pH

For the body to use the nutrients in the food you eat, your digestive system must work properly. Digestion is the chemical process of breaking down food and releasing nutrients in a form suitable for use by the body. You could not digest food if there were not a variety of pH levels within your digestive system.

One of the main digestive juices in the stomach is gastric juice. It is a strong acid, with a pH of 2 or less. The amount of gastric juice produced is regulated so the pH of the stomach remains between 1.5–1.7. The enzymes that digest protein need this highly acidic environment.

Digestion in the stomach involves mainly the breakdown of protein. There is very little digestion of the other nutrients in the stomach.

Stomach acid is so strong that the lining of the stomach must secrete a thick, slimy mucus to prevent damage to the stomach itself. No food is acidic enough to make stomach acid stronger. From the stomach, the food proceeds to the small intestine. The fluid in the small intestine is neutral, with a pH of about 7. This environment is needed for the action of intestinal enzymes.

In the small intestine, carbohydrates and fats are digested. The proteins are further broken down. The products formed by the breakdown of carbohydrate, fat, and protein are absorbed through the walls of the small intestine. Vitamins and minerals are absorbed mostly without being chemically changed.

Fiber, some water, a few mineral salts, and the wastes of digestion move to the large intestine. There, the mineral salts are absorbed, as is some of the water. The remaining materials are excreted.

Digestion is the first step in the process of nourishing the body. Many complex chemical changes occur during digestion. The regulation of pH is a critical factor in the successful digestion of food.

FOOD AND pH

Hydrogen ion concentration, or pH, is very important in the study and preparation of food. Whether a food is acidic or basic affects its properties and how it should be prepared and stored. Rarely is the pH of any ingredient used in food preparation exactly 7. Even distilled water can have a pH slightly below 7 if the water has absorbed carbon dioxide from the air. This causes it to be slightly acidic.

Natural Indicators

An indicator changes color depending on the pH of the solution with which it comes in contact. Although most indicators are commercially prepared, some can be made from food. Certain water–soluble plant pigments or colorings, known as anthocyanins, (an–thoh–SIGH–uh–nins) are very sensitive to pH changes. These pigments are found in foods that are blue and/or shades of red. Anthocyanins can be used as pH indicators, much like litmus paper, which turns pink in acids and blue in bases.

In an acid solution, anthocyanins turn red. In neutral solutions, they turn light violet or colorless. In basic solutions, they turn blue. You can observe this behavior by first adding lemon juice and then baking soda to the juice of red cabbage, concord grapes, or blackberries. The acid will turn the juice bright red, while the base will change the color to blue.

• CAKES

pH is important in preparing food products such as cake. Cakes and other baked goods contain leavening agents. These are substances that help baked products lighten or rise. The type of leavening agent used influences the pH of the cake.

If a recipe calls for a leavening agent that provides too much base, the pH of the cake will be too high. This can cause the cake crumbs to become coarse and the cell walls to be thicker. As a result, the cake will have a grainy texture. The cake will also be flatter and heavier if it is slightly basic. A chocolate cake becomes redder as the pH increases.

pH can affect the texture of a cake.

• CANNING

In canning, pH is important in determining whether food products are safe to eat. *Clostridium botulinum* (klahs–TRID–ee–um boch–uh–LIN–um), written as C. *botulinum*, is the name of an organism that causes **botulism** (BOCH–uh–liz–um), the most serious form of food poisoning known.

The crucial pH for preventing the growth of C. *botulinum* is 4.6. If a food has a pH of 4.6 or less, it is considered a high–acid food and therefore safe from C. *botulinum*. If a food has a pH greater than 4.6, it is considered a low–acid food. C. *botulinum* grows rapidly in a low–acid environment. Therefore low–acid food must be handled in a very specific manner to eliminate the possibility of food poisoning.

Much research has been done to find the safest method of processing canned food that has a pH above 4.6. Because C. *botulinum* is only

C. *botulinum* cannot grow in a high–acid environment where the pH is below 4.6.

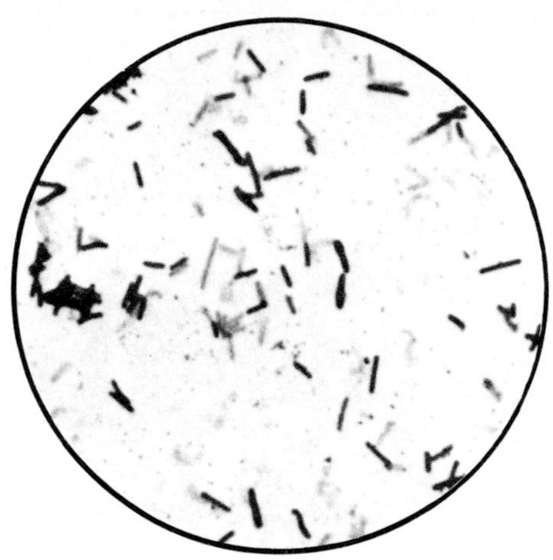

As pH increases, the egg becomes flatter.

destroyed by very high heat, all canned low–acid food must be processed in a pressure cooker. No other processing method produces a high enough heat to destroy C. *botulinum*. It is important to follow recommended times and pressure to be sure that the bacteria are destroyed.

• EGGS

pH is important in handling eggs during storage. If eggs are stored for a week or longer, the pH will change from a normal value of about 7.6 to as high as 9.7. This occurs because carbon dioxide escapes through the shells, leaving the eggs more basic. The increase in pH in the thick egg white causes the breakdown of its structure. This is why old eggs are runnier and have less thick white around the yolk than fresh eggs. Egg producers coat the eggs with an oil film to prevent the loss of carbon dioxide in order to maintain freshness.

pH affects how easy it is to peel a hard-cooked egg. When an egg is hard to peel, it is probably very fresh and still has a pH below 8.7. Once an egg has been stored for several days in the refrigerator, it will have a pH of at least 9.1. Then the egg will be less likely to stick to the shell during peeling.

• WINE

Wine makers use pH as an indicator of when grapes are ready to be harvested to make the best possible wine. If the grapes are too acidic or too basic, the wine will be of a lesser quality.

• FOOD FRESHNESS

The pH of food is one of the factors which affects how long it will stay fresh. Acidic foods do not spoil as quickly as other foods. Buttermilk, sauerkraut, or pickles can be stored for long periods of time because of their low pH.

The main causes of food spoilage are bacteria, yeast, and mold. Bacteria are single–cell organisms. Yeast are one–celled plants. Mold is an organism that grows on organic matter. It gives food a fuzzy appearance.

Bacteria in food grows best at a neutral pH of about 7, although some types can grow in acidic foods. Yeast can grow in a much wider pH range of 4–7. Molds can grow over the wide pH range of 2–8.5.

The pH of a food determines the type of spoilage it will experience in its natural state. Food that has a pH below 4.6, such as most fruit, is often attacked by yeasts and molds. Vegetables, which usually have a pH above 4.6, are more often spoiled by bacteria.

EXPERIMENT 5–1

The pH of Common Foods

The pH of food is important for several reasons. How acidic or basic a food is influences its taste. Acidic pH values tend to prevent food from spoiling. In this experiment, you will test some common foods and food ingredients to determine their pH values.

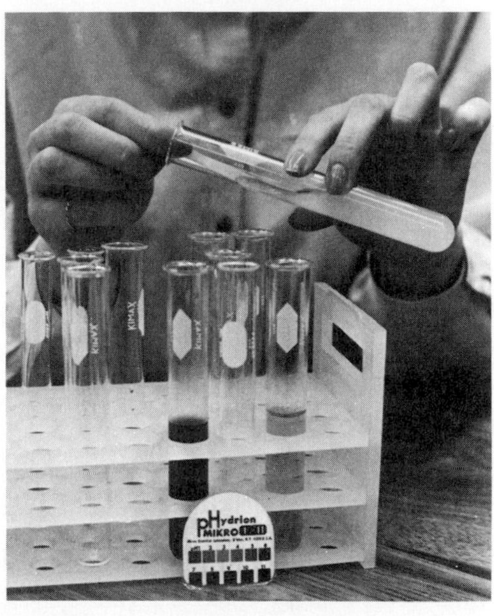

PROCEDURE

1. Working with another laboratory group, prepare half a test tube of each of the 14 substances listed in the data table below. Shake all mixtures to be sure they are dissolved. Label each test tube with the name of the substance it contains.
2. Using pH indicator paper, determine the pH of each solution by dipping the paper into each liquid sample and matching the color to the chart provided. In your data table, record your results.
3. After the pH of all 14 solutions has been tested, combine the contents of test tubes 3 and 4. Be sure to mix thoroughly. Record the pH of the resulting solution.

QUESTIONS

1. Which solutions were acidic?
2. Which solutions were basic?
3. Which solutions were neutral?
4. When an acid and a base were mixed together in step 3, what happened to the pH? What is this process called?
5. What did you observe when you mixed the solutions in step 3? How is this chemical reaction used in preparing some foods?
6. Do you think all tap water has the same pH? Why or why not?

EXPERIMENT 5–1

SAMPLE DATA TABLE

Test Tube Number	Solution	pH
1	tap water	
2	deionized water	
3	vinegar (5% acetic acid)	
4	sodium bicarbonate (a few crystals) dissolved in deionized water	
5	egg white	
6	5 mL honey dissolved in tap water	
7	5 mL molasses dissolved in tap water	
8	buttermilk	
9	lemon juice	
10	cream of tartar (a few grains) dissolved in tap water	
11	lemon–lime soda	
12	cranberry–apple juice	
13	milk	
14	powdered orange drink dissolved in tap water	
3-4	mixture of test tubes 3 and 4	

EXPERIMENT 5–2

Neutralization

Vinegar is a household solution that contains acetic acid. In this experiment, you will compare the acetic acid content of several brands of vinegar. You will do this by titrating equal volumes of the vinegar with the base sodium hydroxide (NaOH). You will determine how much base is needed to neutralize the acid in the vinegar. The more acid present, the larger the quantity of base you will need to neutralize it.

PROCEDURE

1. Wear safety goggles throughout this experiment. The NaOH could harm your eyes if it were accidentally splashed in them.
2. Clamp a clean 50 mL buret to a ring stand. Fill the buret with 1.0 M NaOH solution.
3. Fill a second buret with the brand of vinegar assigned by your teacher.
4. Add 20 mL vinegar from the buret to a clean 250 mL Erlenmeyer flask. Add three drops of the indicator phenolphthalein to the vinegar. The phenolphthalein will change color to show when to stop the titration process. Place the flask under the tip of the buret containing the NaOH.

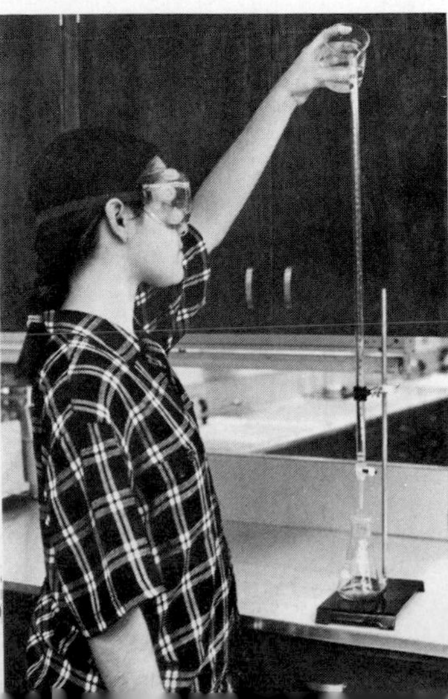

5. Slowly add the NaOH to the vinegar. When a pink color appears where the base first contacts the acid, gently swirl the flask until the color disappears. Add the base drop by drop, swirling after each drop, until one final drop of base turns the solution a pale pink that does not disappear when the flask is swirled.
6. In your data table, record the volume of NaOH used.
7. Wash out the flask, and repeat the titration. If you used more than 25 mL of base, be sure to refill the buret holding the base before you begin the second titration.
8. Again, record the volume of base required. If this is different from your first value, average the two amounts.
9. Report your figures on the chalkboard.
10. In your data table, record the figures for each of the brands of vinegar used by the other experiment groups.

QUESTIONS

1. Do all brands of vinegar contain the same amount of acetic acid? If not, which brand contained the most acid? How do you know?
2. Which brand of vinegar would you choose to use in salad dressing? Why?
3. Which brand of vinegar would be best to use in pickling when it is important to lower the pH as much as possible?

SAMPLE DATA TABLE

Brand of Vinegar	Volume of Base Trial 1	Volume of Base Trial 2	Average Volume

TO SUM UP

- Acids have a sour taste, change the color of indicators, and neutralize bases.
- Bases have a bitter taste, feel slippery, change the color of indicators, and neutralize acids.
- The pH of a solution can be measured by a pH meter, indicator paper, or titration.
- A mole is 6.02×10^{23} items and is the unit of measure scientists use to relate the number of atoms in an element or molecules in a compound to a mass in grams.
- Molarity is the number of moles of a solute in a liter of solution.
- The pH of the fluids in the stomach and small intestine is an important factor in the digestion of food.
- Buffers help regulate blood pH to prevent excessive buildup of hydrogen or hydroxide ions.
- The pH of a food can affect its properties, safety, and freshness.

CHECK YOUR FACTS

1. Write the equation for the ionization of water.
2. List three properties of acids.
3. List three properties of bases.
4. What is the pH of a neutral solution?
5. Is a solution with a pH of 4.8 acidic or basic?
6. What is the pH of pure distilled water?
7. What color would litmus paper turn in lemon juice?
8. What is the end point in titration?
9. What is the atomic mass of carbon? Sulfur? Calcium?
10. How many grams make a mole of oxygen? Phosphorus? Iron? Carbon dioxide (CO_2)?
11. Why is the pH of the fluids in the stomach so low?
12. What is the appropriate pH of the blood?
13. What pH is necessary to ensure that canned food is safe from C. *botulinum*?
14. Why does an egg turn basic during storage?
15. Within what pH range can yeast grow?

CRITICAL THINKING AND PROBLEM SOLVING

1. What determines if a sample of tap water is neutral?
2. If a cleanser causes blackberry juice to turn blue when the two come in contact, is the cleanser an acid or a base?
3. If it takes 15 mL of a base to neutralize 10 mL of vinegar, which solution is more concentrated? How do you know?
4. What is the molarity of a solution that contains 36.5 g of HCl in 1 L of solution?
5. How many grams of calcium carbonate ($CaCO_3$) are needed to make a 1.0 M solution?
6. Look up brownie, muffin, and pound cake recipes, and identify the source of acid and/or base in each.
7. What happens to the pH of a lemon–lime soft drink as it goes flat?

UNIT 2

The Science of Nutrition

In Unit 1, you studied some of the basic scientific information needed by food scientists. In addition, you experimented with equipment and techniques used in food science experiments. Now you are ready to begin your study of the nutrients that are important to your body.

In Chapter 6, you will find information about water. This common substance is essential to life. To understand why water behaves as it does in your body, as well as in food preparation, it is important to learn about its structure and properties.

Chapter 7 will introduce you to the properties of carbohydrates, the most abundant organic molecules on earth. You will learn about sugar and starch, as well as how these substances are used in cooking. In addition, you will read about some of the health problems that arise when the body does not process sugar properly.

Lipids, or fats as they are more commonly called, have an important role to play in a balanced diet. In Chapter 8, you will learn about the uses of fats in cooking, as well as in your body. You will also find information on how the consumption of fat can be related to heart disease.

To be healthy, all human beings need protein in the diet. By studying Chapter 9, you will learn about the structure and composition of protein, how it functions in food, and why it is so important to your body.

Vitamins and minerals are the nutrients you will study in Chapter 10. You will learn what vitamins are and read about those that dissolve in water, as well as those that dissolve in fat. Then you will be introduced to the minerals that are important to good health and discover the reasons they are needed by your body.

Unit 2 concludes with Chapter 11, which is on metabolism. You will learn how your body converts the food you eat into the energy you need. Some of the factors that affect the rate at which your body uses food are also discussed.

CHAPTERS

CHAPTER

6

Water

This chapter will help you . . .

- Explain the properties of water that make it a polar molecule.
- Describe hydrogen bonds and how they differ from covalent bonds.
- Discuss the differences between hard water and soft water.
- Compare and contrast heat of fusion and heat of vaporization.
- Explain the functions of water in food preparation.
- Name the two general types of water in food.
- Identify the functions of water in the body.

Terms to Remember

boiling point
bound water
colloidal dispersions
density
emulsifier
emulsions
free water
hard water
heat of fusion
heat of vaporization
hydrogen bond
immiscible
medium
melting point
metabolism
polar molecule
soft water
solute
solvent
sublimation

Water is an important compound to food scientists, since it affects the look, texture, and flavor of food. It also has many functions in food preparation. Before you go further in your study of food science, you need to take an in-depth look at water—its properties, uses, and nutritional importance.

THE STRUCTURE OF WATER

Water is a molecular compound made up of the two elements oxygen and hydrogen. Each water molecule contains one oxygen atom and two hydrogen atoms, which are bonded to the oxygen at a 105° angle. Water's formula is $\mathbf{H_2O}$.

• A POLAR MOLECULE

Oxygen is an electronegative element. This means it tends to attract the shared electrons in a molecule and become negatively charged. It is much more electronegative than hydrogen. Therefore the electrons that the oxygen and hydrogen share in the covalent bonds exist closer to the oxygen atom than to the hydrogen atoms. As a result, the oxygen end of a water molecule is somewhat negative, while the hydrogen end is somewhat positive.

A molecule such as water, in which there is a division of charge, is called a **polar molecule.** The bonds within such a molecule are referred to as polar covalent bonds. They are called this because they are covalent bonds in which electrons are shared unequally.

• HYDROGEN BONDS

The polar nature of water molecules leads to their attracting each other far more strongly than would be expected. This attraction is caused by a **hydrogen bond.** A hydrogen bond is an attraction occurring in polar compounds in which a hydrogen atom of one molecule is attracted to the negative end of another molecule. This kind of bond exists between molecules in which hydrogen is bonded to either oxygen, nitrogen, or fluorine.

In water, hydrogen bonds exist between a hydrogen end of one molecule and the oxygen end of a neighboring molecule. These hydrogen bonds are much weaker than the covalent bonds within each water molecule. However, they are much stronger than the bonds that exist between nonpolar molecules.

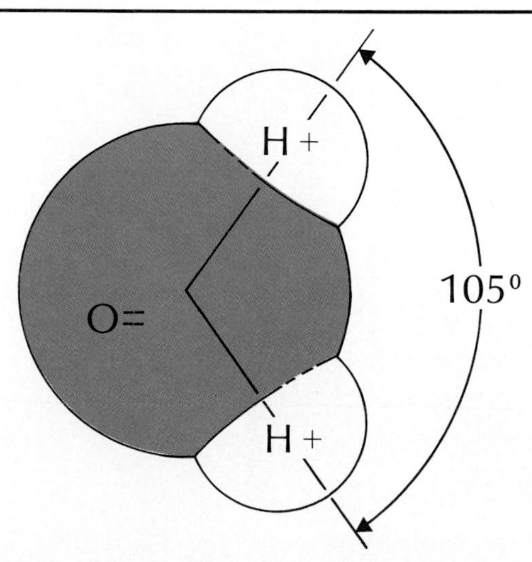

The oxygen end of a water molecule is slightly negative while the hydrogen end is slightly positive.

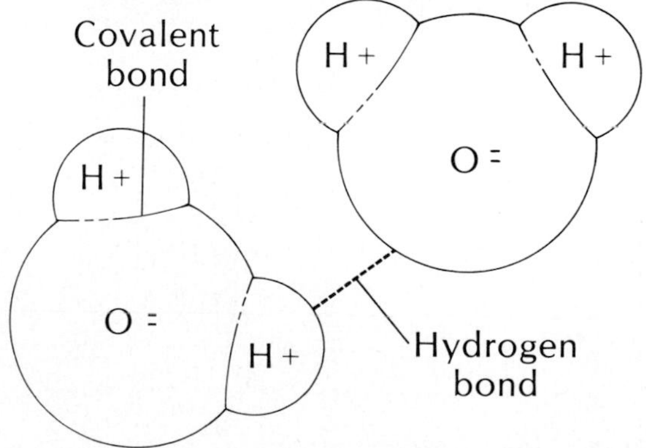

Hydrogen bonds occur in water when the positive hydrogen end of a water molecule is attracted to the negative oxygen end of another water molecule.

Impurities in Water

Even when water is safe to drink, it usually contains dissolved substances that make it chemically impure. The terms "**hard water**" and "**soft water**" refer to whether or not water contains certain metal ions. Hard water is water that contains calcium or magnesium ions; soft water does not contain metal ions.

Whether water is hard or soft can affect the quality of food prepared with it. Beverages such as ice tea may be cloudy if made with hard water. The ions in hard water may interfere with tenderizing certain food. For example, dried beans, peas, or lentils will not become very tender when cooked in hard water.

Hard water does not dissolve soap as effectively as water that does not contain calcium or magnesium ions. As a result, laundry washed in hard water tends to have a grayish film on it. Dishes washed in hard water in a dishwasher often have water spots on them.

Usually, it is best to remove the undesirable ions from hard water. Sometimes the metal ions are present as bicarbonates. The metal ions are bonded to bicarbonate ions, and the compound is dissolved in the water. Water with bicarbonate ions in it is considered temporarily hard water.

Bicarbonates change to insoluble carbonates upon boiling. The compounds formed between the metal ions and the carbonate ions do not dissolve in water. Instead they settle to the bottom of the container. Thus the water can be softened simply by boiling it.

On the other hand, if the metal ions are present as compounds called sulfates, the water is considered permanently hard. Such permanently hard water must pass through an ion exchange filter or undergo chemical treatment to remove the calcium or magnesium ions.

In areas with hard water, many consumers use appliances called water softeners. Water entering the house flows through the water softener to remove the metal ions. The resulting soft water produces cleaner dishes and clothes and more successful food preparation.

Hard water can prevent these dried beans from being as tender as those cooked in soft water.

PHASE CHANGES IN WATER

As you know, water exists as a solid, a liquid, or a gas. When it moves from one state to another, it goes through a phase change. Ice goes through a phase change when it melts into liquid water. Another phase change occurs when the liquid water vaporizes to steam.

Phase changes occur at the **melting point** and the **boiling point** of a substance. Melting point is the temperature at which a substance changes from a solid to a liquid. The boiling point of a substance is the temperature at which its vapor pressure equals the pressure over the liquid. Water has much higher melting and boiling points than many other substances because of its hydrogen bonds.

• MELTING POINT

Generally, pure water exists as a solid below 0°C. When water freezes, the molecules arrange themselves into a crystal structure. The hydrogen bonds cause the water molecules to spread farther apart when they freeze. This causes water to freeze and ice to melt at a higher temperature (0°C) than some other substances freeze and melt. Ice will melt if its surroundings are warmer than 0°C.

Because the molecules in ice are spread apart, ice is lighter or less dense than liquid water. **Density** is the mass per unit volume of a substance. Because ice has less mass than liquid water per unit volume, it floats on liquid water.

The amount of heat required to change 1 g of a substance from the solid phase to the liquid phase is called the **heat of fusion.** For water, the heat of fusion is 80 calories per gram (80 cal/g). This means that it takes 80 calories to change 1 g of water from ice to liquid. The heat of fusion doesn't produce an increase in temperature when it is absorbed by the ice. Instead, it gives the water molecules the energy they need to break out of the crystal structure. You will remember that the heat required to create a phase change without a change in temperature is called latent heat. Therefore heat of fusion is an example of latent heat.

Ice floats because it is less dense than liquid water.

Sublimation occurs when dry ice goes directly from the solid phase to the gas phase.

The heat of fusion and the heat of vaporization are measures of the energy needed to cause phase changes.

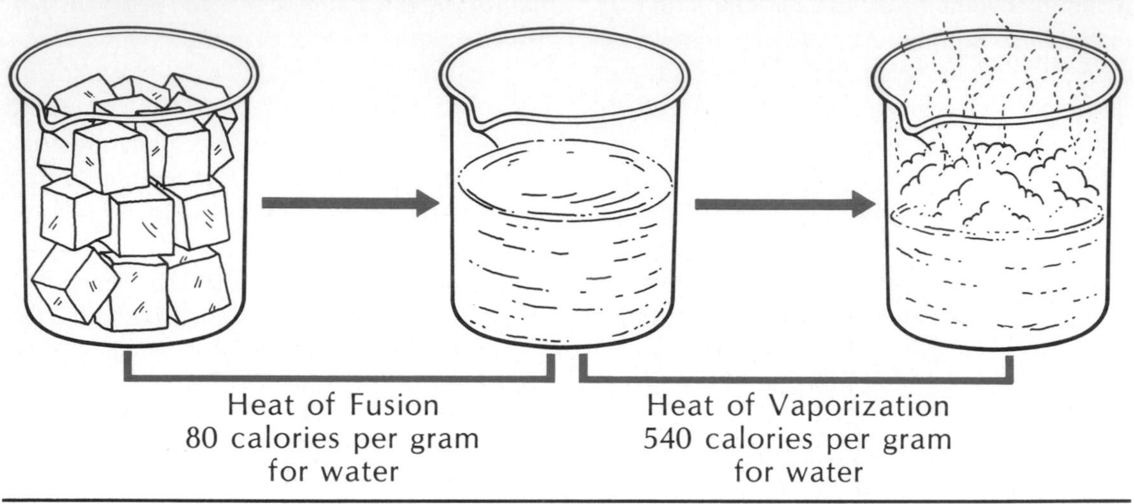

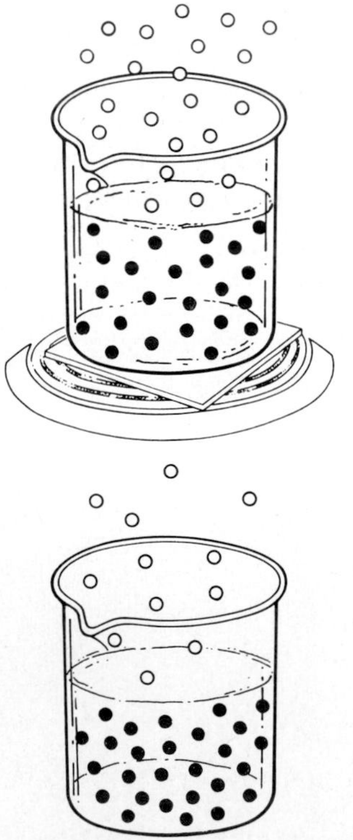

Boiling water causes evaporation to occur more rapidly, but the temperature of the water remains at the boiling point.

The water molecules in ice crystals can pass directly into the gas or vapor phase without melting. This is called **sublimation** (sub–luh–MAY–shun), which occurs when a substance changes from the solid phase directly into the gas phase. Dry ice undergoes sublimation since it changes from a solid to a gas without becoming a liquid. Sometimes products stored for long periods of time in the freezer get freezer burn, which is an unwanted result of sublimation. The food becomes dry and loses color, texture, and flavor.

• BOILING POINT

As you learned in Chapter 3, vaporization is the change of a substance from a liquid to a gas. Water vaporizes when it turns to steam. Evaporation is vaporization that takes place at the surface of a liquid.

Water has a much higher boiling point than would otherwise be expected because of its hydrogen bonds. Its boiling point, 100°C, is high because the hydrogen bonds have to be broken before the liquid water can turn to steam.

Boiling Point and Air Pressure

The boiling point of water depends on the pressure of the air over it. Pressure is a force that acts over a certain area. Air pressure is, therefore, the force that air exerts as it presses on the earth.

Air pressure over liquid water prevents gas molecules from escaping into the air. It is only when the gas molecules gain enough force to equal the force of the air pressure that vaporization occurs. Gas molecules gain the force needed by being heated.

Pure water boils at 100°C at standard atmospheric pressure, which is the pressure of the air at sea level on a clear day. Lowering the air pressure lowers the boiling point. When air pressure is low, bubbles of gas can more easily form in liquid and escape.

At high altitudes, air pressure is lower. As a result, for every 293 m increase in altitude, the boiling point of water drops 1°C. This means that at higher altitudes food prepared in water must cook longer. The proportions of ingredients in recipes, especially water, may need to be altered.

Less drastic changes in air pressure occur with changes in the weather. When the weather is stormy, air pressure is lower. Therefore the boiling point of water is lower on stormy days. The fact that boiling point varies is why it is important to calibrate your thermometer and make adjustments when preparing candy and fruit pectin jellies.

The use of a pressure cooker can help offset the decrease in the boiling point of water that results from lower air pressure. The function of a pressure cooker is to raise the pressure over water that is being heated. The pressure cooker does this by trapping the steam as it leaves the liquid phase. This adds the pressure of the steam to the pressure of the atmosphere. The increased pressure raises the boiling point of the water and allows food to cook faster.

If you were to build a campfire somewhere in this illustration, where could you heat water the fastest for a hot drink?

The **heat of vaporization** is the amount of heat needed to change 1 g of a substance from the liquid phase to the gas phase. The heat of vaporization of water is 540 calories per gram (540 cal/g). This means it takes 540 calories to change 1 g of water from liquid to steam. Like heat of fusion, this is an example of latent heat because it does not produce an increase in temperature.

Once water begins to boil, its temperature remains constant. Therefore boiling water rapidly will cause it to evaporate more quickly, but it will not make the water hotter. It is usually a waste of energy to leave a heating unit on high once water begins to boil.

Water Content in Food

Water makes up a major portion of many foods. Between 70–90 percent of fruits, vegetables, and meats is water. It is not always easy to judge the water content of a food by its appearance.

Some water readily separates from food when the food is sliced, diced, or dried out. Such water is known as **free water.** A slice of bread left uncovered overnight becomes dry because the free water evaporates.

The rest of the water in food, which cannot be easily separated, is called **bound water.** Bound water is tightly held by the various chemical groups in the molecules of food. It is not free to react with other substances the way free water is. It does not freeze until very low temperatures are reached. Bound water does not evaporate the way free water does. Therefore bound water is not involved when food dries out upon standing.

WATER IN FOOD PREPARATION

Water serves a variety of functions in the preparation of food. It is an important **medium** in food preparation. A medium is a substance through which something is transmitted or carried.

• HEAT TRANSFER

Water can be a medium for the transfer of heat from a heating unit to a food. If potatoes, for example, were simply placed in a saucepan over heat, the bottom layer of potatoes would scorch before the rest of the potatoes had cooked. If potatoes are heated in water, on the other hand, the water at the bottom of the pan absorbs the heat first. Heat is transferred throughout the water by conduction and convection. Therefore the potatoes can cook evenly.

• SOLUTIONS

You will recall that a solution is a homogeneous mixture in which one substance is dissolved in another substance. The substance that does the dissolving is called a **solvent** (SAHL–vunt).

The free water readily separates from this orange.

The substance that dissolves is the **solute** (SAHL–yoot). When a substance dissolves in another substance, it is called soluble. Therefore a solute is soluble in a solvent.

Water functions as a solvent in some foods. Because it is a polar molecule, water can dissolve ionic substances. This happens because the charged ends of the water molecules attract ions of the opposite charge, pulling them out of their crystal structure into solution. For example, sodium chloride (table salt) dissolves in water because the negative oxygen end of the water molecule attracts the positive sodium ion. The positive hydrogen ends of the water molecule attract negative chloride ions.

In addition, since water is molecular, it can dissolve many molecular substances, such as sugar, soluble vitamins and minerals, and flavorings. The flavorings in tea leaves or coffee beans dissolve in water to form popular beverages. Sugar added to sweeten strawberries dissolves in the berries' free water to form a sweet syrup. Vitamin C can dissolve into cooking water and be lost during food preparation. You will learn more about solutions in Chapter 13.

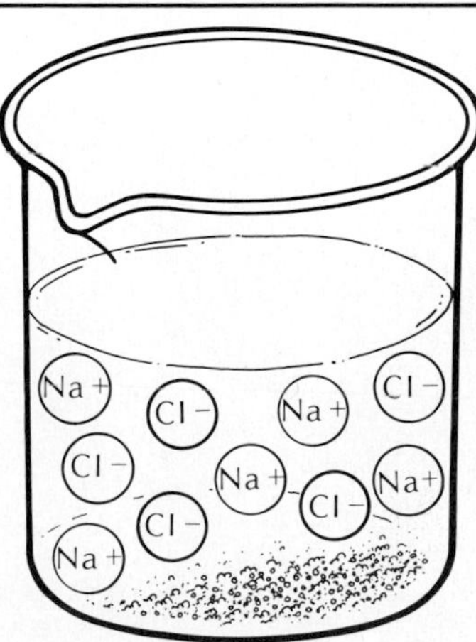

Sodium chloride is the solute and water is the solvent in this beaker of salt water.

• COLLOIDAL DISPERSIONS

Water can also be a medium for **colloidal dispersions** (kuh–LOYD–ul dis–PUR–zhuns). A colloidal dispersion is a homogeneous mixture that is not a true solution. A colloidal dispersion differs from a true solution in the relatively larger size of the solute particles and their larger surface area. These particles are called colloids (KAHL–oyds).

Although colloids are larger than atoms, ions, or molecules, they are still too small to be seen with a microscope. They are not so large that they settle out of the colloidal dispersion. Instead they remain dispersed in, or scattered throughout, the solvent.

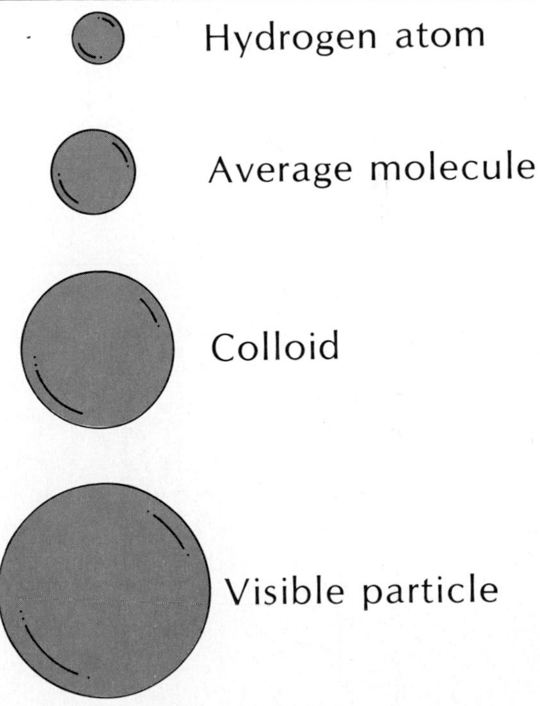

A colloid particle is larger than an atom or a molecule, but still not large enough to be seen.

Proteins as a group form colloidal dispersions. For example, the protein gelatin disperses colloidally in hot water. The first step in making a gelatin salad is to make a colloidal dispersion with gelatin and boiling water. Colloidal dispersions are described more thoroughly in Chapter 13.

• EMULSIONS

Another function of water is that of forming **emulsions** (ih–MUL–shuns). Emulsions are mixtures that contain two liquids whose droplets do not normally blend with each other. Liquids that don't blend or mix are called **immiscible** (ih–MISS–uh–bul). However, an emulsion contains a third substance, known as an **emulsifier** (ih–MUL–suh–fy–ur) or emulsifying agent. The emulsifier coats the droplets of one immiscible liquid so it can remain mixed in another immiscible liquid. Emulsions are often mixtures of water and fat. Mayonnaise, cream, and homogenized milk all contain fat in emulsified form. Emulsions will be explained in more detail in Chapter 13.

This gelatin salad began with a colloidal dispersion.

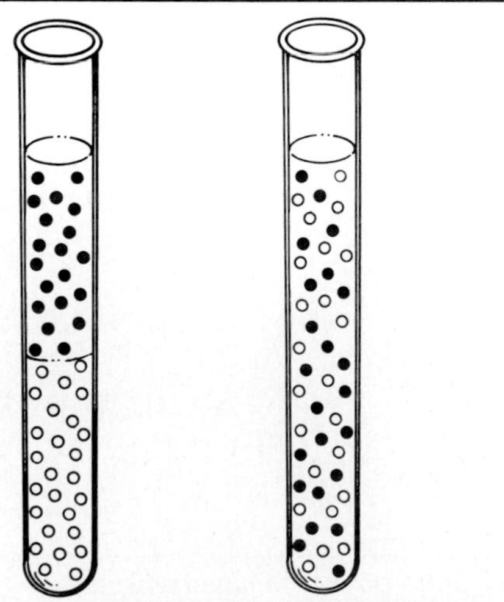

An emulsion is formed when two normally immiscible liquids are mixed with each other.

The evaporation of perspiration cools the body during exercise or illness.

NUTRITION AND YOU

Water: The Essential Nutrient

Water is an absolutely essential nutrient. You cannot live without it. While human beings have been known to survive for many weeks without food, they can live for only a few days without water.

Water has many functions in the body. It dissolves many of the nutrients you consume in your food and transports them to the individual cells in your body. It also carries away the waste materials produced in the cells. Water is a vital part of your body's **metabolism** (muh–TAB–uh–liz–um). Metabolism is the chemical and physical processes occurring within the living cells of the body. Many of the chemical reactions in your body take place in water. In addition, water is an essential reactant in many of those chemical processes.

Water helps your body maintain a constant temperature. Normally, if your body temperature begins to rise, you perspire. This could occur when you exercise or when you are ill with a fever. The perspiration then evaporates off your skin. Energy is required for evaporation to occur, and you are the nearest source of energy. The water removes energy from your body as it evaporates and helps maintain a constant body temperature. When a person becomes ill and loses large amounts of water through vomiting or diarrhea, the body temperature can rise rapidly. Unless fluids can be quickly replaced, death can occur.

The human body is composed of 45–60 percent water by weight. The exact percentage will depend on the amount of fat, bone, and muscle present. Men usually have a slightly higher percentage of water present in their bodies than women. This is because they have a higher proportion of muscle to fat.

Water Requirements

In general, your body obtains water in two ways. It comes from food and liquid you consume or from chemical reactions that take place within your body. Your body helps regulate water intake by causing you to feel thirsty when your body needs more water. Most nutritionists recommend drinking six to eight glasses of liquid a day.

As long as you are healthy, your body maintains a remarkable balance between the amount of water you take in and that which you put out. Normally, you would take in about 800 mL of water a day in the food you eat and another 1000 mL in the liquid you drink. About 300 mL are produced by the chemical reactions taking place within your body. At the same time, you lose about 1300 mL of water a day as urine and another 100 mL as feces. About 50 mL is lost through the skin as perspiration, and you exhale approximately 650 mL as water vapor. On the average, you will add and lose about 2100 mL of water each day.

EXPERIMENT 6–1

Dissolving Solids in Water

Water is an extremely important and effective solvent for many of the substances found in food. How many grams of a particular substance will dissolve in a given amount of water depends on two factors. The first is the substance itself, and the second is the temperature of the water. In this experiment, you will compare the solubility of three compounds. Solubility is the maximum amount of solute that can be dissolved in a definite amount of solvent at a specific temperature. You will find out how much sucrose (sugar), sodium chloride (table salt), and potassium nitrate can dissolve in 10 mL of water at room temperature (20°C) and at 80°C.

PROCEDURE

1. Mass 5.0 g samples of sucrose, sodium chloride, and potassium nitrate. Put each sample in a clean test tube.
2. Gently tap the test tube containing the sucrose on the counter to level the solid. Measure the height of the sucrose in the test tube using a metric ruler. Record the height in your data table.
3. Using your 10 mL graduated cylinder, add 10 mL water to the test tube. Stopper the test tube, and shake for two minutes to dissolve as much sucrose as possible.
4. Allow the undissolved sucrose to settle to the bottom of the test tube. Measure the height of the remaining solid. Record this information in your data table.
5. Repeat steps 2–4 using the samples of sodium chloride and potassium nitrate.
6. Fill a 400 mL beaker half full of water. Heat on a burner set on high. Place all three test tubes in the beaker. Place a thermometer in the test tube containing the sucrose. Heat the test tubes in the beaker until the thermometer reads 80°C. If the test tubes have been in the same water bath for the same amount of time, you can assume that the solutions in each are the same temperature.
7. Remove the test tubes from the water, and place them in a test tube rack. Stir any mixture still containing solid. After the solids settle, measure and record the height of any undissolved solids remaining in each test tube.

EXPERIMENT 6–1

QUESTIONS

1. Which solid dissolved to the greatest extent in room–temperature water? Which one dissolved the least?
2. Heating had the least effect on the solubility of which solid?
3. Were any of the solids less soluble in hot water than in room–temperature water?
4. What can you conclude about the effect of temperature on the solubility of solids?

SAMPLE DATA TABLE

Substance	Height of Original Solid	Height of Solid in 20°C H_2O	Height of Solid in 80°C H_2O
Sucrose			
Sodium chloride			
Potassium nitrate			

EXPERIMENT 6–2

The Boiling Point of Water

Most people know that it takes longer to boil a large amount of water than it does a small amount. Does this mean that the larger amount boils at a higher temperature? In this experiment, you will work to answer this question.

PROCEDURE

1. Pour the amount of liquid assigned you by your teacher into a 250 mL beaker. In your data table, record the temperature of the liquid.
2. Heat the beaker of liquid on the stove, reading and recording the temperature of the liquid every 30 seconds.
3. Continue to heat the liquid until about half of it has boiled away. Be sure to take readings the entire time the liquid is being heated.
4. Make a graph of your results. Plot the temperature of the liquid and the times at which your temperature readings were taken. Compare your results with those of other students.

QUESTIONS

1. Do the graphs of all students in the class have a similar shape?
2. Do all the graphs have a flat section (also called a plateau)?
3. Was the temperature the same in all the beakers once the liquid started to boil?
4. Could faulty thermometers be the cause of any differences in the boiling points in different beakers? Why or why not?
5. Does the boiling point of pure water depend on the amount of water?

SAMPLE DATA TABLE

Time	Temperature

TO SUM UP

- Water is a polar molecule because it has a division of electrical charge.
- Water forms hydrogen bonds when a hydrogen atom of one polar molecule is attracted to the negative end of another polar molecule.
- Hard water contains metal ions, which can affect food, laundry, and dishwashing.
- The heat of fusion and the heat of vaporization are involved in the phase changes of water.
- In food preparation, water acts as a solvent and as a medium for heat transfer, colloidal dispersions, and emulsions.
- Free water and bound water are types of water found in food.
- In the body, water functions as a solvent, a transporter of nutrients, a medium for reactions, a reactant, and a temperature regulator.

CHECK YOUR FACTS

1. Which end of a water molecule is negative?
2. What is the attraction between water molecules called?
3. How can temporarily hard water be softened?
4. Which is more dense, ice or liquid water? Why?
5. What is the heat of fusion of water?
6. Which requires more calories, heat of fusion or heat of vaporization?
7. Does water always boil at 100°C?
8. Name three functions of water in food preparation.
9. Explain the difference between free water and bound water.
10. Name three functions of water in the body.
11. How does the amount of water a person takes in compare to the amount of water put out?

CRITICAL THINKING AND PROBLEM SOLVING

1. Why does hard water leave more deposits in hot water pipes than in cold water pipes over a period of time?
2. Explain why temperature remains constant when ice melts or water boils.
3. Explain why ice is more effective than water at keeping food cool in an ice chest at 0°C.
4. How does the boiling point of water in Denver compare with the boiling point of water in New York City?
5. Why is it important for someone with a high fever to consume large quantities of fluid?
6. Which can be made to taste sweeter, iced tea or hot tea? Why?

CHAPTER

7

Carbohydrates

This chapter will help you . . .

- Explain the chemical reaction that occurs when plants produce carbohydrates.
- Define monosaccharides and disaccharides and name examples of each.
- Describe the normal regulation of glucose level in the blood and the conditions of low and high glucose levels.
- Explain sugar hydrolysis and list the products of the hydrolysis of sucrose and lactose.
- Discuss the process of caramelization.
- Compare the structures of amylose and amylopectin and how these structures affect cooking properties.
- Define the terms gelatinization, paste, retrogradation, and syneresis as used in starch cookery.

Terms to Remember

amylopectin
amylose
caramelization
dehydration
gelatinization
glucose
glycogen
hormone
hydrolysis
hydroxyl group
interfering agents
inversion
paste
photosynthesis
polymer
retrogradation
saccharide
supersaturated
syneresis
viscosity

Carbohydrates are the most abundant organic molecules on earth. They are the main source of energy for all animals, including human beings. In many parts of the world, 80 percent of the kilocalories consumed by humans are in the form of carbohydrates. This percentage is somewhat lower for most people in the United States because Americans tend to eat more meat than do people of other countries. Carbohydrates make up about 50 percent of diets in the United States.

Carbohydrates are molecules made of carbon, hydrogen, and oxygen. They are named for carbon and water—the "hydrate" syllable means that water has been added to the carbon. Carbohydrates studied in food science include sugars, starches, and plant fibers.

Over much of the world, carbohydrates such as these provide a large proportion of kilocalories consumed.

To get quick energy, athletes eat or drink food that contains sugar.

Carbohydrates and Weight

Carbohydrates have a poor reputation among some weight conscious people. Dieters should avoid food in which the carbohydrates are mostly sugar. These foods are often said to provide empty calories because they contain few if any of the nutrients needed to maintain a healthy body.

Foods in which carbohydrates are starches and fibers do have a place in weight reduction programs. Starches such as bread, potatoes, and rice are not high in kilocalories themselves. The butter, jelly, sour cream, or other flavorings added to them often contain more kilocalories than the starch products themselves. Fiber is found in fruits, vegetables, and grain products. It adds volume to the diet, causing the digestive tract to feel full. However, fiber does not provide kilocalories. Therefore food with lots of fiber can help decrease the desire for more calorie–rich foods.

The toppings on this baked potato contain more kilocalories than the potato!

Carbohydrates are one of the best fuels you can provide your body. Each gram of carbohydrate you eat produces 4 kcal of energy. Sugars and starches are the main sources of carbohydrate energy. The carbohydrates in plant fibers do not produce energy in the human body.

PLANTS: NATURE'S CARBOHYDRATE PRODUCERS

Carbohydrates cannot be produced by animals, only by green plants. Using the sun's energy, plants convert carbon dioxide from the air and water taken up by their roots into carbohydrate and oxygen. This process is known as **photosynthesis** (foe–toe–SIN–thuh–sis). The equation for photosynthesis is given below.

$$\underset{\text{Carbon dioxide}}{6CO_2} + \underset{\text{Water}}{6H_2O} + \text{Energy} \rightarrow \underset{\text{Carbohydrate (glucose)}}{C_6H_{12}O_6} \; ; \; \underset{\text{Oxygen}}{6O_2}$$

The green pigment that must be present in plants for photosynthesis to occur is called chlorophyll (KLOR–uh–fill).

The carbohydrate produced in the plant as shown in the equation above is the basic sugar unit called **glucose** (GLOO–kohs). All other carbohydrates are built around the glucose molecule. Once the glucose has been produced, the plant can convert the glucose molecules into other sugars, starches, or fiber. Generally, plants begin by changing the glucose into other sugars. As the plant matures, it converts these sugars into starches. For example, a green pea from a young plant is sweet, while those from older plants have a high concentration of starch. The fiber that is formed gives strength and support to the cell walls of the plants.

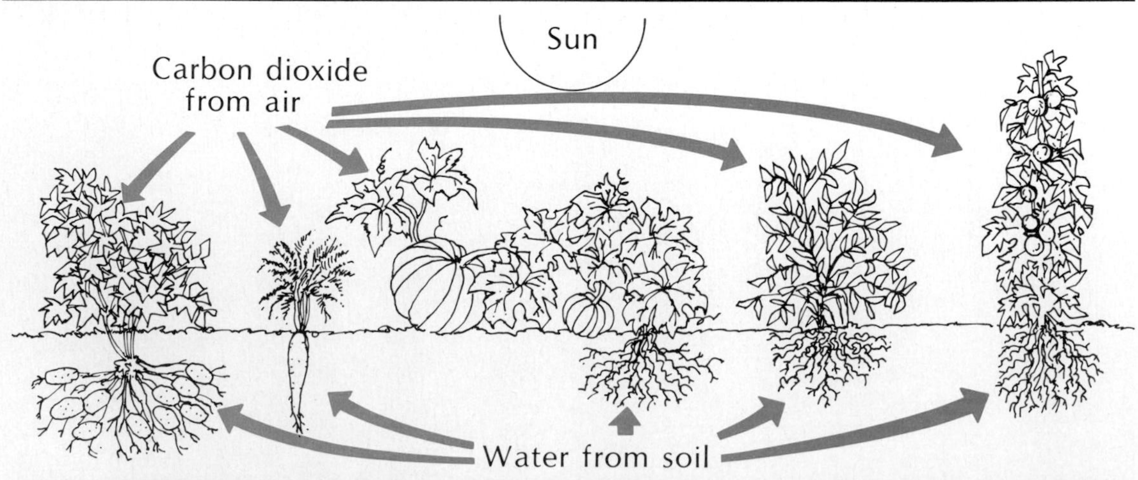

Green plants convert carbon dioxide from the air and water from the soil into carbohydrate and oxygen.

SUGAR

A sugar is a sweet crystalline carbohydrate. The term "**saccharide**" (SAK–uh–ride) is used in discussing sugar. It simply means sugar or a substance made from sugar. The simplest sugars are known as monosaccharides (mahn–oh–SAK–uh–rides), or single sugars. Monosaccharides are the simplest form of carbohydrates. Disaccharides (dy–SAK–uh–rides) are sugars made from two monosaccharides bonded together. Monosaccharides and disaccharides are called simple carbohydrates.

Lactose is the sugar found in milk and milk products.

Sugars contain a combination of hydrogen and oxygen called a **hydroxyl group** (hy–DRAHK–sil). This group is formed of one atom of each element and is written **–OH.** The "–" indicates the bond where the group attaches to a molecule. Organic compounds that contain hydroxyl groups are called organic alcohols. Sugars are alcohols that contain several hydroxyl groups in each molecule.

• GLUCOSE

Glucose is a monosaccharide often called blood sugar because it is the main carbohydrate found in blood. Glucose is the source of the energy used in and by the body. It affects the health and functioning of all the cells in the body. However, its prime function is to provide the brain and nervous system with the

Monosaccharides and Disaccharides

Glucose, fructose (FRUHK–tohs), and galactose (guh–LACK–tohs) are examples of monosaccharides. While glucose does not taste particularly sweet, it is the sugar that is absorbed most quickly by the body. Once it has entered the blood stream, it can be used immediately as a source of energy. Fructose is the sugar found in fruits and the sap of trees. It is the sweetest sugar. Like glucose, fructose can be absorbed directly into the blood stream. However, the liver must chemically change it into glucose before the body can use it as energy. Galactose is not found free in nature. It is always bonded to something else. Small amounts of galactose can be found in milk products such as yogurt and aged cheese.

The two most common food sugars, sucrose (SOO–krohs) and lactose (LAK–tohs), are both disaccharides. Sucrose is the sugar you probably know as common table sugar. Most of the sucrose you consume comes from sugar cane or sugar beets. Lactose is the sugar made by mammals in the mammary glands during milk production. Maltose (MAWL–tohs) is another disaccharide, which is found in cereals and sprouting grains.

energy they need. The level of glucose supplied to the brain by the blood is critical to the ability to think and function.

A healthy body maintains a normal glucose level. It does this through homeostasis (ho–mee–oh–STAY–sis). Homeostasis is the process through which the body regulates itself to maintain normal conditions and a relatively constant internal environment.

The pancreas is the organ that prevents the blood glucose level from getting too high. It does this by secreting the **hormone** insulin. A hormone is a chemical messenger. It affects a specific organ or tissue and brings forth a specific response. In this case, the insulin triggers reactions in the liver and muscle cells. They remove glucose from the blood and store it.

At first, the excess glucose is converted to **glycogen** (GLY–kuh–jun). Glycogen is the form in which carbohydrates are stored in the body. This process also works in reverse. When glucose in the blood drops below a certain level, glycogen stored in the liver can be changed back into glucose to supply the body with energy.

Sometimes more glucose is available than the body needs to store as glycogen. Then the liver can convert the glucose into fat molecules.

Some people have an abnormally low level of glucose in the blood. If the brain is unable to get enough glucose, the person may experience dizziness, weakness, and nausea. This condition is known as hypoglycemia (hy–po–gly–SEE–mee–uh). Only a physician can determine when someone suffers from this condition. If a person does have hypoglycemia, it

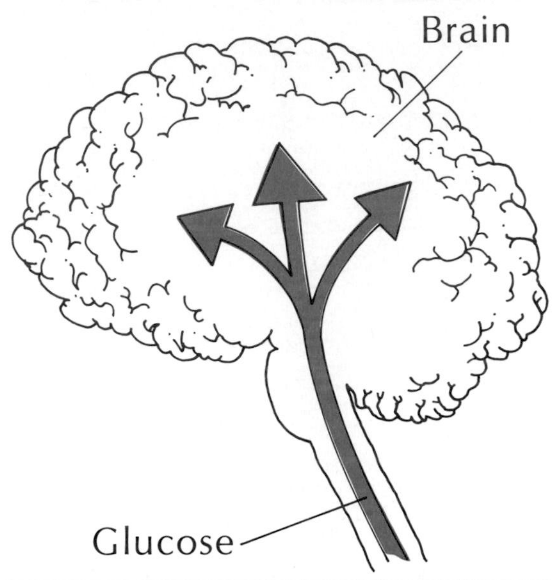

For the human brain to think and function, it needs a steady, adequate supply of glucose.

The hormone insulin carries messages from the pancreas to the liver and muscles to help regulate the level of glucose in the blood.

often can be corrected by a diet and eating schedule prescribed by a doctor.

Just as a lack of glucose in the blood can cause problems, so can too much glucose. A person with an abnormally high blood glucose level has the condition called hyperglycemia (hy–pur–gly–SEE–mee–uh).

There are two main causes of hyperglycemia. First, sometimes the pancreas may not secrete insulin as it should. Secondly, the cells that are supposed to store the glucose may not respond to the insulin that is secreted. As a result, the blood sugar level rises too high. When the excess glucose is not being converted to glycogen or fat, the kidneys go to work. They are the body's backup glucose control mechanism. The kidneys respond to the high glucose level by allowing some of the extra glucose to spill over into the urine.

Diabetes

A person whose body cannot regulate blood glucose level normally has diabetes. There are two types of the disease. The first type, in which the pancreas makes little or no insulin, is known as Type I diabetes. This form of the disease usually occurs in children or young adults. People who have Type I diabetes must take insulin every day. In addition to medication, diet and exercise are very important in this type of diabetes.

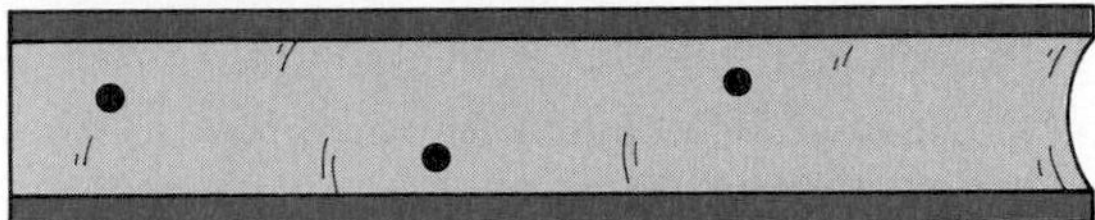

Low blood glucose

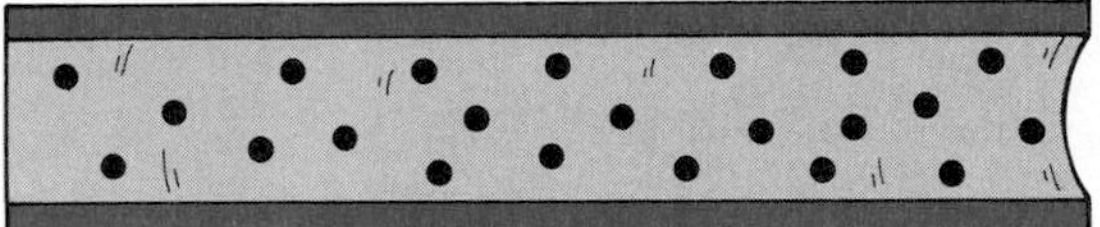

High blood glucose

A person with a low level of glucose in the blood has hypoglycemia, while someone with a high level of glucose in the blood has hyperglycemia.

Exercise can help control Type II diabetes.

Type I diabetes usually occurs in children or young adults.

Type II diabetes, which usually occurs in people over 40, is the most common form of the disease. About 90 percent of all diabetics have Type II diabetes. In this form of the disease, insulin is produced by the pancreas. However, either not enough is produced, or the insulin cannot be used effectively. Sometimes a cell defect prevents the body from using the insulin. Type II diabetes can often be controlled by diet and exercise alone, without any medication being needed. Over half of all diabetics are able to control the disease through diet alone.

Coping With Diabetes

The type of meal plan recommended for diabetics is very like that recommended for most people. Diabetics are urged to count the kilocalories in food they consume, since reducing body weight is often the first treatment for diabetes. In addition, they are supposed to:

- Limit their intake of protein and fat.
- Eat more complex carbohydrates, especially those that contain starch, such as dried peas and beans.
- Increase their consumption of fiber.
- Limit their consumption of salt.

Diabetics are encouraged to eat regularly and avoid becoming overhungry. This provides a constant, steady flow of glucose to the blood stream.

In addition to monitoring what they eat, diabetics are urged to exercise. Through regular exercise, people with Type I diabetes may be able to reduce the amount of insulin they take each day. Those with Type II diabetes, whose bodies produce some insulin, may be able to make their bodies more sensitive to the insulin through exercise.

• HYDROLYSIS OF SUGAR

Sucrose and water are formed when glucose and fructose combine. The word equation for this reaction is shown below.

Glucose + Fructose → Sucrose + Water

This process is reversible through **hydrolysis** (hy–DRAHL–uh–sis). Hydrolysis means the splitting of a compound into smaller parts by the addition of water.

When a dissacharide such as sucrose is hydrolyzed, it will yield the same two sugars from which it was formed. The word equation for the hydrolysis of sucrose is shown below.

Sucrose + Water → Glucose + Fructose

The process of hydrolysis takes place only under certain conditions. You will recall that certain proteins, known as enzymes, control chemical activity in living organisms. The enzyme invertase (in–VUR–tase), also called sucrase (SOO–krase), can cause the hydrolysis of sucrose. Acid and heat can also cause hydrolysis.

Sometimes the hydrolysis of sucrose is called **inversion.** Invert sugar is the name given to the mixture of fructose and glucose that results from inversion. A large proportion of invert sugars may be formed when fruit is sweetened and cooked.

Lactose is hydrolyzed in the body. The enzyme lactase (LAK–tase) breaks down the lactose into two monosaccharides—glucose and galactose. The galactose is then further broken down in the liver to form glucose.

• SWEETNESS AND SOLUBILITY

As you may remember from one of your laboratory experiments, sugars vary in sweetness. According to taste tests like the one you carried out, fructose is the sweetest sugar. Sucrose, glucose, galactose, maltose, and lactose follow

The hydrolysis of maltose yields two molecules of glucose.

Maltose + H_2O → Glucose + Glucose

in that order. Sugars occur in foods in an endless variety of combinations and proportions to give the sweet flavors so many people enjoy.

Honey, for example, is a very concentrated solution of fructose and glucose. Bees make honey by collecting nectar of flowers that contain fructose, glucose, and sucrose. They convert most of the sucrose into fructose and glucose in their bodies.

Sugars are very soluble in water because they contain many hydroxyl groups, which form hydrogen bonds with the water molecules. Interestingly enough, the solubility of sugars in water is the same order as their sweetness: fructose, sucrose, glucose, galactose, maltose, and lactose.

• CARAMELIZATION

Caramelization (kar–uh–mul–uh–ZAY–shun) is a browning reaction that can occur with any kind of sugar. It requires high temperatures and either low or high pH. Caramelization is a very complex chemical process, which is not fully understood.

As sugar is heated, **dehydration** (dee–hy–DRAY–shun) occurs. Dehydration is the loss of water from a substance. In this case, water leaves the sugar molecules. The individual molecules that are left join together into larger molecules. The new molecules have a higher concentration of carbon. This is because hydrogen and oxygen left as water molecules. The carbon gives the new molecules a brown color.

Honey is a concentrated blend of the sugars glucose and fructose.

Caramelization occurs when sugar is heated to a high temperature.

Sucrose, galactose, and glucose all caramelize at 170°C, while maltose does not react until heated to 180°C. Fructose, on the other hand, caramelizes at 110°C, only 10°C above the boiling point of water.

CRYSTALLIZATION OF SUGAR

The making of some kinds of candy is based on the crystallization of sugar. You will recall that a crystal is a solid in which the ions are arranged in a regular repeating pattern. In candy making, crystals are formed from a sugar solution, which is also called a sugar syrup. Crystalline candies include fondant, fudge, panocha, and divinity.

• SUGAR SOLUTIONS

Sugar is extremely soluble in water at any temperature. At 25°C, the solubility of sucrose is 211 g per 100 g of water. This means that 211 g of sucrose will completely dissolve in 100 g of water which is at a temperature of 25°C. As with most solids, the solubility of sugar increases as the temperature rises. Thus the exact amount of sugar that will dissolve depends on the temperature of the solution.

The solubility of sugar increases as the temperature of the solution rises.

If you have more sugar in a beaker than the amount of water present will dissolve, one way to get the sugar dissolved is to heat the solution. As the temperature increases, more and more of the sugar will dissolve. Eventually, you may get all the sugar in solution. If you then cool the solution very carefully, without agitating the mixture in any way, you will have a **supersaturated** (SOO–pur–SACH–uh–ray–tud) solution. A supersaturated solution contains more dissolved solute than it would normally at that temperature.

Candy is made from supersaturated solutions. In candy, the dissolved solute is sugar.

The concentration of a solution is an important factor in the type and quality of candy produced. You will recall that concentration is the amount of a substance in a given unit of volume. In a solution, concentration is the amount of solute dissolved in a certain amount of solvent. As a sugar solution is heated, the sugar dissolves and the temperature increases until the solution boils. As boiling continues, water evaporates. Because the sugar molecules are then dissolved in less water, the concentration of sugar in the solution increases.

In making candy, the sugar solution is boiled until the right concentration is reached. This is measured by temperature. The boiling point of a solution depends on its concentration. The more concentrated a solution is, the higher its boiling point. Candy recipes call for the sugar solution to be boiled until it reaches a certain temperature, which shows that the desired concentration has been reached. The success of the candy depends on heating the solution to the correct temperature. This is why it is critical to calibrate a thermometer the day it is to be used in candy making.

• CRYSTAL FORMATION

Candy is made when crystals separate from a solution. As you just learned, the first step in candy making is to attain the desired concentration of sugar in the solution. The next step is to control the size of the crystals that form when the sugar comes out of solution. The smaller the crystals, the higher the quality of the candy.

Crystallization occurs from a supersaturated solution when particles enter the solution. These particles can be lint or dust or sugar crystals that formed on the sides of the pan and fell into the solution. The sugar in the solution forms crystals around these particles. These newly formed crystals can trigger additional crystallization.

The size of the crystals depends on how many particles are present and how fast the crystals grow around them. The more particles, the smaller the size of the crystals. Crystals that grow rapidly tend to be smaller than those that grow slowly. Small crystals that grow rapidly are most apt to form when a sugar solution is at the right concentration and temperature.

The various sugars form different size crystals. Sucrose crystals tend to be larger than desired in candy. Glucose and fructose form small crystals. Therefore the best quality candy is made when a small part of the sucrose has been hydrolyzed to glucose and fructose.

Interfering Agents

Substances called **interfering agents** can affect crystal growth. Corn syrup, butter, egg white, cream of tartar, and vinegar are interfering agents used to promote the growth of small crystals. Corn syrup is high in glucose which forms small crystals. Cream of tartar and vinegar are acids which can cause the hydrolysis of sucrose creating glucose and fructose. Butter and egg white can completely prevent crystallization if enough is added to the solution. The

Because the boiling point of a sugar solution reflects its concentration, it is important to have accurate temperature measurements in making candy.

This candy is made by the formation of crystals from a sugar solution.

These interfering agents are used in making candy to promote the growth of small crystals.

Continuous agitation of a cool sugar syrup helps create small crystals.

presence of these substances helps create a smooth texture in candy.

Agitation

Crystal formation is also influenced by the amount of agitation the solution is given. Agitation is the stirring or beating of the solution. In addition, the temperature at which this agitation occurs is important. Generally, large crystals tend to form in hot solutions that are only slightly agitated. Smaller crystals form in cooler syrups that are stirred continuously.

Ripening

Some crystal candies, such as fondant, need to age or ripen. This means they should be stored in an air–tight container for 12–24 hours. Ripening tends to produce a softer smoother candy.

STARCH

In addition to forming monosaccharides and disaccharides, glucose also forms polysaccharides (pahl–ee–SAK–uh–rides). These are compounds made from ten or more monosaccharides chemically linked together. Starch and fiber are polysaccharides. They are also called complex carbohydrates.

A polysaccharide is also called a **polymer** (PAHL–uh–mur). A polymer is a large molecule formed when small molecules of the same kind join together to form chains. The process of forming a polymer is called polymerization (pahl–uh–mur–uh–ZAY–shun). Starch is a carbohydrate made from a chain of sugar molecules. Therefore starch molecules are polymers of sugar.

• THE STRUCTURE OF STARCH

Starch is a polymer made from a form of glucose called alpha–D–glucose. A molecule of starch can have anywhere from 400 to several hundred thousand alpha–D–glucose units.

Starch molecules can have either of two structures. One structure is linear, which means it is long and narrow like a line. This type of starch is known as **amylose** (AM–uh–lohs) and is found in rice and in wheat flour. The other structure of starch is a branched form known as **amylopectin** (am–uh–lo–PEK–tin). Amylopectin is less easily mixed in water than amylose, apparently because of its branched structure. Foods containing amylopectin include potato and tapioca.

Amylose is the starch molecule with the greatest thickening power. It can create a solid thickened starch mixture called a gel. A gel is fairly rigid and can hold its shape when formed into a mold. A molded pudding would be thickened with a starch containing amylose. Amylopectin, on the other hand, does not have as much thickening power and does not form gels.

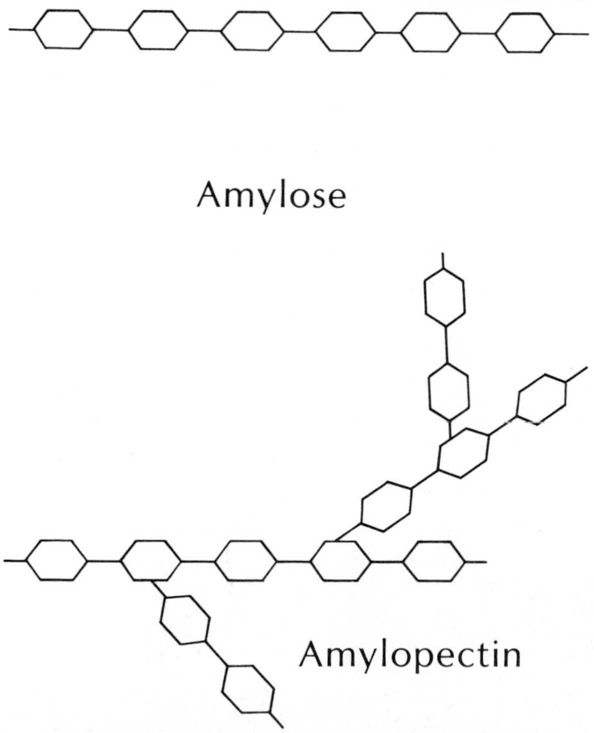

Amylose is a linear polymer of glucose while amylopectin is a branched polymer.

Starches vary a great deal in their ability to thicken food. For example, 30 mL of wheat flour has the same thickening power as 15 mL of rice starch or cornstarch. These differences depend on the proportion of amylose and amylopectin present.

Starches can be chemically changed for specific uses in the food industry. Scientists have produced strains of corn, rice, and barley that contain mainly amylopectin. These starches, called waxy starches, are used for commercial gravies. The gravies will thicken but not form a gel when cooling on your plate. Sometimes starches are changed to eliminate undesirable traits. For example, waxy rice is somewhat stringy in texture. Food scientists have eliminated this quality so that frozen pies made with the starch will have a smooth texture.

• COOKING WITH STARCH

Starches are not water soluble because starch molecules are too large to form true solutions. However, if starches are heated in water, the energy from the water molecules can loosen the bonds between the starch molecules. This makes it possible for hydrogen bonds to form between the starch molecules and the water molecules. The starch granules then absorb water and swell. This process is called **gelatinization** (ju–lat–un–uh–ZAY–shun) and is irreversible. The thickened starch mixture is called a **paste.** A fluid paste is called a sol, and, as mentioned earlier, a solid paste is called a gel.

The temperature at which a paste is formed varies with the type of starch. For example, wheat starch or flour thickens at a somewhat lower temperature than cornstarch.

The thickness of a starch and water mixture will usually increase during the heating that precedes gelatinization. The thickness of the mixture, or its resistance to flow, is called **vis-**

Starch molecules thicken liquids by the process of gelatinization.

Syneresis is most apt to occur with starches that have more amylose molecules.

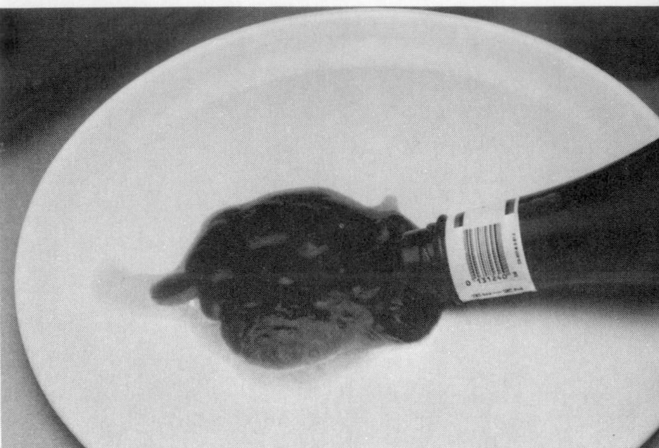

cosity (vis–KAHS–uh–tee). The more starch granules in the water, the more viscous the mixture will be.

Some, but not all, starches have the ability to thicken as they begin to cool. This is known as **retrogradation** (reh–tro–gray–DAY–shun). A familiar example of this process is the thickening of instant pudding as it cools. Starches that have more amylose molecules have a greater ability to retrograde. These starches also have a tendency to form pastes from which water leaks out when the paste cools. This leakage is known as **syneresis** (suh–NEHR–uh–sis). Some brands of ketchup and mustard show this behavior, especially after standing for a period of time.

There are many factors to be considered in selecting a starch to use as a thickening agent in puddings, pies, and frozen desserts. Gelatinization temperature, retrogradation, and syneresis are properties that can affect the preparation and quality of food.

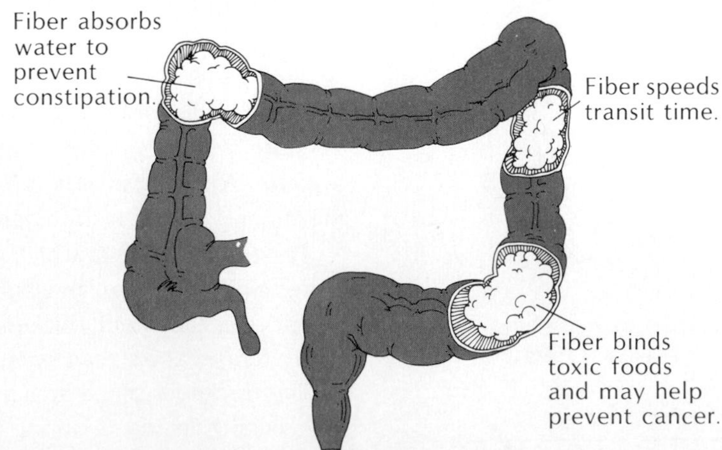

Fiber plays an important role in the healthy functioning of the intestines.

NUTRITION AND YOU

Fiber in the Diet

The main plant fiber eaten in food is cellulose (SELL–yuh–lohs). It is a polysaccharide made from a form of glucose called beta-D-glucose. Cellulose is the main substance of the cell walls and woody parts of plants. Hemicellulose (hem–ee–SELL–yuh–lohs) and pectin are other fibers made from carbohydrate.

Humans cannot digest fiber because they do not have the right enzymes to break the bonds in the fiber molecules. Even though fiber cannot be digested by humans, it serves important functions in the body. Good sources of fiber are fruits, vegetables, nuts, and whole grain breads and cereals.

One property of fiber is its ability to absorb water and swell. Fiber is best known for preventing or relieving constipation. As fiber passes through the intestines, it functions like a sponge, absorbing water as it moves along. This water usually keeps the bowels functioning normally and regularly.

Studies that have been carried out in Finland and Africa indicate that fiber seems to prevent cancer of the bowels. Many nutritionists believe fiber binds with food that has the potential to cause cancer, thereby preventing it from being absorbed into the blood stream. Fiber also speeds up the transit time of food, that is, how long it takes food to pass through the body. This helps reduce exposure to cancer–causing substances.

Fiber itself has little or no nutritive value. However, recent studies suggest fiber may influence the metabolism of some nutrients. People with diabetes are encouraged to eat a high–fiber diet to decrease the amount of insulin their bodies need.

Even though fiber is very important to the body, the average person in the United States eats only 4 g of fiber a day. This is in contrast to other parts of the world. For example, people in developing nations consume close to 30 g of fiber daily.

While there are no Recommended Dietary Allowances (RDA) for fiber, most people do not eat as much fiber as recommended by nutritionists. Some ways to increase your fiber intake are to eat an apple rather than drinking a glass of apple juice, to eat cracked wheat bread rather than white bread, and to consume raw vegetables with their skins on instead of those that have been peeled. The only time a high–fiber diet is not recommended is when a person is recovering from surgery of the stomach or intestines or is suffering from an infection of the lower bowels.

EXPERIMENT 7–1

Making Fondant

In this experiment, you will use sugar as a solute and water as a solvent. You will discover how temperature, agitation, and the presence of interfering agents affect crystal formation.

PROCEDURE

1. Follow the recipe variation assigned by your teacher.

Control Recipe for Fondant	
200 g sugar	120 mL hot water

   a. **Variation 1.** Use the control recipe.
   b. **Variation 2.** Use the control recipe with the addition of 0.3 g cream of tartar.
   c. **Variation 3.** Use the control recipe with the addition of 12 g corn syrup.
   d. **Variation 4.** Use the control recipe but do not cool the solution as instructed in step 6. Go immediately from step 5 to step 7. Beat the mixture until it is white and dry. Then follow the remaining steps.
   e. **Variation 5.** Use the control recipe but use half–and–half instead of water.

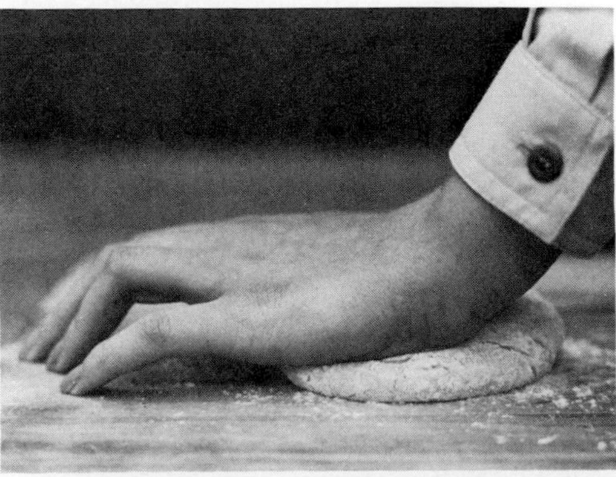

2. Measure the ingredients for the variation you are to make.
3. Place the ingredients in a small saucepan over medium heat. Cover the container and heat until just boiling. This will take about 2 minutes.
4. Remove the cover, and boil until the temperature reaches 114°C. Be sure to use a calibrated thermometer.
5. Remove from heat, and pour onto a heat–proof tray or plate.
6. Cool undisturbed until the bottom of the tray or plate is just warm to the touch.
7. Beat vigorously and continuously with a plastic or wooden spoon until the mixture becomes a creamy white mass.
8. Knead the mixture with your hands by folding, pressing, and squeezing it until it is smooth and elastic. Wrap the fondant in plastic film, and label it with your name, variation, and class period. Place the wrapped sample in the location specified by your teacher.
9. The next day, obtain the sample.
10. Using a toothpick, mix a small amount of the sample with glycerol on a microscope slide. Use a microscope to examine the sample under 10X power.
11. Repeat step 10 with samples from each of the other variations.
12. Sketch the crystals from the five variations. Draw the crystals to scale.
13. Taste a small sample of each variation. Compare the samples on the basis of the feel of the crystals on your tongue, texture, and moistness. Enter the information in your data table.

EXPERIMENT 7–1

QUESTIONS

1. Which variation produced the smallest crystals? The largest crystals? Why?
2. How did the solution's boiling point compare with that of pure water? What happened to the boiling point as time passed?
3. If procedures such as these were used in fudge making, which would produce the smoothest fudge?

SAMPLE DATA TABLE

Variation Number	Feel of Crystals on Tongue	Texture	Moistness
1			
2			
3			
4			
5			

EXPERIMENT 7–2

Thickening Agents

Viscosity is a desirable physical property in many foods. To obtain the desired viscosity in a given recipe, a variety of starches could be used as ingredients. Each of these behaves differently. In this experiment, you will compare how thickening agents used in food can affect the final product.

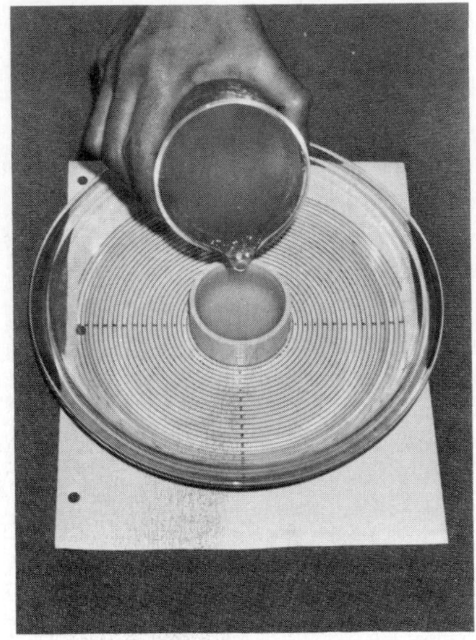

PROCEDURE

1. Obtain a starch from your teacher. Write the name of the starch in your data table.
2. Mass 8 g and 16 g samples of the starch.
3. Put 60 mL cold water in a 400 mL beaker, and stir in the 8 g starch sample. Add 220 mL more water and stir.
4. Heat the beaker of liquid on the stove using moderate heat. Stir slowly but constantly until the mixture boils.
5. Place a glass plate over the line–spread test sheet provided by your teacher. Place a hollow cylinder in the center of the plate, and fill with some of the starch mixture. Lift the cylinder, and allow the starch mixture to flow for 2 minutes. Count the lines covered at each of four points around the circle, and average your four readings. Record this result in your data table and on the chalkboard.
6. Cool the rest of the starch mixture to room temperature by placing the beaker in a pan of cold water.
7. Repeat the line–spread test as described in step 5.
8. Label two paper soufflé cups with your name and the name and amount of starch used in making the sample. Fill each cup with the starch mixture. Cover with plastic film. Refrigerate one and freeze the other until the next class period.
9. Repeat steps 3–8 with the 16 g starch sample.
10. The next day, thaw the frozen starch samples. Examine the thawed and refrigerated samples for retrogradation and syneresis. Record your observations in your data table and on the chalkboard. In your data table, copy the data from the other starches listed on the chalkboard.

EXPERIMENT 7–2

QUESTIONS

1. In what ways were the starches different?
2. Which starch would you choose to:
   a. Give the greatest thickness to a hot product?
   b. Give the clearest thickened fruit sauce?
   c. Give a thick product that is not gelled?
3. What changes occurred when the starches were stored in the refrigerator?
4. What changes occurred when the starches were frozen and thawed?
5. Would you recommend any of these starches as thickening for a cream pie that is to be frozen? Why or why not?

SAMPLE DATA TABLE

Name of Starch	Amount of Starch	Line–Spread Average		Appearance Refrigerated Sample	Appearance Frozen Sample
		Hot	Cold		
	8 g				
	16 g				

R E V I E W

TO SUM UP

- Carbohydrates, which include sugars, starches, and fibers, are an important part of people's diets all over the world.
- Carbohydrates are formed in green plants through the process of photosynthesis.
- Glucose is the basic sugar unit around which all other carbohydrates are formed.
- The body regulates the amount of glucose in the blood through the hormone insulin.
- Important chemical reactions in the study of sugar include hydrolysis, solubility, and caramelization.
- The size of crystals formed from a sugar solution are affected by temperature, the number of particles, the rate of crystal growth, interfering agents, and agitation.
- Starches are polysaccharides, which can have either linear or branched structures.
- Starch cookery is based on the gelatinization of starch molecules and the properties of the pastes that are formed.

CHECK YOUR FACTS

1. What elements are present in carbohydrates?
2. What are the three types of carbohydrate studied in food science?
3. Why are some carbohydrates said to provide empty calories?
4. How are carbohydrates produced?
5. Give an example of a monosaccharide and a disaccharide.
6. Which sugar is considered the sweetest?
7. Which sugar can be used by body cells?
8. Describe two ways the body regulates blood glucose level.
9. List three factors that can cause the hydrolysis of sucrose.
10. What is the order of solubility of sugars?
11. How is sugar caramelized?
12. What factors control the size of sugar crystals in candy making?
13. What is a polymer?
14. What is the difference between amylose and amylopectin?
15. What determines the ability of starches to thicken?
16. Why aren't starches soluble in water?

CRITICAL THINKING AND PROBLEM SOLVING

1. Would tea with a teaspoon of table sugar, tea with a teaspoon of honey, or a glass of milk provide energy quickest? Why?
2. What sugars are present in a bowl of strawberries and whipped cream?
3. Would a diabetic trying to control blood glucose through diet need to monitor anything other than intake of table sugar? Why or why not?
4. Why must the thermometer be calibrated the day you use it for candy making?
5. You are beating candy when you are interrupted by a telephone call. You talk for several minutes and then return to beating. What affect is this apt to have on the quality of the candy?
6. Why can't humans eat wood fiber for an energy source?
7. When you lift the first piece of cherry pie from the pie tin, the filling runs out. You end up spooning the filling from the pie tin to your plate. What might have caused this and how could it have been prevented?

CHAPTER

8

Lipids

This chapter will help you . . .

- Compare the properties of saturated and unsaturated fatty acids.
- Identify foods that contain different types of triglycerides and tell which foods contain saturated and unsaturated fat.
- Discuss the functions of fat in food preparation.
- List ways lipid oxidation can be controlled in food.
- Describe the functions of fat in the body.
- Explain the role of fat, saturated fat, and cholesterol in heart disease.

Terms to Remember

adipose tissue
atherosclerosis
carboxyl group
cholesterol
cracking
double bond
fatty acids
hydrogenation
lipids
lipoproteins
oxidation
plaque
rancid
saturated fat
single bond
smoking point
solidification point
triglycerides
unsaturated fat

Of all the foods people routinely eat, fat probably has the worst reputation. From dieters to those worried about heart disease, people struggle to eliminate fat from the food they eat. However, fat has an important role to play in a well–balanced diet.

PROPERTIES AND COMPOSITION OF LIPIDS

Lipids are a family of chemical compounds, which includes fats and oils. They are one of the main materials found in living cells. Lipids are generally soluble in organic solvents, such as chloroform and acetone. They are only slightly soluble in water. Lipids are present naturally in many foods.

• FATTY ACIDS

Fats are the lipids commonly found in food. Chemically, fats are formed by the reaction of alcohol with organic acids. Organic acids are compounds that contain a **carboxyl group** (kar–BAHK–sul). This group consists of a carbon bonded to an oxygen and a hydroxyl group. It is written **–COOH**, and its structure is shown below.

```
        O
       //
  R — C
       \
        O — H
```

Carboxyl group

The "R" in the carboxyl formula is a type of chemical shorthand. It stands for the rest of the compound. You will note that the carbon is attached to the oxygen with two bonding lines rather than one. This is a special kind of bond, which is described later.

The organic acids which make up fat are called **fatty acids.** These are organic compounds made up of a carbon chain to which hydrogen atoms are attached with a carboxyl group at one end. The carbon chain can vary in length depending on the fatty acid. The simplest fatty acid is acetic acid, a two–carbon fatty acid. Its structure is shown below.

```
     H   O
     |   ‖
 H — C — C — O — H
     |
     H
```

Acetic acid

• SATURATED AND UNSATURATED FATS

Most fatty acids are classified by the type of bond holding the carbon atoms together. A **single bond** is a covalent bond in which each atom donates one electron to form the bond. Thus the atoms are sharing one pair of electrons between them. If all the bonds between carbon atoms in a fat molecule are single bonds, the fat is a **saturated fat.** It is called saturated because it contains the maximum number of hydrogen atoms. The bonding in such a molecule is shown below.

```
   H   H   H
   |   |   |
 — C — C — C —
   |   |   |
   H   H   H
```

Bonding in a saturated fat

The fat on this steak is saturated fat because it contains the maximum number of hydrogen atoms.

On the other hand, fat molecules that contain at least two carbon atoms can be bonded to each other by a **double bond.** A double bond is a covalent bond in which each atom donates two electrons to form the bond. The bonding in this type of fat molecule is shown below.

$$
\begin{array}{ccccccccc}
 & H & & H & & H & & H & \\
 & | & & | & & | & & | & \\
- & C & - & C & = & C & - & C & - \\
 & | & & & & & & | & \\
 & H & & & & & & H &
\end{array}
$$

Bonding in an unsaturated fat

To form the double bond in the molecule shown above, two hydrogen atoms were removed from a fat molecule during a chemical change. Since the molecule does not contain all the hydrogen that it could contain, it is called an **unsaturated fat.**

A monounsaturated fat is one that lacks two hydrogen atoms because it has one double bond between carbons. Oleic acid (oh–LEE–ik) is an example of a monounsaturated fat. A polyunsaturated fat has two or more double bonds between carbons and lacks four or more hydrogen atoms. Linoleic acid (lin–oh–LEE–ik) has two double bonds, while linolenic acid (lin–oh–LEN–ik) has three double bonds. These are both polyunsaturated fats.

• FATS AND OILS

In discussing lipids, the terms "fat" and "oil" are often used interchangeably. However, they are different. A fat is usually a saturated compound that is solid at room temperature. An oil is generally an unsaturated compound that is liquid at room temperature.

One unusual property of fat has to do with melting point. As you know, the melting point of a substance is the temperature at which it changes from the solid state to a liquid. The freezing point is the temperature at which a substance changes from the liquid state to a solid. For most substances, melting and freezing occur at the same temperature. This is not the case, however, for fat.

Fat has what is called a **solidification point.** The solidification point is the temperature at which a melted fat regains its original firmness. A fat's solidification point is lower than its melting point. This means if a fat is melted, it must be cooled to a temperature lower than that at which it was completely melted before it will solidify again.

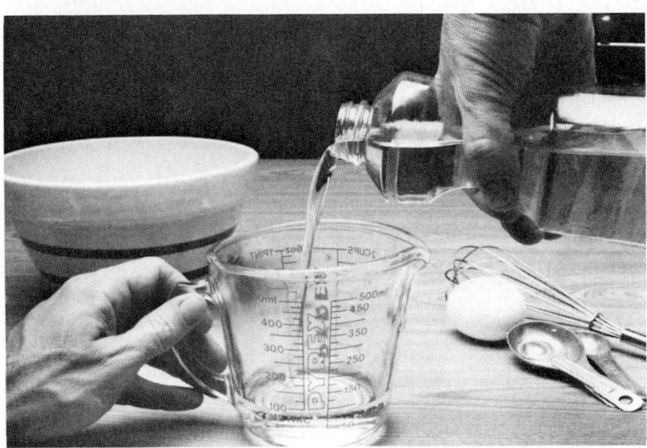

This vegetable oil is an unsaturated fat because it does not contain all the hydrogen atoms it could contain.

The melting point of chicken fat is lower than the melting point of beef fat.

• TRIGLYCERIDES

The **triglycerides** (try–GLISS–uh–rides) are a major class of food lipids. They include nearly all the animal and vegetable fats and oils that people normally eat.

You will recall from earlier in this chapter that fats are formed by the reaction of alcohol with fatty acids. The fats called triglycerides are compounds made up of an alcohol called glycerol (GLISS–uh–rawl) and three fatty acids. Because it is an alcohol, glycerol contains hydroxyl groups (– OH). The structure of glycerol is shown below.

$$
\begin{array}{ccccccc}
 & & H & & H & & H & \\
 & & | & & | & & | & \\
 & & O & & O & & O & \\
 & & | & & | & & | & \\
H & - & C & - & C & - & C & - & H \\
 & & | & & | & & | & \\
 & & H & & H & & H &
\end{array}
$$

Glycerol

When triglycerides are formed, the fatty acid molecules are attached in place of the hydrogens of the hydroxyl groups.

Triglycerides are often divided into seven subgroups. These subgroups include the various types of fats and oils found in food.

Milk fat is a triglyceride that contains short chain fatty acids.

- Milk fat, which is found in the milk from dairy cows. It contains some short–chain fatty acids.
- Fats from the coconut palm. These fats have low melting points and are usually low in unsaturated fatty acids.
- Fats containing linolenic acid, a highly unsaturated fatty acid. Soybeans and wheat germ are the most important sources of these fats in the diet.
- Vegetable butters, which are fats from the seeds of tropical trees. They have a very narrow melting range and are highly saturated. Cocoa butter is a member of this group of fats.
- Fats that contain oleic or linoleic acids. These are unsaturated fats found in corn, peanut, sunflower, olive, and sesame oils. This group of fats is probably the most abundant in diets in the United States.
- Marine (fish) oils, which contain long chains of polyunsaturated fatty acids. Some are also very high in vitamin A and D. Cod liver oil is an example of a marine oil.
- Animal fats, which include the fat found on the edge of cuts of meat as well as the fat dispersed throughout the meat. They are known for their high melting point. Animal fats usually contain a large number of saturated fatty acids as well as oleic acid.

The fat in this pie crust makes it flaky and tender.

COOKING WITH FAT

Fat plays a very important role in cooking. There are five major functions of fat in food preparation.

Hydrogenation

Many naturally occurring vegetable oils undergo a process known as **hydrogenation** (hy–druh–juh–NAY–shun). Hydrogen is chemically added to unsaturated fat molecules causing the double bonds to break and be replaced with single bonds. This changes liquid oil to semi–solid fat.

The food industry uses hydrogenation to change liquid oil to shortening and margarine. Compared to unhydrogenated oil, hydrogenated oil stays fresh longer. It is more stable and will not develop an unpleasant flavor and odor as quickly as most liquid oil.

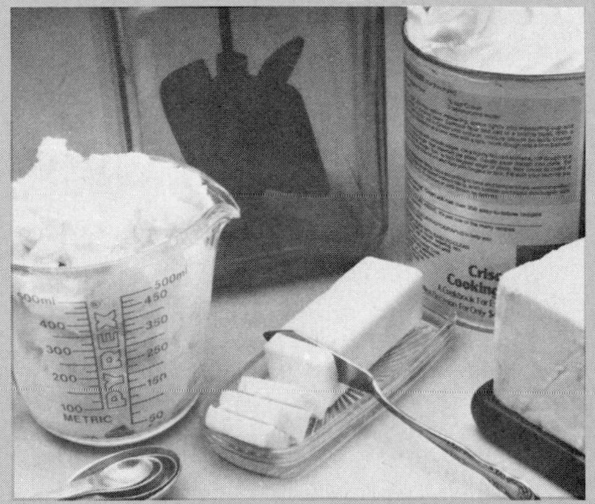

These solid fats were made by hydrogenating vegetable oil.

• TENDERIZING

One of the most important functions of fat is tenderizing. Baked goods, which are made of flour mixtures, are more tender when they contain fat. The fat coats the flour particles, creating a flaky, tender texture. Pie crusts and cakes, for example, would be tough if they did not contain fat.

• AERATION

Fats aerate batters and doughs such as cake batter. To aerate means to add air or gas to a substance. Fat has the capacity to form a bubble around a gas. This property helps incorporate air in a batter. The finely dispersed air bubbles decrease viscosity. This makes batter flow more easily.

• A HEAT MEDIUM

Fats can provide a heat medium that is hotter than water. Fat is heated in a shallow layer to sauté foods, such as potatoes. A deeper layer of fat is used to deep–fry many foods, such as corn dogs.

Fats provide a heat medium for cooking.

The most important factor influencing the use of fat as a heat medium is the temperature at which it produces smoke. This is called the **smoking point** of the fat. Fats that have a lower smoking point are more difficult to cook with than those with a higher smoking point.

Successful frying of food depends on several factors. The food placed in the oil will release some of its own fat as well as other molecules. These will cause the cooking oil to darken and may cause its flavor to change. The high temperatures used for frying may cause volatile substances to be released into the air. High temperatures may also alter the flavor of the food while frying. Finally, foods differ a great deal in the amount of fat they absorb during frying. Shorter contact times and large pieces of food will reduce fat absorption. Large whole pieces of deep–fat fried chicken will contain less fat than smaller chunks of deep–fried chicken.

Small pieces of food absorb more fat during deep–fat frying than larger pieces do.

Repeated heating eventually causes fat to break down, a process called **cracking.** Moreover, heat causes fat to develop an unpleasant flavor much more rapidly than it would otherwise. Therefore the fat used for frying must be replaced periodically.

• IN EMULSIONS

You will recall that emulsions are mixtures containing two liquid phases that do not normally mix. Fats are frequently one of the liquid phases in foods such as mayonnaise. Emulsions can also occur in nature. Milk is an example of a natural emulsion containing fat.

Fat in Food

Some of the fats people eat do not occur in nature. Instead these fats are processed and tailor–made for different functions in cooking. The fats used in food preparation can be divided into two main groups—animal fats and plant fats.

Butter, lard, and beef fat are the commercially important animal fats. Butter is made from milk and is 80–81 percent fat. Lard is made from the fatty tissues of a hog. The fat molecules in lard can be treated or modified so the fatty acids are rearranged. This produces different results in food preparation. Modified lard is a popular product used in the preparation of cakes, pastry, and icings. Beef fat is usually combined with vegetable fats before being used in foods.

Plant fats are used as oils, shortenings, and margarines. Oil seeds are the main source of oil from plants. Vegetable shortenings can be solidified by the hydrogenation of oils. Margarine is a hydrogenated oil to which salt, skim milk, emulsifiers, preservatives, and color have been added. It is used as a substitute for butter.

FLAVOR

Fats contribute flavor. For example, olive oil may be used for flavor in a salad. Different fats and oils have characteristic flavors. Butter, bacon fat, and olive oil are all examples of fats that provide distinctive flavors to food. The flavors contributed by fats can be desirable or undesirable depending on how the food is handled.

Undesirable flavors are usually the result of **oxidation** (ahk–suh–DAY–shun). Oxidation is a chemical change in which a substance loses electrons. When fat oxidizes, it loses its electrons by combining with oxygen. The oxidation of fatty acids is a very complex series of chemical reactions that food scientists are still studying in an effort to understand them completely.

Lipid oxidation is one of the main causes of food spoilage. The term "**rancid**" is used to describe the unpleasant flavors that develop during the oxidation of fat. Linolenic acid, an unsaturated fatty acid, oxidizes easily and causes unpleasant flavors in many rancid foods. However, because foods contain different fats, oxidation can be a different chemical change in each food product. Thus rancid walnuts taste differently from rancid meat or rancid potato chips.

Frying Safety

When you fry food, it is important to use the proper equipment. A deep–fat fryer should be properly designed. It needs to be well–insulated with high sides and a reliable thermostat. If a frying pan is used on the top of the stove, it should be a heavy–duty pan with sides high enough to prevent oil from spilling onto the heating element.

Fat that comes in contact with a heating element can cause a fire. Should such a fire occur, do not throw water on it! Water will spread a grease fire. Instead, smother the fire with the lid of the frying pan or with another pan.

Be sure to dry food thoroughly before immersing it in hot fat. Water will cause the fat to spatter. Spattering fat can burn the person who is frying.

It is crucial to use the correct temperature for the type of food being fried. Use a deep–fat thermometer, and watch the temperature. Do not leave the pan unattended. This is important to ensure that the food will cook completely but not absorb too much fat. Finally, it is important to keep frying equipment clean and to filter or change oil frequently.

BODY FAT AND YOU

You consume fats or lipids in many forms in your diet. The obvious sources for most people are butter, margarine, lard, shortening, and vegetable oils. However, to one extent or another, fat is a part of most food.

Most people eat lipids in the form of butter or margarine.

• FUNCTIONS OF FAT

The main function of body fat is to maintain body temperature at a reasonably constant level. This is accomplished by a thin layer of fat under the skin. Fat is a poor conductor of heat. Therefore the insulation provided by the fat under the skin helps maintain a constant body temperature.

One function of body oil is to keep hair glossy and healthy.

There are areas of the body that contain pockets of fat, which serve specific functions. These pockets of fat are made up of fat cells, which are also called **adipose tissue** (ADD–uh–pohs). For example, under each of the kidneys is a fatty cushion that helps keep them from being bumped or damaged.

The natural oil excreted by the skin keeps it from drying out and flaking off. Body oil also helps nourish hair and make it glossy and healthy. Hair that does not get enough oil from the body is dry and brittle.

Two fatty acids, linoleic and linolenic, are necessary for the production of some of the body's hormones. They are called essential fatty acids because they are required by the body. In addition, fat is a source of essential vitamins.

Controlling Oxidation

There is much research going on in the food industry to find ways to control fat oxidation. For example, potato chips are packaged in pure nitrogen instead of air to prevent oxidation and the resulting rancid flavor.

The food industry employs many tests to determine how much and how fast oxidation takes place in food. Food scientists can then develop methods of food preservation and packaging that will minimize the oxidation process.

As with other chemical reactions, the rate of oxidation increases as the temperature increases. Therefore keeping food cool can retard oxidation. However, the reaction does continue even at freezing temperatures, just more slowly. Since oxidation occurs on the surface of a food, it can be retarded by decreasing the area exposed to the air.

Adding water often slows down the rate of oxidation. This occurs because the water molecules interfere with oxygen molecules coming in contact with the fatty acids present in food. Thus drying a food causes it to become rancid faster than it would if it had not been dried. Substances to prevent oxidation, called antioxidants, are used in dried food to help maintain flavor.

As you know from Chapter 7, glucose and carbohydrates are the main source of energy for the human body. However, fat is a concentrated source of energy. A gram of fat provides 9 kcal. Therefore it supplies more than twice as many calories of energy as a gram of carbohydrate, which provides only 4 kcal per gram. A fat molecule thus provides much more energy than the same size carbohydrate molecule.

It is important to note that while the body can use fat for energy, it cannot break down fat into the glucose needed by the brain and nervous system. Therefore when the body needs glucose, it begins to break down stored protein to meet a part of its needs. An overweight person who is fasting could possibly die from the breakdown of protein tissue long before all the available fat has been used. Fasting is not a safe method for losing weight.

• FAT IN THE DIET

Americans consume about 45 percent of their calories in the form of fat. That is approximately 150 g of fat for a person who normally consumes 1300 kcal per day. This differs drastically from the fat intake of people from less industrialized countries. They generally consume only 30 g of fat per day. On a yearly basis, these people consume approximately 8 kg of fat, while people from the United States take in 50 kg. The percentage of fat in the typical diet here is much higher than at any earlier time in history.

The health benefits of eating unsaturated rather than saturated fat are causing many people to substitute margarine for lard and butter in their diets. However, the long–term impact of these dietary changes is unknown and so is being carefully studied. Current dietary guidelines recommend limiting the kilocalories from fats to less than 30 percent of the total kilocalories consumed.

• FAT AND HEART DISEASE

One of the greatest health concerns today is the effect of fat intake on the heart. Too much saturated fat and total fat in the diet are believed to be contributing factors in heart disease.

In addition, **cholesterol** (kuh–LESS–tuh–rawl) is thought to affect the heart. It is a fatty alcohol that can be made from glucose or saturated fatty acids. Cholesterol is a complex molecule whose formula is $\mathbf{C_{27}H_{45}OH}$. Cholesterol is constantly produced in the body by the liver. It is found in all cell membranes and is also a basic component in sex hormones and

Which plate of food contains the most fat?

Plaque can build up in arteries until it interferes with or stops the flow of blood.

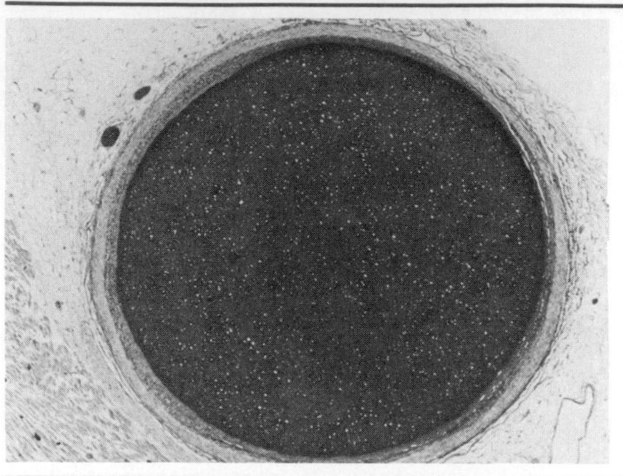

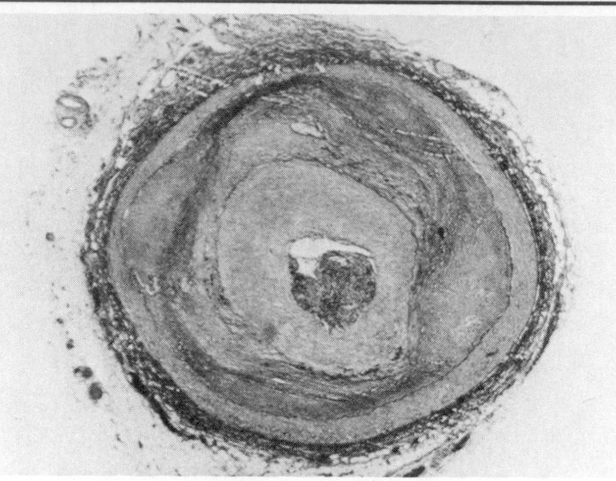

other hormones. Since cholesterol is produced in the body, it is not necessary to consume it. Because it can be made from saturated fatty acids, cholesterol levels in the blood are related to the amount of saturated fat eaten.

Cholesterol in the blood is thought to be a contributing factor in the body's manufacture of **plaque** (PLAK). A plaque is a mound of lipid material mixed with calcium and smooth muscle cells. Plaque lodges in the artery walls in and around the heart. Eventually, it may cause **atherosclerosis** (ath–uh–ro–skluh–RO–sis). This heart disease is often called hardening of the arteries because of the buildup of plaque along the inner walls of the arteries.

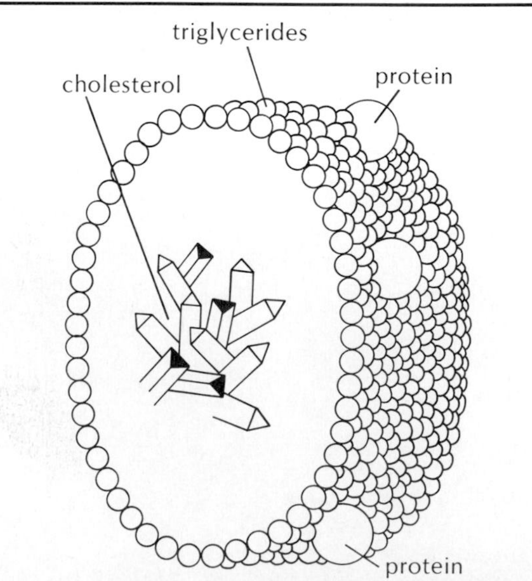

Lipoproteins transport cholesterol and other fats in the body.

In the body, cholesterol and other fats are transported as substances called **lipoproteins** (lip–oh–PRO–teens). A lipoprotein is a large complex molecule of lipids associated with protein. To move around the body through the blood, fats combine with protein to form lipoproteins. The more protein in a lipoprotein molecule, the more dense the molecule is. The more fat contained in the lipoprotein, the less dense it is.

The lipoproteins that transport cholesterol from the liver to other tissues are known as low–density lipoproteins. They are referred to as either LDL or beta lipoproteins. LDL carry about 75 percent of the cholesterol that moves about the body in the blood.

Lipoproteins returning to the liver from other parts of the body are high–density lipoproteins. These are referred to as either HDL or alpha lipoproteins. The HDL are thought to carry cholesterol from storage places back to the liver for disposal. HDL carry only about 25 percent of the cholesterol in the body.

A higher than normal LDL level indicates that a person has a high risk of heart disease. This is because the LDL have a higher percentage of cholesterol. A raised HDL level usually indicates a low risk of such problems. Thus, if blood tests indicate either low HDL or high LDL levels, a person needs to limit consumption of fat, especially saturated fat.

NUTRITION AND YOU

Preventing Heart Disease

Recent research has shown that consuming marine oils on a regular basis can reduce the chances of suffering from heart disease. This is believed to be due to fatty acids, referred to as Omega 3 fatty acids, found in some fish.

Scientists think that Omega 3 fatty acids help prevent heart disease in two ways. First, they make it more difficult for the plaque to form or clump together. Second, these fatty acids make plaque less sticky and therefore less likely to collect in the arteries.

Ocean fish, such as sardines, salmon, tuna, and herring, contain the highest levels of Omega 3 fatty acids. Cod stores its fatty acids in its liver so eating cod does not have the same benefit as eating the other fish mentioned. In the past, it was common for cod liver oil to be given to young children in the winter to help them stay healthy. The high level of Omega 3 in the cod's liver is apparently the reason that giving children cod liver oil has been beneficial.

Eating fish at least twice a week may be beneficial in preventing heart disease. For example, Eskimos in areas such as Greenland eat a steady diet of food high in cholesterol and fat. However, they have a low rate of heart disease, apparently because of the large quantities of fish they eat.

What You Can Do

To help prevent heart disease, you can avoid too much fat, saturated fat, and cholesterol. You can do this by:

- Choosing lean meats, poultry, fish, and dried beans or peas as protein sources.
- Eating liver and eggs only occasionally.
- Using skim milk and skim milk cheeses.
- Limiting how much butter, cream, shortening, lard, and hydrogenated margarine you eat.
- Trimming excess fat from your meat.
- Baking, boiling, and broiling foods rather than frying them.
- Reading labels to discover the amounts and kinds of fat in foods.

One of the most important factors in heart disease is heredity. You can't change your family's medical history. However, you can change your own behavior and dietary practices. This may help you reduce the chances of having the same health problems that have afflicted other members of your family.

By monitoring what and how much you eat, you may be able to reduce your chances of suffering from heart trouble. However, no formula or specific diet can guarantee that any particular person will be free of heart disease.

EXPERIMENT 8–1

Comparison of Lipids in Cake

In this experiment, you will observe the effects of several different lipids on a basic cake recipe.

PROCEDURE

1. Follow the recipe variation assigned by your teacher.

Control Recipe for a Basic Cake	
150 g sugar	120 mL milk
108 g cake flour	2 mL vanilla
1.8 g salt	41 g egg (1)
3.5 g double-acting baking powder	
47 g hydrogenated shortening	

   a. **Variation 1.** Use the control recipe.
   b. **Variation 2.** Use 47 g margarine instead of 47 g hydrogenated shortening.
   c. **Variation 3.** Use 47 g lard instead of 47 g hydrogenated shortening.
   d. **Variation 4.** Use 47 g vegetable oil instead of 47 g hydrogenated shortening.

2. Measure all ingredients for the variation you are to make. They should be at room temperature.
3. Sift dry ingredients into a mixing bowl.
4. Add shortening.
5. Add 80 mL of the milk.
6. Beat for 2 minutes at medium speed with an electric mixer or 300 strokes by hand.
7. Add egg and the remainder of the milk.
8. Beat 2 minutes or 300 strokes more.
9. Bake in a 23 cm (9–in.) round cake pan at 185°C (365°F) for about 20 minutes.
10. Let the cake cool for 10 minutes; then remove from pan and place on a cooling rack. When it is cool, wrap in plastic wrap. Label with your name, variation, and class period. Place in the location specified by your teacher.
11. The next day, slice the cake in half, forming two half circles. Measure the height of the cake at the center using a metric ruler. Record the height in your data table, and write it on the chalkboard. In your data table, copy the height of the other variations.
12. Cut a 0.3 cm slice of cake, wrap it in plastic wrap, label, and give to your teacher. This sample will be frozen and evaluated later.
13. Cut the rest of the cake into small pieces. Put the pieces on a paper labeled with the variation number.
14. Place the cake pieces out for taste testing.
15. Taste samples of each variation, and evaluate for texture, tenderness, flavor, and moistness. Record your evaluations in your data table.

EXPERIMENT 8–1

QUESTIONS

1. Which sample had the finest grain? The most tender texture?
2. Which sample seemed the lightest? The moistest?
3. Did you notice any flavor differences among the samples? Which did you like best?

SAMPLE DATA TABLE

Variation	Height	Texture	Tenderness	Flavor	Moistness
1					
2					
3					
4					

EXPERIMENT 8–2

The Tenderizing Effect of Lipids

Lipids are an important ingredient in pastries as well as cakes. In this experiment, you will compare the tenderness and mouthfeel of pie crusts prepared with several different lipids.

PROCEDURE

1. Follow the recipe variation in step 3 as assigned by your teacher.

Control Recipe for a Cherry Pie	
1 454 g	can pitted tart cherries, drained (save juice)
80 mL	juice from cherries
50 g	sugar
10 g	tapioca
10 g	butter
5 drops	red food coloring
145 g	flour
5 g	salt
85 g	hydrogenated shortening
	water

2. Combine the cherries, cherry juice, sugar, tapioca, butter, and red food coloring in a mixing bowl. Let stand for 10 minutes.
3. Sift together the flour and salt.
   a. **Variation 1.** Use the control recipe. Cut the hydrogenated shortening into the flour–salt mixture.
   b. **Variation 2.** Use 85 g lard instead of 85 g hydrogenated shortening. Cut the lard into the flour–salt mixture.
   c. **Variation 3.** Use 85 g margarine instead of 85 g hydrogenated shortening. Cut the margarine into the flour–salt mixture.
   d. **Variation 4.** Use 85 g vegetable oil instead of 85 g hydrogenated shortening. Mix the vegetable oil into the flour–salt mixture.
4. Slowly sprinkle water on the dough, and mix with a fork until the dough is moistened and can be formed into a ball.
5. Roll the dough into a large circle. Fit the dough into a pie pan. Cut off excess dough.
6. Pour the pie filling into the pie crust.
7. Bake pie for 50 minutes at 200°C (400°F). Remove from oven and cool.
8. Cut the pie into small pieces and set out for taste testing.
9. Taste a sample of each variation and evaluate for texture, tenderness, and flavor. Record your evaluations in your data table.

QUESTIONS

1. Which pie crust had the most crisp, flaky texture?
2. Which pie crust was the most tender?
3. Which pie crust had the best flavor?
4. Did the same lipid produce the best pie crust that produced the best cake?

SAMPLE DATA TABLE

Variation	Texture	Tenderness	Flavor
1			
2			
3			
4			

TO SUM UP

- Lipids are important in health and body functioning.
- Fatty acids are a part of all fats, including triglycerides, the fats most commonly found in food.
- Saturated fats contain the maximum number of hydrogen atoms, while unsaturated fats do not contain all the hydrogen they can because of double bonds between carbon atoms.
- In food preparation, fat is used to tenderize, aerate, form emulsions, and add flavor.
- Fat is an important heat medium for sautéing or deep–frying food.
- Fat develops a rancid flavor when it oxidizes, or loses electrons by combining with oxygen.
- In the body, fat regulates temperature, provides energy, promotes healthy skin and hair, provides vitamins, and is needed for hormone production.
- Reducing the amount of total fat, saturated fat, and cholesterol eaten can help prevent heart disease.

CHECK YOUR FACTS

1. What is the general chemical structure of fatty acids?
2. What is a carboxyl group? In what organic compound is it found?
3. What is a triglyceride, and how is it formed?
4. Which group of triglycerides is most abundant in diets of people in the United States?
5. Name two reasons marine oils are considered nutritious.
6. List three commercially important animal fats.
7. Why are fats included in cake recipes?
8. List three fats often used for their flavor.
9. Which fatty acid is often responsible for rancid flavors?
10. Why are potato chips packaged in nitrogen?
11. Name three functions of body fat.
12. Why can eating marine oils reduce the risk of heart disease?

CRITICAL THINKING AND PROBLEM SOLVING

1. What is the difference between saturated and unsaturated fat?
2. Explain what happens during hydrogenation of fats.
3. How does the solidification point of a fat compare with its melting point?
4. Discuss the pros and cons of using lard as opposed to vegetable oil in cooking.
5. Why does the oil used for deep–fat frying in restaurants need to be changed frequently?
6. Your doctor tells you that your level of HDL is very low and that your LDL level is abnormally high. How do these levels affect your chances of having heart disease?
7. List the ingredients in three brands of margarine. Which is the best for you? Why?
8. Record the amounts of all the oils and fats you consume during a two–day period. How could you reduce your total fat intake?

Protein

This chapter will help you . . .

- Name the groups of elements that identify an amino acid.
- Describe the chemical structure of protein.
- Explain what happens during the denaturation of protein and how the process occurs.
- Describe ways in which protein is used in food preparation.
- Discuss the composition of eggs and how they should be stored.
- List factors that affect the stability of an egg foam.
- Identify the functions of protein in the body.
- Compare and contrast complete and incomplete protein.

Terms to Remember

albumin
amine group
amino acids
amphoteric
antibodies
chalaza
coagulation
complete protein
denaturation
essential amino acids
fibrous protein
foams
globular protein
high–quality protein
incomplete protein
macromolecules
peptide bond
polypeptide
toxins

One of the most important types of food needed by the body is protein. In this chapter, you will study the structure and function of protein to understand why protein is so important to a healthy body.

STRUCTURE AND COMPOSITION OF PROTEIN

Protein molecules are very large and complex. They are made up of hydrogen, carbon, oxygen, nitrogen, and sometimes other elements. Because of their large size, they are often called **macromolecules** (mak–ro–MAHL–uh–kyools). A macromolecule is a large molecule containing many atoms. Because of their size, protein molecules can make up to 50 percent of the dry weight of a body cell.

Protein is made up of chains of substances called **amino acids** (uh–MEE–no). Amino acids are a type of organic acid. You will recall that organic acids are molecules that contain a carboxyl group (–COOH). In addition to the carboxyl group, amino acids also contain an **amine group** (uh–MEEN). An amine group contains two atoms of hydrogen and one atom of nitrogen and is written **$-NH_2$**. The structure of an amine group is shown below.

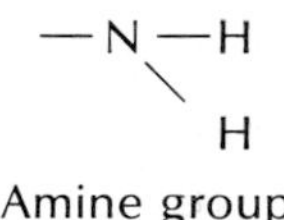

Amine group

Three Categories of Protein

Protein falls into three categories according to its function:

- The first type of protein is structural protein. This is the protein that makes up the skin, muscles, organs, and cell membranes.
- The second type of protein controls body processes. These proteins are enzymes, hormones, and **toxins** (TAHK–sins). As you know, enzymes are proteins that control chemical activity in living organisms. Hormones are chemical messengers that affect specific organs or tissues. Toxins are poisonous proteins harmful to biological systems.
- The third type of protein is food protein. It is the protein with which this chapter is concerned. Food protein is digestible, nontoxic, and available for human consumption. Meat, eggs, peanuts, and milk are examples of food containing protein.

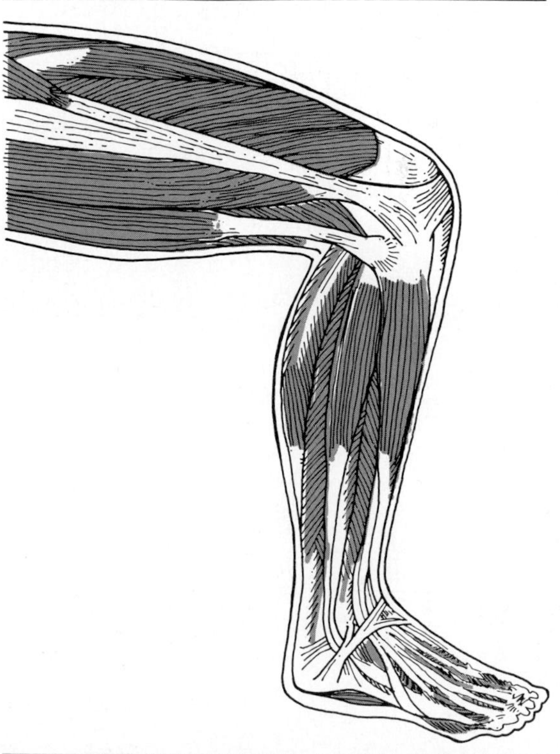

Structural protein is an important part of your muscles, skin, and organs.

A simple amino acid, glycine, has the following structure. You will note the carbon atom bonded to hydrogen, the carboxyl group (–COOH) on the right, and the amine group ($-NH_2$) on the bottom.

```
  H       O
   \      ||
  H—C —C—O—H
   /
  N
 / \
H   H
```

Glycine

The proteins in this bread and cheese are made from different combinations of amino acids.

There are 20 different amino acids. They are called the building blocks of protein because they can be combined in millions of different ways to form protein. This means a tremendous variety of protein exists.

When amino acids link together to form protein, one of the hydrogen atoms attached to the nitrogen atom in the amine group comes off. This leaves a place for a second amino acid to attach to the first. The bond between two amino acids is called a **peptide bond**. It occurs between the nitrogen of one amino acid and the carbon of the second amino acid. Peptide bonds create molecules that contain chains of amino acids.

The protein molecule that is created when many peptide bonds form a single molecule is known as a **polypeptide**. The shortest protein chains contain 20 amino acids. However, most protein molecules contain 100 to 500 amino acids, and some contain thousands.

Polypeptides do not exist as long straight, flat chains of amino acids. Rather, the chain coils, folds, and tangles—looking something like a wadded–up ball of string. The order of the amino acids in the chain determines how the molecule is folded.

You will recall that a polar molecule is one with a division of charge in the molecule. Amino acids are polar molecules. As a result, polypeptides are a web of positive and negative charges. These charges allow protein molecules to form hydrogen bonds like the hydrogen bonds formed in water.

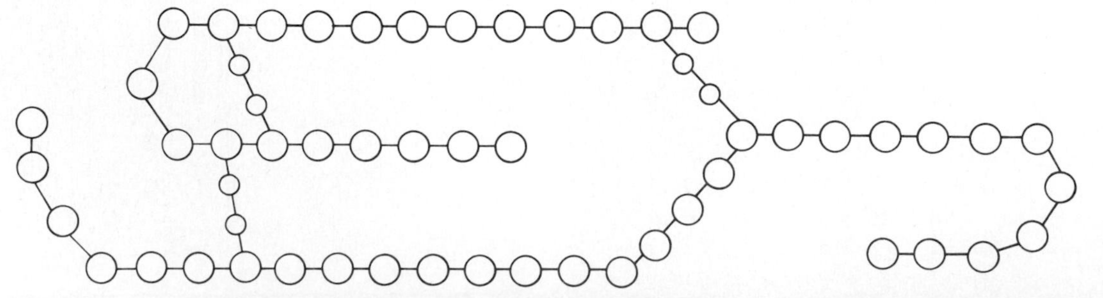

The peptide bonds between amino acids create this polypeptide, which is the hormone insulin.

DENATURATION OF PROTEIN

Denaturation (dee–nay–chur–AY–shun) is a process that changes the shape of a protein molecule without breaking its covalent bonds. Denaturation breaks the hydrogen bonds so the normal structure of the protein molecule is replaced by a looser, less compact structure. This kind of change is unique to protein. In denaturation, some of the original properties of the protein are diminished or eliminated.

What happens is that the protein molecule unfolds. Because each protein is unique, the denaturation process varies from one protein molecule to the next.

Fibrous and Globular Protein

Some protein molecules are shaped like a coiled metal spring. These form ropelike fibers and are called **fibrous protein**. Because they are very strong, they serve as connective tissue. Collagen (KAHL–uh–jun), myosin (MY–uh–sin), keratin (KER–uh–tun), and elastin (ih–LAS–tin) are fibrous proteins.

Another type of protein molecule is known as **globular protein** (GLAHB–yuh–lur). These protein molecules are not as strong as fibrous protein. They are shaped more like a ball of steel wool. Hemoglobin (HE–muh–glo–bun), the protein cells that carry oxygen in the blood, and casein (KAY–seen), a milk protein, are examples of globular protein.

Because proteins are such large molecules, they generally form colloids, rather than true solutions, with water. The folded shape of protein molecules also helps prevent their dissolving in water.

Denaturation is the first step to **coagulation** (ko–ag–yuh–LAY–shun). Coagulation means to change a liquid into a soft semisolid clot or solid mass. Coagulation occurs when the polypeptide bonds unfold during denaturation, collide with other protein molecules, and clump together to form a solid.

For example, an egg white is a clear, runny

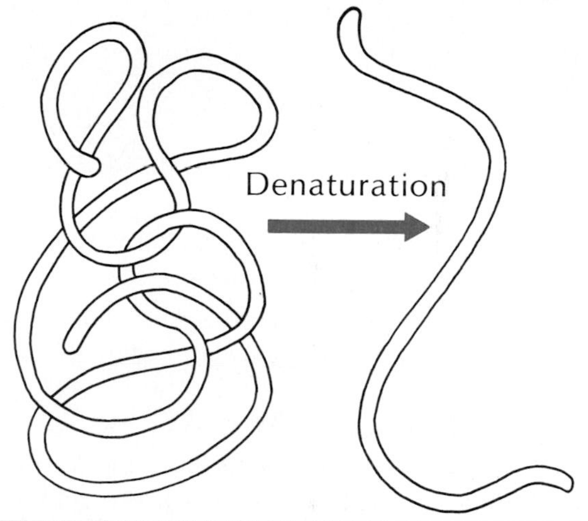

When a protein molecule is denatured, the hydrogen bonds are broken, which allows the molecule to unfold.

These deviled eggs could not have been prepared without the denaturation and coagulation of the protein in the eggs.

Denaturation often can be reversed if coagulation has not occurred.

substance before it is cooked. When heated, the substance becomes a white solid. This is because the protein in the egg white has been denatured by the heat and has coagulated.

• DENATURATION BY HEAT

Heat is the most common means of denaturing protein. How much and how fast the protein denatures depends on both the temperature and the structure of the protein. Since each protein has its own structure, each is affected by heat in a slightly different way. The chart on page 151 shows that most kinds of protein denature at temperatures between 47°-67°C.

The rate at which protein denatures increases 600 times for every 10°C increase in temperature. This is why temperature is important when cooking eggs and why they can be overcooked so quickly.

• OTHER MEANS OF DENATURATION

Denaturation is caused not only by heat. Freezing, pressure, sound waves, irradiation, and the addition of certain compounds can also produce denaturation. A very high or very low pH will often cause proteins to denature. Mechanical treatments, such as beating or whipping foods, can cause denaturation. Common examples of denaturing protein in this manner are beating egg whites and kneading bread.

Certain metal ions also cause protein molecules to unfold. Sodium and potassium ions are the ones most commonly involved in this process. However, other metal ions, such as copper and iron, can also denature protein molecules.

Sometimes, if coagulation has not occurred, denaturation is reversible. This is why egg whites that have been slightly whipped and then allowed to stand will become liquid again. Coagulation is never reversible.

PROTEIN IN FOOD

Protein is involved in a variety of ways in food preparation. Proteins can serve as emulsifiers. This is because the amino acid molecule is polar. One end of it is soluble in water, while the other end is soluble in fat and oil. Mayonnaise is an example of an emulsion in which egg protein stabilizes the oil and water.

Protein aids in the formation of **foams**. A foam is formed when a liquid is whipped, trapping air in the liquid. Meringue (muh–RANG) and whipped cream are examples of foams. Protein in the egg and cream surrounds the air bubbles during beating to form the foam.

The gelatin used in desserts and salads is a protein product. It is a colloidal dispersion in hot water. When cool, the protein forms a network that turns the liquid colloidal dispersion to a firm, semisolid mass.

Gluten (GLOO–tun) is an elastic, stretchy protein found in wheat. It gives bread its final shape and structure. When bread dough is kneaded, the gluten is developed. The dough becomes smooth and stretchy, creating an elastic mesh. When the yeast in the bread produces carbon dioxide, the cell walls of the gluten stretch. The gluten cells rise and expand as the carbon dioxide forms small

Protein Coagulation Temperatures

Protein coagulates at various temperatures. The chart below shows the temperatures at which different proteins coagulate.

Protein	Coagulation Temperature
Egg albumin	56°C
Milk albumin (bovine)	67°C
Legumelin (pea)	60°C
Myosin (rabbit)	47°–56°C
Casein (bovine)	160°–200°C

The gelatin and whipped cream both contain protein.

holes in the dough. These holes remain after the bread is baked because the heat coagulates the gluten, causing it to become a solid structure.

In this text, meat refers to the edible portion of mammals. It is approximately 15–20 percent protein. The muscle, or lean part, of the meat is composed of fibrous proteins called actin (AK–tin) and myosin. These proteins form tiny bundles of fibers in the muscles. The bundles are held together by connective tissue made up of the proteins collagen and elastin. These are long, strong molecules. When you cook meat slowly, as in a stew, the heat breaks down some of the collagen, making the meat more tender.

EGGS

Eggs are complex biological systems. Although eggs are considered a protein food, they contain every vitamin and mineral human beings need except vitamin C. The reason vitamin C is missing is that chickens, like most animals, make their own vitamin C in the body. The chick that is developing in the egg can manufacture vitamin C when it is needed. Therefore, vitamin C does not have to be supplied in the egg with the other nutrients. The calcium in eggs, however, is present only in the shells. Therefore you would have to eat the shells to get your calcium from eggs!

• COMPOSITION OF EGGS

An egg is composed of:

- A thick outer shell.
- An inner and outer shell membrane.
- Egg white.
- **Chalaza** (kuh–LAY–zuh), a ropelike structure that keeps the egg yolk centered.
- Egg yolk.

The egg shell is made of interwoven protein molecules and calcium in the form of calcium

The egg is a complex biological system.

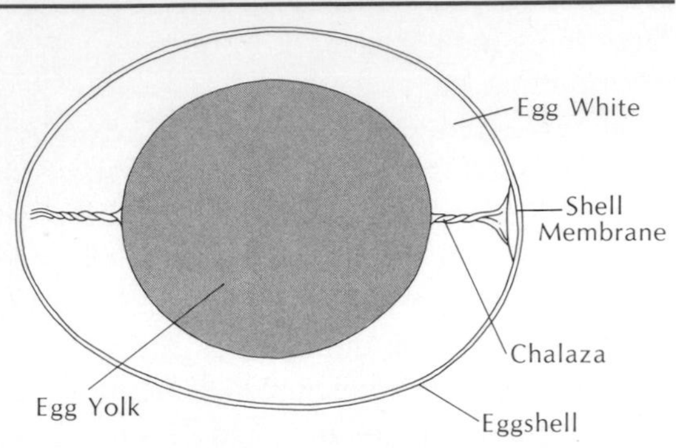

carbonate crystals. It contains pores, which allow a developing chick to breath.

Although the composition of eggs can vary, the edible portion is generally two–thirds egg white and one–third yolk. The egg white is often referred to as the **albumin** (al–BYOO–mun) because that is the name of the main protein present in it. The egg yolk, the yellow middle portion of the egg, has a very different composition from the egg white. It is a highly nutritive substance rich in iron, phosphorus, vitamin A, thiamin, and riboflavin.

• STORING EGGS

How eggs are stored is important in maintaining their quality. Physical and chemical changes occur as an egg deteriorates. Physically, the egg white becomes less viscous and more watery. The water from the white moves into the yolk, making it thinner also. Because the shell is porous, water will evaporate and carbon dioxide will escape. This causes an increase in the pH. As a result, the protein begins to break down and other changes occur. Coating eggs with a light mineral oil immediately after the eggs are laid helps prevent these changes. If the eggs are not coated, the normal pH of 7.6 can increase to over 9.

Because the egg shell is porous, eggs can pick up odors and flavors. If stored covered, eggs are less apt to develop an undesirable flavor.

Temperature is extremely important in egg storage. Eggs seem to retain their quality best if the temperature during long–term storage is -1°C.

• COOKING WITH EGGS

Eggs have countless uses in traditional menus from all over the world. They are eaten alone, as well as being used in a variety of ways in cooking.

One role eggs play is in making foams. Foams are important in many recipes because they make food light and fluffy. Foams are usu-

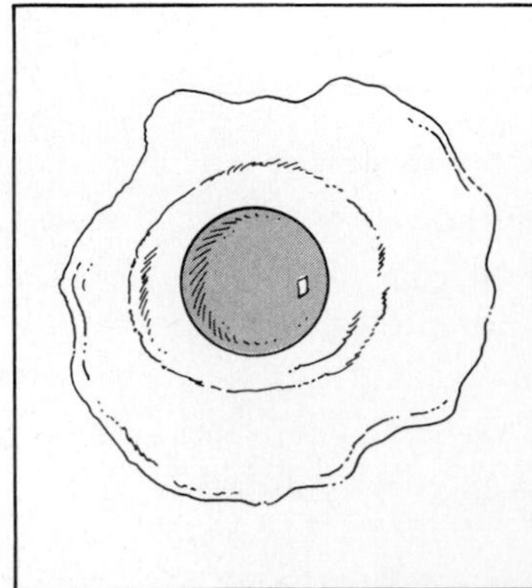
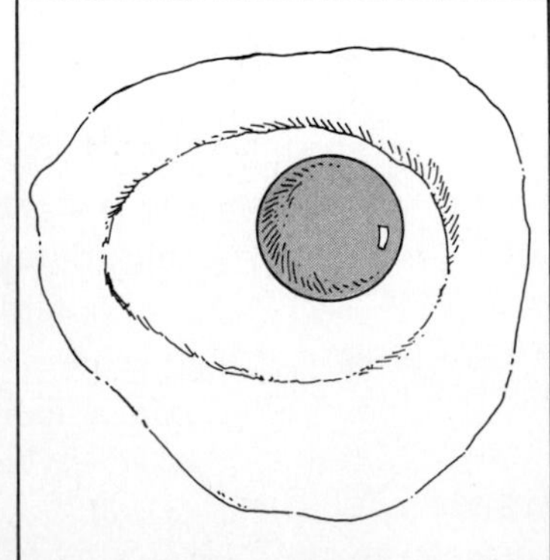
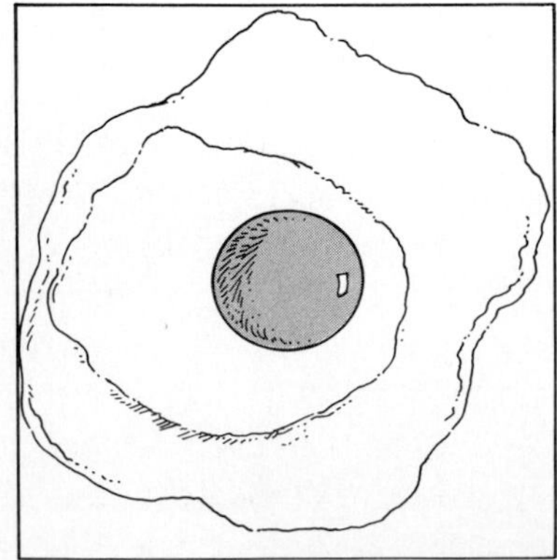

As an egg ages, the white becomes less viscous and more watery, and the yolk becomes thinner.

ally composed of egg white and air. Egg white is well suited to foam making because it can form a colloidal dispersion. The bubbles of air in the foam are surrounded by the protein molecules from the egg white. These have been denatured and therefore are stable, yet elastic.

Many factors influence the formation of foams, including:

- The type of beating and how long it lasts.
- The temperature of the egg white.
- The pH of the egg.
- The quality of the egg white.
- The presence of other substances, such as cream of tartar, fat, and sugar.

In making a foam, the faster the beater is moving, the faster the foam will form. The volume of a foam depends on the amount of air incorporated during beating. The more air, the greater the volume of the foam. To determine when a foam has been beaten enough, but not too much, it is necessary to evaluate the foam volume and stability. If the egg whites are overbeaten, the protein may unfold to the point where it loses its elasticity. The result is a less stable foam. You will evaluate foams in Experiment 9–1.

A room–temperature egg white will whip faster and produce a larger volume of foam than a cooler one will. The fresher the egg, the better its quality, and the better the foam will be. Freshness influences the pH of the egg white. An egg white will form the best foam if its pH is 4.6–4.8.

The presence of extra substances can help or hinder foam formation. Because pH is so important, cream of tartar is often added to lower pH. This stabilizes the protein and produces a higher quality foam. Sugar increases the stability of egg foams but delays foaming. The directions in many recipes say to beat the egg whites until foamy before adding sugar. If any egg yolk or other type of fat is present, the egg foam will not be as stable and may not even foam. Many recipes recommend not using plastic bowls because leftover fat can be present even after washing. This will interfere with foam formation.

A low pH is also important in other kinds of egg cooking. For example, recipes for poaching eggs often recommend adding vinegar to the water in which the eggs are to be cooked. As soon as the egg white enters the vinegar–water mixture, it begins to denature. This causes it to hold together better than it would in plain water.

Protein molecules from egg white surround air bubbles to create the meringue for this pie.

Lifting the beater from an egg foam is one way to test the stability of a foam.

PROTEIN AND NUTRITION

While there are 20 amino acids, only 8 are considered **essential amino acids**, which must be included in the human diet. The other 12 are not considered essential because the human body can manufacture them. However, all 20 amino acids must be present to make body protein.

Food protein is often classified as complete and incomplete. A **complete protein** contains all eight essential amino acids. An **incomplete protein** is lacking one or more of these essential amino acids.

A **high–quality protein** contains all the essential amino acids. In addition, it contains them in amounts proportional to the body's need for them. Egg protein is the standard by which the quality of all other proteins are measured.

Protein can be obtained from both animal and vegetable products. Animal protein generally contains complete protein. Most vegetables contain only incomplete protein.

Vegetarians must carefully plan their diets to ensure that they consume all eight essential amino acids. By combining foods, they can consume the equivalent of complete protein. Eating grains with seeds, such as beans with rice or wheat with soy, is a way to get all the essential amino acids. Otherwise, vegetarians' bodies would not be able to build proteins because certain amino acids would be lacking.

Most people in the United States consume more protein that their bodies actually need. In many parts of the world, however, food containing protein is too expensive for most people. These people are malnourished and their health suffers. An adequate supply of protein is needed to maintain good health.

The protein in this fish is complete because it contains all eight essential amino acids.

Essential Amino Acids

The eight amino acids that adults must consume to be healthy are:

- Methionine (muh–THIGH–uh–neen).
- Threonine (THREE–uh–neen).
- Tryptophan (TRIP–tuh–fan).
- Isoleucine (eye–suh–LOO–seen).
- Leucine (LOO–seen).
- Lysine (LYE–seen).
- Valine (VA–leen).
- Phenylalanine (fen–ul–AL–uh–neen).

Infants also require the amino acid histidine (HISS–tuh–deen) for proper development. Histidine may also be essential for adults during illness.

Combining whole wheat bread and peanut butter helps provide the essential amino acids.

Protein Recommended Dietary Allowances

The Recommended Dietary Allowances (RDA) for protein depend on a person's stage of development. Growing children need more protein per kilogram of body weight than the average adult.

The RDA state that each day a healthy adult should consume 0.8 g of high–quality protein per kilogram of ideal body weight. A woman who weighs her ideal weight of 55 kg would need about 44 g of protein a day (55 kg × 0.8 g/kg = 44 g). A man whose ideal weight is 70 kg would need 56 g of protein each day (70 kg × 0.8 g/kg = 56 g).

In contrast, five–year–old children should consume 1.5 g of protein per kilogram of body weight. Children ages 11–14 need about 1 g per kilogram of body weight. Women who are pregnant or nursing require an additional 20–30 g of protein each day to keep themselves and their babies healthy.

NUTRITION AND YOU

Nature's Body Builder

Protein has many functions in your body. One of the most important is to be nature's body builder. You need protein to build body tissue for new growth and to replace worn–out cells.

Your need for new tissue was obvious when you were a growing child. However, now you need new tissue to form a scar if you cut yourself, to replace blood lost when you donate blood, or to grow new hair and nails. Replacement cells are needed on the inside of your intestinal tract about every three days. Your red blood cells must be replaced every three or four months. The cells of your skin are constantly rubbing off and need to be replaced.

Protein molecules are both specific and versatile. While protein in general does many jobs, different proteins serve different purposes. Specific proteins are involved in controlling growth, healing, blood replacement, the formation of hair and nails, and the replacement of cells throughout the body.

Food protein is needed so your body can build other proteins. Most of your body processes are controlled by proteins called enzymes and hormones. A single cell may contain over 1000 different enzymes. Hormones regulate many of your body processes. For example, in Chapter 7, you learned that the hormone insulin regulates the glucose level in your blood. **Antibodies** are a form of protein that help your body fight disease. Proteins are needed to form lipoproteins so lipids can be transported in your blood.

Proteins are crucial in helping your body systems maintain stable pH levels. They can do this because they are **amphoteric** (am–fuh–TER–ik). This means they can react either as an acid or a base depending on what they are reacting with.

Protein can be used by your body as a source of energy. This happens if your body has an insufficient supply of carbohydrate or fat to supply the energy you need. Protein can also be used for energy if you eat more protein than your body needs.

EXPERIMENT 9–1

Egg Foam Stability

An egg foam is formed by beating egg white. The beating denatures the egg protein, which forms a colloidal dispersion with the air beaten into the egg white. There are several factors that influence the stability of a foam. These factors are listed on page 153. In this experiment, you will add sugar at different points in the beating process and observe the effect on the foam.

PROCEDURE

1. Mass 25 g sugar.
2. Separate one egg white from its yolk, and put the white into a small glass mixing bowl.
3. Follow the variation assigned by your teacher.
   a. **Variation 1.** Add sugar before beating. Omit step 4 below.
   b. **Variation 2.** Add sugar when egg is foamy.
   c. **Variation 3.** Add sugar when soft peaks form in the foam. When you withdraw the beater, the tips of soft peaks will bend somewhat. The foam will still look shiny and moist.
   d. **Variation 4.** Add sugar when stiff peaks form in the foam. The tips of the peaks will not bend, and the foam will not slip if the bowl is tipped.
   e. **Variation 5.** Add no sugar. Omit step 4 below. In step 5, beat until stiff peaks form in the foam.
4. Begin beating the egg white. Time how long you beat the egg white before adding sugar, and record this information in your data table.
5. Sprinkle the sugar over the egg whites at the point indicated in step 3, and beat slowly until the foam forms slightly rounded peaks when the beater is withdrawn. Time how long you beat the egg white, and record the time in your data table.
6. Measure the average height of the foam with a plastic metric ruler by immersing the ruler in the foam. Record the height in your data table.
7. Put 75 mL foam into a funnel supported in a graduated cylinder. Cover and let stand for 20 minutes. In your data table, record the volume of the leakage.
8. Determine the total beating time, and record it in your data table.
9. Record your data on the chalkboard. In your data table, copy the data from the other variations.

EXPERIMENT 9–1

QUESTIONS

1. Which sample gave the greatest height (largest volume) of foam?
2. Which sample required the longest beating time?
3. Which sample had the greatest amount of leakage?
4. When is the best time to add sugar when making a foam from egg whites?

SAMPLE DATA TABLE

Variation	Time Before Adding Sugar	Time After Adding Sugar	Total Beating Time	Height in cm	Leakage in mL
1	———				
2					
3					
4					
5	———	———			

EXPERIMENT 9–2

The Effect of Acid on Protein

In this experiment, you will compare the behavior of egg white in pure water and in an acid, vinegar, as temperature increases. You will be able to draw some conclusions about the effects of acids on protein in egg white during cooking.

PROCEDURE

1. Obtain an egg white from your teacher.
2. Pour white vinegar into a 100 mL beaker to a depth of about 3 cm. Pour room–temperature water into a second 100 mL beaker to exactly the same depth as the vinegar.
3. Scoop up 5 mL egg white. If possible, use the liquid part and avoid the chalaza, the clear stringy tissue. Gently add the white to the beaker of water, using a minimum of dropping or stirring. Try to keep the egg white together. Add 5 mL egg white to the beaker of vinegar in the same manner.
4. Pour tap water into a large saucepan to a depth of about 3 cm. Heat until water boils.
5. Pour cold tap water into a second large saucepan to a depth of about 2 cm. Place both 100 mL beakers in this saucepan. Stir the cold water in the saucepan as you slowly add the boiling water. Do not pour any water in the beakers. Stop adding boiling water when the water in the pan is about twice as deep as the liquid in the beakers.
6. Observe the egg samples while they are warming after 1 minute and again after 3 minutes. Record your observations in your data table.
7. After about 5 minutes, remove both beakers from the water bath. Hold them up so you can examine the samples from the side. Record your observations in your data table.

QUESTIONS

1. In which treatment did a "skin" first form over the egg white?
2. What caused the differences between the egg white cooked in water and the egg white cooked in vinegar? Why did these differences occur?
3. Which cooking medium—water or vinegar—would make the most appetizing poached egg? Why?
4. What substance other than vinegar could you use in the water to produce a similar effect?

SAMPLE DATA TABLE

Time	Egg White in Water	Egg White in Vinegar
1 minute		
3 minutes		
5 minutes		

TO SUM UP

- Proteins are made up of chains of amino acids joined by peptide bonds.
- Protein molecules are denatured by heat and other factors.
- Protein is found in a variety of foods and reacts in many ways during food preparation.
- Eggs are a nutritious food, which need proper storage to retain their quality.
- Foam formation depends on the temperature, pH, and quality of the egg; the type of beating; and the presence of other substances.
- In the body, food protein is used for building and repairing tissues, making proteins that regulate body processes, maintaining pH, and providing energy.
- Complete proteins are needed in the diet to provide the eight essential amino acids.

CHECK YOUR FACTS

1. Why are protein molecules called macromolecules?
2. What is a carboxyl group? An amine group?
3. How are peptide bonds formed?
4. Name two examples of fibrous protein.
5. Name three factors that can cause denaturation.
6. What metal ions most commonly denature protein?
7. When is denaturation reversible?
8. List the parts of an egg.
9. Name three factors that influence formation of foams.
10. Why is protein called nature's body builder?
11. Why are only 8 of the 20 amino acids essential?
12. Which incomplete protein foods combine to provide all essential amino acids?

CRITICAL THINKING AND PROBLEM SOLVING

1. Explain why protein must be denatured before coagulation.
2. Why is egg yolk such an effective emulsifier in making mayonnaise?
3. Explain why slamming an oven door when bread is partially baked may cause the bread to fall flat.
4. Why don't chicken eggs contain vitamin C?
5. Why does albumin pH go up if eggs are stored without being coated with oil?
6. Why do many food scientists not recommend storing eggs in the special compartment in the refrigerator door?
7. You are making a meringue for a banana pie. You take the eggs from the refrigerator, separate them, add sugar, and start beating the whites. Would you expect to get a large volume of foam? Why or why not?
8. Why do victims of malnutrition take longer to heal after an injury than a well–nourished person would?
9. Plan menus for a day for a vegetarian so that all the essential amino acids will be consumed.

Vitamins and Minerals

This chapter will help you . . .

- Describe water– and fat–soluble vitamins and list the main vitamins in each category.
- Explain why megadoses of fat–soluble vitamins can be toxic.
- Discuss the functions of vitamins and minerals in the body.
- Describe food sources for the various vitamins and minerals.
- Identify deficiency diseases and explain their causes.
- Distinguish between major and trace minerals and list examples in each category.
- Identify some interrelationships among nutrients.

Terms to Remember

anemia
beriberi
carotene
deficiency diseases
fat–soluble vitamins
major minerals
megadoses
osteomalacia
osteoporosis
pellagra
precursors
provitamins
rickets
scurvy
trace minerals
water–soluble vitamins

This chapter will discuss the properties of vitamins and minerals. You will learn their functions in maintaining your health, as well as how they interact.

WHAT ARE VITAMINS?

Vitamins are complex organic substances vital to life. They are needed in very small amounts by the human body. Unlike the other nutrients you have studied, vitamins do not provide energy. Instead, they perform specific functions in the body, which will be described later in this chapter.

Vitamins were not discovered until this century. Vitamin A was the first to be discovered, in 1915. The last was vitamin B_{12}, in 1948. The

These foods are good sources of vitamin A, the first vitamin discovered.

Vitamin Recommended Dietary Allowances

Different people need slightly different amounts of each vitamin. Therefore in setting up the Recommended Dietary Allowances (RDA) for vitamins, the government has taken average amounts for each vitamin. The following chart gives the RDA of several major vitamins for persons of various ages.

Vitamins	Children 1–3	Children 7–10	Males 15–18	Females 15–18	Males 23–50	Females 23–50
Vitamin A (RE)*	400	700	1000	800	1000	800
Vitamin D (μg)**	10	10	10	10	5	5
Vitamin E (mg)	5	7	10	8	10	8
Vitamin C (mg)	45	45	60	60	60	60
Thiamin (Vitamin B_1) (mg)	0.7	1.2	1.4	1.1	1.4	1.0
Riboflavin (Vitamin B_2) (mg)	0.8	1.4	1.7	1.3	1.6	1.2
Niacin (mg)	9	16	18	14	18	13

*Retinol equivalent
**micrograms

main reason vitamins were discovered so recently is that the body needs such tiny amounts of each one. It took complex knowledge of chemistry and biology to discover vitamins. Until early in this century, scientists did not have the techniques to identify substances needed in such small amounts. Because the energy nutrients are needed in larger amounts, scientists discovered them much earlier than vitamins. While the body requires hundreds of grams of energy nutrients each day to stay healthy, it needs only a millionth of a gram of some vitamins.

Most vitamins are not produced by the body. As a result, they must be consumed on a regular basis if a person is to remain healthy. Vitamins are a necessary part of the human diet. They are available from food, but different foods are good sources of different vitamins.

Certain diseases result from the lack of specific nutrients. These are called **deficiency diseases**. There is no proof that vitamins actually cure illnesses other than those that result from vitamin deficiency. Vitamins are not cure–alls.

Vitamins cannot cure colds or other illnesses except those that are caused by a vitamin deficiency.

Vitamins are often divided into two main categories. **Water–soluble vitamins** will dissolve in water and therefore are only stored in the body in small amounts, if at all. They must be consumed on a daily basis. **Fat–soluble vitamins** do not dissolve in water but, instead, in fats or lipids. Fat–soluble vitamins can be stored in the body for long periods of time. Therefore consuming excessive amounts of these vitamins can be harmful, rather than helpful, to the body.

• WATER–SOLUBLE VITAMINS

The water–soluble vitamins include thiamin (THIGH–uh–min), riboflavin (RY–bo–flay–vin), niacin (NY–uh–sin), vitamin B_6, pantothenic acid (pan–tuh–THE–nik), biotin (BY–uh–tin), folacin (FAWL–uh–sin), vitamin B_{12}, and vitamin C. The major B vitamins—thiamin, riboflavin, and niacin—and vitamin C are nutritionally the most important water–soluble vitamins.

Thiamin

Thiamin, or vitamin B_1, is needed for the metabolism of carbohydrates. Since carbohydrates are the body's main source of energy, thiamin plays a vital role in human metabolism. Thiamin is also involved in the transmission of high–speed impulses in the nervous system. Thiamin is present in yeast, peas, pork, wheat germ, and peanuts and is found in smaller amounts in other food.

Thiamin is easily destroyed by oxygen through the oxidation process. It can also be damaged by heat, especially if the pH is high.

Thiamin is the vitamin that prevents **beriberi** (ber–ee–BER–ee), a disease of the nervous system. Beriberi can cause partial paralysis of the arms and legs, weakness, mental confusion, and death. Beriberi is found mostly in eastern and southern Asia where food that contains thiamin is sometimes not available. In the United States, the only people who develop beriberi are those who drink large amounts of alcohol on a regular basis.

Riboflavin

Riboflavin, or vitamin B_2, is important to growth. It is needed for the metabolism of protein and for tissue repair. Riboflavin is found in both animal and vegetable foods, such as broccoli, asparagus, beef liver, and milk.

Riboflavin affects many chemical reactions in the body. It makes up part of the molecular structure of several enzymes that:

- Allow the release of energy from glucose.
- Help convert the amino acid tryptophan to niacin.
- Help form red blood cells.

Riboflavin is more stable than thiamin since it is not affected by acids, heat, or oxidation. However, riboflavin is unstable in high pH conditions and is destroyed by light. If a clear container of milk is left in the light for over four hours, 75 percent of the riboflavin in the milk will be gone. This is the main reason milk is sold in cardboard cartons.

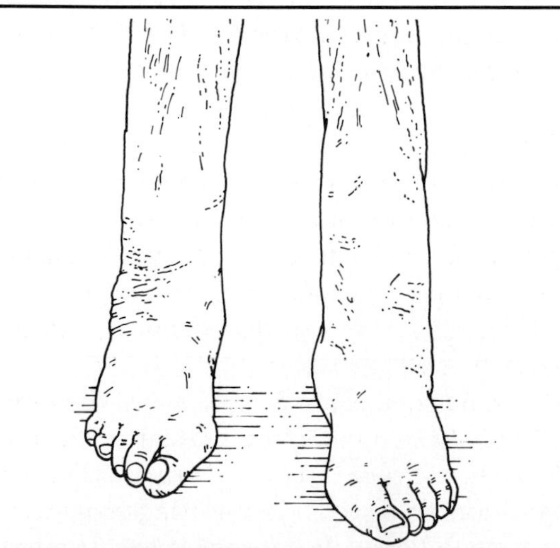

A deficiency of thiamin causes beriberi.

The riboflavin in this milk will be destroyed by the sunlight.

Vitamin Precursors

Some vitamin needs are met by **precursors** (pri–KUR–surs). A precursor is a compound that can be changed into a vitamin in the body. These substances are not vitamins themselves, but they can be changed into vitamins by the body. Vitamin precursors can also be called **provitamins.** One example of a precursor is **carotene** (KAIR–uh–teen), an orange plant pigment, which can be changed into vitamin A in the intestines and liver. A vitamin D precursor is made in the liver. It is converted into vitamin D when it is exposed to ultraviolet sunlight absorbed through the skin. Tryptophan is an amino acid precursor that can be converted into niacin in the liver.

Niacin

Niacin is required by all living cells, not just by higher organisms such as humans. It plays a crucial role in the release of energy from carbohydrate, fat, and protein. It is needed for the formation of deoxyribonucleic acid (dee–ahk–see–ry–bo–noo–KLAY–ik), also known as DNA. This is the compound that controls the type of cells that are produced. Niacin is found in dried peas and beans, peanut butter, liver, chicken, and fish.

Niacin is a very stable vitamin. It is not affected by light, heat, oxidation, acids, or bases. As a result, very little niacin is lost during food processing.

Niacin is known for its role in preventing **pellagra** (puh–LAY–gruh). This disease causes skin eruptions, digestive and nervous disturbances, and eventual mental deterioration. Pellagra was a major health problem in the late 1800s, especially in areas where the diet consisted mostly of corn, molasses, and salt pork. This is because the niacin in corn cannot be used by the body since it is bound to the protein in the corn.

Pellagra is still found in parts of the world, such as Romania, Egypt, Yugoslavia, and India, where the diet is based primarily on corn. Even though Mexicans and other Central Americans have a corn–based diet, they do not suffer from pellagra. This is because they use soda lime in the preparation of the corn for tortillas. The soda lime chemically frees the niacin from the corn protein to which it is bound.

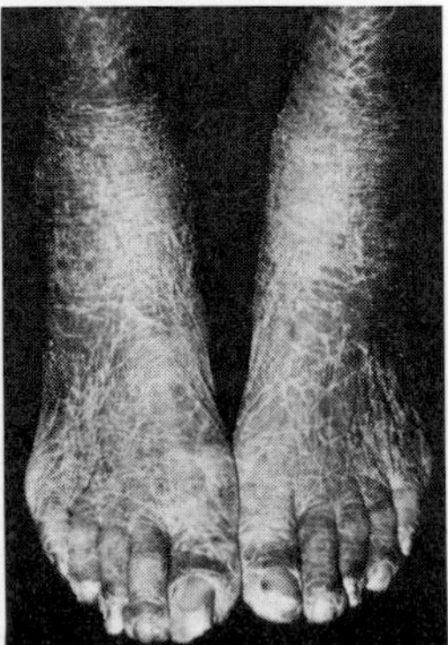

Pellagra is a deficiency disease caused by a lack of niacin.

Vitamin C is often added to food during processing.

Other B Vitamins

There are a number of other B vitamins closely related to the ones discussed here. These include vitamin B_6, vitamin B_{12}, folacin, pantothenic acid, and biotin. They are generally found in the same foods as the other B vitamins and are important in the release of energy from food and in other molecular changes in cells.

Vitamin C

Vitamin C is present in all citrus fruits (such as oranges, lemons, and limes), as well as in potatoes, broccoli, and cabbage. Because it has so many functions in the body and is water soluble, it is important that vitamin C be consumed on a daily basis.

The main function of vitamin C in the body is to assist in forming the protein collagen in connective tissue. Collagen is part of the material that holds cells together, including bone and blood vessels. Vitamin C is also involved in the formation of the dentin layer of the teeth. This is the hard dense layer beneath the enamel, or outer layer.

Vitamin C is stable in the presence of acids, but it is destroyed by oxidation, light, heat, and bases. The fact that vitamin C is so easily broken down is why it is added to so many foods after processing.

Most animals produce vitamin C in their systems. However, humans, monkeys, guinea pigs, and trout must rely on food to provide the vitamin C needed.

Vitamin C is perhaps the best known vitamin today. Supposedly, vitamin C can cure colds if taken in excessively large amounts called **megadoses**. However, there is no conclusive evidence that vitamin C actually does this. In fact, there is concern that megadoses of any vitamin may be harmful to health. Megadoses of vitamin C can, for example, cause kidney stones in some people and diarrhea in others.

• FAT–SOLUBLE VITAMINS

Fat–soluble vitamins are found mostly in lipids and are not soluble in water. They are easily stored in the body. The main fat–soluble vitamins are A, D, E, and K.

Vitamin A

Vitamin A can be consumed directly or acquired from its precursor carotene. The active form of vitamin A in food is called retinol (RET–un–awl). It is found in animal products, such as liver, butter, egg yolk, and cheese. Vitamin A as carotene is found in large amounts in carrots, spinach, broccoli, sweet potatoes, apricots, and liver.

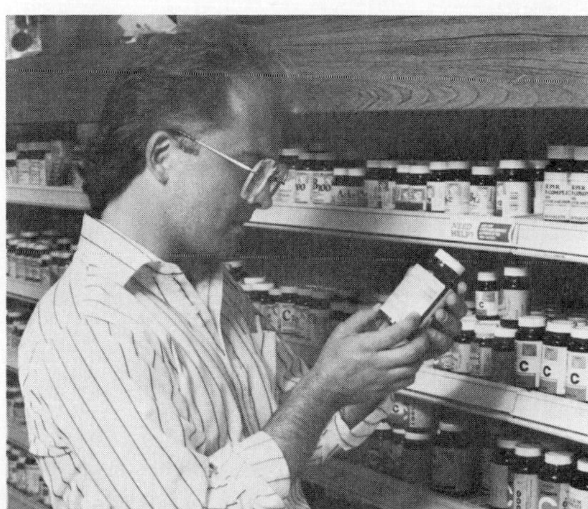

Megadoses of vitamin pills can be toxic to the body.

Vitamin A is essential for good vision. Most of the vitamin A needed by the body is used to maintain mucous membranes. These membrane cells secrete mucus, which protects the walls of the respiratory and digestive systems. During the growth years, vitamin A affects the length to which bones grow. It also helps in the manufacture of red blood cells, plays a role in forming important hormones, and is involved in reproduction.

Scurvy and Vitamin C

Vitamin C is known for its role in preventing the deficiency disease called **scurvy.** Scurvy keeps the blood from carrying as much oxygen as the body needs. Scurvy causes weakness, leaky blood vessels, and spongy gums that often result in the loss of teeth. Most scurvy victims die.

Scurvy has plagued sailors throughout history. During the 1500s, two–thirds of the crew of a ship that made an around–the–world voyage died of the disease. However, in 1747, a British doctor carried out a dietary experiment with two groups of sailors. Those who ate oranges and lemons while on ship did not get scurvy. The condition of those who had the disease improved as soon as they began to eat these fruits.

British sailors are known as "limeys." This nickname dates back to when the British navy required that lime juice be provided to all their ships' crews to prevent scurvy. Scientists now know, of course, that it was the vitamin C present in citrus fruits that cured the sailors and prevented others from suffering from scurvy.

The health of the eyes depends on an adequate supply of vitamin A.

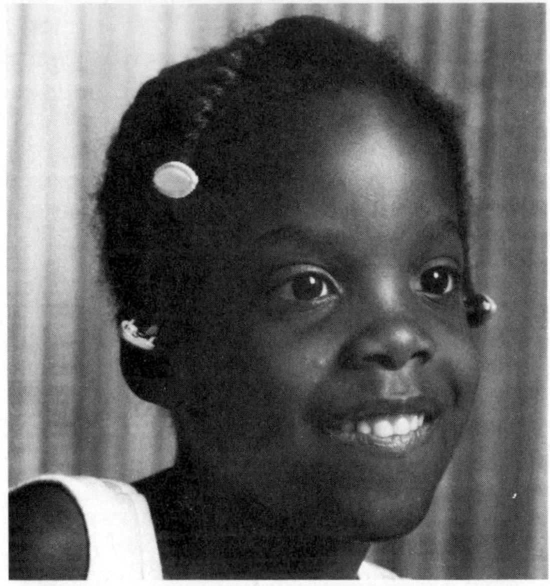

Sunlight on the skin promotes the formation of vitamin D.

Because vitamin A plays a role in such complex systems in the body, its exact function in each case is not clearly understood. It is known, for example, that vitamin A helps people see in the dark. However, while deficiency of vitamin A can cause poor vision, extra vitamin A does not increase visual ability.

The body can store up to a year's supply of vitamin A in the liver. Therefore it is possible to go without vitamin A for long periods of time without any noticeable effects. On the other hand, too much vitamin A is toxic to the body. Joints can become painful, and the clotting of blood is affected. Vomiting and diarrhea often occur, and the person becomes irritable, tired, and weak. It is difficult to get too much vitamin A through the diet. However, people who take megadoses of vitamin A pills are apt to have problems.

Studies have shown that up to 50 percent of the vitamin A used in the body comes from carotene. This is the pigment that gives color to many red and yellow fruits and vegetables. It is also present, though hidden, in green vegetables. Carotene is used by the food industry as a food coloring. The pure form is bright yellow and is used to color margarine, soft drinks, and cake mixes.

Vitamin D

Vitamin D was discovered in 1919. The active form of vitamin D is called cholecalciferol (ko–luh–kal–SIFF–uh–rawl). Foods high in vitamin D are certain animal foods, such as eggs, liver, and fish oils. Sunshine is another important source. Vitamin D is generally added to milk in the United States.

Vitamin D is essential to the growth and repair of strong bones. It makes the minerals calcium and phosphorus available in the blood so they can be deposited as bone tissue. One of the reasons vitamin D is added to milk is that milk has a high content of calcium and phosphorus, both of which are crucial to bone formation.

Vitamin D is sometimes called the sunshine vitamin because the body can manufacture it from the ultraviolet rays in sunlight. The liver manufactures a vitamin D precursor. This precursor circulates in the blood until it is exposed to sunlight through the skin. The sunlight begins the chemical process that converts the precursor into vitamin D.

Young people who do not get enough vitamin D may develop the deficiency disease called **rickets**. These children have bowed legs and soft bones. In the past, children who lived in northern regions where they were exposed to very little sunlight were given cod liver oil. Because the oil was high in vitamin D, it helped prevent rickets.

Adult rickets is called **osteomalacia** (ahs–tee–oh–muh–LAY–shuh). It occurs most often in women who do not spend much time in the sun or who have had a high number of pregnancies. During pregnancy, vitamin D, calcium, and phosphorus from the woman's body are used for bone formation in the baby. Repeated pregnancies can cause a deficiency of vitamin D in the woman, leading to osteomalacia.

Vitamin D is stored in the fatty tissue of the body. Too much vitamin D can cause kidney stones and other problems with excess calcium deposits. It is not possible to build up too much vitamin D from exposure to sunlight. This is because the body will only convert as much of the precursor into vitamin D as it needs.

Vitamin E

What is called vitamin E is actually at least eight different chemicals. The scientific name of vitamin E is tocopherol (toe–KAHF–uh–rawl). Vitamin E is primarily found in vegetable oils, but small amounts are present in fruits, vegetables, and grains. Soybean oil and wheat germ oil are good sources of vitamin E.

Vitamin E helps stabilize cell walls and protect vitamin A in the body. It has an important role in regulating oxidation during metabolism.

Because vitamin E is found in so many foods, there are few, if any, cases of deficiency. Vitamin E is relatively nontoxic, but megadoses can cause nausea and intestinal distress.

At the time vitamin E was discovered in 1922, it was found to be needed for reproduction in at least 20 animal species. As a result, vitamin E became known as the vitamin affecting sterility. However, it has never been proved that it actually influences human reproduction.

Vitamin K

Vitamin K is vitally important to blood clotting. The process of producing a blood clot is a complex one involving many chemicals. If any one of these, such as vitamin K, is missing, a person could bleed to death. Vitamin K is found in milk, liver, and many dark green vegetables.

Osteomalacia can cause a softening of the bones and often occurs in women who do not spend much time in the sun.

The human body cannot produce vitamin K. However, bacteria that normally live in the intestines can produce this chemical. Thus vitamin K is produced *in* the body but not *by* the body.

The bacteria that produce vitamin K can be killed by antibiotics. People on such medication need to be sure to eat food rich in vitamin K. If they are on a restrictive diet, they may have problems with poor blood clotting.

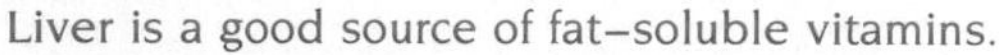

Liver is a good source of fat–soluble vitamins.

The copper in this wire is the same mineral needed by the body.

Mineral Recommended Dietary Allowances

The following chart gives the Recommended Dietary Allowances (RDA) of several minerals for persons of various ages.

Minerals	Children 1–3	Children 7–10	Males 15–18	Females 15–18	Males 23–50	Females 23–50
Calcium (mg)	800	800	1200	1200	800	800
Phosphorus (mg)	800	800	1200	1200	800	800
Magnesium (mg)	150	250	400	300	350	300
Iron (mg)	15	10	18	18	10	18
Zinc (mg)	10	10	15	15	15	15
Iodine (μg)*	70	120	150	150	150	150

*micrograms

WHAT ARE MINERALS?

Minerals are elements that the body needs in varying amounts. Those needed in amounts of 0.1 g or more each day are known as **major minerals.** These include sodium, calcium, phosphorus, chlorine, potassium, sulfur, and magnesium. Minerals the body needs in amounts of 0.01 g or less each day are known as **trace minerals.** Iron, zinc, iodine, copper, manganese, fluorine, chromium, selenium (sih–LEE–nee–um), and molybdenum (muh–LIB–duh–num) are some of the trace minerals.

• SODIUM

Sodium, a highly reactive metallic element, is found in the body as positive sodium ions. Sodium is important because it helps maintain the balance that allows water to flow freely in and out of cells.

Table salt is the primary source of sodium for most people. Excessive amounts of sodium can be a problem to those with high blood pressure or heart disease. In fact, excessive sodium may contribute to the onset of these problems. Therefore it is recommended that most people limit their salt intake. This can be difficult because many processed foods are high in sodium. In addition, many people enjoy the flavor salt adds to food.

Sodium is one mineral many people get too much of.

• CALCIUM

Calcium is important in many ways in the body. It is one of the main components of teeth and bones. It is needed to build and maintain strong bones. It also circulates in the body and helps maintain cell membranes. Calcium ensures proper muscle action, a regular heartbeat, and a steady concentration of ions both inside and outside body cells. It also plays a role in blood clotting. All milk products are high in calcium.

Calcium deficiency symptoms are similar to vitamin D deficiency symptoms. This is because the two are so closely interrelated in the chemical processes of the body. A lack of calcium can cause **osteoporosis** (ahs–tee–oh–pore–OH–sis). This is a condition where the bones become thinner and less dense, and therefore more fragile. Osteoporosis results in bone fractures, especially in people over age 65.

Calcium is perhaps the most important mineral during the growth years. It is also important

Calcium, which is an important mineral for women, is found in milk and milk products.

for women throughout their lives. The hormonal changes that take place as women age cause them to lose calcium.

• OTHER MAJOR MINERALS

Phosphorus is closely linked with calcium. These two minerals combine to form the compound calcium phosphate, which gives bones their strength and rigid structure. Phosphorus also has other functions in the body, since many processes within body cells involve phosphorus. Any type of animal protein is an excellent source of phosphorus. The mineral is plentiful in animal muscle tissue.

Potassium is crucial in regulating the heartbeat. It also helps maintain the fluid volume inside cells. Potassium is abundant in many foods, such as orange juice, bananas, dried fruits, and potatoes.

The element chlorine is a highly poisonous gas. However, people consume it as negative chloride ions, which are attached to sodium ions in table salt. Chloride ions are used by the body to control blood pH and to form hydrochloric acid. This is a compound used in the stomach for the digestion of food.

Sulfur is important in the formation of skin, hair, and nails. It is a part of several amino acids. Therefore meat and other protein foods are good sources of sulfur. There has never been any reported deficiency of this mineral.

Magnesium is involved in making protein and in releasing energy. Good sources are nuts, grains, dark green vegetables, seafood, and chocolate. Deficiencies in magnesium rarely occur.

Bananas are a good source of the mineral potassium.

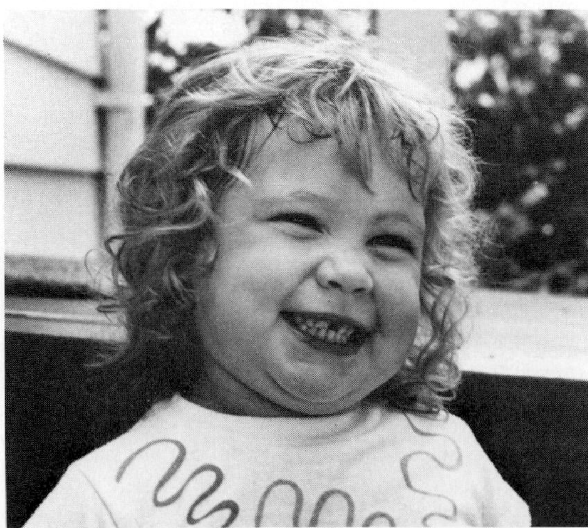

Fluoride ions are important in the formation of teeth.

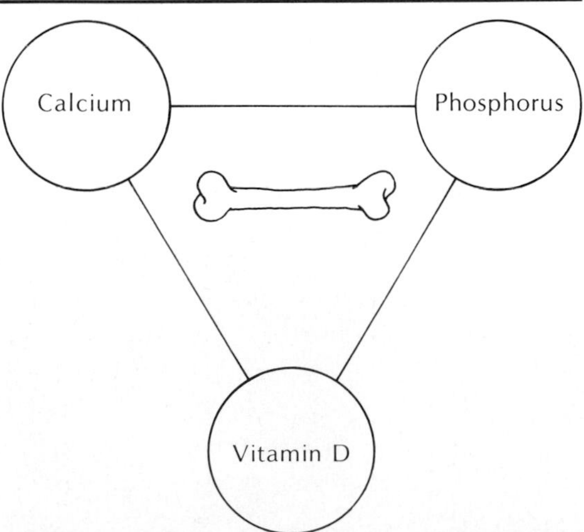

The interaction among calcium, phosphorus, and vitamin D is needed to build strong bones.

• TRACE MINERALS

There are a variety of trace minerals needed for proper body functioning.

- Iron is a vital part of red blood cells that carry and release oxygen.
- Iodine is a component of thyroid hormones important in metabolism.
- Zinc is involved in many enzymatic reactions and forms part of the structure of bone.
- Copper is used in breathing, energy release, and the production of red blood cells.
- Manganese is involved in metabolic processes and formation of bone.
- Fluoride ions from fluorine are important in the formation of bones and teeth.
- Chromium is needed for the action of insulin.
- Selenium functions as part of certain enzymes.
- Molybdenum is a working part of several enzymes.

Scientists are continuing to study other minerals to see whether they are important in the functioning of a healthy body.

NUTRITION AND YOU

Nutrient Interaction

Balance is the key to good nutrition. Vitamins and minerals are important to the body not only for what they do individually, but also because of their interaction with each other.

Vitamin C affects the absorption of iron and copper. Having vitamin C present in the same meal as food high in iron will let the body absorb up to three times as much of this mineral. This is especially important to people who suffer from the iron deficiency disease call **anemia** (uh–NEE–mee–uh). On the other hand, vitamin C interferes with the absorption of copper in the body.

Iron is also involved in other interrelationships. Drinking tea while eating iron–rich food will inhibit the body's ability to absorb the iron. Too much manganese makes an iron deficiency worse. An iron deficiency makes a person more apt to suffer from lead poisoning.

Zinc and vitamin A are closely related. In fact, zinc deficiency has all the symptoms of vitamin A deficiency. This is because zinc is a necessary portion of the protein that takes vitamin A from the liver when it is needed by the body.

Calcium and phosphorus are absorbed better by the body if consumed together. Eating equal amounts of each mineral is considered best. Vitamin D is needed to help the calcium and phosphorus be deposited in the bones.

Another interrelationship with calcium involves magnesium. Magnesium helps hold calcium in the enamel of the teeth.

Vitamin E helps prevent vitamin A and polyunsaturated fatty acids from being destroyed by oxygen. Vitamin E also helps vitamin A be absorbed by the body. Selenium can be used to prevent the oxidation of vitamin E.

Protein also affects some vitamins and minerals. Vitamin A depends on protein for its functions and for transportation in the body. High protein levels can prevent absorption of iron and cause the body to excrete calcium in the urine.

Scientists are discovering new ways that nutrients interact with each other. The best way to get a good balance of all the required nutrients is to eat a variety of food.

EXPERIMENT 10–1

Titration of Vitamin C

Vitamin C is an acidic compound. This is because one of the major forms of vitamin C is ascorbic acid. The amount of vitamin C in a substance can be calculated by finding out how much acid is in it.

As you know, titration is a way to find the concentration of one substance by using a known amount and concentration of another substance. In this experiment, you will use a base made for titration to find out the level of vitamin C in a juice sample. The amount of base used to neutralize the juice sample is proportional to the amount of acid in the juice.

Certain factors cause vitamin C to break down into other compounds. This experiment will test the effect of heat on vitamin C content in apple and orange juice.

PROCEDURE

1. Wear safety goggles throughout this experiment.
2. Obtain 50 mL apple juice or 50 mL orange juice from your teacher.
3. Follow the variation assigned by your teacher.
   a. **Variation 1.** Use the refrigerated orange juice as is. Add 50 mL deionized water to the sample.
   b. **Variation 2.** Heat the orange juice sample for 5 minutes on medium heat (1½ minutes in a microwave oven). Add 50 mL deionized water to the sample.
   c. **Variation 3.** Use the refrigerated apple juice as is.
   d. **Variation 4.** Heat the apple juice sample for 5 minutes on medium heat (1½ minutes in a microwave oven).
4. Clamp a clean 50 mL buret to a ring stand. Fill the buret with the titration base. In your data table, record the initial buret reading. Accurate measurements are very important in titration.
5. Place 10 mL diluted orange juice or undiluted apple juice into a 250 mL Erlenmeyer flask, and add 15 mL oxalic acid solution.
6. Place the Erlenmeyer flask under the tip of the buret. Slowly add 2.6 dichlorophenolindophenot solution (it is a blue oxidizing agent) to the juice solution. When a pink color appears, gently swirl the flask until the color disappears. Add the base drop by drop, swirling after each drop, until 1 drop turns the solution a pink color that does not disappear when the flask is swirled. In your data table, record the final buret reading.
7. Repeat your titration two more times, for a total of three titrations. In your data table,

EXPERIMENT 10–1

record your initial and final buret readings for each titration. Average the volumes used for your three trials and record the average in your second data table.

8. Write your average volumes on the chalkboard. In your second data table, record the average volumes from the other variations.
9. Calculate the milligrams of vitamin C in 100 mL of juice (an average serving) for each sample using the equation below. Your teacher will tell you what number to use for "difference in buret readings for standard solution."

$$\frac{\text{mg vitamin C}}{\text{in 100 mL juice}} = \frac{10 \times \text{difference in buret readings}}{\text{difference in buret readings for standard solution}}$$

Enter this information in your data table.

QUESTIONS

1. Which sample contained the most vitamin C? The least?
2. Did heat reduce the vitamin C content of the juices? By how much? Which juice was affected more, orange or apple?
3. What type of storage procedures would you recommend for apple and orange juice to maintain high levels of vitamin C?

SAMPLE DATA TABLES

Trial	Individual Buret Readings			Mg Vitamin C in 100 mL Juice
	Initial	Final	Difference	
1				
2				
3				

Variation	Average Class Buret Readings			Mg Vitamin C in 100 mL Juice
	Initial	Final	Difference	
1				
2				
3				
4				

EXPERIMENT 10–2

Calcium in Milk

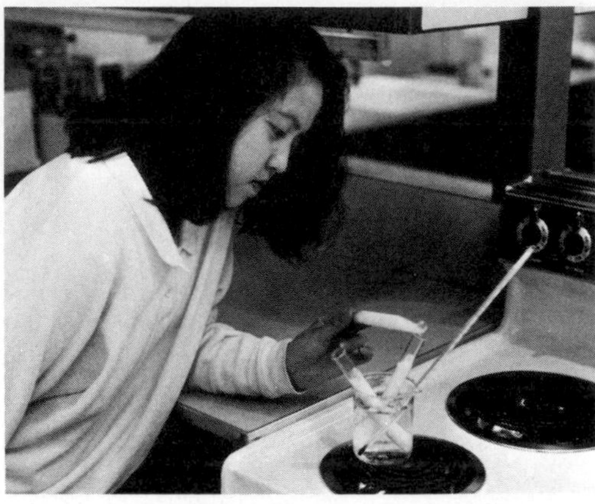

In this experiment, you will observe the effects of calcium ions on the coagulation of milk. The enzyme rennin causes milk to coagulate by converting the milk protein casein into a compound called paracasein. However, for rennin to work, calcium ions must be present. When calcium ions are removed from milk, coagulation is suppressed. When calcium ions are restored, coagulation proceeds as usual.

PROCEDURE

1. Fill three test tubes three–fourths full of whole milk. Label them A, B, and C.
2. Heat water in a 400 mL beaker to a temperature of 37°C, and place all three test tubes in the water. Maintain heat at 37°C.
3. Add 0.1 g of rennet, a substance that contains the enzyme rennin, to tube A. Add 0.1 g of rennet and 0.1 g of sodium citrate to tube B. This compound reacts with calcium ions to produce the insoluble substance calcium citrate. Tube C will be a control. A control in an experiment is the standard with which other samples are compared.
4. Stopper the tubes, and allow them to sit for 5 minutes.
5. After 5 minutes, examine the contents of the test tubes. Turn them upside down, but do not shake them. Record your observations in your data table.
6. Add 4–5 drops calcium chloride solution to tube B. Replace it in the water bath with the other tubes for an additional 5 minutes. Again, record your observations in your data table.

QUESTIONS

1. Compare test tube A with test tube C. How do they differ?
2. What happened to the calcium ions in test tube B?
3. Explain what happened when the calcium chloride was added to test tube B.

SAMPLE DATA TABLE

Test Tube	Appearance After 5 Minutes	Appearance After 10 Minutes
A		
B		
C		

REVIEW

TO SUM UP

- Vitamins and minerals perform specific functions in the body that are vital to life.
- Deficiency diseases resulting from a lack of vitamins or minerals are beriberi, pellagra, rickets, osteomalacia, scurvy, osteoporosis, and anemia.
- Different foods are good sources of different vitamins and minerals, so it is important to eat a variety of foods to get your Recommended Dietary Allowances of each.
- Water–soluble vitamins dissolve in water, are not stored in the body, and must be eaten every day.
- Fat–soluble vitamins dissolve in lipids, are stored in the body, and can be toxic if taken in megadoses.
- Major minerals are needed in larger amounts in the body than trace minerals.
- Vitamins and minerals interact in body processes, so a deficiency of one affects the functioning of others.

CHECK YOUR FACTS

1. What are vitamins?
2. What is the precursor of niacin?
3. Which vitamin is important in growth and tissue repair?
4. Which is the most stable of the water–soluble vitamins?
5. Why don't people from Mexico suffer from pellagra even though their diets are based on corn?
6. What vitamin prevents people from getting scurvy?
7. What vitamin precursor is used as a food coloring?
8. What are the functions of vitamin D?
9. What vitamin is important in blood clotting?
10. What is the difference between major and trace minerals?
11. Why should people limit their intake of salt?
12. What minerals are part of enzymes in the body?

CRITICAL THINKING AND PROBLEM SOLVING

1. Why don't many animals get scurvy?
2. Who would need to eat more foods high in vitamin D—a resident of Anchorage or a resident of San Diego?
3. Which vitamin and mineral work together to prevent rickets?
4. Explain the following statement: Vitamin K is produced *in* the body but not *by* the body.
5. Why are people on a restrictive diet who are also taking antibiotics apt to bleed excessively if they are injured?
6. Would it be best to take an iron supplement with tea, orange juice, or water? Why?
7. Plan a typical daily menu for a three–year–old, a teenager, and an inactive older person. Use what you learned about sensory evaluation as well as what you now know about nutritional requirements.

Metabolism

This chapter will help you . . .

- Define anabolism and catabolism, the two opposite processes of metabolism.
- Describe conditions needed for metabolism to occur.
- Explain the process of osmosis and the role it plays in metabolism.
- Discuss basal metabolism and factors that affect it.
- Identify various levels of voluntary activity and how these affect the need for kilocalories.
- Describe metabolic changes that can occur during fasting and their effect on the body.
- Explain why lactic acid builds up in the muscles during exercise and how this can be prevented or treated.

Terms to Remember

adenosine triphosphate
ammonia
anabolism
basal metabolic rate
basal metabolism
catabolism
cold–blooded
ketones
lactic acid
membranes
metabolic rate
osmosis
protoplasm
semipermeable
voluntary activities
warm–blooded

You have learned that the food you eat is turned to energy in your body. This energy is used to maintain metabolism and to carry out **voluntary activities**. You may recall that metabolism is the chemical and physical processes occurring within the living cells of the body. Voluntary activities are your physical actions and movements, such as walking, talking, or conducting food science experiments. This chapter will look at how the body uses food and what determines how much food the body needs.

Energy is needed for voluntary activities.

THE PROCESS OF METABOLISM

The main component of animal and plant cells is **protoplasm** (PRO–tuh–plaz–um). This is a colloidal substance consisting of water, protein, lipids, carbohydrates, and inorganic salts. During the process of metabolism, food becomes protoplasm. In addition, metabolism can also break down protoplasm into simpler substances and waste matter.

Metabolism thus consists of two opposite body processes, each of which has its own name. **Anabolism** (uh–NAB–uh–liz–um) is the chemical processes involved when molecules combine to build larger molecules. An example of an anabolic (an–uh–BAHL–ik) reaction would be amino acids joining to form protein. Anabolism uses energy. **Catabolism** (kuh–TAB–uh–liz–um) involves the chemical reactions in which large molecules break down into smaller molecules. These reactions generally release energy. The breakdown of glucose to carbon dioxide and water is a catabolic (kat–uh–BAHL–ik) reaction.

Energy Sources—A Review

The three energy sources used by human beings are carbohydrates, lipids, and protein. The body uses each of these nutrients in a unique manner.

As you may recall, the main function of carbohydrate is to provide energy to body cells. It is broken down into glucose, which can be used immediately, stored in the body as glycogen, or converted to fat. When used immediately, the glucose is broken down to carbon dioxide, water, and energy.

Lipids in the diet are also stored in the body until they are needed for energy. They are stored as adipose tissue.

During digestion, protein is broken down into amino acids. These amino acids can be used to build the body's own protein. Sometimes amino acids are broken down to meet energy needs. This occurs if there is an excess of amino acids or if the body needs more energy than it can get from glucose and glycogen.

Adenosine Triphosphate

Metabolism involves both the use and release of energy. When energy is released, it is carried by molecules known as **adenosine triphosphate** (uh–DEN–uh–seen try–FOS–fayt), or ATP. ATP is the carrier of energy in living cells. When energy is needed, the ATP releases the energy it has carried.

ATP is composed of a compound called adenosine to which phosphate groups can be added. Phosphate groups contain one atom of phosphorus and four atoms of oxygen and are written **$-PO_4$**. One, two, or three phosphate groups can be attached to the adenosine. When more than one phosphate group is attached to the adenosine, the groups chain together. When three phosphate groups are attached, the compound is ATP, which can be shown as A–P–P–P. When only two phosphate groups are attached, the compound is adenosine diphosphate, or ADP. It can be shown as A–P–P.

The bonds between the phosphate groups are where the energy is carried. These are called high energy bonds. Energy is primarily carried between the second and the third phosphate groups. When the bond between the second and third phosphate groups is broken, the third phosphate group is transferred to another molecule. In addition, energy is released for work in the cells. When this occurs, the ATP has become ADP.

$$\text{ATP} \rightarrow \text{ADP} + \text{Energy}$$

Because ATP is constantly being used up in the cells, it must be remade. ADP uses energy provided by the breakdown of glucose to link with another phosphate group to again become ATP.

How fast the chemical processes of metabolism take place is known as the **metabolic rate** (met–uh–BAHL–ik). This rate varies from person to person.

For metabolism to occur, there must be enough oxygen and water. There must also be a way to rid the body of waste products, which can be toxic if allowed to build up. Body temperature must be within an acceptable range. Finally, dissolved substances in the blood and cells must be at appropriate levels.

• REGULATION OF CHEMICALS

The cells in the body are mostly protoplasm surrounded by thin layers of tissue called **membranes**. The membranes of the cell walls are **semipermeable** (sem–ee–PUR–me–uh–bul). This means that varying amounts of certain substances can pass through the membranes. Because the cell walls are semipermeable, there is a constant interchange of molecules across the membrane of every cell in the body. If metabolism is to occur normally, there must be a proper concentration of chemicals on each side of the cell membrane. Because chemical imbalances between the cells can occur, some kind of control mechanism is needed.

Certain ions in the body help regulate the concentration of body chemicals by **osmosis** (os–MOH–sis). Osmosis is the movement of fluid across a semipermeable cell membrane so there is an equal concentration of solute on both sides of the membrane.

Sodium and chloride ions are the principal minerals in blood. Potassium and phosphate ions are the most abundant minerals in cell protoplasm. If there is an increase in sodium

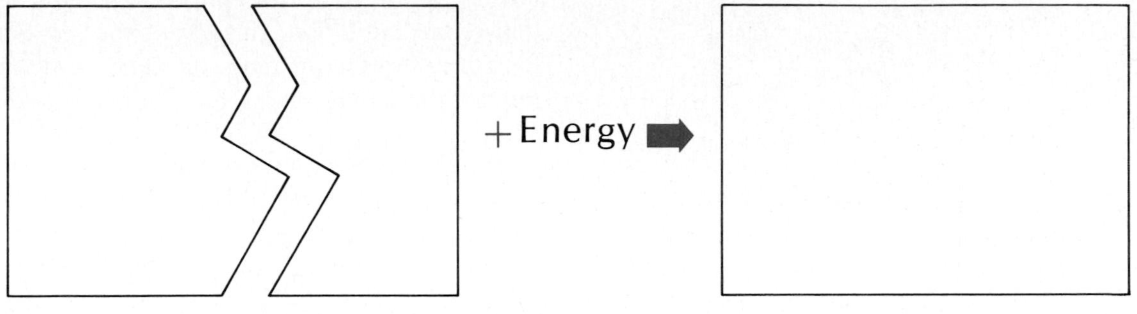

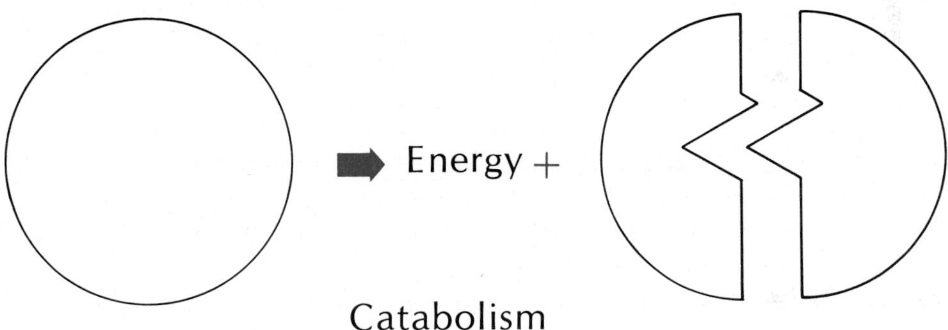

Anabolism uses energy to build larger molecules from smaller ones, while catabolism releases energy when large molecules break down to smaller ones.

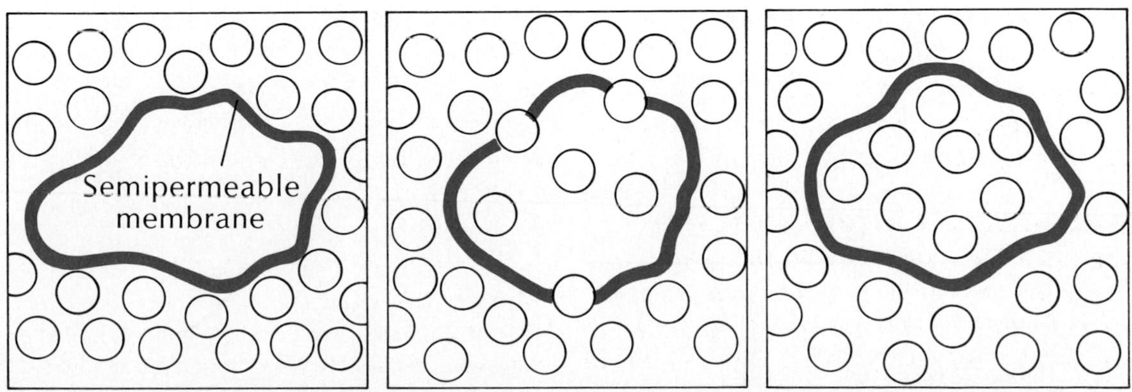

Molecules of certain substances can pass through a semipermeable membrane.

ions in the blood, water from the cells will be drawn into the blood. This lowers the sodium ion concentration. At the same time, it raises the potassium concentration inside the cells.

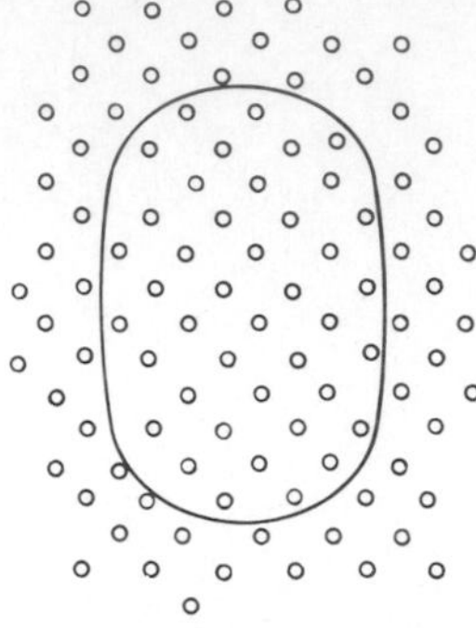

A.

B.

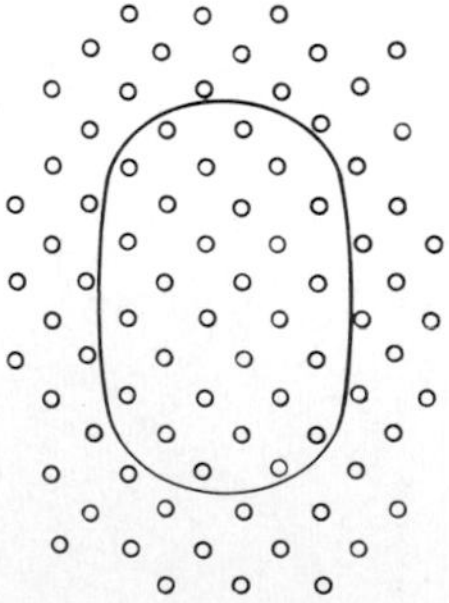

C.

In A, a cell contains the same concentration of a solute as does the area around it. In B, more solute is added outside the cell, increasing the concentration. In C, water moves out of the cell (causing it to become smaller) to equalize the concentration of the solute.

Animals and Metabolic Rate

Metabolic rate varies in humans from person to person. It also varies among different kinds of animals. The metabolic rate of animals depends on a variety of factors.

All animals, except mammals and birds, are **cold–blooded.** This means that body temperature varies with the surroundings. Since temperature affects the rate of chemical reactions, it also affects metabolism. When cold–blooded animals are in a warm setting, their metabolism functions at a certain rate. This rate becomes much slower if the surroundings cool because body temperature cools also.

Warm–blooded animals, including humans, have mechanisms that maintain a more or less constant internal body temperature. In humans, this mechanism involves perspiring if the surroundings become too warm. If the surroundings cool down, the body produces more heat. Because body temperature stays the same, the metabolic rate in warm–blooded animals is relatively constant.

The size of an animal affects metabolic rate. The metabolic rate of small mammals is much faster than that of larger ones. Small mammals must work harder than larger mammals just to stay warm. This means their blood must circulate faster, which requires the heart to beat faster. Small mammals breathe more often per minute than larger ones. Mice, for example, take 150 breaths a minute. The average human breathes 16 times a minute, while an elephant breathes only 6 times.

By controlling the movement of water, the body also controls the concentration of the substances dissolved in it.

• BASAL METABOLISM

Basal metabolism is the amount of energy needed by a body at rest to maintain the automatic activities that support life. These include:

- Regulation of body temperature.
- Maintenance of breathing.
- Control of the heartbeat.
- Breaking apart molecules, building muscle tissue, and other metabolic reactions taking place in the cells.

A body at rest uses energy for the automatic activities that support life.

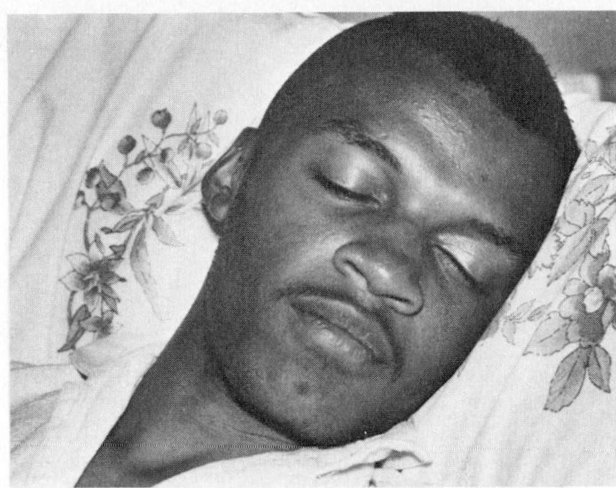

Calculating Basal Metabolic Rate

Accurate measurements of basal metabolic rate (BMR) require special equipment and testing procedures. However, there is a shortcut method to get a rough approximation of the energy spent on BMR.

On the average, males use about 1 kcal per kilogram of body weight per hour for BMR. Females use about 0.9 kcal per kilogram per hour. The following steps show how to calculate your BMR.

1. Convert your weight in pounds (lb.) to kilograms by using the following equation.

$$\frac{\text{weight in pounds}}{2.2} = \text{weight in kilograms}$$

For example, if you weigh 150 lb., the calculation would be as follows.

$$\frac{150 \text{ lb.}}{2.2} = 68 \text{ kg}$$

2. To find out how many kilocalories you use per hour, use the following equation. If you are a female, your BMR factor is 0.9. If you are a male, the BMR factor is 1.

$$\text{kcal used per hour} = \text{weight in kg} \times \text{BMR factor}$$

For example, a female who weighs 68 kg would use 61 kcal per hour ($68 \times 0.9 = 61$). A male of the same weight would use 68 kcal per hour ($68 \times 1 = 68$).

3. To find out how many kilocalories you use per day, use the following equation.

$$\text{kcal used per hour} \times 24 = \text{kcal used in BMR per day}$$

The 68 kg female would thus need 1464 kcal per day for basal metabolism ($61 \times 24 = 1464$). The 68 kg male would need 1632 kcal for basal metabolism ($68 \times 24 = 1632$).

Approximately how many kilocalories do you need a day for basal metabolism?

The BMR of this child is higher than that of her mother.

Basal metabolism uses about two–thirds of the energy the body produces. It varies from person to person, depending on a number of factors.

Basal metabolism is measured by the **basal metabolic rate**, also known as BMR. BMR is the rate at which energy is used by a body at rest after a 12–hour fast. It is scientifically measured in humans as heat given off per time unit—kilocalories per hour. Accurate BMR measurements are taken with a portable laboratory machine.

Factors Affecting BMR

A person's age affects BMR. The younger a person is, the higher the BMR. Scientists think that cells must function at a rapid rate to build the new material needed for growth. The BMR decreases about 2 percent per decade after growth stops.

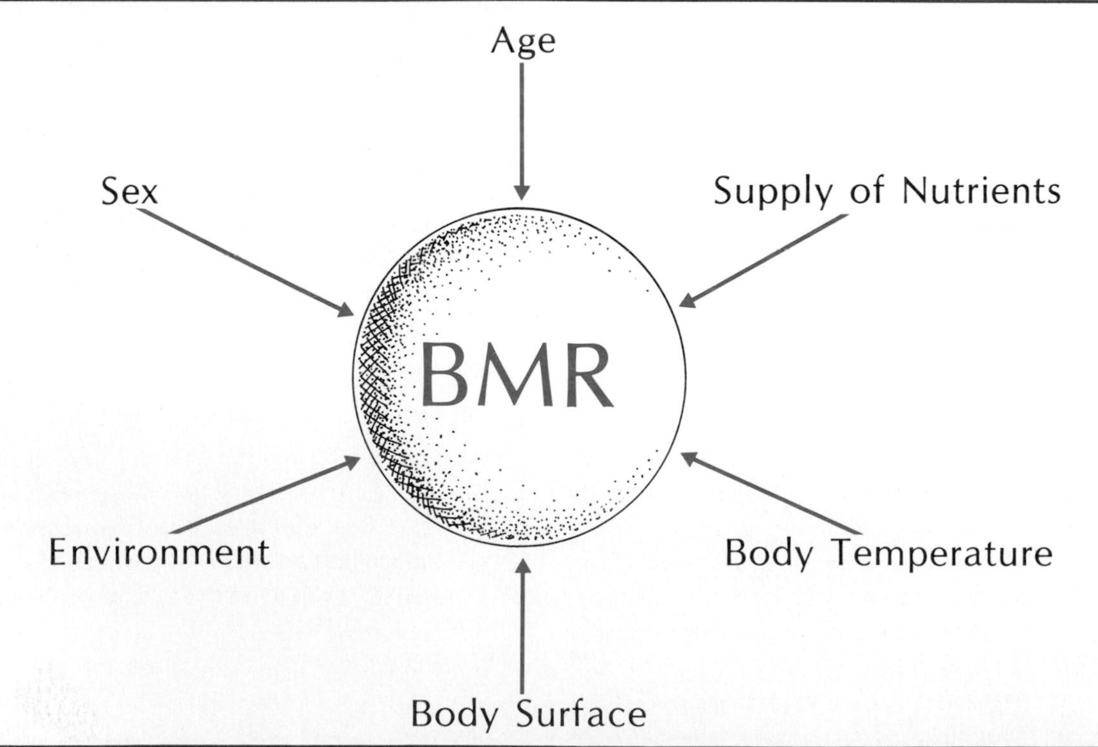

How do each of these factors affect BMR?

Voluntary Activities

You have unique energy needs based on your size, age, and level of activity. The total number of kilocalories you need each day is based on the energy you need for basal metabolism and the voluntary activities in which you participate.

Voluntary activities vary tremendously in the number of kilocalories they need. Both the time spent in an activity and the physical work it requires affect the number of kilocalories used.

Sedentary activities involve sitting. These include activities such as reading, watching television or movies, playing cards, typing and eating. These activities burn about 80–100 kcal per hour.

Light activities use 110–160 kcal per hour. Some light activities are preparing food, ironing, walking slowly, and attending to personal care.

Making beds, doing laundry, walking moderately fast, light gardening, and carpentry work are examples of moderate activity. These use 170–240 kcal per hour.

Vigorous activities use 250–350 kcal per hour. These include such activities as polishing a car, walking fast, bowling, golfing, gardening, and scrubbing the floor.

Finally, strenuous activities include swimming, playing tennis, playing football, running, bicycling, and dancing. These activities burn 350 or more kcal per hour.

Most people participate in all of these types of activities at some time or another. However, each person's life-style can be classified according to which level of activity is most common for that person. To estimate the number of kilocalories needed for voluntary activities, multiply the following percentages times BMR.

- Sedentary life-style—20 percent.
- Life-style of light activity—30 percent.
- Life-style of moderate activity—40 percent.
- Life-style of vigorous activity—50 percent.
- Life-style of strenuous activity—varies but at least 50 percent.

To find the total kilocalories you need each day, add the kilocalories from your BMR to those from your voluntary activities. Eating this number of kilocalories daily will let you maintain a constant weight.

Body surface also affects metabolic rate. Since heat is lost through body surface, a small person will have a slower BMR than a large person. This is true even if a short overweight person weighs the same as a tall thin person. The tall person has more surface area than the shorter person of the same weight. The tall person thus has to produce more heat per unit of body weight to maintain body temperature.

Males have a higher metabolic rate than females. This is apparently because males have a lower percent of body fat and a greater proportion of active lean tissue than females. Fat tissue is much less active metabolically. Therefore the BMR for females tends to be lower than for males.

The environment can have some effect on BMR, though not a great deal. Prolonged exposure to cold will cause a person's body to burn more kilocalories. This will help maintain

Watching television is a sedentary activity that does not burn many kilocalories.

Strenuous activities like tennis can burn 350 or more kcal per hour.

a steady body temperature. In very hot weather, metabolism may slow to avoid increasing body temperature.

When someone is ill and fever increases body temperature, metabolic rate changes. Running a fever can cause the BMR to increase as much as 4 percent for every °C that body temperature increases.

Just as running a fever can increase metabolic rate, other factors can cause it to decrease. For example, if the body does not receive adequate nutrients, the BMR will slow down. This can occur from intentional fasting or from malnutrition caused by a lack of an adequate food supply. The lowered BMR is a survival mechanism, since using calories more slowly will help prolong life. For this reason, fasting is usually not recommended to those who want to lose weight. The body will simply slow down to the point where less weight will be lost than if small quantities of a variety of foods were eaten.

The body needs lots of glucose for activities like volleyball.

THE METABOLISM OF FASTING

Occasionally, a person will decide to fast. Fasting means consuming nothing but fluids, usually water. Since glucose is not available from the diet, the body gets energy from stored glycogen. However, the glycogen stored in the body will supply only about a day's worth of energy. Once this is gone, the body begins to use its supply of stored fat. Protein molecules from muscle are also used to supply energy.

The brain requires a constant supply of glucose. If glucose and glycogen are not available, the body breaks down protein to obtain the needed glucose. During protein metabolism, **ammonia** and **ketones** are formed. Ammonia **(NH_3)** is formed from the amine group. Ketones are compounds that contain a carbon atom double bonded to an oxygen atom with additional single bonds to two other carbons. The general structure of a ketone molecule is shown below.

$$R_1 - \underset{\displaystyle O}{\underset{\|}{C}} - R_2$$

Ketone

Ammonia and ketones are waste products of the breakdown of protein. If allowed to accumulate, ketones can have a serious effect on health by lowering the blood pH. Therefore large quantities of water must be consumed to flush ketones out of the blood.

In addition, a fasting person may experience:

- An increase in blood cholesterol.
- An increase in uric acid, an acid found in urine.
- A decrease in hormones needed by the thyroid gland.

All of these changes can be harmful and can make the fasting person ill.

People can become ill because of the harmful changes that occur in the body during fasting.

METABOLISM AND EXERCISE

Muscles use the same fuel as other cells—glucose, if it is available. When you are sitting typing or walking to class, your muscles can get the energy they need from glucose in the blood. However, if you go mountain climbing, play basketball, or engage in other vigorous exercise, your muscles require great quantities of glucose. At this point, your body must break down some of the glycogen stored in the muscles. The glycogen is turned into glucose, which in turn breaks down into water, carbon dioxide, and the energy needed.

Lactic acid buildup can cause a burning sensation in the muscles.

Sometimes people exercise to the point where they feel a burning sensation in their muscles or where they experience extreme muscle fatigue. This burning sensation or fatigue is caused by a buildup of **lactic acid** in the muscles. Lactic acid is a waste product formed when glucose is not completely metabolized. Lactic acid buildup occurs when there is not enough oxygen for the cells to completely break down the glucose.

When lactic acid builds up, the person simply needs to rest. Resting will replenish the oxygen supply to the body. This will allow the lactic acid to combine with oxygen to complete the glucose metabolism. In addition, the lactic acid can be carried away in the bloodstream to the liver.

Those who exercise regularly are less likely to experience lactic acid buildup. Well–conditioned muscles burn food fast and efficiently. In addition, muscles accustomed to frequent physical exercise build up a supply of the enzymes needed to process glucose and fat at a fast rate. Thus, during exercise, the body can effectively draw on both glucose and fat for energy.

Complex carbohydrates are good sources of kilocalories for athletes.

NUTRITION AND YOU

Nutritional Needs of Athletes

You have learned that strenuous activity requires more kilocalories than light activity. People who participate in athletics obviously need more kilocalories than others do.

Complex carbohydrates—starches—seem to be the best form for the added kilocalories. Foods such as pasta, pancakes, breads, and cereals are recommended as good sources of kilocalories for athletes.

Some athletic events involve a short time of high–intensity activity. These might be sprints and short races. Endurance events, such as marathon races, require sustained effort over a long time. Both kinds of activities draw on glycogen in the muscles for energy. Low–carbohydrate, high–fat diets tend to hinder performance, especially in endurance events.

To increase muscle glycogen, some athletes have tried a technique called carbohydrate loading. Carbohydrate loading manipulates dietary carbohydrate. Several days before an event, the athlete reduces carbohydrate in the diet, then uses up glycogen stores through exercise. The night before the event, the athlete eats a huge amount of complex carbohydrate. The muscle glycogen stores rebound to about twice the normal limit, providing fuel for the endurance event. However, carbohydrate loading has unhealthy side effects. The athlete may suffer an abnormal heartbeat, swollen and painful muscles, and weight gain. Some athletes now eat extra carbohydrate before the event, but they avoid the dangerous reduction in carbohydrate intake beforehand.

Probably the most important nutrient for athletes is water. The regulation of body temperature through perspiration makes it important for an athlete to drink plenty of liquid. If water balance is not maintained, dehydration can occur, which brings fatigue.

Protein is not a good fuel for athletic activity. There is no evidence that extra protein increases strength, endurance, or speed.

In general, there is no need for extra vitamins, minerals, protein, or lipids in the diet of an athlete. Additional carbohydrate and water are the main nutritional needs for athletic activity. The increased intake of kilocalories due to the extra carbohydrate will ensure an adequate supply of essential nutrients.

EXPERIMENT 11–1

Osmosis—Travel Through a Membrane

Osmosis is the passage of water and other liquids through a semipermeable membrane. In metabolism, it acts to regulate the concentration of substances on both sides of the membrane.

Eggs contain a membrane through which osmosis can take place. In this experiment, you will determine whether water flows primarily in or out of an egg by observing changes in liquid level and the size of the egg.

PROCEDURE

1. Place an egg (still in the shell) in a 250 mL beaker containing enough vinegar to cover the egg. Let stand for three days.
2. Pour out vinegar and carefully rinse any remaining shell off egg, leaving the egg sac.
3. Carefully place the egg (which now has no shell) in a clean 250 mL beaker. Follow the variation assigned by your teacher.
   a. **Variation 1.** Add water to completely cover the egg.
   b. **Variation 2.** Add vinegar to completely cover the egg.
   c. **Variation 3.** Add corn syrup to completely cover the egg.
   d. **Variation 4.** Add a salt–water solution to completely cover the egg.
4. Measure the height of the liquid in the beaker, and record it in your data table.
5. After 30 minutes, measure the level of the liquid in the beaker and note any appearance changes in the egg and the liquid. Record these in your data table.
6. Label the beaker with your name, variation number, and class period. Cover it with plastic wrap. Leave it overnight in the location designated by your teacher.
7. The following day, measure the liquid level and observe the appearance of the egg and the liquid. Note any evidence of layers separating in the liquid. Record the information in your data table.
8. Record the heights of your liquid and the appearance of the egg and the liquid on the chalkboard. In your data table, record the height and appearance information for the other variations.

EXPERIMENT 11–1

QUESTIONS

1. Did more water go into or out of your egg membrane?
2. Describe the appearance of any eggs that lost water.
3. Which eggs lost the most water? Gained the most? Why?

SAMPLE DATA TABLE

Variation	Initial Liquid Height	Height/ Appearance After 30 Minutes	Height After 24 Hours	Appearance of Egg After 24 Hours	Appearance of Liquid After 24 Hours
1					
2					
3					
4					

EXPERIMENT 11–2

Kilocalories in Food

You have been studying how food is converted into energy during metabolism. Sometimes it is difficult to imagine that a food can actually produce energy. In this experiment, you will burn nuts to see how much heat energy is released per gram of nut burned.

PROCEDURE

1. Stick the eye of a needle in the narrow end of a cork. Mount the shelled nut assigned by your teacher on the point of the needle. The cork, nut, and needle are called the nut assembly.
2. Determine the mass of the nut assembly. Record it in your data table.
3. Remove both ends of a large can, and punch holes in the sides near the bottom. The large can will serve as a chimney to minimize heat loss during the experiment.
4. Remove one end of a small aluminum can. Punch two holes in the sides of the can near the top. The holes should be opposite each other.
5. Pour exactly 100 mL tap water into the small can. Take the temperature of the water in the can and record it in your data table.
6. Insert a glass stirring rod through the holes in the sides of the small can. Use the glass rod to balance the small can within the large can.
7. Place the nut on a nonflammable surface, and ignite it with a match. Immediately place the large can around the nut assembly so the small water can is above the nut.
8. Allow the nut to burn for 2 minutes or until it goes out.
9. Stir the water with the thermometer. In your data table, record the water's highest temperature.
10. Mass the nut assembly, and record it in your data table.
11. Write your information on the chalkboard. Copy the information for the other kinds of nuts in your data table.

EXPERIMENT 11–2

CALCULATIONS AND QUESTIONS

1. Calculate the calories of heat from the burning nut. The 100 mL of water has a mass of 100 g. Use the following equation to make the calculation.

$$\text{calories} = \text{grams water} \times \text{temperature change} \times 1 \frac{\text{calorie}}{\text{degrees–gram}}$$

2. Divide the calories from question 1 by the change in mass of the nut. This determines the calories released per gram of nut burned. Record this value on the chalkboard in kilocalories.
3. Which kind of nut released the most heat per gram? The least? Do these results agree with information in standard calorie tables provided by your teacher?
4. Why do you suppose the calculated values for calories per gram are less than the values listed in the calorie table?

SAMPLE DATA TABLE

Kind of Nut	Mass			Temperature		
	Original	**Final**	**Change**	**Original**	**Final**	**Change**

R E V I E W

TO SUM UP

- Energy is needed by the body for metabolism and voluntary activities.
- In metabolism, molecules can be combined or broken down through the processes of anabolism and catabolism.
- Osmosis regulates the concentration of chemicals dissolved in the blood and cells through the movement of fluid through cell membranes.
- Basal metabolism is the amount of energy needed by a body at rest to maintain the automatic activities that support life.
- Basal metabolism is measured by the basal metabolic rate, which uses kilocalories per hour to measure the heat produced by a body at rest after a 12 hour fast.
- Voluntary activities use varying amounts of kilocalories depending on the physical work involved and the time spent.
- Fasting can be dangerous because it disrupts the normal metabolic processes.
- Extreme muscle fatigue during exercise is the result of the buildup of lactic acid because of a lack of enough oxygen to completely break down glucose.

CHECK YOUR FACTS

1. What is the body's source of instant energy?
2. What is the relationship among metabolism, anabolism, and catabolism?
3. Name three conditions that must be present for metabolism to occur.
4. Explain the process of osmosis.
5. What is basal metabolism? Basal metabolic rate?
6. Name three factors that influence metabolic rate.
7. Identify the levels of voluntary activity and the number of kilocalories each uses per hour.
8. How long can a person exist on the energy produced from the glycogen stored in the muscles?
9. What symptoms warn a person who is exercising that lactic acid has built up in the muscles?
10. Why are people who exercise regularly less likely to have lactic acid buildup during exercise?

CRITICAL THINKING AND PROBLEM SOLVING

1. Why are semipermeable cell membranes needed for osmosis?
2. Why is the BMR factor for males higher than the BMR factor for females?
3. Imagine two men, both of whom weigh 90 kg. One man is 1.9 m tall, while the other is 1.5 m tall. If you used the steps on page 181 to figure BMR, both men would have the same BMR. Is this likely? Why or why not?
4. What happens to the metabolic rate of a young person who grows taller without gaining weight?
5. How would the basal metabolism of someone living in the Arctic compare with that of someone living near the equator?
6. Calculate the number of extra kilocalories you would require per week if you ran one hour a day.
7. Calculate your projected weight loss per week if you eat as you do now but begin running one hour a day.

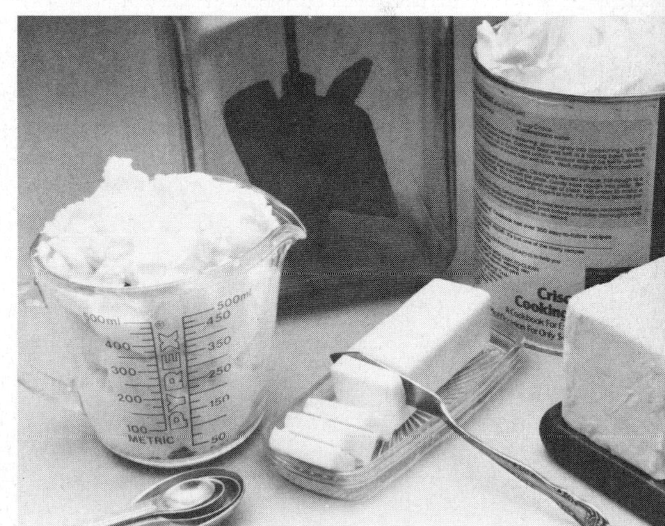

Which nutrients discussed in Unit 2 are found in the foods pictured above?

UNIT 3

The Science of Food Preparation

To remain healthy, you need to eat a balanced diet that contains all the nutrients described in Unit 2. One factor that influences how likely you are to eat a particular food is how it is prepared. Unit 3 presents information on food preparation.

As you read Chapter 12, you will learn how enzymes function in your body, as well as how they cause changes in food before the food is eaten. You will also discover some of the factors that affect enzyme activity. You will identify how these factors can be used to control enzymatic changes during food preparation.

Very few foods you eat and drink are pure substances. Instead, nearly all foods are mixtures. Solutions, colloidal dispersions, and emulsions are the topic of Chapter 13. As you study this chapter, you will learn about food products that are examples of each of these kinds of mixtures.

Chapter 14 contains information on how gas and air are used to give foods a light and consistent texture. Leavening agents, as you will learn, are critical to food quality. You will read about both chemical and natural leavening agents and how they affect the foods that contain them.

Food can be prepared in many ways. One technique, which influences flavor as well as how long food can be stored, is fermentation. Many foods you regularly consume have been fermented. In Chapter 15, you will look at bacteria and yeast fermentation. This chapter will help you understand the basic principles of fermentation.

Unit 3 concludes with Chapter 16. You will read about the complex composition of milk, the methods used in processing milk, and the many types of milk products available. You will learn how to use these products in food preparation.

CHAPTERS

CHAPTER

12

Enzymes

This chapter will help you . . .

- Describe how enzymes act as catalysts in chemical reactions.
- Explain the relationship between an enzyme and a substrate.
- Compare the functions and activities of enzymes and coenzymes.
- Discuss various enzymes involved in digestion.
- Identify factors that affect enzyme activity.
- Explain how enzyme reactions are involved in food preparation.

Terms to Remember

activation energy
active site
blanched
catalyst
coenzymes
curd
enzymatic browning
papain
substrate

You have learned that enzymes are proteins that control chemical activity in living organisms. Therefore enzyme activity is vital to good health. In addition, it is important in nutrition because enzymes break down food into compounds the body can use. Enzymes also act on food products, affecting food processing and preparation. In this chapter, you will learn more about enzymes and how they work.

ENZYMES AND CHEMICAL REACTIONS

Enzymes are involved in a variety of chemical reactions that take place in the body. They work on breaking down and putting together other compounds. Enzymes play a crucial role in the reactions in which they take part.

An enzyme is called a protein **catalyst** (KAT–ul–ist) by scientists. A catalyst is a substance that helps a chemical reaction take place. While a catalyst participates in the chemical reaction, it is not a reactant or a product. The catalyst is not used up or destroyed as the reaction proceeds. It is available to take part in the reaction again.

• PROPERTIES OF ENZYMES

Enzymes, like catalysts in general, are very specific. Each enzyme has only one particular function. Although there are millions of reactions taking place in the body, each enzyme has one reaction that it influences. It is as if an enzyme is a key and the substance with which it reacts is a lock. The "lock," or the substance on which the enzyme acts, is called a **substrate.** Only one enzyme "key" will work in each substrate "lock."

Each enzyme has an **active site.** This is the part of the enzyme molecule that actually attaches to the substrate during the reaction. The

Just as only one key can open a lock, only one enzyme can act on a substrate.

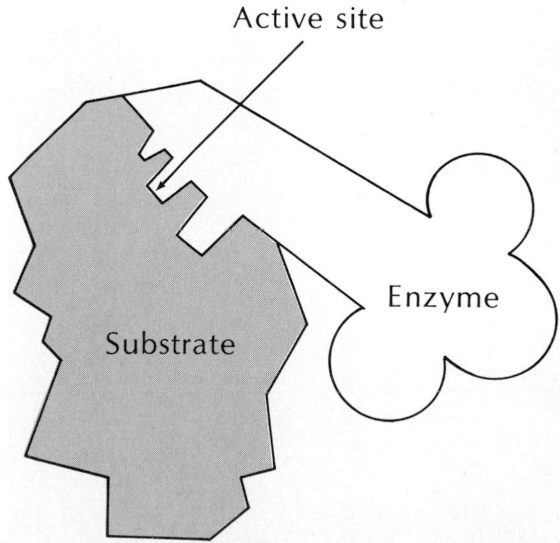

During a chemical reaction, the active site of the enzyme attaches to the substrate.

The enzyme sucrase, named for the substrate sucrose, acts as a catalyst in the hydrolysis of sucrose.

$+ H_2O +$ → $+ H_2O$ → $+$

Sucrose + Water + Sucrase → Sucrose-Sucrase Combination + Water → Glucose + Fructose + Sucrase

Invert Sugars

active site is the part of the enzyme surface where the reaction takes place.

Most enzymes are named for the specific reactions in which they participate. The beginning of the enzyme name is the same as the substrate with which it reacts. Most enzymes have names ending in "–ase." Therefore amylase is the enzyme that breaks down the starch amylose, while maltase attacks the sugar maltose.

What was the activation energy which started this chemical reaction?

Activation Energy

Any chemical or biological reaction requires energy to get started. This is known as **activation energy.** When you strike a match, you are using friction to give the substances on the head of the match enough energy to burst into flame. Some reactions, like the burning match, will keep releasing energy until the reacting substances are used up. Other reactions will continue only if energy is supplied from an outside source.

One function of a catalyst is to lower the amount of activation energy needed for a reaction. The heat required to start most cell reactions without a catalyst is so great that the cell would be killed. Even if it were possible to get such a reaction started, it would proceed very slowly.

Enzymes, acting as catalysts, reduce the activation energy required for a reaction. The enzymes allow the reaction to proceed at a more rapid rate at lower temperatures.

• COENZYMES

In certain reactions, enzymes temporarily join with other molecules known as **coenzymes.** Coenzymes are heat–stable organic molecules. They must be loosely associated with an enzyme for the enzyme to function. Coenzymes are usually smaller than enzymes themselves. Like enzymes, they are not used up during a reaction and so can be reused.

Coenzymes work with enzymes in several ways. They often alter the shape of the enzyme's active site so the enzyme "fits" the substrate better and the reaction can take place. Sometimes coenzymes serve as transfer agents of atoms, electrons, or groups of atoms during a reaction. For example, in a reaction, an enzyme might remove a hydrogen atom from a molecule. The coenzyme would accept this hydrogen atom until it could donate it to another substance. If the coenzyme were not available, the reaction could not take place.

Some very important coenzymes are made from vitamins or fragments of vitamins. If a person does not consume enough of the needed vitamin, the coenzyme cannot be made. Then certain cellular reactions cannot take place. For example, thiamin functions as a coenzyme. It acts as a coenzyme in reactions in which the body stores energy.

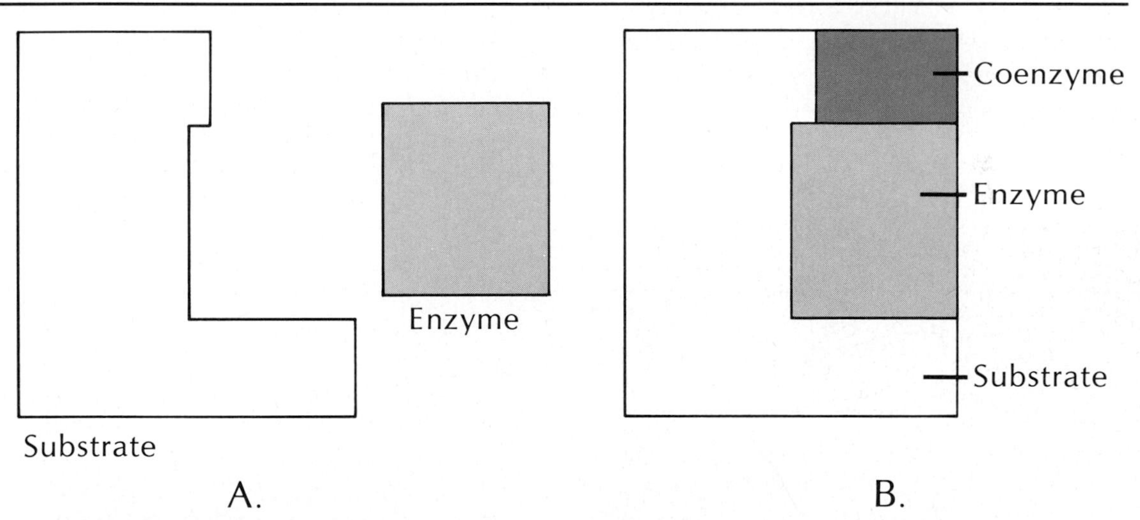

No reaction can occur in A because the enzyme does not fit the substrate. In B, the presence of the coenzyme allows the reaction to proceed.

Through the action of various enzymes, this sugar can be turned into protein to build and repair body tissues.

ENZYMES IN THE BODY

How you digest and use the food you eat depends upon the enzymes present in your system. Every minute, millions of enzymes are taking apart molecules and putting them together in different combinations in your body.

An example of how enzymes change compounds in living cells involves glucose. During metabolism, glucose can be changed to glycine, an amino acid. This change, brought about by enzymes, involves a series of steps.

You know that glucose is a six–carbon sugar whose formula is $C_6H_{12}O_6$. The structure of glucose is shown below.

```
                           H
                           |
              H   H   H    O   H   O
              |   |   |    |   |   ‖
     H — O — C — C — C — C — C — C — H
              |   |   |    |   |
              H   O   O    H   O
                  |   |        |
                  H   H        H
```

Glucose

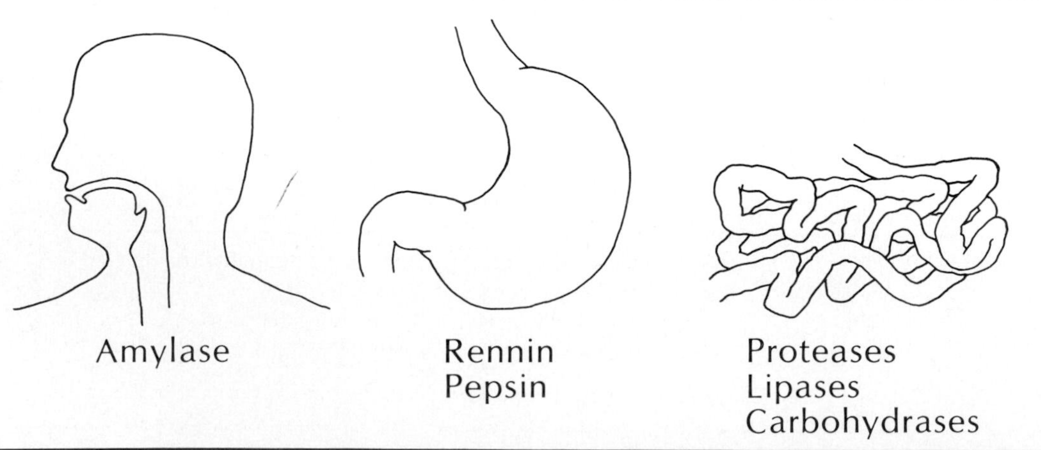

Digestion occurs because of the action of various enzymes in the mouth, stomach, and small intestine.

After the body breaks down carbohydrates into glucose, enzymes work on the glucose molecule. They add a phosphate group, alter the arrangement of atoms, and break the compound in two. In addition, atoms are removed, an amine group is added, and other changes are made. Each change is a step in the metabolism of glucose brought about by enzymes. Finally, the enzymes produce the amino acid glycine. This compound may be used by the body to produce protein.

```
      H
      |
   H—N    O
      |    ||
   H—C—C—O—H
      |
      H
```

Glycine

NUTRITION AND YOU

Enzymes and Digestion

Enzymes play a valuable role in the digestive process. Without them, your body would not be able to use the nutrients in food.

Digestion begins in your mouth. Saliva contains amylase, an enzyme that breaks down the starch amylose. Amylase begins converting amylose to the sugar maltose in the mouth. One way to detect this change is to take a piece of bread and slowly chew it. You should notice that it eventually begins to taste sweeter. The breakdown of amylose to maltose in the mouth is why the latest dental research shows that starches can cause cavities as easily as sugars.

Protein foods are chewed and mixed with saliva in the mouth. It is only after they reach the highly acidic environment of the stomach that their digestion begins. Two of the enzymes found in the stomach are rennin and pepsin. Rennin curdles milk protein and prepares it for pepsin. The pepsin acts to denature protein by attacking the peptide bonds that hold the amino acids together.

It would seem reasonable that since enzymes are proteins, the stomach enzymes would be attacked by stomach acid. In fact, they are the only proteins in the body designed to be protected from acid. They actually become most active in strong acid.

Food proceeds from the stomach to the small intestine. There, other enzymes break down the complex molecules found in food into small molecules, which can be used by the body. The proteases work on protein, the lipases break down lipids, and the carbohydrases work on carbohydrates. Specific enzymes within each group break down specific molecules. The enzyme lactase, which breaks down lactose, is an example of a carbohydrase. Phospholipase is a lipase enzyme that acts on phospholipids.

The intestinal enzymes do not function effectively in an acidic environment. Therefore pancreatic juice, which contains sodium bicarbonate, helps neutralize the partly digested food as it leaves the stomach and enters the small intestine.

FACTORS AFFECTING ENZYME ACTIVITY

In addition to their importance in the body, enzymes are also important to food scientists. In some cases, food scientists use enzymes to cause desirable changes in food, such as making meat more tender. At other times, they look for ways to denature or inactivate enzymes. This allows food scientists to stop those processes that lead to overripe or spoiled food. Understanding the factors affecting enzyme activity allows food scientists to control enzymatic reactions.

• TEMPERATURE

One of the most vital factors affecting the activity of enzymes is temperature. Usually, enzymes function very slowly at temperatures below freezing. The activity of enzymes increases as temperature increases, reaching a peak between 30°– 40°C. Once the temperature rises past 45°C, most enzymes are inactivated. This occurs because their protein is denatured.

If enzymes continue to react in frozen food, the food develops a bitter flavor. To deactivate enzymes, fruits and vegetables are **blanched** before freezing. Blanching means briefly immersing food in boiling water. The high temperature of the water or steam denatures the enzymes.

The unique flavors and textures of these cheeses are the result of desirable enzyme activity.

Desirable Enzyme Activity

There are times when continued enzyme activity is desirable. For example, rice grains stored for long periods of time are less sticky after cooking than are unstored rice grains. This is apparently because the enzyme amylase acts on the starch amylose, breaking down the amylose chains. The broken chains are less sticky than the longer chains.

Enzymes are also used in making hard cheese, such as Cheddar or Swiss. The enzymes are first involved in coagulating milk to make a solid called a **curd.** The curd is the basis of the cheese. It is treated and allowed to age. A number of chemical and physical changes take place in the cheese during aging. These changes are caused by the activity of enzymes. The flavor of the cheese becomes stronger, and desirable changes in texture occur.

• pH

Another factor that influences enzyme activity is pH. Most enzymes function best at a pH of about 8.5, though they can react even when the pH ranges from 7–10. However, activity decreases if the pH falls or rises beyond this

Although the activity of enzymes slows in dried food, it will continue unless the food was blanched before being dried.

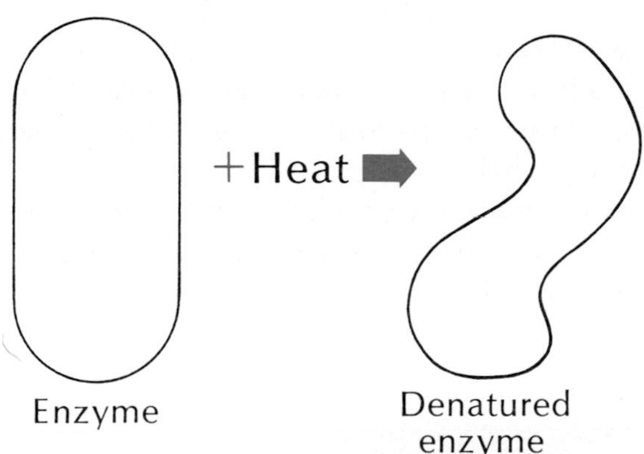

When heat denatures an enzyme, the enzyme changes shape and is inactivated because it no longer fits its substrate.

Enzymes and Food Scientists

Food scientists work to understand the factors that control enzyme activity in food. The rate of enzyme reaction is affected by temperature, pH, and the amount of enzyme used. Food scientists can adjust these factors to produce the most desirable product.

Food scientists must deal with the fact that enzymes are specific. Sometimes scientists wish to slow down a certain process. They must first determine exactly what enzyme controls the reaction. Then they must find a way to eliminate either the enzyme or the substrate with which it reacts. Only then will the reaction slow or stop.

For example, sugar cane is harvested for its sucrose. The tassel of sugar cane contains sucrase, which will break down sucrose. Therefore great care is taken to separate the tassels from the cane during harvesting so the sucrase won't hydrolyze the sucrose.

At other times, food scientists add enzymes during food processing to produce a particular reaction. In cheese making, for example, enzymes are added to create the flavor and texture associated with a particular cheese.

range. Most enzymes become completely inactive if the pH drops below 6.2 or rises above 10.8.

• WATER

Water is important to enzyme activity. It acts as a medium in which enzymes and their substrates can interact. If water is removed, it becomes much more difficult for the enzyme and substrate to react. While a low water level tends to limit enzyme activity, it does not stop it completely.

Even though the water level is low in dried food, enzyme activity will continue until the food has an unpleasant aroma. Therefore vegetables and fruits to be dried also need to be blanched. This will stop the undesirable enzyme activity.

ENZYME ACTIVITY IN FOOD

Enzymes serve a variety of functions in food preparation. The two experiments you will perform in this chapter involve the reactions of enzymes in food.

• BAKING YEAST BREAD

The enzyme sucrase plays a role in baking yeast bread. Yeast cells contain sucrase, which acts as a catalyst for the breakdown of sucrose to simple sugars. As the simple sugars break down further, they produce carbon dioxide, which causes the bread dough to rise. The process stops as the bread bakes because the temperature rises to the point where the yeast cells are killed.

The enzyme sucrase is important in making yeast bread rise.

• TENDERIZING MEAT

Another use of enzymes is in meat tenderizers. Three enzymes, which come from the fruit called the papaya, are diluted with salt in a dry powder called **papain** (puh–PAY–in). The enzymes in papain attack the connective tissue in muscle fiber. By breaking down the muscle fiber, they make meat more tender to eat.

Enzymes produce discoloration in fruits and vegetables that are bruised or cut.

• ENZYMATIC BROWNING

Enzymes produce discoloration in fruits and vegetables. This process is called **enzymatic browning.** Pears, apples, bananas, figs, peaches, plums, avocados, and potatoes all change color when bruised or cut. Their normal color turns to a gray or brown when the cell tissues are injured.

The color change of enzymatic browning always involves three substances—a substrate, an enzyme, and oxygen. To stop enzymatic browning, one of the three substances must be eliminated or limited. The food itself is the substrate, so it can't be eliminated. Denaturing the enzyme, however, can be done by:

- Using heat, as in blanching prior to freezing.
- Lowering the pH.
- Using sulfur dioxide, a gas that affects enzymes.
- Lowering the temperature to slow down the chemical reaction.

Finally, enzymatic browning is slowed by excluding oxygen. This can be accomplished by placing vegetables in salt water or fruits in sugar water. The solutions prevent oxygen from contacting the food. When oxygen is excluded, enzymatic browning does not take place.

Lowering the pH of the banana slices with lemon juice helps slow enzymatic browning.

EXPERIMENT 12–1

Enzymatic Browning

Fruit leather is a snack that is easy to make using either fresh or canned fruit. Light-colored fruit leather, such as apple or pear, will tend to darken during drying because of enzymatic browning. In this experiment, you will test three substances and heat for effectiveness in maintaining the color of fruit leather.

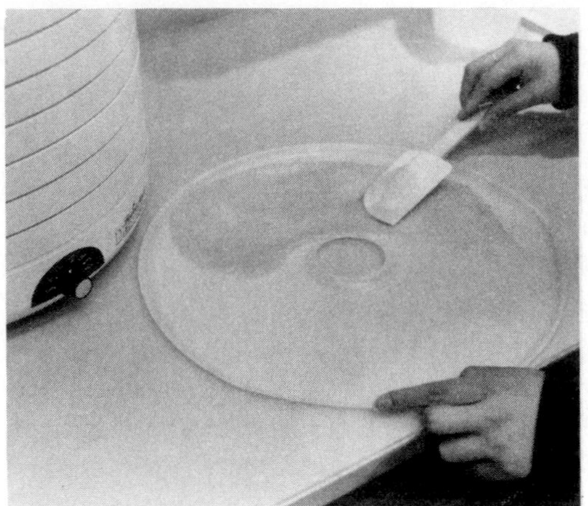

PROCEDURE

1. Wash the fruit provided by your teacher.
2. Peel and core the fruit, cutting away blemishes.
3. Cut the fruit into cubes about 1 cm per side.
4. Follow the variation assigned by your teacher.
   a. **Variation 1.** Cook the pieces of fruit in a saucepan over medium heat for 15 minutes, stirring constantly. A higher temperature may cause the fruit to scorch. Remove from heat, and cool at room temperature for 5 minutes. Crush 375 mg ascorbic acid tablets. Add to fruit.
   b. **Variation 2.** Crush 375 mg ascorbic acid tablets. Add to cubed fruit.
   c. **Variation 3.** Cook fruit as described in variation 1. Add 0.5 g sodium bisulfite to fruit. Since some people have an allergic reaction to bisulfite, *you will not eat the fruit leather containing the bisulfite.*
   d. **Variation 4.** Add 0.5 g sodium bisulfite to the cubed fruit.
   e. **Variation 5.** Cook fruit as described in variation 1. Add 2 mL lemon juice to fruit.
   f. **Variation 6.** Add 2 mL lemon juice to cubed fruit.
5. Puree the fruit by mashing it through a strainer or food mill or by using a blender or food processor. The puree should be the thickness of applesauce.
6. Pour the puree on plastic wrap, and spread to 0.5 cm thickness. Label the plastic wrap with your name, variation number, and class period.
7. Dry in dehydrator. The temperature of the dehydrator should be maintained at 117°-122°C (135°-140°F). The plastic wrap will not melt at the low drying temperatures used. Drying time will vary from 4–8 hours.
8. When done, the leather should feel tacky but should not contain any moisture.
9. Evaluate all fruit leathers for color. Taste the fruit leathers made with ascorbic acid and lemon juice, and evaluate texture and flavor. Do not taste the fruit leathers made in variations 3 and 4. Enter the information in your data table.

EXPERIMENT 12–1

QUESTIONS

1. In which fruit leather did the most enzyme activity occur? The least? How do you know?
2. Was the color of the fruit preserved better when the fruit was cooked or uncooked? What does this tell you about enzyme activity?
3. Which of the three additives was most effective in preserving the fruit color?
4. Of the samples tasted, which seemed to have the best flavor?
5. Were there any differences in texture among the samples?
6. Of the methods tested, which produced the overall best fruit leather?

SAMPLE DATA TABLE

Variation	Color	Texture	Flavor
1			
2			
3			—
4			—
5			
6			

EXPERIMENT 12–2

Effect of Blanching on Enzymes

Freezing is a relatively simple method of preserving food. Although freezing slows down enzyme activity, it does not stop it. If frozen food is not pretreated, enzyme activity will continue. Blanching is a way to deactivate enzymes with heat. In this experiment, you will observe the effects of blanching on the quality of frozen vegetables.

PROCEDURE

1. Prepare the sample of vegetables as instructed by your teacher.
2. Rinse the vegetables thoroughly in cold water. Divide the vegetables into two samples.
3. Fill a large saucepan with water. Heat the water to a rolling boil.
4. Blanch half the vegetables by putting them in the boiling water for 3 minutes. Immediately place the vegetables in ice water. Cool the vegetables in the ice water for 5 minutes; then dry them.
5. Leave the other half of the vegetables unblanched. Dry them.
6. Pack the vegetables in small plastic bags. Label the bags with your name, class period, and whether the vegetables are blanched or unblanched.
7. Freeze the vegetables at –18°C, and hold in frozen storage 3 weeks or longer.
8. After the holding period, add water to two saucepans to a depth of 1 cm. Bring the water in both pans to a boil, and add a pinch of salt to each. Add the package of blanched frozen vegetables to one saucepan and the unblanched vegetables to the other. Reduce heat to low, cover, and cook until the vegetables are done.
9. Evaluate the vegetables for color, aroma, taste, and texture. Record the information in your data table.

QUESTIONS

1. What does blanching do to the vegetables?
2. Why were the vegetables cooled after blanching?
3. Which treatment yielded a vegetable with a better color? Aroma? Texture? Taste?
4. Account for any differences observed between the two vegetable samples.

SAMPLE DATA TABLE

Treatment	Color	Aroma	Taste	Texture
Blanched				
Unblanched				

TO SUM UP

- Enzymes are protein catalysts that break down and put together other compounds.
- Enzymes perform specific functions on specific substrates.
- In many chemical reactions, small molecules called coenzymes are needed for an enzyme to function.
- A variety of enzymes are active during digestion to break down food so nutrients can be used by the body.
- Enzyme activity is affected by temperature, pH, and water.
- Enzymes play a desired role in baking yeast bread, tenderizing meat, and making cheese.
- Food scientists work to retard the activity of enzymes that cause enzymatic browning and food spoilage.

CHECK YOUR FACTS

1. What is the type of protein that helps control chemical activity in living organisms?
2. Why are enzymes important in nutrition?
3. Why do scientists call enzymes protein catalysts?
4. What happens to enzymes during chemical reactions?
5. What is a substrate?
6. Explain how most enzymes are named.
7. Why are coenzymes important in body reactions?
8. Describe two functions of enzymes in the body.
9. What are three factors that affect enzyme activity in food preparation?
10. What pH is the best for enzyme activity?
11. List three ways food scientists use enzymes in food processing.
12. Identify three methods for denaturing enzymes.

CRITICAL THINKING AND PROBLEM SOLVING

1. With what substances do the enzymes called disaccharidase, galactase, and peptidase react?
2. Explain how enzymes affect activation energy in cellular reactions.
3. Compare and contrast the proteases in the stomach with those in the small intestine.
4. Explain why food is blanched prior to freezing or drying.
5. Would enzyme activity continue in cucumbers after they are pickled in vinegar? Why or why not?
6. Explain the role of the enzyme sucrase in bread making.
7. Why is papain used in meat tenderizers?
8. When fresh pineapple is added to gelatin, the gelatin does not set, but remains a liquid. Why do you think this occurs? When canned pineapple is used, the gelatin sets normally. Why does this occur?
9. Based on the results of your fruit leather experiment, suggest a method for preventing browning of a banana leather product.

CHAPTER

13

Solutions, Colloidal Dispersions, and Emulsions

This chapter will help you . . .

- Identify the solvent and solute in a given solution.
- Discuss the effect of a solute and its concentration on the boiling and freezing points of a solution.
- Calculate the concentration of a solution using mass percent.
- Compare and contrast unsaturated, saturated, and supersaturated solutions.
- Describe the properties of colloidal dispersions.
- Explain the three parts of an emulsion and their relationship to each other.
- Identify various food emulsions and tell the type of emulsion each is.

Terms to Remember

aggregates
continuous phase
dispersed phase
homogenization
mass percent
phospholipids
saturated
surface tension
Tyndall effect
unsaturated

As you learned in Chapter 6, water can combine with many of the substances found in food. In acting as a solvent, water dissolves other substances to form solutions. In addition, water can serve as a medium for colloidal dispersions and can form emulsions. This chapter will look at each of these types of mixtures.

SOLUTIONS

Solutions are important to nutritionists and food scientists. Many reactions in the body take place in water solutions. For example, glucose and the water–soluble vitamins are in solution when they are carried in the blood. Common food solutions include coffee, tea, and carbonated beverages. In Chapter 7, you worked with a sugar solution in making fondant.

Solutions, you may remember, are homogeneous mixtures in which one substance, the solute, is dissolved in another, the solvent. A solution is the same in every part of a given sample. This can be shown by taking 1 mL samples from the bottom, middle, and top of a 100 mL sample of salt water. The 1 mL samples can be evaporated and the remaining salt massed. The same amount of salt will be found in each sample.

Each sample of a specific solution has the same composition. However, samples of various solutions will differ from each other. If the procedure described above were repeated with another saltwater solution, equal amounts of salt would be found in the three samples. However, these amounts might not be the same as in the first solution. In other words, there is no set formula for a solution.

Solutions are always composed of at least two substances—the solvent and the solute. Solvents can be solids, liquids, or gases. However, in food science, the solvent is almost always a liquid—most often water. Solutes can also be solids, liquids, or gases. Examples of solid solutes in food science are salt, sugar, or vitamin C. A fruit syrup is a solution of sugar and water. The alcohol in an alcoholic beverage is an example of a liquid solute. Gases, such as the carbon dioxide (CO_2) dissolved in carbonated beverages, can also be solutes.

Most beverages are solutions.

The gas dissolved in this soft drink is a solute.

The salt added to the ice in this ice cream freezer lowers the freezing point, increasing the speed at which the ice cream freezes.

Solutions of a solid dissolved in a liquid boil at higher temperatures and freeze at lower temperatures than the pure solvent does. The more concentrated the solution, the higher the boiling point or the lower the freezing point. You will study the effect of a solute on boiling point in Experiment 13–1.

Which carrots—the diced, sliced, or whole—will lose more nutrients during cooking?

Vitamins and Minerals in Solution

Whenever food is cooked in water, some of the water–soluble vitamins and minerals dissolve in the water as the cooking proceeds. The amount of nutrients lost depends on at least two factors.

The greater the surface area, the greater the vitamin and mineral loss. Surface area, as you know, depends on the size of the cooking pieces. Thus thinly sliced pieces of potato will lose more nutrients than potatoes boiled whole.

The amount of cooking time also affects the amount of vitamins and minerals dissolved in the water. Long cooking times remove most of the vitamins and minerals in the food. Fewer nutrients dissolve during shorter cooking times.

If the vitamins and minerals are not deactivated by heat, they remain in the cooking water. When the cooking water is thrown away, the dissolved vitamins and minerals are wasted. However, if the water is used, they can be saved and consumed. Some recipes suggest using potato water when mashing potatoes to take advantage of the vitamins and minerals dissolved in it.

• CONCENTRATION OF SOLUTIONS

You know that concentration is the amount of a substance in a unit amount of another substance. In solutions, concentration is the amount of solute in a unit amount of solvent. There are several ways to express the concentration of solutions. The method used most often in food science is called **mass percent**. This system of calculating concentration uses the following equation. In this equation, the solute is called solute A.

$$\text{Mass percent of solute A} = \frac{\text{mass of solute A} \times 100}{\text{total mass of the solution}}$$

If you dissolve 15 g of sodium chloride (NaCl) in 85 g of water, your calculations would be as follows.

$$\text{Mass percent of NaCl} = \frac{15\text{ g} \times 100}{85\text{ g} + 15\text{ g} = 100\text{ g}} = 15\text{ percent}$$

• TYPES OF SOLUTIONS

When you first add sodium chloride to a beaker of water, the salt dissolves. At this stage, when the solution contains less solvent than it can possibly hold at a given temperature, it is called **unsaturated**. However, for any given amount of water, a point is eventually reached when no more salt will dissolve. A solution that contains all the solute it can possibly hold at a given temperature is a **saturated** solution. A glass of iced tea with a layer of sugar on the bottom that won't dissolve is a saturated solution.

You will recall that solubility is the maximum amount of solute that can be dissolved in a definite amount of solvent at a specific temperature. Temperature can have a drastic affect on solubility.

The solubility of gases, when used as a solute, decreases as temperature increases. This

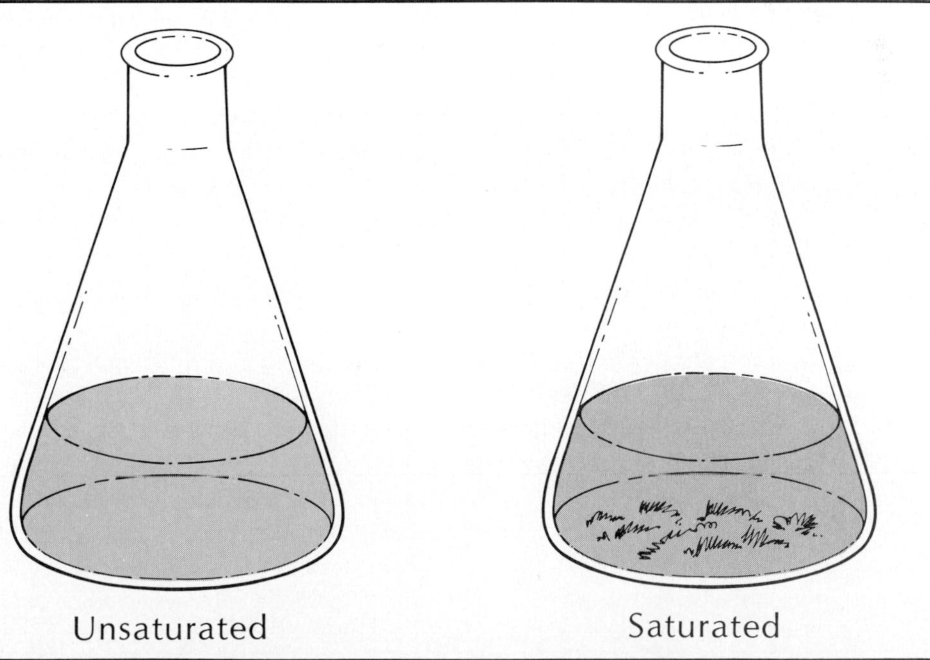

A solution is saturated when no more solute will dissolve in it.

is why a carbonated beverage goes flat much faster if opened while at room temperature than if it has been cooled before opening. It is also why water that has been boiled has little flavor. The gases that had been dissolved in the water were driven off in the heating process.

On the other hand, the solubility of most solids increases when the temperature increases. If you have more solid in a beaker than the amount of water present will dissolve, one way to get the solid dissolved is to heat the solution. As the temperature increases, more and more of the solid will dissolve.

Heating a mixture to dissolve additional solute, then cooling it undisturbed makes a supersaturated solution. You remember that this is a solution that contains more dissolved solute than it would normally at that temperature. As you may recall from Chapter 7, crystallization from a supersaturated sugar solution is an important step in candy making.

NUTRITION AND YOU

The Solution Is Fluoride

Earlier in this book, you learned about the importance of water to the human body. Water is necessary for survival. One of its functions in the body is to carry dissolved nutrients. Fluorine is a trace mineral that is in solution in the body as fluoride ions.

Fluoride ions are often found naturally in water. When fluoride is present in water in concentrations greater than one part per million, there is a noticable decline in the rate of tooth decay among those who drink the water. This is important since tooth decay is considered a major public health problem.

Fluoride helps in the formation of enamel, the outer layer of a tooth. Numerous studies and tests have shown that fluoride helps make the enamel more resistant to decay. Recent studies also show that fluoride may slow the loss of bone in osteoporosis.

The American Medical Association, the National Institute of Dental Health, and the National Cancer Institute all endorse fluoridation of drinking water. Over 5000 communities throughout the United States have fluoridated their water. As a result, nearly 100 million people consume fluoride in their drinking water.

However, many communities do not add fluoride to the water. Some people are afraid that consuming too much fluoride could be harmful. It is true that when fluoride ions are present in excess of 2.5 parts per million, the excessive fluoride can cause mottled, or discolored, enamel. The mottled teeth are not harmed and, in fact, are very resistant to decay. Other people argue that it is unnatural to add fluoride ions to the water supply.

If you live in an area that does not have fluoride in its water supply, you have several options to protect your teeth against decay. You can use a fluoride toothpaste, take fluoride tablets, or have your dentist treat your teeth with a fluoridated substance. Dental fluoride treatments are generally carried out only on people who are 3–16 years of age.

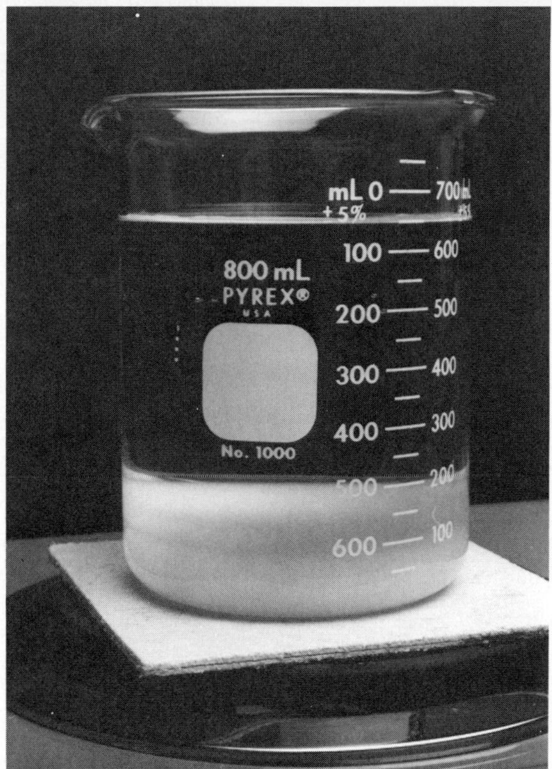

Heat can change a saturated solution to an unsaturated one.

COLLOIDAL DISPERSIONS

You will recall that a colloidal dispersion is a mixture in which the solute particles don't dissolve the way they do in a true solution. The particles, called colloids, are distributed or dispersed in a medium, rather than dissolved in it. Milk, egg white, gelatin, and jelly are common food colloidal dispersions. Any protein in liquid forms a colloidal dispersion. This is because of the large size of the protein molecules.

Colloidal dispersions may appear clear and homogeneous, just like true solutions. However, colloidal dispersions are different from true solutions. The main difference is particle size.

In solutions, the solute is dispersed as individual ions or molecules. In colloidal dispersions, the solids exist in either very large molecules, such as protein, or in **aggregates** (AG–ruh–gits) of ions or molecules. An aggregate is a group or dense cluster of ions or molecules. Vitamin B_{12} molecules form aggregates in a colloidal dispersion.

Using fluoridated toothpaste can help prevent tooth decay.

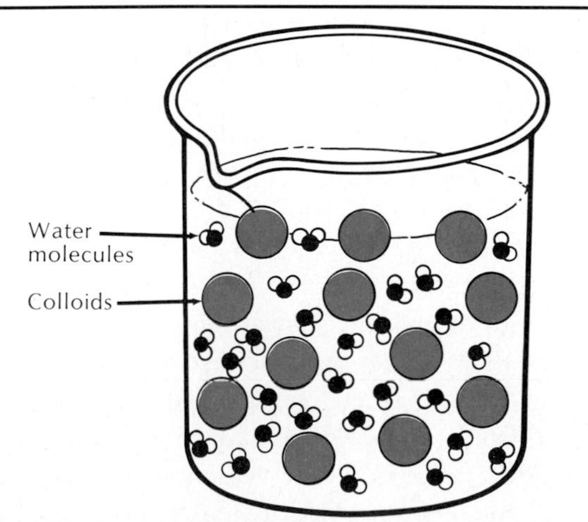

The particles in a colloidal dispersion can be large molecules, as in this drawing, or aggregates of ions or molecules.

Light passes through a true solution, but is scattered by a colloidal dispersion.

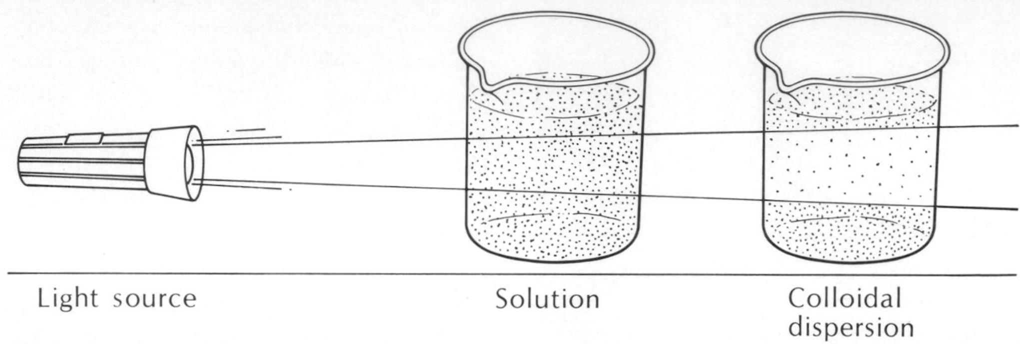

The particles in a colloidal dispersion are large enough to scatter, or deflect, visible light. Therefore when a light beam passes through a colloidal dispersion, it is possible to see the path of the light. This is known as the **Tyndall effect**.

The Tyndall effect can be easily seen in a colloidal dispersion of gelatin in water or pectin in jelly. You may also have seen the Tyndall effect if you have noticed how a sunbeam shining through a window is visible. This occurs because dust particles suspended in the air scatter the light so that the beam can be seen. True solutions do not exhibit the Tyndall effect because the individual particles present are too small to scatter the light waves.

As you know, the concentration of a solute affects the boiling and freezing point of a solution. However, the solids present in colloidal dispersions have almost no effect on boiling or freezing point.

Even though the particles in a colloidal dispersion are larger than those in a true solution, they are still small enough that they will not settle out. They will remain indefinitely suspended in the liquid. For example, the calcium and magnesium phosphates that are colloidally dispersed in milk do not settle out upon standing. In this way, dispersions are similar to true solutions.

Even though the particles in a colloidal dispersion do not settle out, many colloidal dispersions are unstable. This is because of the size of the particles involved. The curdling of milk, for example, is due to the instability of the protein casein.

EMULSIONS

You will recall that an emulsion is a mixture of two liquids whose droplets do not normally blend with each other. The two liquids that are not able to mix are called immiscible.

Emulsions are a special class of colloidal dispersions. An emulsion is simply a liquid–in–liquid dispersion. The particles in an emulsion are large enough to deflect light rays from their normal path through the surrounding liquid. This is what gives emulsions an opaque, milky appearance.

• FORMING AN EMULSION

One factor in making liquids immiscible in each other is **surface tension**. This is a property of liquids that occurs because the molecules at the surface are attracted toward the other molecules within the liquid. This attraction causes a contraction, or shrinking, at the surface of the liquid, which makes it behave as if it had a skin. The contraction is called surface tension.

Oil and water are immiscible liquids. When they are poured together, the oil floats on the water. Surface tension causes the oil molecules to attract each other and the water molecules to attract other water molecules. At the same time, the oil and water molecules tend to repel each other. As a result, the two liquids arrange themselves to have the least possible surface area exposed between them. The best way to do this is to form a single mass of oil on top of a single mass of water.

If the mixture is shaken, the oil and water temporarily mix. After a short time, the oil floats out of the water and once again sits on top of it. However, by forming an emulsion, the oil and water can be mixed more permanently. When the mixture is agitated so the oil is broken into tiny droplets, an emulsifier can be added that will coat the oil droplets so they cannot join back together. An emulsion like this is known as an oil–in–water emulsion because the oil is dispersed in the water as very tiny droplets. Many emulsions in food science are oil–in–water emulsions.

These drops of water form because of surface tension.

The substance existing in droplet form in an emulsion is called the **dispersed phase**. The other liquid, in which the droplets are dispersed, is known as the **continuous phase**. The volume of the dispersed phase can vary a great deal. In milk, it is 2–3 percent, while it ranges from 65–80 percent in mayonnaise.

An emulsifier, the substance that keeps the immiscible liquids mixed, is an active compound that absorbs or sticks to the surface of the dispersed substance. It lowers the surface tension so the many tiny droplets in the emulsion cannot stick together. As long as the droplets are separate, they can remain dispersed in the continuous phase, rather than separating out.

An emulsifier would keep this oil-and-vinegar salad dressing from separating into an oil layer and a vinegar layer.

Emulsifiers usually are molecules that have a polar end, which dissolves well in water, and

EXPERIMENT 13–2

Making an Emulsion

Mayonnaise is an emulsion of oil in water. This experiment is designed to illustrate one of the factors that influences the formation of emulsions.

PROCEDURE

1. Follow the recipe variation in step 2 as assigned by your teacher.

Control Recipe for Mayonnaise

2	egg yolks	250 mL salad oil
4.2 g	salt	45 mL vinegar
1 g	dry mustard	

2. Place egg yolks, salt, mustard, and 5 mL vinegar in a small bowl, and beat with an electric mixer at medium speed until the egg yolks are sticky.
   a. **Variation 1.** Add the oil drop by drop, beating constantly until you have added 125 mL oil. Continue beating constantly as you add the remaining oil in a thin steady stream.
   b. **Variation 2.** Add the oil 5 mL at a time, beating constantly until you have added 125 mL oil. Continue beating constantly as you add the remaining oil in a thin steady stream.
   c. **Variation 3.** Add the oil 15 mL at a time, beating constantly until you have added 125 mL oil. Continue beating constantly as you add the remaining oil in a thin steady stream.
   d. **Variation 4.** Add the oil 125 mL at a time, beating constantly until all the oil has been added.
3. Stir the mixture as you add the remaining vinegar in a slow steady stream.
4. Inspect and sample all four variations of the mayonnaise. Record your observations in your data table.

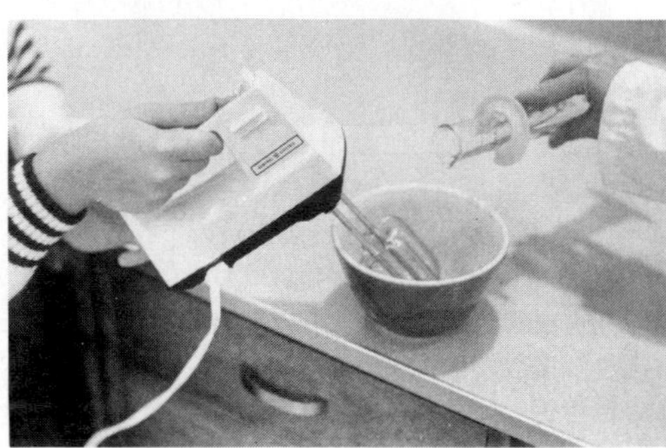

QUESTIONS

1. Were there any differences in color among the four samples? Appearance? Flavor? Texture?
2. What affect did the rate of adding oil have on the quality of the mayonnaise?
3. Which variation produced mayonnaise most similar to the commercial mayonnaise found in supermarkets?
4. How does the emulsifying agent keep the oil and water from separating?

SAMPLE DATA TABLE

Variation	Color	Appearance	Flavor	Texture
1				
2				
3				
4				

TO SUM UP

- Solutions are homogeneous mixtures in which a solute is dissolved in a solvent.
- The concentration of a solute affects the solution's boiling and freezing points.
- The concentration of a solution can be measured by calculating mass percent.
- Gas–in–liquid solutions become less soluble when heated, while solid–in–liquid solutions become more soluble when heated.
- The particles in a colloidal dispersion are larger than those in a solution and will scatter light in the Tyndall effect.
- An emulsion consists of a dispersed phase mixed in a continous phase, with an emulsifier to hold the two phases in the mixture.
- Oil–in–water emulsions include salad dressings and mayonnaise, air–in–liquid emulsions include egg foams and whipped cream, while butter and margarine are water–in–oil emulsions.

CHECK YOUR FACTS

1. Calculate the mass percent of sugar if 40 g sugar are dissolved in 50 g water.
2. What does it mean when a carton of orange drink says it contains 10 percent orange juice?
3. Can more sugar be added to iced tea or hot tea before the solution is saturated? Why?
4. You are making a sugar syrup for fruit, but when you combine and stir the sugar and water, the sugar forms a thin layer on the bottom of the container. How can you get the sugar to dissolve?
5. Explain how solutions and colloidal dispersions differ.
6. Describe the function of an emulsifying agent.
7. Why is it necessary to agitate the mixture when an emulsifier is added to form an emulsion?
8. How can you remake gravy from which some of the fat has separated?
9. Explain how soap, which is an emulsifier, helps get fats and oils off dishes.

CRITICAL THINKING AND PROBLEM SOLVING

1. Identify the solvent and solute in sweetened water.
2. How do the freezing and boiling points of water solutions compare with those of pure water?
3. What is the method used in food science to calculate the concentration of a solution?
4. Explain the differences among unsaturated, saturated, and supersaturated solutions.
5. How does the solubility of a gas–in–liquid solution change when heated? A solid–in–liquid solution?
6. What is the Tyndall effect?
7. Will salt water produce the Tyndall effect? Why or why not?
8. Are water and vinegar immiscible? Why or why not?
9. Is mayonnaise a solution, colloidal dispersion, or emulsion? How do you know?
10. What substance is the continuous phase in mayonnaise?
11. What is the emulsifying agent in gravy?

CHAPTER

14

Leavening Agents and Baked Goods

This chapter will help you . . .

- Describe the purpose of leavening agents in baked goods.
- List the four major leavening agents.
- Explain why baking soda is used with an acid in baked goods.
- Identify the types of doughs and batters used in making quick breads.
- List the ingredients in baking powder.
- Discuss how air and steam act as leavening agents.
- Describe the properties of yeast as a leavening agent.
- Name three types of wheat and a product made from each.

Terms to Remember

baking powder
baking soda
double–acting baking powder
fermentation
nutrient dense
quick breads
single–acting baking powder

Baked products are a part of the diet in most cultures. Baked goods usually are leavened, a process that causes them to be light and porous. Leavening involves producing a gas that expands as the batter or dough is heated, leaving holes as the batter or dough structure sets during baking.

As you learned in Chapter 5, a leavening agent is a substance included in baked goods to lighten or aerate them. The most common leavening agents are air, water vapor or steam, yeast, and chemical agents. Chemical agents and yeast leaven by producing carbon dioxide gas (CO_2). Yeast, air, and steam are sometimes called natural leavening agents.

CHEMICAL LEAVENING AGENTS

Most recipes for cakes and cookies call for the addition of chemical leavening agents as a source of carbon dioxide. Those most widely used are **baking soda** and **baking powder.** Baking soda is the chemical compound sodium bicarbonate. Baking powder is a compound that contains baking soda, dry acids, and starch or some other filler.

The tiny holes in this bread were produced by a gas from a leavening agent.

Ammonium Bicarbonate

Baking soda and baking powder are the most common chemicals used to produce carbon dioxide during baking. However, there are some other substances used for this purpose. One of these is ammonium bicarbonate, a product often used by commercial manufacturers of cookies and crackers.

The decomposition of ammonium bicarbonate produces carbon dioxide according to the following equation.

$$\underset{\text{Ammonium bicarbonate}}{NH_4HCO_3} \xrightarrow{\text{heat}} \underset{\text{Ammonia}}{NH_3} + \underset{\text{Carbon dioxide}}{CO_2} + \underset{\text{Water vapor}}{H_2O}$$

In this reaction, there is no solid product formed, only the three gases shown. However, the ammonia gas produced may affect the taste of the final product.

Ammonium bicarbonate is usually used only in crackers and certain types of cookies. Because these products are thin and have a large surface area, the ammonia gas can escape completely. Therefore the products do not have the unpleasant ammonia taste.

Ammonium bicarbonate is used commercially to leaven thin, flat products.

• BAKING SODA

Sodium bicarbonate, or baking soda, is a salt, whose formula is $\mathbf{NaHCO_3}$. It is formed from sodium hydroxide, a strong base, and carbonic acid, a weak acid. Because sodium hydroxide is stronger than carbonic acid, the salt formed by their interaction is basic.

Baking soda releases carbon dioxide when heated. The equation for the breakdown of sodium bicarbonate by heat is shown below.

$$\underset{\text{Sodium bicarbonate}}{2NaHCO_3} \xrightarrow{\text{heat}} \underset{\text{Carbon dioxide}}{CO_2} + \underset{\text{Sodium carbonate}}{Na_2CO_3} + \underset{\text{Water vapor}}{H_2O}$$

The sodium carbonate produced by this reaction has an unpleasant effect on a baked product. In addition to a bad taste, sodium carbonate gives a yellowish color to the final product.

To prevent the formation of sodium carbonate, baking soda is always used with an acid. This alters the chemical reaction to avoid producing sodium carbonate. Acid ingredients that can be used with baking soda are sour milk, vinegar, lemon juice, or cream of tartar.

For example, a recipe might call for cream of tartar. This is an acidic compound named potassium bitartrate, whose formula is $\mathbf{KHC_4H_4O_6}$. When cream of tartar is added, the breakdown of the baking soda becomes a two-step reaction. In the first step, the baking soda reacts with the cream of tartar to produce a salt called sodium potassium tartrate and carbonic acid.

$$\underset{\text{Sodium bicarbonate}}{NaHCO_3} + \underset{\text{Potassium bitartrate}}{KHC_4H_4O_6} \xrightarrow{\text{water}} \underset{\text{Sodium potassium tartrate}}{KNaC_4H_4O_6} + \underset{\text{Carbonic acid}}{H_2CO_3}$$

In the second step, the carbonic acid breaks down into carbon dioxide and water.

$$\underset{\text{Carbonic acid}}{H_2CO_3} \rightarrow \underset{\text{Water}}{H_2O} + \underset{\text{Carbon dioxide}}{CO_2}$$

The combination of baking soda and cream of tartar produces the carbon dioxide needed for leavening the baked product. Since sodium carbonate is not produced, unwanted side effects are avoided.

Sodium bicarbonate is made from sodium hydroxide and carbonic acid.

These acids can be used with baking soda to prevent the formation of sodium carbonate.

Quick Breads

Bread products made with baking powder or baking soda are often called **quick breads** because they do not need time to rise, as do yeast products. Muffins, coffee cakes, and biscuits are all examples of quick breads. All quick breads contain flour, liquid, and salt. Depending on the recipe, they may also contain a chemical leavening agent, fat, sugar, and eggs.

There are four categories of quick breads. These are based on the ratio of flour to liquid in the product. The categories include pour batters, drop batters, soft doughs, and stiff doughs.

Foods, such as popovers, pancakes, waffles, and cream puffs, are made from pour batters. Pour batters are made with an equal ratio of liquid to flour by volume. A recipe for popovers that calls for 480 mL flour will also call for 480 mL liquid, usually water. If salt is added to the recipe, there will generally be 2.5 mL salt for every 240 mL flour.

Drop batters produce baked goods such as muffins and some cookies. These batters use two parts flour to one part liquid. Drop batters are often the most difficult to prepare because cooks tend to overmix them. To produce a light product, such as a muffin, it is crucial not to mix too long. Too much mixing will overdevelop the gluten protein found in the flour. This will cause tunnels in the baked product. Drop batter recipes usually say to mix only until the ingredients are moist. Stirring should stop at this point, even if the batter is still lumpy.

Soft doughs use three parts flour to one part liquid. These need more mixing to develop gluten. Some may require kneading to develop the gluten. You will recall that kneading means mixing and working a dough into a mass by folding over, pressing, and squeezing. Soft doughs are used to make baking powder biscuits.

Stiff doughs contain more flour and are drier than soft doughs. Stiff doughs use six to eight times as much flour as liquid. They are used to produce pie crusts, pasta, and some cookies.

A chemical leavening agent was used to make this banana bread.

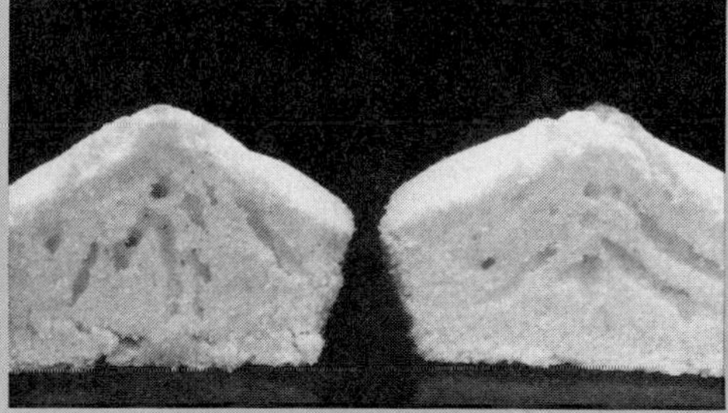

Overmixing muffin batter will cause tunnels in the final product.

Baking powder biscuits are made from a soft dough.

Pasta is made from a stiff dough.

Most of the carbon dioxide from the double–acting baking powder in this cake will be released by the oven heat.

• BAKING POWDER

As mentioned earlier, baking powder is a mixture of baking soda, dry acids, and a filler. The filler is usually cornstarch or calcium carbonate. Homemade baking powder can be made from baking soda and cream of tartar. There are two types of commercially prepared baking powders.

Single–acting baking powder begins to release carbon dioxide as soon as a liquid is added to it. The liquid may be water, milk, potato water, or orange juice. The baking powder reacts quickly because the acid in it is soluble in a cold liquid. Homemade baking powder is a single–acting baking powder. Few single–acting baking powders are sold in the United States.

Double–acting baking powder is the type in common use in the United States. It contains two acids—one that reacts with cold liquid and one that reacts with heat. Some carbon dioxide is released as soon as liquid is added to a double–acting baking powder during mixing. However, most of the carbon dioxide is produced after the batter has been placed in the oven and heated.

Commercially prepared double–acting baking powder is often a combination of sodium bicarbonate and phosphate compounds. One common double–acting baking powder contains sodium bicarbonate, monocalcium phosphate ($CaH_4(PO_4)_2$), and sodium aluminum sulfate ($NaAl(SO_4)_2$).

Carbon dioxide is the only gas produced by chemical leavening agents used in the United States. By law, baking powder must yield at least 12 g carbon dioxide for every 100 g baking powder. Since the carbon dioxide is formed from the breakdown of the baking soda, the soda must be at least 25 percent of the volume of the baking powder to yield the carbon dioxide needed.

Leavening in Cakes

Cakes are a popular baked product, which can be leavened in a variety of ways. The leavening used affects the properties of the cake.

Cakes that contain fat or lipid are called shortened cakes. Examples of shortened cakes are the familiar white, yellow, and chocolate cakes. They usually contain a chemical leavening agent, which produces carbon dioxide to make the cake rise. Air is also a minor leavening agent in shortened cakes. It is added when the fat and sugar are mixed together, as well as when the ingredients are blended. Air is also added if the recipe calls for beaten eggs. Fat and eggs tenderize the cake batter so it expands easily.

Pound cakes are leavened with air and steam. The air is incorporated when the batter is mixed. Heat changes the liquid in the batter to steam. The steam enlarges the air bubbles created when the batter was mixed and causes the cake to rise.

Unshortened cakes are also called sponge cakes. This type of cake includes yellow sponge cakes and angel food cakes. Unshortened cakes depend on the air beaten into an egg foam for leavening. Steam is also a minor leavening agent for sponge cakes.

This shortened cake is leavened with a chemical leavening agent and air.

An angel food cake is leavened with air beaten into an egg foam.

Cream puffs are made from a pour batter and are leavened with steam.

Beating this cake batter adds air, which acts as a leavening agent.

NATURAL LEAVENING AGENTS

Yeast may be the best known natural leavening agent. However, steam (water vapor) and air are also natural leaveners.

• STEAM

All recipes for baked goods contain some liquid, which produces steam when heated. Steam is the primary leavening agent in the pour batters used to make popovers and cream puffs. Pour batters are the only batters that contain enough water to provide the steam needed to leaven the final product. Steam is also a minor leavening agent in batter cakes and pie crusts.

To prepare recipes in which steam is a primary leavener, it is necessary to use a very hot oven. Such recipes usually require at least 204° C (400° F) to convert the liquid to steam.

The structure of the products leavened by steam is formed by eggs and by gluten, the protein substance found in flour. As the steam is formed, the batter expands around the steam. Baking coagulates the protein to set the structure of the product.

• AIR

Air is incorporated into baked products by mixing. It is the principal leavening agent in meringues and angel food cakes. These products are based on egg foams, where beating egg whites introduces air into the batter. The denaturation of protein plays an important part in the leavening process because the protein traps the air bubbles in the foam. The air leads to a light and fluffy product.

Air can also be added to baked goods in other ways. Blending fat and sugar, sifting flour, and beating the batter are all ways of adding air. Although air is not the main leavening agent in most baked goods, it provides some leavening in many products.

Yeast is a microscopic plant that works as a leavening agent through the **fermentation** (fur–men–TAY–shun) process. Fermentation is a chemical reaction that splits complex organic compounds into simpler substances. You will learn more about fermentation in Chapter 15.

During fermentation, yeast converts sugar, usually glucose, into ethyl alcohol and carbon dioxide. The chemical equation for the reaction is given below.

$$\underset{\text{Glucose}}{C_6H_{12}O_6} \xrightarrow{\text{yeast}} \underset{\text{Ethyl alcohol}}{2C_2H_5OH} \quad \underset{\text{Carbon dioxide}}{2CO_2}$$

The ethyl alcohol evaporates during baking, while the carbon dioxide causes the product to rise. Since the yeast is killed by the high

Yeast Throughout History

Yeast has been used for thousands of years to leaven bread. The very first yeast dough probably occurred by accident. Yeast, which is everywhere in the environment, landed on some dough. The yeast caused it to rise, forming a lighter bread than had previously been known.

In ancient Egypt, the first leavening agent was a piece of leftover dough in which yeast was growing. Eventually, the Egyptians used beer froth, which contains yeast, to leaven their bread. The word "yeast" originally meant the froth or sediment of a fermenting liquid (such as beer).

In ancient Rome, the people also leavened bread by saving a piece of old dough. In addition, during the grape harvest, wheat bran or the grain called millet was mixed with grape juice. These mixtures were fermented to develop yeast growth and then dried in the sun. The cakes that were formed were soaked in water when needed for leavening. The Romans thought that raised bread made the body strong. They considered it a particularly nutritious food.

During the 1700s, little had changed from ancient times. The preferred leavening in England was beer froth, just as it had been in ancient Egypt. The English dried the beer froth slowly. When it was needed, they mixed it with water, flour, and sugar and allowed it to stand for a day.

The English also used old pieces of yeast dough for leavening, especially when they were at sea. This was a less popular method of leavening because it produced a sourness in the bread. This sourness was due to the yeast and other microorganisms that grew in the bread while it was stored.

While the British found sourness in bread undesirable, less than a century later American gold miners made sourdough bread a mark of distinction. The sourdough bread associated with the Old West was made by using a starter. The cook kept the yeast alive by keeping some dough from one batch of bread to start the next batch.

Today, sourdough bread contains other organisms in addition to yeast, one of which is a bacteria called *Lactobacillus*. These organisms give sourdough bread a distinctive flavor.

baking temperatures, the fermentation process stops once the product becomes hot in the oven.

The rate and quantity of carbon dioxide produced by yeast is crucial in bread making. Some recipes call for a large amount of yeast to speed up the process of making the bread. Gas production by yeast can also be increased by adding sugar to encourage yeast growth. The best temperature for yeast fermentation is 27°C.

On the other hand, yeast gas production can be decreased by adding excess salt. While some sugar increases gas production, too much sugar can decrease it. A sudden temperature change, either high or low, can also decrease gas production.

The yeast used in bread making is *Saccharomyces cerevisiae*. It is sold in granular and compressed forms. The granular or pellet form can last for long periods of time at room temperature because it usually contains less than 9 percent water by weight. This lack of moisture makes it stable over time. The compressed yeast usually needs to be refrigerated or frozen. This is because it contains more moisture. It usually is 70 percent water by weight.

Carbon dioxide produced by yeast causes these rolls to rise.

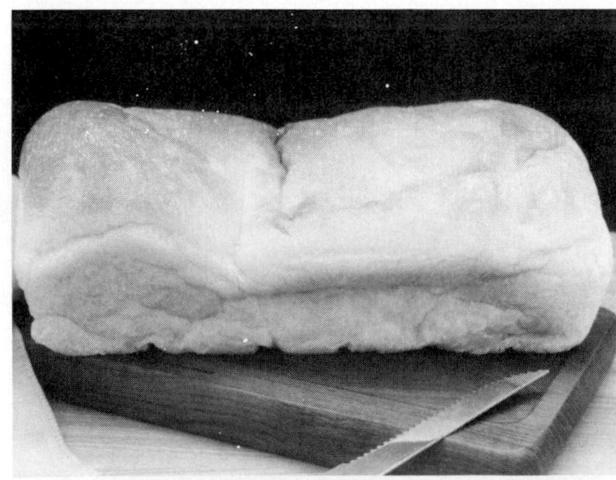

A low–quality product can result from poor gas production by yeast.

Granular and compressed forms of yeast are available for baking.

NUTRITION AND YOU

Wheat in the Diet

Human beings first began cultivating wheat about 10,000 years ago. As early as the fifth century B.C., the Greek historian Herodotus described Egyptian bread baking in his writings. Today, wheat is still one of the most important grains known. Nearly one–third of the world's population depends on wheat for nourishment. It is the basic grain in the diet of some of the people who live on every continent on earth.

Ninety percent of all wheat consumed today can be divided into three main groups—common, club, and durum. Common wheat is best for making bread. Club wheat is used for flour for general baking purposes, such as making cakes. Durum wheat is used in making macaroni, spaghetti, and noodles.

Wheat has the highest protein value of any cereal grain. However, it contains incomplete protein. To provide the body with all the amino acids needed, it is necessary to combine wheat with a legume or seed product. Whole grains and whole grain products are good sources of dietary fiber.

Many baked products are made with wheat flour. Most bread is made from wheat. Bread is sometimes called a **nutrient dense** food. This means it provides a relatively high quantity of one or more nutrients with a relatively low number of kilocalories.

Bread can vary greatly in its nutritional value. For example, bread made with eggs and milk is more nutritious than bread made with only flour and water. Bananas, pumpkin, nuts, and raisins added to bread increase its nutritional value. Whole grain bread is more nutritious than white bread because of the extra fiber it contains. When buying bread, it is important to check the ingredient list so you can choose a nutritious product.

Even though bread is nutritious, it should make up only a part of your diet. It is important to eat moderate amounts of a variety of nutritious foods.

Breads and other baked goods are usually made with wheat flour.

EXPERIMENT 14–1

Comparison of Leavening Agents

This experiment will allow you to test and compare the effects of various baking powders. You will make the same cake recipe you used during Experiment 8–1.

PROCEDURE

1. Follow the recipe variation assigned by your teacher.

Control Recipe for a Basic Cake	
150 g sugar	120 mL milk
108 g cake flour	2 mL vanilla
1.8 g salt	41 g egg (1)
3.5 g double-acting baking powder	
47 g hydrogenated shortening	

   a. **Variation 1.** Use the control recipe.
   b. **Variation 2.** Use 4.7 g baking powder instead of 3.5 g.
   c. **Variation 3.** Use 1.7 g baking powder instead of 3.5 g.
   d. **Variation 4.** Use 2 g sodium bicarbonate plus 3.9 g cream of tartar instead of 3.5 g baking powder.
   e. **Variation 5.** Use 2 g baking soda instead of 3.5 g baking powder, and use 15 mL vinegar and 105 mL milk instead of 120 mL milk. Mix the vinegar and milk together well.
   f. **Variation 6.** Use 1 g baking soda instead of 3.5 g baking powder, and use 120 mL buttermilk instead of regular milk.
2. Measure all ingredients for the variation you are to make. They should be at room temperature.
3. Sift the dry ingredients into a mixing bowl.
4. Add shortening and 80 mL of the liquid.
5. Beat for 2 minutes at medium speed with an electric mixer or 300 strokes by hand.
6. Add egg and remainder of the liquid.
7. Beat 2 minutes or 300 strokes more.
8. Bake in a 23 cm (9–in.) round cake pan at 185°C (365°F) for 20 minutes.
9. Let the cake cool for 10 minutes; then remove from pan and place on a cooling rack. When it is cool, wrap in plastic wrap and label with your name, variation, and class period. Place the cake in the location specified by your teacher.
10. The next day, slice the cake in half, forming two half circles. Measure the height of the cake at the center using a metric ruler.
11. Record the height in your data table, and write it on the chalkboard. Copy the heights of the other variations in your data table.
12. Cut a 0.3 cm slice of cake, wrap in plastic wrap, label, and give to your teacher. This sample will be frozen and evaluated later.
13. Cut the cake into small pieces. Put the pieces on a paper labeled with the variation number. Place the pieces out for taste testing.
14. Taste samples of each variation and evaluate for texture, tenderness, flavor, and moistness. Record your evaluations in your data table.
15. Mix one piece of each variation with enough deionized water to make a smooth suspension. Use pH paper to determine the pH. Record information in your data table.

EXPERIMENT 14–1

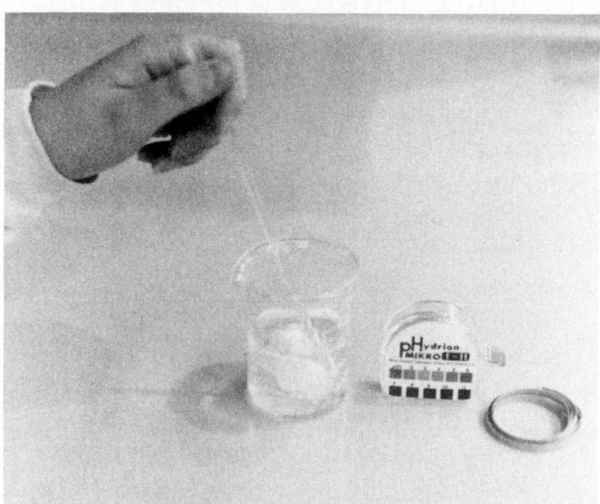

QUESTIONS

1. Which leavening agent produced the tallest cake? The shortest?
2. What effects did the various leavening agents have on texture? Tenderness? Flavor? Moistness?
3. How does the pH of the cake samples compare with the pH of the leavening source used in each cake? Why are these different? (Note: pH values for leavening agents were tested in Experiment 14–1.)
4. Of the six samples, which did you prefer? Why?

SAMPLE DATA TABLE

Variation	Height	Texture	Tenderness	Flavor	Moistness	pH
1						
2						
3						
4						
5						
6						

EXPERIMENT 14–2

Production of Carbon Dioxide Using Baking Powders

As you know, baking powder releases carbon dioxide gas. In this experiment, you will identify sources of leavening gases and compare the approximate amounts of carbon dioxide produced by each.

PROCEDURE

1. Place 15 mL of the albumen solution supplied by your teacher in each of three 250 mL beakers.
2. On squares of paper, mass 3.5 g of two different brands of baking powder.
3. Mass 2 g sodium bicarbonate and 3.9 g cream of tartar. Combine to form a homemade baking powder. Mix well.
4. Place tap water in a shallow container to a depth of about 3 cm. Bring water to a boil. Lower the heat and simmer.
5. Pour the baking powders into the three 250 mL beakers at the same time (one powder in each beaker). Stir quickly but only enough to disperse the baking powder. Too much stirring allows loss of the gas that is forming.
6. At 1–minute intervals for 5 minutes, measure the height of the foam in each beaker. After you have measured the foam, test the liquid with pH paper to determine its pH. Record this information in your data table.
7. After 5 minutes, place the three beakers in the shallow container of simmering water.
8. Heat the beakers for 5 minutes. Measure the height of the foam each minute, and observe changes during that time. Again, test the liquid with pH paper to determine its pH. Record this information in your data table.

QUESTIONS

1. What are the two essential ingredients in baking powder?
2. Which baking powder produced the most foam at room temperature? When heated?
3. Which baking powder was most acidic? Basic?
4. How did heating affect the pH of the solutions?

SAMPLE DATA TABLE

	Height at Room Temperature			pH at Room Temperature			Height in Warm Water			pH in Warm Water		
Time	#1	#2	#3	#1	#2	#3	#1	#2	#3	#1	#2	#3
1 minute												
2 minutes												
3 minutes												
4 minutes												
5 minutes												

TO SUM UP

- Leavening involves the production of gas to cause baked goods to rise and become light and porous.
- The most common leavening agents are chemical agents, air, steam, and yeast.
- Baking soda is combined with acid to produce carbon dioxide in a two–step process.
- Baking powder is made from baking soda, dry acid, and a filler, usually cornstarch or calcium carbonate.
- Quick breads are classified as pour batters, drop batters, soft doughs, and stiff doughs depending on the ratio of liquid to flour.
- Double–acting baking powders react first with cold liquid and then with heat.
- Most products leavened primarily with air are made with egg foams.
- Yeast ferments sugar to produce the carbon dioxide used in leavening.

CHECK YOUR FACTS

1. What is the purpose of leavening agents in baked goods?
2. What are the most widely used chemical leavening agents?
3. What is the disadvantage of using only sodium bicarbonate as a leavening agent?
4. What are the four categories of quick breads?
5. How can baking powder be made at home?
6. What is the difference between single–acting baking powder and double–acting baking powder?
7. Identify types of cakes leavened with air, steam, and chemical leavening agents.
8. Where does the steam used as a leavening agent come from?
9. What gives sourdough bread its distinctive flavor?
10. What happens to the ethyl alcohol produced by the yeast during the fermentation process?
11. How can gas production by yeast be increased?
12. Why must compressed yeast be refrigerated?

CRITICAL THINKING AND PROBLEM SOLVING

1. Why is an acid always used with baking soda?
2. If a recipe called for baking soda and vinegar, but you had no vinegar, what could you substitute for the vinegar?
3. When baking soda and cream of tartar are used as a leavener, what happens to the sodium potassium tartrate that is a product of the reaction?
4. Would a single–acting or double–acting baking powder last longer in a humid climate? Why?
5. Explain why baking powder must contain at least 25 percent baking soda.
6. Why do batters need to be thin when steam is the leavening agent?
7. When making angel food cake, what holds the air used as the leavener in the batter?
8. Why does yeast fermentation stop during baking?
9. If a yeast bread recipe consistently produced bread that was too heavy, what changes could you make to produce a lighter bread?

Fermentation and Food

This chapter will help you . . .

- Explain anaerobic respiration and how it is involved in both metabolism and food science.
- List three reasons why food is fermented.
- Identify bacteria used to ferment food.
- Compare fresh–pack pickling and brine pickling.
- Discuss how lactic acid bacteria create sauerkraut from cabbage.
- Describe the process of making vinegar.
- Identify the purposes of the ingredients used in making yeast breads.

Terms to Remember

aerobic
anaerobic
anaerobic respiration
brine
brine pickling
cell respiration
fresh–pack pickling
indigenous microorganisms
microbes
microorganisms
pasteurization

You have learned how your body uses glucose to provide energy. Glucose is the main source of energy for living systems in general, not just human beings. The energy from glucose is released when the glucose molecule is taken apart in the cell. This process is known as **cell respiration.** The process of cell respiration involves many complex steps.

Some chemical reactions require air or oxygen. These reactions are called **aerobic.** However, the first series of steps in cell respiration always occurs in the absence of air or oxygen. A reaction that takes place in the absence of oxygen is called **anaerobic.** Therefore respiration that occurs without oxygen is called **anaerobic respiration.**

Another name for anaerobic respiration is fermentation. As you learned in the last chapter, fermentation is a chemical reaction that splits complex organic compounds into relatively simpler substances. During fermentation, sugar (usually glucose) is changed to carbon dioxide and alcohol or various organic acids.

The delicious taste of chocolate is a result of fermentation.

Fermentation is an important step in the metabolism of glucose in the body. However, it is also an important process in food science since it is used in preserving and preparing many of the foods you eat.

Food is fermented for three basic reasons. First, fermentation extends the time food can be stored without spoiling. Second, it makes some food more enjoyable to eat. Wild rice, for example, is fermented to make it easier to

An aerobic reaction requires oxygen, while an anaerobic reaction takes place without oxygen.

chew. Finally, fermentation makes some food more usable. Few people would like the taste of chocolate or coffee if they were not fermented and processed before being eaten. Not all fermentations are desirable. However, many provide safe and improved foods.

Fermentation in food involves a change in the raw food material. It can occur in either animal or vegetable foods. It is brought about by the growth of **microorganisms** (my–kro–OR–gun–iz–ums). Microorganisms are single cells of microscopic size. They cannot be seen by the human eye but can be studied through a microscope. Microorganisms are also called **microbes** (MY–krohbs). The microorganisms involved in fermenting food can be bacteria, yeast, or mold, or a combination of these.

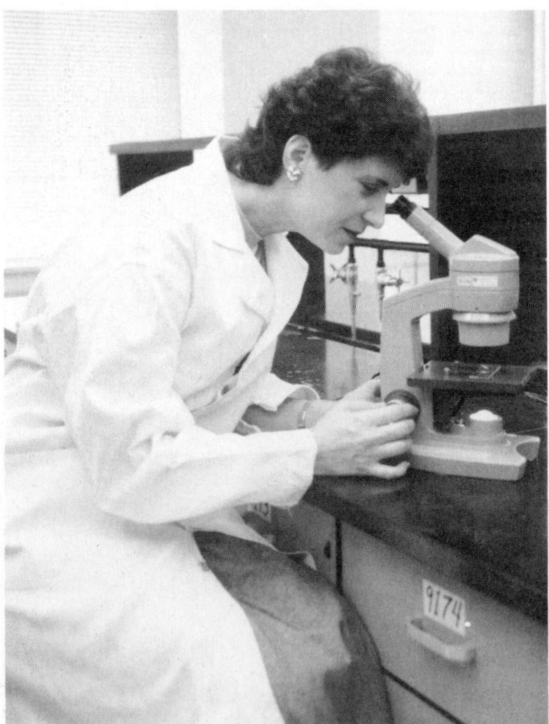

Some organisms, called microorganisms, are so small they can be seen only through a microscope.

Fermentation in History

Fermentation has been used in food processing since before recorded history. Tribes of nomads learned that, under certain conditions, milk would change to a solid material—cheese—or a semisolid material—yogurt. Although these nomads did not know it, the changes in milk resulted from fermentation by bacteria.

For centuries, people have been using yeast to ferment fruit juices to produce alcoholic beverages. In the 1850s, the French wine industry was having serious trouble with wine that had spoiled. French emperor Napoleon III called in scientist Louis Pasteur to help. Pasteur knew that the fermentation that produced wine was caused by yeast. But certain bacteria in the wine were also fermenting. Pasteur discovered that the fermentation by bacteria spoiled the wine because it produced vinegar instead of the alcohol produced by yeast. Pasteur suggested that the wine makers heat the wine for a short time to destroy the bacteria. At first, they were horrified. However, they found that a heat treatment destroyed many of the bacteria that were spoiling the wine. This process, known as **pasteurization**, is still used today, especially for milk.

BACTERIA FERMENTATION

Bacteria are the microorganisms used in the fermentation of food such as pickles, sauerkraut, and yogurt. Of the many types of bacteria that can cause fermentation, there are three that are commonly used to ferment food. These three are lactic acid bacteria, acetic acid bacteria, and carbon dioxide–producing bacteria. Proteolytic bacteria are also used in food fermentation, although they are less common. Proteolytic bacteria differ from other fermenting bacteria because they break down protein rather than carbohydrate.

Yogurt is made from milk by fermentation bacteria.

• LACTIC ACID BACTERIA

Lactic acid bacteria are used in the production of foods such as sour cream, cottage cheese, cheddar cheese, dill pickles, olives, sauerkraut, and vanilla. These bacteria carry out the same reaction that takes place in muscle cells. In both cases, glucose is converted into lactic acid and energy. The equation for the reaction is shown below.

$$\underset{\text{Glucose}}{C_6H_{12}O_6} \xrightarrow{\text{bacteria}} \underset{\text{Lactic acid}}{2HC_3H_5O_3} + \text{Energy}$$

During lactic acid fermentation, the acid formed lowers the pH of the solution. This continues until no more glucose is available for reaction and fermentation stops. When the pH goes below 4.5, other bacteria, which could spoil the food, normally die. Sometimes the fermentation does not go on long enough to lower the pH below 4.5. Then the bacteria remain alive and can make the food inedible.

The distinctive flavors of Cheddar cheese and olives are caused by lactic acid bacteria fermentation.

Pickles

Pickles are usually made from cucumbers. However, other foods can be pickled, such as watermelon, cauliflower, onions, or okra. Making pickles involves the use of **brine**, a water–

and–salt mixture that contains large amounts of salt. Pickling is currently carried out in two ways.

One process for pickle making is known as **brine pickling.** This requires that the pickles remain in the brine for several weeks. During this time, fermentation by lactic acid bacteria takes place until an acceptably low pH is reached. Changes occur in the appearance and texture of the food being fermented. Green vegetables change to an olive or yellow–green color and become translucent, or partly transparent. The texture of the food becomes firm and crisp, but tender. Characteristic flavors develop.

The other process of making pickles is known as **fresh–pack pickling.** The pickles are not fermented as in brine pickling. Instead, the food is placed in brine for only a few hours or overnight, if at all. Then the food being pickled is drained and immersed in a boiling mixture of vinegar (acetic acid) and spices. The high temperature of the solution combined with the low pH of the vinegar kill undesirable bacteria, while the vinegar and spices give flavor to the pickles.

Brine pickling requires several weeks of fermentation by lactic acid bacteria.

Sauerkraut

Sauerkraut, made from cabbage, is another food fermented by lactic acid bacteria. Salt added to the cabbage pulls water and sugar out of the cabbage. Then lactic acid bacteria convert the sugar into lactic acid in the sauerkraut. The lactic acid is what gives sauerkraut its sour taste.

There are three factors involved in successfully making sauerkraut. First, the salt that is used inhibits the growth of many bacteria that could spoil the sauerkraut. Secondly, soil–borne lactic acid bacteria present on the surface of the cabbage produce the acid that lowers the pH of the sauerkraut. Third, 21°C is the best temperature for the growth of lactic acid bacteria.

It is important to wash the cabbage prior to shredding when making sauerkraut. This actually encourages the growth of the lactic acid bacteria and decreases the percentage of undesirable bacteria.

Ordinarily, the pH of fresh vegetables like cabbage is 5.5–6.5. This pH is perfect for growing microorganisms such as spoilage bacteria, yeast, and mold. Therefore when the salt and cabbage are first combined many microorganisms grow. Soon the lactic acid bacteria produce enough acid that the pH is lowered to between 3–4.6. Once the pH is below 4.6, the solution is too acid for anything except fermenting bacteria to grow. The other microorganisms die, while the fermenting bacteria continue to multiply. The end result is a safe and flavorful sauerkraut.

When making sauerkraut, washing the cabbage encourages the growth of lactic acid bacteria.

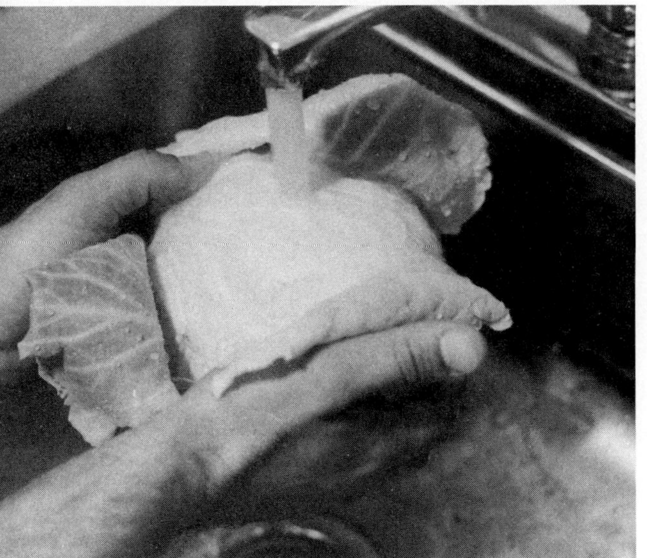

A low pH results in the fermentation of a safe and flavorful sauerkraut.

The lactic acid bacteria found on cabbage and cucumbers as they grow are called indigenous bacteria.

• ACETIC ACID BACTERIA

Acetic acid bacteria are those used to make vinegar. Vinegar can be produced from most fruits. A two-step process is involved in the production of vinegar. First, sugar must be fermented to ethyl alcohol (C_2H_5OH). This step is carried out by yeast. Then the alcohol undergoes the process known as oxidation, which leads to the production of acetic acid. As you know, oxidation is a chemical change in which a substance loses electrons. In this case, oxidation occurs when the ethyl alcohol combines with oxygen. This second step is carried out by acetic acid bacteria.

Sources of Bacteria

Some bacteria are found in nature on plants used as food. For example, cucumbers and cabbage have bacteria on them when they are harvested. The microorganisms found on foods such as these are called native or **indigenous microorganisms** (in–DIJ–uh–nus). Indigenous means found naturally in a particular environment. Indigenous bacteria are used in making pickles from cucumbers or sauerkraut from cabbage.

There are other foods in which indigenous bacteria are not suitable. They are not used in making yogurt because it is impossible to know whether the bacteria present in a given sample of milk are the best ones for making yogurt. So the milk is heated to kill the bacteria that may be present. Then a known microbe is added to the milk. In yogurt, lactic acid bacteria are added. The scientific names of these bacteria are *Streptococcus thermophilus* and *Lactobacillus bulgaricus*. This technique allows yogurt producers to have more control over their end product.

The microbes that are added to make yogurt or other fermented products are produced commercially. They have been preserved through drying, freeze–drying, or concentrating and freezing. The uniform quality of the commercially prepared microbes helps produce quality food products.

Proteolytic bacteria help ferment the cacao beans to make chocolate.

• OTHER FERMENTING BACTERIA

Bacteria that produce carbon dioxide are used in making Edam, Gouda, and Swiss cheeses. You will learn more about cheese making in the next chapter.

Proteolytic bacteria are used in the production of chocolate. Cacao beans, which are actually seeds, are fermented from 3–13 days. This removes the outside pulp from the beans and gives them aroma, flavor, and color. These changes are the result of both enzyme reactions and fermentation caused by microorganisms, including the proteolytic bacteria. The process is quite complicated. It involves many stages, which must be carefully controlled to produce a quality chocolate product.

There are some food products whose production involves the use of more than one type of microorganism. Thus bacteria, yeast, mold, or enzymes may be involved in their production. Soy sauce, coffee, Camembert cheese, and many sausages belong in this category.

YEAST FERMENTATION

As described in the last chapter, fermentation is carried out by yeast as glucose is converted into ethyl alcohol and carbon dioxide. In addition to glucose, yeast can also ferment maltose, sucrose, and fructose. However, it can't ferment lactose, the sugar found in milk.

Yeast grow and produce carbon dioxide at different rates. The challenge in using yeast fermentation in cooking is to determine what conditions will allow the yeast to grow at a rate and for a length of time that will produce the best food product.

• YEAST BREADS

Yeast breads are made from a soft dough that is leavened by carbon dioxide produced during yeast fermentation. Yeast dough is actually a type of foam. The bubbles of carbon dioxide are surrounded by the starch and proteins of the flour dough.

The basic ingredients in yeast dough are flour; a liquid, which is usually either water or milk; yeast; and salt. Sometimes sugar, fat, or eggs are added to produce a specific flavor or texture.

Bubbles of carbon dioxide are surrounded by starch and protein molecules of the dough to create holes in this yeast bread.

Fermented Food From Around the World

Most cultures of the world enjoy some fermented foods. In the Orient, people enjoy paw tsay, a dish consisting of fermented turnips and radishes. Soy sauce, saki, and kimchi, which is fermented cabbage, are also popular fermented foods in the Orient. The Japanese have been preparing fermented fish for centuries.

In Hawaii, the famous dish called poi, which is served at luaus, is prepared from the fermented taro root. This root grows in the moist valleys found throughout the Hawaiian islands.

Fermented foods originally prepared in Europe include sausages, salami, bologna, and hundreds of cheeses. In addition, buttermilk is a favorite in Bulgaria.

The flour used in making bread provides starch and protein, especially gluten. Flour varies in its gluten content. For making yeast bread, flour that has a high gluten content is best. The starch grains in the flour are trapped by the gluten. Thus when the bread is baked, these starch grains surround the gas cells and form the solid structure of the bread.

The starch in flour is also used as food for the yeast in bread making. Although yeast need sugar to produce carbon dioxide, too much sugar will slow down the fermentation process. Therefore the starch molecules in flour are broken down into sugars usable by the yeast.

Eggs are often added to yeast bread dough when making breads for special occasions.

The liquid used in bread making provides a medium in which the other ingredients can dissolve and be transported to the yeast cells. Milk is usually the liquid used. This is because it provides additional nutrients not supplied by liquids such as water or potato water. Milk also helps bread stay fresh longer. During baking, the steam formed by the liquid combines with the carbon dioxide produced by the yeast to cause the bread to expand and rise.

Salt is an important ingredient in bread. It not only adds flavor, but it also inhibits enzymes that break down protein. A yeast dough made without salt would be very sticky and difficult to work with.

Sugar is added for flavor and to provide an easily fermentable food for the yeast. Sugar also helps the crust on bread to brown. Fats make breads more tender. Eggs are generally added to breads only for special occasions to make the breads richer in texture and flavor.

• BEVERAGES

The beverage industry has been using yeast fermentation for thousands of years. Most alcoholic beverages are fermented products. The fermentation of barley produces beer and ale. Corn and rye can also be fermented to produce alcoholic drinks. Most wine is made from fermented grapes, although apples, blackberries, and other fruit can also be used to make wine.

Records indicate wine was produced in the Middle East as early as 3000 BC. In the beginning, it is quite possible that grapes fermented accidentally before they were eaten. This could happen because the yeast were present naturally on the surfaces of the grapes.

Since then, however, wine making has become a highly scientific process. It employs elaborate systems of stainless steel tanks, electronic monitors, and computerized temperature controls. This is an example of how science has transformed a process that

Coffee

Coffee is a beverage produced in part by fermentation by bacteria and enzymes. Coffee can be processed by either a wet or dry method.

In the wet method, the coffee berries are washed and placed in machines that remove the outer pulp. The berries are soaked in tanks of water and left to ferment for 12–24 hours. They are then sprayed with water until the sticky coating that has formed on them has been removed. Finally, they are allowed to dry in the sun.

The dry method is the older and more natural method. The berries are washed and then spread in thin layers to dry for two or three weeks. During this time, fermentation occurs. The beans are raked several times each day to ensure uniform drying. About 60 percent of all the world's coffee is produced using the dry method.

After the beans are processed with either the wet or dry method, they are roasted. This develops their flavor and aroma. During roasting, the beans become drier and their oils become water soluble. Finally, the beans are ground for brewing.

Coffee beans are processed, roasted, ground, and brewed to create the beverage people enjoy.

was once considered an art. Wine making is still an art, but science is making it a more controllable art.

Wine makers carefully monitor and test the growing grapes. In deciding when to harvest, they look at the sugar levels in the growing grapes. Differences in sugar content cause differences in the amount of alcohol produced during fermentation. However, even the most careful scientific testing cannot remove all the mystery from wine making.

No two batches of wine are ever exactly the same. While the fermentation process is consistent, factors such as temperature, fermentation time, and nutrients in the grape juice all affect the final product. In addition, the grapes are never exactly the same two years in a row. The grapes are affected by the amount of rain-

Many factors, such as rainfall and the weather when grapes are growing, affect the quality of the wine produced.

fall, whether the summer is long and hot or short and cool, and dozens of other variables. These factors make it difficult for the wine maker to know ahead of time whether the grape harvest will produce a mediocre wine or one of premium quality.

MOLD AND ENZYME FERMENTATION

Molds are important in the fermentation of some food products. Molds contain enzymes that can split cellulose molecules. As you know, the human body cannot metabolize cellulose. This is because the body does not contain the enzymes that can break down cellulose. Therefore mold fermentation of cellulose allows humans to digest some foods that would otherwise be indigestible. For example, many grains have a cellulose or hemicellulose coating. Through fermentation carried out by molds, these coatings can be broken down so the body can use the nutrients in the grains. Nuts and seeds can also be made more digestible by mold fermentation.

Molds often alter the texture of foods and make them more pleasing to eat. Molds are important in the fermentation of many cheeses, such as Cheddar cheese. Mold fermentation is also needed to produce soy sauce.

A variety of enzymes are used in fermentation. As mentioned above, enzymes are involved in mold fermentation. The enzyme sucrase is needed to break down sucrose molecules during yeast fermentation. Sucrase also speeds up the fermentation process. Tea is fermented by enzyme oxidation of tea leaves. By controlling the fermentation process, tea can be made with color variations and subtle flavor differences.

Variations in fermentation of tea leaves produce subtle color and flavor differences.

NUTRITION AND YOU

Nutrition and Fermented Food

The nutrients in food can be affected by the process of fermentation. Water-soluble vitamins dissolve in brine and then can be lost during pickling. The amount of energy (kilocalories) present in a food may decrease during fermentation. This occurs because the food releases energy as it is fermented. Some of this energy is used by the bacteria that cause the fermentation.

Some foods are more nutritious after fermentation than before. Certain microorganisms involved in fermentation produce vitamin B_{12} and riboflavin. Enzymes in mold can ferment the fiber coatings of grains, nuts, and seeds, so the nutrients in these foods can be used by the body.

More commonly, the nutritional value of fermented foods is similar to that of the foods from which they were made. Fat-soluble vitamins, protein, and carbohydrate usually are not changed much by the fermentation process. The following chart will let you compare the nutritional value of three common fermented foods with similar size servings of their unfermented sources.

Food	Kcal	Riboflavin	Vit. A	Vit. C	Calcium
Cucumber	5	0.01 mg	70 I.U.	3 mg	8 mg
Pickle	15	trace	30 I.U.	1 mg	8 mg
2% Milk	120	0.42 mg	450 I.U.	2 mg	297 mg
2% Yogurt	145	0.44 mg	170 I.U.	2 mg	415 mg
Cabbage	20	0.04 mg	120 I.U.	42 mg	34 mg
Sauerkraut	40	0.09 mg	120 I.U.	33 mg	85 mg

EXPERIMENT 15–1

Lactic Acid Fermentation

In this experiment, you will prepare sauerkraut from cabbage. As the fermentation process proceeds, you will monitor changes in the color and texture of the cabbage and the appearance and pH of the brine.

PROCEDURE

1. Remove and discard the outer leaves from a firm, mature head of cabbage. Use one head of cabbage for every two laboratory groups. Wash, drain, and cut the head in half. Remove and discard the core.
2. Each group should shred half the head of cabbage using a sharp knife. Pieces should be no thicker than a dime. Place the shredded cabbage in a mixing bowl.
3. Sprinkle 18.2 g sodium chloride over the shredded cabbage, and mix thoroughly by hand. The salt will pull water from the cabbage to form a brine.
4. Pack the cabbage into a clean jar, pressing the cabbage down firmly with a wooden spoon. Fill the jar to 5 cm from the top. Be sure the brine covers the cabbage. If you need more brine, obtain it from your teacher.
5. Fill a plastic bag with brine solution provided by your teacher, and seal tightly. Place the plastic bag on top of the cabbage to hold it down. Wipe the top of the jar and put on the lid. Do not seal the lid tightly.
6. Label your jar with your name and class period, and place in the location indicated by your teacher.
7. Every few days:
   a. Check to see that the cabbage is covered with liquid. If necessary, add a weak brine made by dissolving 28.8 g salt in 1 L water.
   b. Skim off any film that may form.
   c. Record the following information in your data table: color of the cabbage/sauerkraut; texture of the cabbage/sauerkraut; appearance of the brine (clear, cloudy); and pH of the brine as tested with pH paper.
8. Allow the fermentation process to continue for about 5 weeks or until the pH of the brine is 3.5 or below for at least a week. Do not taste the sauerkraut if the pH remains above 4.

QUESTIONS

1. What changes occurred in the color and texture of the cabbage as it fermented?
2. What changes occurred in the appearance of the brine as the cabbage fermented?
3. What is the final pH of the brine solution?
4. Is the pH low enough to preserve the sauerkraut? If not, what could you do about it?

SAMPLE DATA TABLE

Date	Color	Texture	Brine Appearance	Brine pH

EXPERIMENT 15–2

Yeast Growth

One of the most important challenges in making bread is to determine the conditions that will allow yeast to grow at a rate and for a length of time that will produce the best bread. In this experiment, you will grow yeast in a variety of environments to determine how each affects yeast growth.

PROCEDURE

1. Add 100 mL water to a 250 mL beaker. Heat the water to 30°C over medium heat.
2. Put a small saucepan half full of water on a second burner over low heat.
3. When the temperature of the water in the beaker has reached 30°C, remove it from the heat. Add 3.2 g dry yeast to the beaker and mix thoroughly so that all the yeast dissolves.
4. Follow the variation assigned by your teacher.
   a. **Variation 1.** Add nothing to the yeast and water mixture.
   b. **Variation 2.** Add 4.3 g sugar to the yeast and water, and mix well.
   c. **Variation 3.** Add 6.6 g salt to the yeast and water, and mix well.
   d. **Variation 4.** Add 4.3 g sugar and 6.6 g salt to the yeast and water, and mix well.
5. Remove the saucepan from the stove. Determine the temperature of the water in the saucepan.
6. Add cool water if necessary to adjust the temperature of the water to 25°C. Place the beaker containing the yeast mixture in the warm water in the saucepan for 15 minutes.
7. After 15 minutes, remove the beaker from the saucepan, and measure the height of the yeast mixture. In your data table, record the height of the mixture for the variation you followed.
8. Observe the odor and consistency of your mixture, and record this information in your data table.
9. Write the information for your variation on the chalkboard. In your data table, copy the information for the other variations.

QUESTIONS

1. In which environment did the yeast grow best? Worst? Why?
2. Why wasn't the beaker placed directly on the heating element during yeast growth?
3. Check at least three different bread recipes to determine if the ingredients used and directions given seem reasonable according to the results of this experiment.

SAMPLE DATA TABLE

Variation	Height	Odor	Consistency
1			
2			
3			
4			

REVIEW

TO SUM UP

- Cell respiration is a multistep process that involves the breakdown of glucose and the release of energy.
- Anaerobic respiration, also called fermentation, is the first step in the breakdown of glucose and occurs without oxygen.
- Fermentation in food can be caused by bacteria, yeast, mold, and enzymes.
- Food can be fermented by lactic acid bacteria, acetic acid bacteria, carbon dioxide–producing bacteria, or proteolytic bacteria.
- Pickles can be made using either brine pickling or fresh–pack pickling methods.
- Yeast dough is a type of foam where bubbles of carbon dioxide produced by yeast are trapped in the dough by the starch and protein in flour.
- Yeast ferments grain and fruit to produce alcoholic beverages.

CHECK YOUR FACTS

1. What is anaerobic respiration?
2. List three reasons for fermenting food.
3. Name at least two types of microorganisms that cause food fermentation.
4. How are proteolytic bacteria different from other fermenting bacteria?
5. Which bacteria carry out the same reaction in food fermentation as takes place in muscle cells?
6. What happens to pH during pickling?
7. Which pickling method takes longer? Why?
8. How is the growth of spoilage bacteria, yeast, and mold stopped in making sauerkraut?
9. What kind of bacteria are used in producing vinegar?
10. What type of bacteria are involved in the fermentation of chocolate?
11. Why is yeast dough considered a foam?
12. What is the name of the main protein found in flour?
13. Why is the sugar level in grapes important in wine making?

CRITICAL THINKING AND PROBLEM SOLVING

1. How does anaerobic respiration differ from cell respiration?
2. What would happen if cucumbers were blanched before pickling?
3. Why must *Lactobacillus bulgaricus* or *Streptococcus thermophilus* be added during yogurt making?
4. Why can't yeast ferment milk?
5. Why is steam more important than carbon dioxide in causing bread to rise while it is baking?
6. If you added twice the salt called for in a bread recipe, what would happen?
7. Why would unripe grapes be unsuitable for wine making?
8. Why does wine ferment even after the bacteria in it are killed by pasteurization?
9. Describe the changes that take place when fresh cider ferments.

CHAPTER

16

Dairy Products and Processing

This chapter will help you . . .

- List the components of milk and explain how each is dispersed in the milk.
- Describe what happens when milk protein is coagulated.
- Discuss the processing of milk and how it is treated when it is pasteurized, homogenized, and fortified.
- Compare and contrast skim milk, low–fat milk, whole milk, half–and–half, and various creams.
- Differentiate between evaporated milk, condensed milk, and dried milk.
- Identify factors that affect the ability of cream to form a foam.
- Explain the changes that occur when milk is heated.
- Describe the process of making a fermented or cultured milk product and list examples of these products.

Terms to Remember

carrageenin
creaming
culture
fortification
incubation period
inoculation
lactose intolerance
micelles
milk solids
precipitate
serum proteins
shelf life
starter
whey

Milk and milk products play an important role in the diet. The most common milk consumed by people today is cow's milk, although the milk of other animals is consumed in some parts of the world. This chapter will focus on the composition and properties of cow's milk and products made from it.

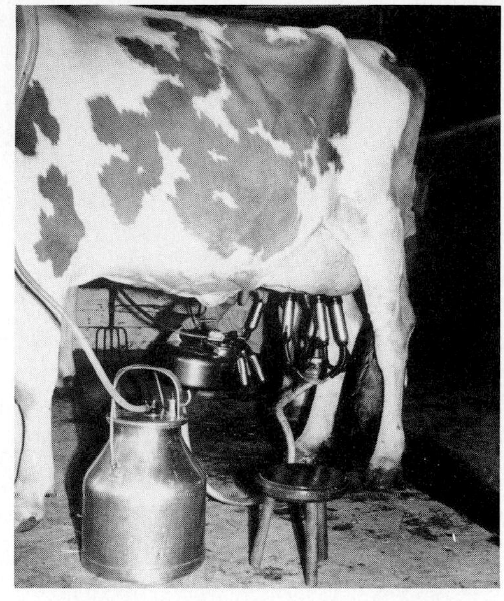

Most of the milk you drink is cow's milk.

The Complex Nature of Milk

Milk is a very complex substance. There are over 250 chemical compounds found in milk.

Milk is a solution that is 87 percent water. Dissolved in the water are water–soluble vitamins, the milk sugar lactose, and many trace minerals and mineral salts.

The water phase of milk is also a colloidal dispersion. The colloids include milk proteins whose molecules are too large to dissolve.

Finally, milk is not only a solution and a colloidal disperson but also an emulsion. The fat in milk is present as small droplets or globules whose size depends on the breed of cow producing the milk. These fat globules are prevented from coming together by a thin coating of protein emulsifiers.

This milk contains over 250 different chemical compounds.

COMPOSITION OF MILK

Milk contains all the major nutrients. It is a source of protein, fat, carbohydrate, vitamins, and minerals.

• PROTEIN

There are two main proteins that are dispersed as colloids in milk. These are casein and **whey.**

About 80 percent of the milk proteins are caseins. The caseins of the milk are associated with each other and with some of the minerals in milk in structures called **micelles** (my–SELLS). A micelle is an aggregation, or group, of molecules, often found in colloidal dispersions. The micelles in milk are more or less spherical. Light reflected from micelles gives milk its white color.

Casein can be coagulated by acids. This causes the protein to settle out as white clumps, which separate from the liquid. These clumps are called curds or clots. When these form, the milk is said to be curdled. Milk tends to curdle when mixed with acidic foods, such as tomatoes. Curdling can be prevented by thickening the milk or the food to be added to it with starch. The starch surrounds the casein and prevents it from coagulating when the foods are combined.

While caseins are sensitive to acids, they are quite stable in heat. However, the casein in milk can be destabilized by the enzyme rennin. Rennin is used to clot milk in the first stage of cheese making.

Also suspended colloidally in milk are the whey proteins, which are also called **serum proteins.** These proteins make up the other 20 percent of milk protein.

Whey proteins are found in the liquid left after fat and casein have been removed from the milk. Whey proteins are easily coagulated by heat.

Milk also contains a number of enzymes, which are protein molecules. Most of these are denatured during pasteurization.

Fat

Protein

Bound Water

Micelles are groups of molecules found in colloidal dispersions.

Curdled milk can be caused by the coagulation of casein by acids.

If the curds from curdled milk are strained through a cheesecloth, the liquid remaining contains whey proteins.

Cream rises to the top of freshly drawn milk.

• FAT

Cow's milk contains the most complex lipids known. There are over 400 different fatty acids found in the lipids in cow's milk. However, only 20 individual fatty acids account for most of the fat in milk. Milk fat contains very little cholesterol compared with egg yolk. The cholesterol that is present is in the membrane that surrounds the fat globules. The fats in milk influence its flavor, texture, and price. The greater the percentage of milk fat, the more costly the milk is.

In freshly drawn milk, the fat droplets are emulsified and suspended throughout the milk. However, they do not stay this way but, instead, associate in clusters. Eventually the clusters become large enough that their lower density causes them to float to the top of the milk, a process called **creaming.** Cream is simply milk that is extra rich in emulsified fat droplets.

To eliminate creaming, milk is homogenized. You will remember that during homogenization the fat globules in milk are reduced in size. This is done by forcing the milk through small openings under pressure. This breaks down the fat particles to a size that will remain uniformly distributed throughout the milk, rather than rising to the top.

• SUGAR

Lactose is the sugar found in all varieties of milk. It is made only by cells of the lactating mammary gland. Lactose has many functions in milk. It:

- Provides food energy.
- Makes milk delicately sweet.
- Provides a substrate for the formation of lactic acid by the enzyme lactase.
- Adds body to milk.

Lactose reacts with amino acids when milk is heated. This chemical reaction is what causes the tan color and slightly caramelized flavor of cooked milk products.

This machine uses pressure to reduce the size of fat particles in milk during homogenization.

One of the symptoms of lactose intolerance is stomach cramps.

Some individuals are unable to digest lactose. This is due to the absence of lactase in their intestines. This problem is known as **lactose intolerance.** When lactase is missing, the milk lactose remains undigested. Intestinal bacteria then ferment the lactose, producing acids and gas. The symptoms of lactose intolerance are bloating, diarrhea, and stomach cramps.

• MINERALS AND VITAMINS

Most of the minerals present in milk are in the form of salts. While there are a number of different salts in milk, they are present in very small quantities. Usually, the salts make up less than 1 percent of milk. These salts include chlorides, phosphates, and citrates of potassium, calcium, sodium, and magnesium.

The calcium and magnesium ions in milk help make the casein micelles stable. When the pH of milk is lowered, the acid removes the calcium ions from the casein micelles. This curdles the milk and allows the formation of curds and whey. When the enzyme rennin is added to milk for making cheese, it coagulates the milk faster if there are fewer salts present.

Among the trace elements present in milk are cobalt, copper, iodine, iron, magnesium, nickel, and molybdenum. The exact amounts of the minerals present depend upon the soil conditions in the area where the cows were fed.

Of the four vitamins in milk, riboflavin is present in the largest amount. It has a greenish tint that can only be seen in milk that contains no fat. Riboflavin is sensitive to light, which is the reason milk should be stored in cardboard or plastic containers.

The other vitamins in milk are thiamin, niacin, and vitamin A. In addition, milk is usually fortified. **Fortification** is the addition of a nutrient to a food. In this case, vitamin D is added during the processing of milk.

Most milk is fortified with vitamin D.

All three of these foods contain the same amount of protein.

MILK PROCESSING

Milk should have good flavor, a high nutritive value, and a satisfactory **shelf life.** Shelf life is the time a food product can be safely stored before deteriorating. Local health departments carefully regulate the processing and sale of milk and milk products. Most milk sold today is pasteurized, homogenized, and fortified during processing.

As you learned in the last chapter, Louis Pasteur developed the process of pasteurization, which ensures the safety of milk. Pasteurization has been used for over 100 years to kill harmful bacteria present in milk. In this process, milk is heated to high temperatures for a short time to destroy harmful bacteria.

Pasteurization also denatures the enzymes present in milk. In fact, one method of testing milk to see if it has been pasteurized is to test for the specific enzyme alkaline phosphatase. If the enzyme is present, the milk has not been pasteurized. This is known as the phosphatase test.

The shelf life of milk is the time it can be safely stored without deteriorating.

Milk Storage

It is the responsibility of the dairy industry to provide consumers with milk products of consistently high quality. Those who purchase milk products can maintain that quality by careful handling at home.

Fresh milk should be stored in the refrigerator. It will retain its quality for one to three weeks when properly stored. After milk is used, it should be returned immediately to the refrigerator. Leaving milk on the table during meals or letting it sit on a kitchen counter causes rapid growth of bacteria and hastens spoilage.

Storing milk in a closed container will help prevent unpleasant flavors from developing. In addition, because exposure to light causes the breakdown of riboflavin, a closed container will help preserve the nutritional value of the milk.

Sometimes milk is pasteurized at ultra–high temperatures for a short period of time. This milk, called UHT milk, has few bacteria and a long shelf life. When properly packaged, UHT milk can be stored unrefrigerated for 6–8 weeks.

Some UHT milk can be stored unrefrigerated for 6–8 weeks.

Most milk sold in the United States is homogenized. This reduces the size of the fat particles, as described earlier in this chapter.

Finally, most milk is fortified by adding vitamin D. Milk can be fortified by exposing it to ultraviolet light. This changes some of the fat components in the milk to vitamin D. Vitamin D concentrate can also be added to the milk prior to pasteurization.

Leaving milk on the table during meals causes rapid growth of bacteria.

NUTRITION AND YOU

The Nutritional Value of Milk

Milk contains most of the substances needed for good nutrition. It is an important part of a healthy diet from infancy to old age.

Milk is a good source of protein because it contains all the essential amino acids needed by humans. It is a complete protein, so it can be the only source of protein at a meal. Milk supplements the incomplete proteins found in cereal when milk and cereal are eaten together.

Milk is also a good source of energy. One cup of milk provides 12 g carbohydrate in the form of the sugar lactose. Lactose is also important because it increases the absorption of calcium, phosphorus, magnesium, and zinc.

Calcium is the most important mineral found in milk. In fact, milk is the most important source of dietary calcium. The form of calcium found in milk is readily used by the body. Milk also contains significant amounts of phosphorus. This is important because phosphorus must be present for the body to absorb calcium.

Milk is a good source of vitamins. The main B vitamins in milk are riboflavin, thiamin, and niacin. These are water–soluble vitamins. Milk is also a source of fat–soluble vitamin A. Skim milk, which contains no fat, is not as good a source of vitamin A.

Milk is not a good source of vitamin C, iron, or copper. This is why vitamin C and egg yolk are added to a baby's diet early in life.

Pasteurization has a small effect on the nutritional value of milk. It creates a slight loss of thiamin, vitamin B_{12}, and vitamin C. Some of the calcium becomes insoluble, thus not usable by the body. Some people claim that raw milk (unpasteurized) is more nutritious. These claims have not been supported by scientific research. The benefits of pasteurization for health and safety far outweigh the slight decrease in nutritional value it causes.

Cheese is also a very nutritious food, since it is made from concentrated milk. For example, the protein in 85 g cheese is equal to the protein in 85 g ground beef or in three eggs.

Cream and butter, even though made from milk, are not especially nutritious. They contain little carbohydrate and few other nutrients found in milk. They are considered fats rather than milk products.

TYPES OF MILK PRODUCTS

Fresh fluid milk is divided into categories according to its fat content. The level of fat in each type of milk is set by law. Skim milk has had all fat removed. Low–fat milk contains from 0.5–2 percent milk fat. In most states, whole milk contains a minimum of 3.5 percent milk fat.

Cream can also be divided according to the amount of fat it contains.

- Half–and–half is 10 percent fat.
- Coffee cream contains 18 percent fat.
- Light whipping cream has 30 percent fat.
- Heavy whipping cream contains a minimum of 35 percent fat.

Whipping cream often bears the label UHT. As with milk, this label means that the product has been pasteurized at an ultra–high temperature for a short time to increase its storage life.

Evaporated milk is whole milk that has been heated at low pressure. This causes up to 60 percent of the water in the milk to evaporate at temperatures well below the normal boiling point of milk. The result is a concentrated form of milk that is usually homogenized, sterilized in processing, and sealed in a tin. **Carrageenin** (kair–uh–GEE–nun), a vegetable gum, is often added to evaporated milk prior to processing to stabilize the casein proteins. Evaporated milk has a slight tan color. This is due to the chemical reaction of lactose with amino acids, which occurs because of the temperatures needed to sterilize the product.

Condensed milk is processed by removing 50 percent of the water in the milk, adding sugar, and canning it. Condensed milk is 44 percent sugar. The milk does not need to be sterilized because the large amount of sugar present prevents the growth of harmful bacteria. The sugar produces a high osmotic pressure, which draws the water left in the milk away from the nutrients needed for bacterial growth. This makes it impossible for bacteria to grow.

Dried milk is available in powder form. The milk used to make dried milk is pasteurized, and then the water is removed leaving a dry

Milk is sold according to the amount of fat it contains.

Evaporated, condensed, and dried milk all have water removed during processing.

solid material. These solids that remain are called **milk solids.** They are the protein, carbohydrate, fat, minerals, and vitamins that were dissolved in the liquid portion of the milk.

Fermented milk can be buttermilk, sour cream, or yogurt. Fermented milks have a distinctive flavor because of the breakdown of lactose by bacterial action.

COOKING WITH MILK

Milk is often used as is for a beverage or on cereal. It also has many uses in food preparation. Milk can be whipped, heated, or combined with other ingredients to create a variety of nutritious foods.

• FOAMS

Cream is commonly used as a foam when it is whipped. You know that a foam consists of bubbles of gas trapped in a liquid. There are several factors that affect the ability of cream to form a foam.

The amount of fat in the cream is important in making a foam. The higher the fat level, the better the foam is apt to be. Whipping cream is usually 35 percent fat. Cream containing 30 percent fat will produce a less stiff foam than cream of 40 percent fat. Viscosity, or the thickness of the cream, is increased by the extra amount of fat. This improves the quality of the whipped cream.

Temperature is crucial in making a good foam. Cold temperatures increase the viscosity of the cream. Temperatures below 7°C produce the best foams. For best results, the beaters and bowl used for whipping cream should also be cold.

The amount of cream affects the quality of the foam. Whipping small amounts usually produces better results than whipping large amounts.

The quality of whipped cream depends on its fat content and its temperature when whipped.

Finally, adding sugar decreases both the volume and stiffness of the foam, as well as increasing the time it takes the foam to form. Therefore it is best to add sugar after the cream is at the desired stiffness.

• HEATING MILK

Heat causes a variety of reactions in milk. Some of these reactions are desirable, while others are not. Therefore milk must be handled carefully when heated.

Heat denatures and coagulates the whey proteins of fresh milk, causing them to **precipitate** (prih–SIP–uh–tayt). To precipitate means to cause a solid substance to separate from a solution. Some of the calcium phosphate in milk also precipitates with the protein. The solids, which settle on the bottom of the container in which the milk is being heated, scorch easily in high temperatures. To prevent scorching, milk must be heated either over low heat or in a double boiler.

When milk is heated in an open container, a skin forms on the surface. This is due to the concentration of casein as the water surrounding it evaporates. If this skin is removed, milk solids are likewise removed.

The skin tends to hold in steam, making it more likely that the milk will boil over. A foam on the surface of hot milk minimizes the formation of a skin. This is the reason hot chocolate is often whipped to produce a foam. Serving hot chocolate with a marshmallow or whipped cream on it also helps prevent the formation of a skin.

Finally, heating milk can cause it to curdle. Curdling generally occurs only at high temperatures when other factors that affect milk are also present. High levels of salt in hot milk, a low pH, or the presence of certain enzymes can cause curdling. For example, fresh pineapple contains an enzyme called bromelin, which causes milk to clot or curdle. Adding sodium bicarbonate (baking soda) to the milk can prevent curdling by raising the pH.

In general, it is best to use fresh milk, low temperatures, and nonacid foods when cooking with milk. This will prevent curdling in foods such as custards or cream soups.

To precipitate means to cause a solid substance to separate from a solution.

As water evaporates, the concentration of casein on the top of heated milk causes a skin to form.

FERMENTED MILK PRODUCTS

The fact that raw milk will ferment and curdle if not consumed almost immediately has been known for thousands of years. While fermented milk has a sour taste, it can be stored without spoiling for longer periods of time than milk itself. As a result, people all around the world have developed a taste for fermented milk products. Each region uses a unique system for preparing such products.

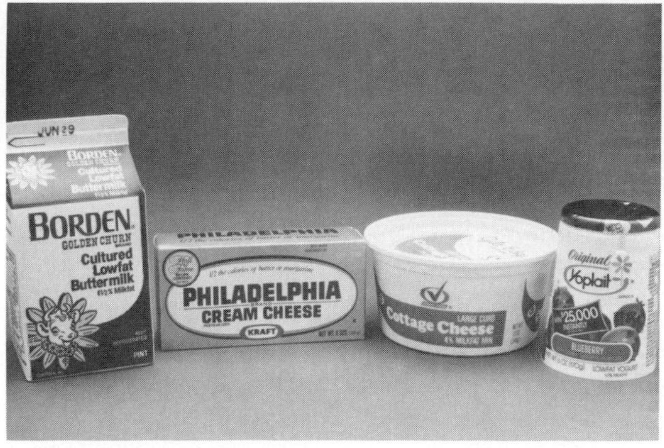

Fermented milk products can be stored longer than milk itself.

• MAKING FERMENTED MILK PRODUCTS

As discussed in the last chapter, lactic acid bacteria cause milk to sour. However, the low pH of the sour milk inhibits the growth of other bacteria. If allowed to grow, the other bacteria could cause the milk to spoil as well as cause disease in those who consume it.

Today, fermented milk products are commercially made. Cultured milk is the term used for any milk product fermented to produce a desired flavor or texture. The fermentation is caused by a **culture,** also known as a **starter.** This is a controlled bacterial population that is added to milk. It produces acid and flavors that are characteristic of a specific fermented milk product. The starter bacteria used in fermented milk products also inhibit the growth of common bacteria that cause disease.

In preparing a cultured milk product, the producer first selects and prepares the specific starter culture. Generally, the milk is pasteurized. The starter is added to the milk, a step known as **inoculation.** Then time is allowed for the bacteria to grow and ferment the milk. This is known as the **incubation period.** The product is sometimes agitated. Finally, it is cooled to stop or slow down the bacterial growth.

Commercially fermented milk products are made with a culture to produce their characteristic flavors.

• TYPES OF CULTURED MILK PRODUCTS

There are a number of cultured milk products sold in stores today. Buttermilk, yogurt, cream cheese, and other cheeses are popular.

Originally, buttermilk was the fluid left over during the production of butter. After the butter was formed and removed from milk, what was left was buttermilk. It was a popular beverage on farms. Today, buttermilk is a cultured product prepared from skim or low–fat milk. Buttermilk is also sold in a dry form, similar to dried milk, for use in baking.

Another cultured milk product is sour cream. This popular product is used alone or in dips. It contains fewer calories and fats than mayonnaise or salad oils.

Sour cream is often used in dips for vegetables and chips.

Yogurt is an eastern European food, which has become popular in the United States. It can have the thickness of a beverage or a gel. Yogurt, which is made from a milk base, contains lactose, lactic acid, B vitamins, and high concentrations of protein. Yogurt is usually low in calories.

Making Yogurt

Yogurt is prepared by adding a bacterial culture to milk that has been heated. Heating the milk not only kills unwanted bacteria but also denatures the whey proteins. Denaturation increases the capacity of the proteins to bind water and promote the growth of the fermenting bacteria.

The bacteria used in the preparation of yogurt must be incubated between 41°– 45°C. An eight–hour incubation period seems to produce yogurt with the smoothest gel. Commercial yogurt makers often add gelatin or a vegetable gum to guarantee a firm final product. The body or firmness of yogurt can also be increased by adding additional milk solids. Flavoring material such as fruit is also often added.

Cheeses are prepared by coagulating the casein protein found in milk. There are many variables that affect the final cheese product. These variables include:

- The types and number of microorganisms present.
- The types and quantities of enzymes present.
- The degree of souring.
- The incubation temperature.
- How much of the liquid is drained from the final product.
- The conditions for storing the cheese while it ripens, or ages.

Ripening plays a major role in producing cheese. The cheese is held in a temperature– and humidity–controlled environment for at least 60 days while ripening. The chemical reactions that occur during ripening change the flavor, texture, and appearance of the cheese.

There are four main categories of ripened cheese. These include:

- Very hard cheeses, such as Parmesan and Romano.
- Hard cheeses, such as Cheddar, colby, and provolone.
- Semisoft cheeses, such as Muenster, Roquefort, and Stilton.
- Soft cheeses, such as Brie, Camembert, and mozzarella.

Unripened cheeses, such as cottage and cream cheese, are eaten fresh within a few weeks. These cheeses tend to be higher in moisture and lower in fat than other cheeses.

Cheese is a popular food throughout the world.

EXPERIMENT 16–1

Making Yogurt

Yogurt is a cultured milk product made by the fermentation of lactic acid bacteria. The milk is first heated to kill any undesirable bacteria that may be present and to denature the milk protein. This results in a firmer, more custardlike body and texture in the finished product. Then lactic acid bacteria are inoculated into the milk, and the milk is incubated. This experiment allows you to observe the changes caused by lactic acid bacteria while making yogurt.

PROCEDURE

1. Obtain the yogurt base (milk) from your instructor. There will be three different yogurt bases used in this experiment.
2. Heat the yogurt base in a saucepan or double boiler to 82°C. Maintain this temperature for 15–20 minutes.
3. Cool the heated yogurt base to 43°C.
4. Use the yogurt–making equipment as instructed by your teacher.
5. Add 30 mL yogurt starter culture to the 43°C yogurt base. Mix with a gentle stirring motion to minimize the addition of air.
6. Fill yogurt containers and cover.
7. Put filled containers in either a yogurt maker or setting pans. Maintain the temperature at 43°C.
8. Check the temperature frequently. Do not exceed 46°C. Temperatures of 46°C and above will kill the culture.
9. When the milk has coagulated and formed a firm gel, remove the yogurt containers and cool them immediately by setting them in ice or putting them in the refrigerator.
10. Save an unopened container in the refrigerator to use as a starter.
11. Measure the pH of a sample of each yogurt base and record in your data table.
12. Test taste a sample of each yogurt base for color, texture, and taste. Record your observations in your data table.

EXPERIMENT 16–1

QUESTIONS

1. If there were differences in color among the samples, which looked the most appetizing?
2. Were there any differences in texture among the samples?
3. Which, if any, of the samples had an unpleasant aftertaste?
4. Which sample was the most acidic?
5. Is there any correlation between the level of acidity and aftertaste?
6. All factors considered, which base produced the best yogurt?
7. Which do you prefer, the best homemade yogurt or the commercial yogurt? Why?

SAMPLE DATA TABLE

Yogurt Base	pH	Color	Texture	Taste/Aftertaste

EXPERIMENT 16–2

Evaluation of Commercial Yogurts

There are a number of important factors in judging the quality of yogurt. First, yogurt should have a smooth, uniform texture. There should not be any graininess, lumpiness, or liquid whey present. Good yogurt should not have an unpleasant aftertaste. In this experiment, you will evaluate the quality of commercially prepared yogurt.

PROCEDURE

1. Evaluate the yogurt samples provided by your teacher on the basis of color, texture, and taste. Record your observations in your data table.

2. After you have finished the taste test, obtain the brand and unit cost information for each sample and record in your data table.

QUESTIONS

1. Which yogurt sample did you think had the best appearance?
2. Which yogurt sample tasted the best to you? Why?
3. Did the brand of yogurt with the highest unit cost seem worth the additional money? Why or why not?
4. After reading the labels on the containers:
   a. List the yogurts that contained live bacteria.
   b. List those that did not contain live bacteria.
   c. List the yogurts that had added coloring.
   d. List the information given on the container of yogurt you liked best.
   e. Did all brands of yogurt contain the same number of calories per serving? Which brand was the highest? Which was the lowest?

SAMPLE DATA TABLE

Sample	Color	Texture	Taste	Unit Cost	Brand

TO SUM UP

- Milk and milk products are sources of protein, fat, carbohydrate, vitamins, and minerals.
- Milk is a complex product that has substances in solution, in colloidal dispersions, and in emulsions.
- Lactose intolerance results from the absence of lactase in the intestine to digest the lactose in milk.
- Milk is pasteurized, homogenized, and fortified during processing.
- Fresh fluid milk products are classified according to fat content.
- The ability of cream to form a foam depends on the fat content of the cream, the temperature, the amount of cream, and the point at which sugar is added.
- Heat denatures and coagulates the protein in milk and can cause the milk to curdle.
- Fermented milk products are commercially made from pasteurized milk inoculated with specific starter cultures, which produce the desired flavor or texture.

CHECK YOUR FACTS

1. What are the two main milk proteins?
2. What gives milk its white color?
3. Which type of milk protein can be curdled by acid?
4. How is creaming eliminated?
5. Name the functions of lactose in milk.
6. List the main vitamins found in milk.
7. What is the phosphatase test used for?
8. What does the label UHT on milk indicate?
9. Why shouldn't milk be left out of the refrigerator for long periods of time?
10. What is the difference between skim milk, whole milk, and coffee cream?
11. What is the difference between condensed milk and evaporated milk?
12. When should sugar be added to whipped cream?
13. List the steps in making a cultured milk product.
14. How are ripened and unripened cheeses similar and different? List two examples of each.

CRITICAL THINKING AND PROBLEM SOLVING

1. Explain how milk can be a solution, a colloidal dispersion, and an emulsion.
2. Should milk be avoided in a low–fat, low–cholesterol diet? Why or why not?
3. Some drug stores sell a product containing lactase. Who might buy this product and why?
4. Look up the nursery rhyme about "Little Miss Muffett." What was she eating? How was it made?
5. Describe what happens to milk when it is pasteurized, homogenized, and fortified.
6. Why shouldn't a family store its milk in a glass pitcher, which will look attractive when set on the table during meals?
7. Why does whipped cream liquify when left standing too long?
8. How is the nutritional value of hot chocolate affected when the skin that forms on top is removed?
9. Why is it important to heat milk before making yogurt?
10. Which milk products have the longest shelf life? Why?

4

The Science of Food Processing

The science of processing food has developed as a result of the complex nature of food combined with the ever–increasing distances between where food is produced and where it may be consumed. Unit 4 presents information on maintaining the quality of food.

Food safety, the topic of Chapter 17, is of ultimate importance in both processing and preparing food. As you read this chapter, you will learn about the causes and means of preventing the main types of food poisoning. This chapter also contains information on the government agencies that assist in maintaining food safety.

In Chapter 18, you will examine one of the oldest known methods of processing food—dehydration. You will learn why this is a popular method of preserving food and how food must be prepared prior to dehydration. You will become familiar with several methods of dehydration and how each influences the quality of the end product.

Chapter 19 explores home and commercial canning. You will learn about the equipment needed for home canning, as well as how to use it to prepare and process food. You will also discover how food is canned commercially.

You will get a glimpse of some of the newest methods of food processing and preservation in Chapter 20. In this chapter, you will find information about freezing, freeze drying, and irradiation. You will discover how the food industry controls the composition of the gases inside packages. This extends the time packaged food maintains its quality.

Unit 4 concludes with a chapter on food additives. In Chapter 21, you will learn what additives are, as well as how they are used in foods. Additives make the wide variety of foods available today possible. This chapter will help you understand the information on food labels, so you can decide whether or not you want to consume a given food.

CHAPTERS

CHAPTER

17

Food Safety

This chapter will help you . . .

- Name and describe the properties of the microorganisms that cause food spoilage.
- Differentiate between food intoxication and food infection.
- List specific organisms that can cause foodborne illness.
- Discuss sanitary and food–handling practices that can help prevent food poisoning.
- Identify United States government agencies that keep the food supply safe.
- Describe information required on a food label.

Terms to Remember

additives
adulterated
cross contamination
food infection
food intoxication
foodborne illnesses
GRAS list
parasites
pathogenic
pesticides
residue
spores

For people to be well nourished and healthy, the food they eat must be safe and of good quality. Unless steps are taken to preserve fresh or raw food, it will undergo chemical and physical changes. Such changes will make the food unappetizing and possibly even dangerous to eat.

MICROORGANISMS AND FOOD SPOILAGE

Various types of microorganisms are involved in food spoilage. You have learned that the main causes of spoiled food are mold, yeast, bacteria, and enzymes.

One microorganism that grows on food samples is mold, which gives the food a fuzzy appearance. Mold is aerobic, meaning it requires air to survive. It can grow well in pH environments from 2–8.5. Mold grows best in moist environments at moderate temperatures ranging from room temperature, which is 20°C, to 35°C. Some mold can grow, though more slowly, at temperatures as low as 0°C.

Yeast are one–celled plants. Like mold, most yeast are aerobic, although the yeast involved in fermentation can grow without air. Yeast requires a moist environment and grows well only at a pH range of 4–6.5. It grows best at temperatures between 20°–38°C. The growth of yeast can be inhibited by low temperatures or by sugar levels of 65 percent or more. Yeast can form **spores**, which are microorganisms in a dormant, inactive, or resting state. Yeast spores are destroyed at temperatures of 100°C.

Bacteria are single–cell organisms found in air, soil, water, and food. They can grow in both aerobic and anaerobic environments depending on the specific bacteria. This means that certain bacteria can flourish even in sealed containers. Like yeast, bacteria grow within a fairly limited pH range of 4.5–7. They do best at temperatures ranging from 20°–50°C and require moist environments. Most bacteria are destroyed in boiling water. However, some bacteria are more resistant to heat, so very high temperatures are needed for their complete destruction.

Enzymes can also cause food spoilage. You learned about the effects of enzymatic action on food in Chapter 12.

Mold gives food a fuzzy appearance.

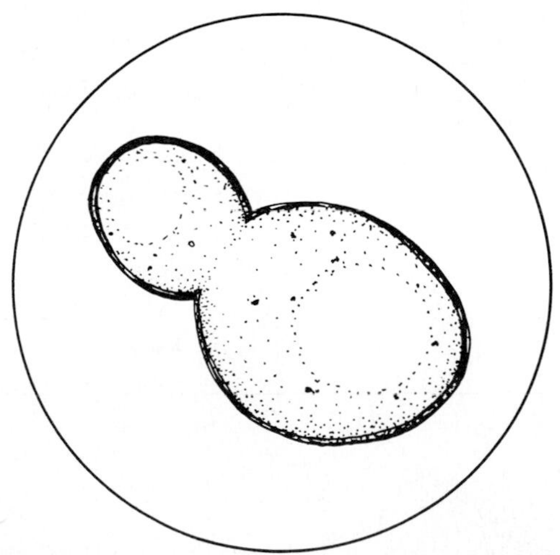

Yeast plants can go into a dormant, inactive state by forming spores.

Only bacteria that grow under anaerobic conditions can grow in these sealed cans.

The nutritional value of this overripe food declines as the food deteriorates.

Food processing and preservation can help prevent the growth of microorganisms that cause spoilage in food. You will learn more about these topics in the other chapters in this unit.

TYPES OF FOOD POISONING

The microorganisms described above cause undesirable changes in food quality. Sometimes they also cause illnesses known as food poisoning. Food poisoning is the everyday term used to describe a wide variety of **foodborne illnesses.** These are illnesses caused by eating food contaminated by:

- Toxic chemicals.
- Toxins produced by microorganisms.
- **Pathogenic** (path–uh–JEN–ik) (disease–carrying) microorganisms.
- Animal **parasites** or their eggs. A parasite is an organism that grows and feeds on another organism.

Food poisoning produces a variety of symptoms. These can range from mild indigestion caused by food left out too long at a picnic to serious problems caused by improper food processing.

● FOOD INTOXICATION

One type of foodborne illness is **food intoxication.** This is caused by toxins present in the food. These toxins can be either chemical or bacterial.

Most chemical toxins in food are there because of accidental contamination. For example, some toxic chemicals used by farmers in growing food may remain on or in the food during processing. On the other hand, some chemicals added on purpose may be toxic in some circumstances. Monosodium glutamate, a flavor enhancer, can cause allergic reactions in some people.

NUTRITION AND YOU

Declining Nutritional Value

Spoiled or deteriorating food can be unsafe to eat. In addition, such food is not a good source of nutrients, since the nutrient value of food declines over time.

Fruits and vegetables that have been taken from a garden or picked from a tree at their prime have the highest nutritional value possible. As time passes, nutritional value steadily decreases. This is due to the natural breakdown that takes place in living matter once it has been harvested.

All food deteriorates from the time it is harvested, slaughtered, or manufactured. The rate at which food deteriorates and eventually becomes inedible varies greatly. For example, crackers last a long time if properly packaged, while fresh strawberries spoil in a few days. The causes of deterioration can include light, high or low temperature, enzymes, radiation, dry air, microorganisms, industrial contaminants, insects, parasites, rodents, and the oxygen in air.

Storing food at the right temperature is critical in maintaining food safety and nutritional value. Many foods, such as meat, milk, and leafy vegetables, will be unfit for human consumption if stored at room temperature for more than two days. Indeed, perishable cooked food becomes unsafe if left at room temperature more than two or three hours.

Sometimes frozen food may be higher in nutritional value than fresh food. If the frozen food was processed immediately after harvesting, its nutritional value would be high. Fresh food in the produce section of a grocery store may have spent time at room temperature during transportation and handling. Therefore the fresh food has had more chances to decline in quality and nutritional value.

Toxins can be produced by a variety of bacteria. There are about 20 bacteria that can cause foodborne illness, although not all of these produce toxins. Three toxin–producing bacteria that can cause food intoxication are *Clostridium perfringens* (klahs–TRID–ee–um pur–FRIN–jens), *Staphylococcus aureus* (STAF–uh–lo–kahk–us OR–ee–us), and *Clostridium botulinum*.

Food taken on a picnic needs to be stored safely to prevent food poisoning.

Clostridium Perfringens

Clostridium perfringens is a foodborne bacteria that can cause illness. This organism is always present to some extent in the intestinal tract, but it does not grow there. To cause illness, large numbers of these bacteria must be ingested. Once in the body, C. *perfringens* produces toxin and spores. It is the toxin, rather than the bacteria itself, that causes the illness. The toxin can be produced by C. *perfringens* only in the body, so it has never been found in food.

Since C. *perfringens* is present almost everywhere, it is difficult to keep out of the food supply. This problem is compounded because the bacteria produce heat–resistant spores. Therefore steps must be taken to be sure that cooked food is kept very hot (60°C) or is refrigerated promptly so that the C. *perfringens* cannot grow.

C. *perfringens* is anaerobic; that is, it grows without air. Foods where C. *perfringens* grows well include turkey, meat gravy, dressing, stews, and casseroles. These are foods that are cooked and then often held at temperatures below 52°C.

It has also been found that C. *perfringens* can grow rapidly at the temperatures used in low–temperature, long–time cooking, such as that done in a slow cooker. This method of food preparation can result in a food that contains large numbers of C. *perfringens*. When the food is eaten, the bacteria release their toxin and an outbreak of C. *perfringens* food poisoning occurs.

Pesticides and Food

The United States Food and Drug Administration (FDA) works with both the United States Department of Agriculture (USDA) and the Environmental Protection Agency (EPA) in setting levels of **pesticides** that can be used on crops. Pesticides are chemicals that are used to kill insects and rodents. Some of these pesticides leave a **residue** on the crop. A residue is the matter remaining after a chemical or physical process. Many pesticide residues, also called residuals, are toxic to humans.

Once food is harvested, the FDA checks it to be certain that the set levels of residues have not been exceeded. Obviously there are so many food products and food producers that the FDA cannot check every food sample. However, by doing spot checks, the FDA works to keep pesticide residuals to a minimum.

Governmental agencies control the use of pesticides by farmers to help keep the food supply safe.

C. *perfringens* produces toxins that cause illness.

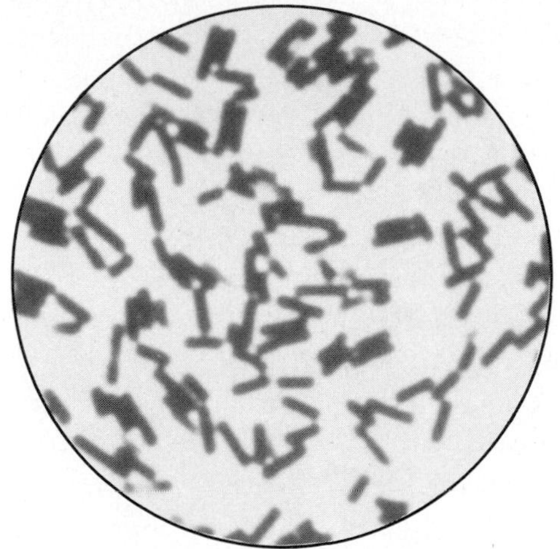

Outbreaks of food poisoning caused by C. *perfringens* usually involve large numbers of people. In fact, C. *perfringens* is a problem of the food service industry because most outbreaks involve mass-feeding operations.

Symptoms of this illness include stomach cramps, diarrhea, and occasional nausea. The symptoms generally appear 4–22 hours after eating and may last one to five days. Rarely does anyone die from this type of foodborne illness. In fact, most cases of this illness are never reported or are misdiagnosed as stomach flu or a virus.

C. *perfringens* grows well in roast turkey that is held at room temperature.

Staphylococcus Aureus

Staphylococcus aureus, better known as staph organisms, are bacteria found in the body's nasal passages and on the skin. These organisms can be spread in the air in drops of moisture during breathing, talking, sneezing, and coughing. Staph organisms usually enter food from a human or animal source.

Like *Clostridium perfringens,* staph bacteria do not actually cause an infection. Instead, they produce a toxin that causes illness. Staph bacteria grow best in moist meat dishes and starchy foods. Sliced roast beef or ham that is stored unsafely can become incubators for the bacteria, allowing them to grow and produce toxin. The prevention of foodborne staph poisoning is achieved by keeping perishable food cold (below 4°C) or hot (above 60°C).

The symptoms of the food poisoning caused by the staph toxin tend to occur sooner and to be more acute than the other types. Diarrhea, vomiting, and stomach cramps may appear within 1–7 hours after eating and may last for 24–48 hours.

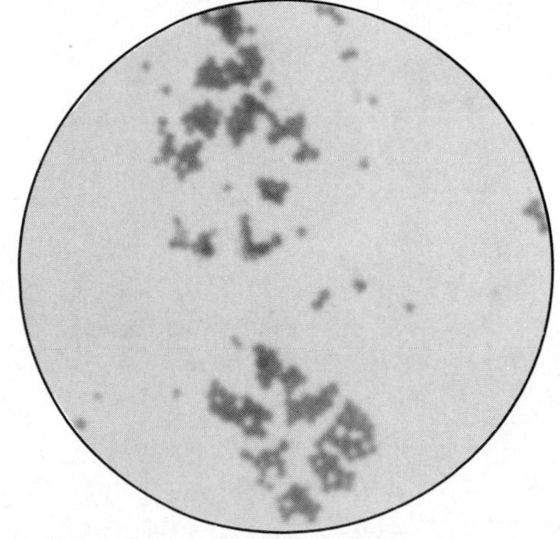

Staphylococcus aureus is found on the skin and in the nasal passages.

Clostridium botulinum most often grow in improperly home–canned food.

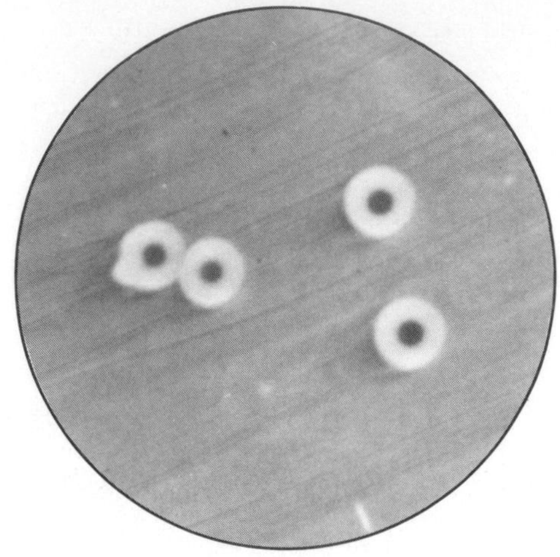

Salmonella bacteria are found in raw food, such as meat and fish.

Clostridium Botulinum

Clostridium botulinum is a well–known bacteria that produces toxin. As discussed in Chapter 5, botulism is the most serious form of food poisoning. This foodborne intoxication, which can be fatal, is caused by the toxin produced by *Clostridium botulinum*. These bacteria most often grow in improperly home canned food.

• FOOD INFECTION

Another type of foodborne illness is **food infection.** This occurs when pathogenic organisms enter the body with the food eaten. These organisms may be present in the food but not actually growing there. However, once they enter the body, they can grow and cause illness.

Salmonella

Salmonellosis (sal–muh–nel–OH–sis) is the most common food infection. It is caused by the *Salmonella* (sal–muh–NEL–uh) bacteria. They are found in raw food, such as poultry, meat and meat products, fish and shellfish, and cracked eggs. *Salmonella* are killed when heated to a temperature of 71°C. However, the bacteria survive if food is eaten raw or is undercooked.

Generally, *Salmonella* must be present in large numbers to cause illness. Since the bacteria grow best at room temperature, *Salmonella* infection most often occurs when food is allowed to sit unrefrigerated.

Problems can occur because of **cross contamination.** This happens when bacteria are transferred from one food to another. For example, *Salmonella* can be transported from one food to another by flies, roaches, or rats. In addition, during food preparation, hands, utensils, or work surfaces can transfer the bacteria to foods that are ready to eat.

Once food containing the *Salmonella* has been eaten, it takes from 5–72 hours for symptoms to appear. The time involved depends on the quantity of food ingested and the rate of digestion of the food. Symptoms of *Salmonella* poisoning include nausea, vomiting, abdominal pain, and diarrhea. Some people also experience headaches, fever, drowsiness, muscle weakness, and chills.

Animal Parasites

Another cause of food infection can be animal parasites or their eggs. Raw pork contains a parasite called *Trichinella spiralis* (trih–kuh–NEL–uh spuh–RAL–is). It is a tiny worm that lives in pork muscle. If infected pork is eaten, the parasite grows in the intestine and causes illness. Mild infection may involve diarrhea, fever, fatigue, and muscle pain. Heart and brain damage leading to death can occur in severe infections. T. *spiralis* is killed if pork products are cooked to an internal temperature of 77°C so there is no trace of pink left in the meat.

Flies can cross contaminate food by transporting bacteria from one food to another.

Trichinella Spiralis

Trichinella spiralis, found in raw pork, is killed if the meat is cooked to an internal temperature of 77°C.

PREVENTING FOOD POISONING

The most common cause of food poisoning is negligence. If food is properly prepared, handled in a sanitary manner, and stored safely, most types of food poisoning can be avoided.

Most food poisoning is caused by bacteria that are literally everywhere in the environment. These bacteria and the toxins they produce cannot be seen, smelled, or tasted while you are eating a contaminated food. It is only later, when symptoms appear, that you realize something was wrong with the food. Therefore it is crucial to do all you can to keep food poisoning from occurring.

• FOOD HANDLING

Once heated, food should be eaten while hot. Food to be served hot should be kept above 60°C until served. Food not eaten hot should be chilled rapidly and refrigerated at 7°C or below.

It is important to remember that refrigeration does not kill bacteria. It simply keeps

To be safe, hot food should be served hot.

them inactive so they do not multiply. If a food sample is allowed to sit at room temperature for a period of time, bacteria will multiply. These bacteria will remain in the food when it is put in the refrigerator. The food will be just as likely to cause illness when it is finally eaten as it would have if eaten before being refrigerated. This means hot food should not be permitted to cool slowly to room temperature before being refrigerated. Cooked food is more frequently the cause of foodborne illness than raw food because of improper refrigeration.

Good food–handling practices will prevent most kinds of food poisoning. In addition, such practices will minimize food spoilage caused by the growth of other types of microorganisms.

Sanitary Practices

People who handle food must keep themselves and the area in which they work clean. Good sanitary practices can help prevent food poisoning.

It is crucial that people wash their hands with hot soapy water before and after touching food. In class, you should always wash your hands before doing any laboratory work involving food. After washing your hands, it is important not to recontaminate them by touching your hair or blowing your nose. If this should happen, or if you should handle raw food or an object unrelated to food, you should wash your hands again.

Food should be placed only in clean containers and manipulated with clean utensils. If something falls to the floor, be sure to wash it before continuing its use. Never put a tasting spoon back in a sample of food.

Be sure to use soap and water to wash all surfaces before and after using them. This is particularly important with cutting boards. It is recommended that cutting boards be sterilized with hot soapy water containing one part chlorine bleach to eight parts water. This is especially important after using a cutting board to cut raw meat, fish, or poultry. Sterilization will ensure that most microorganisms have been killed. Surfaces treated in this way should be rinsed with clear water before being used.

It is also important when handling raw meat that you not allow the liquid that has dripped from the meat to drip on other food. This liquid could contaminate the food. Never place cooked meat on the same tray that was used for the raw meat unless the tray has been washed.

Food poisoning can be prevented by good sanitary practices.

Hot food should not be left out to cool slowly to room temperature but should be refrigerated promptly.

• CHEMICAL CONTAMINATION

Contamination of food with harmful chemicals occurs rarely and usually is an accident. In the kitchen or the processing plant, it is important to store disinfectants and pesticides in a separate area, away from all food. Containers that have held food should never be used to store cleaning powders or pesticides. Someone could accidentally eat or drink these compounds thinking they were food.

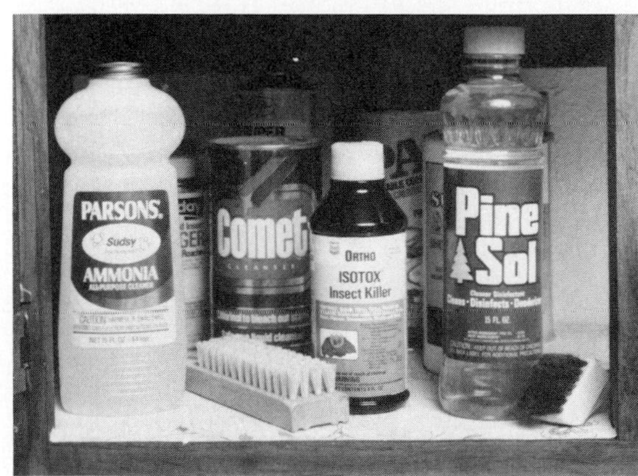

Always store poisonous substances in properly marked containers.

THE GOVERNMENT AND FOOD SAFETY

In the United States, the federal government is responsible for the safety of the food supply. The United States Department of Agriculture (USDA) monitors meat and poultry products. The Food and Drug Administration (FDA) monitors the food supply in general. The FDA, which is a part of the Department of Health and Human Services, assures consumers that the food they buy is safe to eat, nutritious, and honestly represented.

• FOOD PROCESSING

The FDA oversees food processing and establishes guidelines and regulations. These are

The USDA inspects meat and poultry products to be sure they are safe to eat.

The FDA is responsible for seeing that commercially processed food is safe to eat.

designed to prevent outbreaks of food poisoning, especially in commercial settings.

When the FDA says that food is safe, it means the food is free from any hazards. One of the main hazards is foodborne disease. The FDA closely monitors food processing to ensure that commercially processed food has been safely processed.

The FDA also tests for the presence of environmental contaminants. These can be toxic metals, such as mercury and lead, or other industrial chemicals. At one time, for example, swordfish were removed from the market nationwide because unacceptable amounts of mercury were found in samples of these fish. Once the mercury levels dropped, the FDA allowed swordfish to again be marketed. The mercury content of these fish continues to be carefully monitored.

International Agencies

The United Nations has established two organizations concerned with food control on an international level. These are the Food and Agricultural Organization (FAO) and the World Health Organization (WHO). These organizations are not primarily enforcement agencies but exist to identify problems and make recommendations to maintain food wholesomeness throughout the world.

The FAO was formed in 1944 with two main objectives—eliminating hunger and improving nutrition. The hope was that this organization could accomplish these goals throughout the world.

WHO was founded in 1948. The primary purpose of WHO is to foster cooperation among nations in all areas related to health. WHO spends a large part of its budget on solving international problems related to nutrition. WHO works closely with the FAO to promote nutrition research worldwide. FAO and WHO produce joint reports that recommend and encourage research into the nutritional requirements of people throughout the world.

WHO publishes the magazine *World Health* ten times a year in English, French, Portuguese, Russian, and Spanish. *World Health* features articles with colorful photographs and illustrations which highlight current global health issues.

The quality of food sold in any given country is controlled by that country itself. In some underdeveloped nations, the quality of the food is not as much of a concern as the quantity available. Many international agencies help with the distribution of food to areas that have undernourished populations. Many privately funded foundations are also working to eliminate world hunger.

• ADDITIVES

Another area of responsibility for the FDA is food **additives.** An additive is a substance added in small amounts to something else to improve, strengthen, or alter it. Additives will be considered in detail in Chapter 21.

Virtually anything can be considered an additive. Therefore the FDA has compiled a list of over 600 ingredients considered safe and not designated as additives. These substances appear on the **GRAS list.** GRAS stands for Generally Recognized As Safe. Examples of substances on the GRAS list are sugar, table salt, and cinnamon. While never tested, these substances are generally recognized as safe to eat.

• FOOD LABELING

The FDA also monitors the labeling of food. In the late 1800s, many foods were **adulterated** (uh–DULL–tuh–ray–tud). This means they were made impure by the addition of improper ingredients. Since there were no laws regulating labeling, consumers did not know whether they were buying pure or adulterated food.

The Wiley Food and Drug Act of 1906 was passed to regulate food processed in the United States. It was replaced in 1938 with the Federal Food, Drug, and Cosmetic Act. This law specifies what a label is: "a display of written, printed, or graphic matter upon the immediate container."

The law requires that all ingredients, including water, be listed on the label in order of quantity. Any product that makes nutritional claims must provide information on the label regarding serving size, servings per container, calories, protein, carbohydrate, and fat content. In addition, the U.S. RDA for up to 12 vitamins and minerals must appear.

In July 1986, sodium labeling became mandatory on food labels because many people are on diets that restrict sodium intake. The laws regarding food and labeling are constantly being evaluated and changed when the FDA decides this is necessary.

Sodium labeling on food helps people who must limit their sodium intake for health reasons.

Federal laws regulate the information that can or must appear on a food label.

EXPERIMENT 17–1

Growing Cultures

Although single microorganisms are not visible, colonies of microorganisms, called cultures, can be seen. Cultures are grown in the laboratory on a gelatinlike substance called nutrient agar (AY–gar), which is made to promote bacterial growth. In this experiment, you will have the chance to discover just how widespread microorganisms really are.

PROCEDURE

1. On the bottom of a Petri dish containing nutrient agar, use a felt–tip pen to draw two intersecting lines that divide the dish into quarters. Number the quarters 1–4.
2. Using the procedure outlined in steps 3–7 below, test the three surfaces in the group assigned to you by your teacher.

Group 1	**Group 2**
your shoulder	your hair
sink bottom	clean dish
cutting board	countertop

Group 3	**Group 4**
refrigerator shelf	table top
washed finger tip	floor
unwashed finger tip	doorknob

3. Obtain a 10 cm strip of cellophane tape. Fold over about 2 cm of the tape to make a nonsticky end to hold.
4. Holding the tape at the folded end, put the sticky side on one of the three surfaces on your list. Pull the tape from the surface, and immediately place it on the agar surface on the number 1 quarter of the dish. Remove and discard the tape.
5. In your data table, record the source from which you took the sample and the number of the area in the dish in which you put it.
6. Repeat steps 3, 4, and 5 for each of the other two surfaces on your list, putting each sample in a new section of the dish.
7. As a control, obtain a fourth piece of tape and touch it to the agar without letting the end that touches the agar touch any other surface, including your fingers. Repeat step 5.
8. Incubate the Petri dish at room temperature for three or four days in the place designated by your teacher.
9. Observe the Petri dish daily. Describe in your data table and on the chalkboard any growths that have appeared on the agar.
10. In your data table, copy the information on the growths reported by the other groups.

EXPERIMENT 17–1

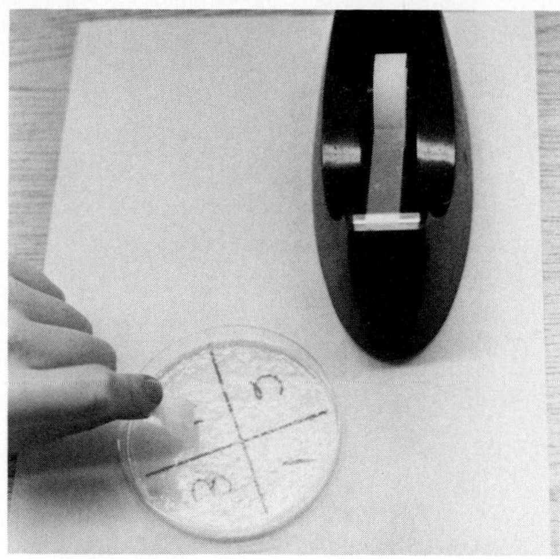

QUESTIONS

1. Was the tape itself free of microorganisms?
2. Were any of the surfaces tested free of microorganisms? Which ones?
3. Which surfaces produced the most bacterial growth? Why do you think this occurred?
4. How can you minimize the likelihood of food poisoning?

SAMPLE DATA TABLE

Surface Tested	Area Number	Agar Day 1	Agar Day 2	Agar Day 3

EXPERIMENT 17–2

Bacteria in Milk

When milk is produced by a healthy cow, it is a completely sterile fluid. However, during the milking process, it passes through ducts that are routinely contaminated with bacteria. Unless great care is taken, many types of bacteria will enter the milk during milking. If the milk is cooled immediately and kept cold, these bacteria will multiply very slowly. When milk is pasteurized, all forms of harmful bacteria are killed.

One way of testing for the presence of bacteria in milk is to add the indicator called methylene blue. This blue substance becomes colorless in the absence of oxygen. Since bacteria use up the oxygen present in milk, the rate at which the methylene blue loses its color is a measure of the number of bacteria present in the milk. In this experiment, you will compare the bacteria populations in fresh raw and pasteurized milk, as well as in samples that have been kept for one week or longer.

PROCEDURE

1. Label four test tubes 1–4. To the first, add 10 mL fresh raw milk; to the second, add 10 mL fresh pasteurized milk; to the third, add 10 mL week–old raw milk; and to the fourth, add 10 mL week-old pasteurized milk.
2. To each test tube, add 0.5 mL methylene blue solution. Stir each sample to mix the indicator throughout the milk. Be sure to thoroughly wash the stirring rod after stirring each sample to avoid cross contaminating the samples.
3. Incubate the test tubes in a beaker of water heated to 37°C. Maintain the water at this temperature throughout the experiment. Check the test tubes periodically during the next 24 hours. In your data table, record the time required to completely decolorize the indicator. Milk that loses its color in less than half an hour is badly contaminated. A sample that retains its color for more than 8 hours is of excellent quality.

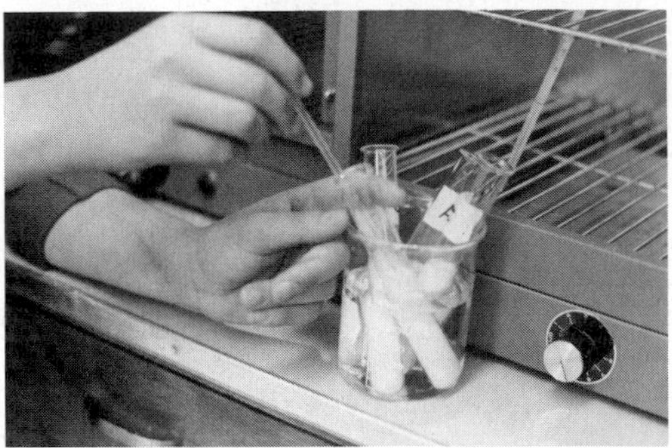

QUESTIONS

1. Which sample had the fewest bacteria present? The most?
2. What does this experiment indicate about the importance of pasteurization?
3. What steps can be taken to prevent growth of bacteria in milk for as long as possible?

SAMPLE DATA TABLE

Test Tube	Time Required to Decolorize Methylene Blue
1	
2	
3	
4	

TO SUM UP

- Mold, yeast, bacteria, and enzymes can cause physical and chemical changes in food, which make it unappetizing and possibly dangerous to eat.
- Foodborne illness can be caused by toxic chemicals, toxins produced by microorganisms, pathogenic microorganisms, and animal parasites or their eggs.
- *Clostridium perfringens, Staphylococcus aureus*, and *Clostridium botulinum* are bacteria that produce toxins that cause food intoxication.
- The major cause of food infection is the bacteria called *Salmonella*.
- Food poisoning can be prevented by proper sanitary and food–handling practices.
- The Food and Drug Administration is the federal agency responsible for monitoring the general food supply.
- The GRAS list includes over 600 ingredients generally recognized as safe in food.
- The information required on food labels is strictly regulated by law.

CHECK YOUR FACTS

1. Identify four types of organisms involved in food spoilage.
2. What are four causes of foodborne illness?
3. Name the two types of foodborne illness.
4. Name four bacteria that can cause foodborne illness.
5. When is food poisoning caused by C. *perfringens* most likely to occur?
6. How can food intoxication caused by staph bacteria be prevented?
7. What is the most serious form of bacterial food poisoning? Why?
8. Which bacteria is involved in food infections from raw or undercooked food?
9. How should cutting boards be treated before and after cutting raw meat?
10. How does the taste of food contaminated with bacteria compare with uncontaminated food?
11. What government agencies are primarily responsible for the safety of the food supply?
12. What is the GRAS list?
13. Why were laws passed regulating labels on food?

CRITICAL THINKING AND PROBLEM SOLVING

1. Why is cheese apt to develop mold cultures during refrigeration?
2. Are yeast or mold apt to spoil dried fruit? Why or why not?
3. Compare and contrast food intoxication and food infection.
4. Explain why scientists know that C. *perfringens* bacteria themselves do not cause food poisoning.
5. Give two examples of situations in which cross contamination could occur.
6. Describe how a dish of egg salad taken to a picnic should be handled to prevent any risk of food poisoning.
7. If a freezer containing bread, raw beef, berries, cooked beef stew, and raw ears of corn breaks down, which food should be dealt with first to prevent food poisoning? Why?
8. Suppose you were a food manufacturer thinking of developing a new granola bar. Of what use would the GRAS list be to you?
9. Evaluate the information on three food labels. Which do you think is the best label? Why?

CHAPTER

18

Dehydration

This chapter will help you . . .

- List the purposes of dehydration.
- Explain why food is pretreated before dehydrating.
- Compare and contrast sulfiting, sulfuring, and blanching.
- Describe the different types of blanching that can be used as pretreatment methods.
- Discuss why air temperature and movement play an important role in successful dehydration.
- Identify four methods of dehydration and explain how they are similar and different.
- Describe how dried food should be stored.

Terms to Remember

caseharden
dehydrator
dehydrofreezing
reconstitution
rehydration
steam blanching
sulfiting
sulfuring
syrup blanching

Various methods of food preservation are used to stop the action of microorganisms. As you learned in Chapter 15, fermentation is one method of preserving food. In fermentation, pH is lowered to control the growth of microorganisms and the activity of enzymes. Another method of food preservation that has been used for thousands of years is dehydration. Dehydration refers to any process that drives water out of food samples. It is also called drying. Although meat and fish can be preserved by drying, this chapter will discuss the dehydration of fruits and vegetables.

PURPOSES OF DEHYDRATION

There are three basic reasons for drying food. First, drying preserves the food so it can be kept longer without fear of spoilage. Dried apple slices have a longer shelf life than fresh apples. Second, drying decreases the weight and bulk of food, which makes it easy to transport. It costs less to ship a package of dried apricots than it does to ship the same number of fresh apricots. Third, food is dried for convenience. Instant coffee and the potato flakes used to make instant mashed potatoes take less time to prepare than regular coffee or fresh potatoes.

Dehydration in History

Dehydration has a long history of use as a method of food preservation. The ancient Greeks and Egyptians took dried food on their sea voyages. Dried wheat placed in tombs over 3000 years ago is still edible today.

Ancient civilizations used the sun for drying food, a method still used throughout the world. However, a number of mechanical methods of drying food have been developed over the years. The French first used a mechanical method of drying in 1795.

Large scale dehydrating was begun during World War I. It was used to preserve food for the armies involved in the fighting. Dried food is excellent for military purposes because it is lightweight, compact, and lasts for a fairly long time.

The ancient Egyptians dehydrated food for sea voyages and to put in the tombs of royalty.

PREPARATION FOR DEHYDRATION

When drying food, it is important to use unblemished fruits and vegetables that are not overripe. Otherwise, one piece of spoiled food can negatively affect an entire tray of drying food.

Most food is sliced into thin pieces to accelerate the drying process. Such slices have more surface area per unit of mass. This means moisture can escape more rapidly from a slice than it could from a larger piece. The moisture within the food has a shorter distance to travel to get to a surface.

Many convenience foods are dehydrated.

Sliced food dries faster than larger pieces of food.

Before food can actually be dried, it should be pretreated. Such pretreating reduces fat–soluble vitamin loss, flavor loss, enzymatic browning, and deterioration during storage.

Vegetables deteriorate more rapidly than fruit during storage because enzymes present in them continue to function. Pretreating most vegetables before drying will decrease the chances of spoilage and increase their quality and storage life.

There is less enzyme action in fruit because of its higher sugar content and acidity. In fact, some fruits do not need to be pretreated prior to drying. Grapes, figs, and plums are examples of such fruits.

• SULFITING

The enzymes present in most fruit can cause fairly rapid browning as oxygen in the air reacts with compounds in the fruit. One way to prevent browning in fruit and light–colored veg-

Grapes and plums are not usually pretreated before being dried to become raisins and prunes.

etables is **sulfiting.** This involves soaking food in a solution of water and sodium metabisulfite or sodium bisulfite. Mixing either of these compounds with water releases sulfur dioxide gas. The gas penetrates the surface of the food, slowing oxidation and enzymatic browning.

Since food can become mushy if soaked too long, sliced food should be soaked for only 10 minutes. Halves of fruit or large pieces of vegetable should soak for a maximum of 30 minutes. After soaking, the food should be drained thoroughly before drying. One disadvantage of sulfiting is that it extends drying times 15–20 percent because of the water the food absorbs during soaking.

Sulfiting fruit before drying helps prevent oxidation and enzymatic browning.

Rehydration

While dehydration refers to removing water from food, **rehydration** involves replacing the water that was previously removed. Rehydration is also called **reconstitution** (ree–kahn–stih–TOO–shun), which means restoring to a former condition by adding water.

Fruit that has been dried is often eaten in its dehydrated form. However, many recipes call for rehydration of dried fruit. There are two main methods for rehydrating fruit:

- Place the fruit in boiling water that has been removed from the heat. Soak the fruit for 5–10 minutes, drain, and pat dry with a paper towel.
- Place the fruit in a steamer over boiling water for 3–5 minutes. Pat the fruit dry with a paper towel.

Once the fruit has been rehydrated, it must be used fairly quickly or it will spoil. If the fruit is not used right away, it should be placed in the refrigerator.

Vegetables take longer to rehydrate than fruit because of the larger amounts of water lost during drying. Soaking vegetables for a long period of time makes them more tender than they would otherwise be. When rehydrating vegetables, it is best to soak them overnight.

Some recipes suggest that vegetables be soaked in boiling water, then placed in the refrigerator to soak in the water for several more hours. It is best not to soak vegetables for more than 2 hours at room temperature because bacteria can begin to grow in the mixture. Vegetables vary in how they should be rehydrated, so it is important to follow recipe instructions carefully when rehydrating vegetables.

Dried beans need to soak overnight before they are cooked.

• SULFURING

The method used by most commercial fruit dryers to prevent browning is **sulfuring**, another way of adding sulfur during dehydration. The process involves placing the food on large trays that are stacked together and covered. Fumes from burning sulfur, which contain sulfur dioxide gas, circulate around the food.

The sulfuring process usually takes from 1–4 hours. The sulfur dioxide fumes produced during this process should not be inhaled, since they are harmful to the lungs.

The amount of sulfur used is determined by the weight and type of food to be processed. For example, pears, peaches, and apples require twice the amount of sulfur per kilogram as the same quantity of apricots.

After sulfuring, food should be placed outside to sun dry or put in a dryer that is outside. This helps remove the harmful sulfur fumes.

Sulfuring is considered the best commercial pretreatment method because the food maintains its original shape and color and remains pliable. Vitamins A and C are not affected by this process. In addition, sulfuring not only prevents browning, but also shortens drying time, repels insects, and inhibits mold growth.

• BLANCHING

Many fruits and vegetables are blanched prior to drying. Blanching is used to stop enzyme activity, especially in vegetables. It shortens drying and rehydration time by relaxing the tissue walls so moisture can escape or reenter more rapidly. Blanched vegetables take less time to cook because they are already partially cooked. However, blanching is the harshest possible pretreatment for fruit, since it destroys the natural flavor and texture of the fruit, as well as vitamin C. While blanching is the least effective method of pretreating fruit for drying, it is used by people who prefer not to use sulfur dioxide.

The most common form of blanching is water blanching. The prepared food is placed in boiling water to denature enzymes. This checks the ripening process and prevents undesirable flavor changes. You used this process in Experiment 12–2 when you blanched vegetables.

Steam blanching, or steaming, involves placing the food in a perforated basket over boiling water so that the steam blanches the food. Steam blanching is generally preferable to water blanching before dehydrating vegetables. Blanching the vegetables in water adds more moisture to the food than steaming does. The added moisture increases drying time. Smaller quantities of water–soluble vitamins and minerals are lost during steaming than during water blanching.

A sweet fruit with a soft texture is produced by **syrup blanching.** In this process, cut fruit is soaked in a hot solution of sugar, corn syrup, and water. It is then drained and dried. The main disadvantage of this method is that sugar is added to already sweet fruit. Other problems are that the texture and natural flavor of the fruit tend to suffer and the heat of the solution reduces the amount of vitamin C in the fruit.

Steam blanching is preferable to water blanching vegetables before drying.

METHODS OF DEHYDRATION

All methods of dehydration heat food in some way so that moisture is driven off. This heat can be provided by the sun or some other source.

• SUN DRYING

Sun drying is the oldest method of drying food and is still popular today. Most commercially prepared dried fruit, such as peaches, apricots, raisins, and figs, are sun dried. The cost of sun drying is low, since large quantities of food can be dried at one time and the only equipment needed are drying trays. The sun's ultraviolet rays have a sterilizing effect, which inhibits the growth of microorganisms.

Sun drying requires many consecutive days during which the temperature is 29°C or higher with relatively low humidity. As with other drying methods, it is important to maintain good air circulation and ventilation.

A modern innovation added to this ancient drying method is the use of solar dryers. These devices concentrate the sun's warmth and protect the food from insects and pollution.

Dehydrators produce good–quality dried food.

• DEHYDRATORS

A popular and efficient way to dehydrate food at home is to use a **dehydrator.** A dehydrator is a small appliance that has drying trays where food can be placed for drying. Many dehydrators are constructed so the number of drying trays can be changed.

Dehydrators are equipped with thermostats, so they can be set for exactly the temperature needed. They maintain low temperatures and have a fan that circulates air

Sun drying, the oldest method of drying food, is used today in commercial fruit drying operations.

In commercial spray dryers, a liquid food is sprayed into the dryer where the hot air evaporates the liquid, leaving the dry food product.

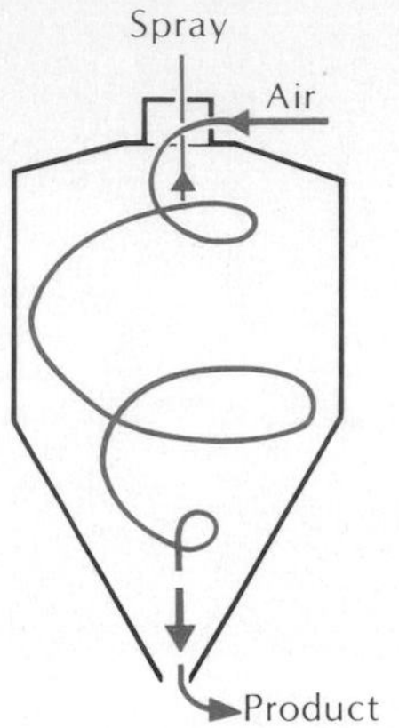

continually. They require very little monitoring, so food can be dried 24 hours a day in a sanitary and consistent environment. Generally, dehydrators produce the best quality home–dried food.

Commercial dehydrators function in the same manner as home dehydrators but are larger. There are several types of commercial dehydrators. The type of dryer used depends on the food being dried. Drum and vacuum driers are usually used to dry purees and liquids. Food cut into pieces is almost always dried in kiln or tunnel driers. Milk is dehydrated in a spray drying system. Commercial dryers can handle large volumes of food.

Air Temperature and Movement

In drying food, it is important to control air temperature to prevent spoilage. Drying temperatures are not high enough to kill bacteria. Instead, the drying process removes enough moisture from the food so that it is not as suitable an environment for bacteria growth. However, if food is dried too slowly, there is time for bacteria to grow, which can cause the food to spoil.

If a sample is dried at too high a temperature, it is possible to cook or **caseharden** the outside of the food. This means that a hard outer layer forms, which traps moisture in the food. This moisture can then support bacteria growth, again causing spoilage.

Good air circulation is also important in dehydration. The more rapid the air movement, the faster the moisture will be swept away from the food. The air must be from an outside source, so the moisture removed from the food is not recirculated. If this happens, the air will eventually become saturated, be unable to hold any more moisture, and the food will not dry. When food is commercially dried, the humidity of the air is closely monitored to ensure quality control.

Good air circulation around drying food promotes faster drying.

• ROOM AND OVEN DRYING

People wishing to dry food at home without a dehydrator may use room or oven drying. These methods have been used since pioneer days with varying degrees of success.

In room drying, food is set out and allowed to dry at room temperature. It is important to select a warm spot with good air circulation to prevent the growth of mold. Room drying is the least effective method of dehydrating food at home. The dried food produced is of low quality because it is nearly impossible to maintain constant conditions during the entire drying process.

Not all ovens can be set at a low enough temperature for oven drying food.

Water Content of Fresh Fruits and Vegetables

Fruit	Percentage of Water	Vegetable	Percentage of Water
Apple	84	Broccoli	89
Apricot	85	Carrot	88
Banana	65	Cabbage	92
Coconut	51	Celery	94
Blueberry	83	Cucumber	95
Cranberry	88	Mushroom	90
Peach	89	Onion	89
Papaya	89	Potato	80
Pineapple	86	Tomato	94
Strawberry	90	Zucchini	94

Which of these foods has the highest percentage of water? The lowest?

The dried fruit has a higher nutritional value per gram compared with the fresh and canned fruit.

Oven drying is popular with those who dehydrate small amounts of food at home. It takes longer than drying food in a dehydrator but is faster than sun drying. The food must be rotated because of the lack of good ventilation in the oven. Food dehydrated in an oven tends to be of a low quality.

Temperatures between 38°–60°C (100°–140°F) are best for oven drying. If the temperature rises above 63°C (145°F), more of the vitamins will be destroyed and case-hardening may occur. Some older ovens are not able to maintain such low temperatures, since 93°C (200°F) may be their lowest setting. This temperature is too high for dehydrating food.

Fruit that has been sulfured should never be oven dried because of the irritating fumes produced. These gases may even discolor the inside of the oven.

• DEHYDROFREEZING

Dehydrofreezing is a method used by the food processing industry to preserve food. It combines drying and freezing to preserve food by removing some of the moisture and then freezing the food.

Food treated by dehydrofreezing is as moist as commercially dried food but does not mold. The partially dried food occupies less than half as much space in a freezer as food that is simply frozen. Fruits and vegetables processed by dehydrofreezing have good flavor and color. They reconstitute in about half the time required for fully dried food.

DRIED FOOD

Whatever method of drying is used, it is important not to overdry food. Fresh food varies in moisture content. After drying, food should contain 15–20 percent of its original moisture. If more moisture is removed, the product loses color, flavor, nutrients, and texture quality. Most dried fruit should be chewy and leatherlike, while vegetables are often brittle or crisp.

Once food is dried to the correct moisture content, it should be sealed in glass jars, heavy plastic bags, or metal cans. This will prevent moisture in the air from reentering the food.

Dried food should never be stored uncovered in the refrigerator because of the moisture present. It generally will last the longest if kept dry and stored at room temperature. Dried food needs to be checked periodically for mold, and if any is present, the food should be discarded.

Dried food should be stored in sealed containers.

NUTRITION AND YOU

The Nutritional Value of Dried Food

Dried food is often called a nutritional powerhouse. This is because of its high nutritional value per gram. Eating dried food is a way of taking in vitamins and minerals in a very concentrated manner.

Some nutrients are lost during the drying process. For example, some of the vitamin A and vitamin C content is lost during drying, but more is lost during the pretreatment of the food. Blanching causes most of the vitamin and mineral loss from dried food. Sulfuring causes the least vitamin and mineral loss of the various pretreatment methods.

In general, foods lose more nutritional value during normal cooking than they do during dehydrating. Moreover, because drying is done at lower temperatures than canning, fewer vitamins are lost during drying than during canning.

The following table gives some examples of the nutritional content of various fresh, canned, and dried foods.

Peaches	**Fresh**		**Canned**		**Dried**	
Amount	2		250	mL	250	mL
Mass	200	g	244	g	160	g
Calcium	18	mg	10	mg	71	mg
Vitamin A	266	RE*	110	RE	624	RE
Riboflavin	0.1	mg	0.07	mg	0.3	mg
Niacin	2	mg	1.5	mg	8.5	mg
Vitamin C	14	mg	7	mg	29	mg
Apricots	**Fresh**		**Canned**		**Dried**	
Amount	3		250	mL	250	mL
Mass	107	g	258	g	130	g
Calcium	18	mg	28	mg	87	mg
Vitamin A	289	RE	449	RE	1417	RE
Riboflavin	0.04	mg	0.05	mg	0.21	mg
Niacin	0.6	mg	1	mg	4.3	mg
Vitamin C	11	mg	10	mg	16	mg
Grapes	**Fresh**		**Canned**		**Dried**	
Amount	30		250	mL	250	mL
Mass	150	g	150	g	145	g
Calcium	18	mg	12	mg	90	mg
Vitamin A	15	RE	10.5	RE	3	RE
Riboflavin	0.06	mg	.015	mg	0.12	mg
Niacin	0.6	mg	.30	mg	0.7	mg
Vitamin C	6	mg	3	mg	1	mg

*RE = Retinol Equivalent

EXPERIMENT 18–1

Dehydrating Fruits and Vegetables

In this experiment, you will test the moisture content of various fruits and vegetables by dehydrating them and determining their loss of mass. You will assume this loss of mass is due to a loss of water.

PROCEDURE

1. Wash, peel, and core the fruit or vegetable provided by your teacher. Pat dry with a paper towel.
2. Place the food on a cutting board and slice the food into 0.3 cm slices.
3. Take one slice of your fruit or vegetable and soak it for 5 minutes in the sodium bisulfite solution provided by your teacher. Remove the fruit slice and rinse it lightly under cold tap water. Place it on the rack or drying tray specified by your teacher for the sodium bisulfite samples.
4. Mass the remaining food, and record its mass in your data table.
5. Spread the food you have massed on your rack or drying tray.
6. Place your samples in the dehydrator, following the directions given by your teacher.
7. The next day, mass your dried food and record the mass in your data table.
8. Calculate the percent of the original sample that was water. This is the percent of the original mass lost during drying. It can be determined by using the following equation.

$$\text{Percent of original mass lost as water} = \frac{\text{fresh mass} - \text{dried mass}}{\text{fresh mass}} \times 100$$

9. Obtain your pretreated food slice and compare its appearance with that of the rest of your dried sample. Report your observations in your data table.
10. Write your figures, calculations, and observations on the chalkboard. In your data table, copy the information from the other food samples.
11. Place your dried food in a plastic bag and label with your name and class period.
12. Store the bag in the place designated by your teacher.

EXPERIMENT 18–1

QUESTIONS

1. What effect did the sodium bisulfite have on the fruit or vegetable slice?
2. Which fruit or vegetable lost the most water by mass?
3. Which fruit or vegetable lost the highest percent of water?
4. Which fruit or vegetable originally had the highest moisture content?
5. How did you determine the highest moisture content?
6. Do you think 100 percent of the water in the fresh sample was removed? Why or why not?

SAMPLE DATA TABLE

Food	Mass of Original Sample	Mass of Dried Sample	Mass Lost by Original Sample	Percent of Original Mass Lost as Water	Appearance of Pretreated Slice

EXPERIMENT 18–2

Reconstituting Fruits and Vegetables

Rehydration and reconstitution refer to returning water to dried food. In this experiment, you will reconstitute the fruit or vegetable sample you dehydrated in Experiment 18–1. You will see whether it will reabsorb all the water it originally lost.

PROCEDURE

1. Place your dehydrated vegetable or fruit in a 1000 mL beaker filled with water. Soak the food for 40 minutes. Drain, and pat the pieces dry with a paper towel.
2. In your data table for this experiment, enter the mass of the dried food sample from the data table of Experiment 18–1.
3. Mass the reconstituted samples. Record the reconstituted mass in your data table.
4. Calculate the amount of water reabsorbed by the reconstituted food. Record this value in your data table.
5. Calculate the percent of the reconstituted sample that is water. This is the same as the percent of the reconstituted mass gained during the soaking process. It can be calculated using the following equation.

$$\text{Percent of mass gained as water} = \frac{\text{reconstituted mass} - \text{dried mass} \times 100}{\text{reconstituted mass}}$$

6. Write your figures and calculations on the chalkboard. In your data table, copy the information from the other food samples.

SAMPLE DATA TABLE

Food	Mass of Dried Sample	Mass of Reconstituted Sample	Mass Gained by Reconstituted Sample	Percent of Reconstituted Mass Gained as Water

QUESTIONS

1. Which fruit or vegetable absorbed the most water by mass?
2. Which fruit or vegetable gained the highest percent of water?
3. Did any fruit or vegetable restore to the original mass?
4. Do you think soaking the food for a longer time would have changed the results? Why or why not?

TO SUM UP

- Dehydration is a preservation method that removes water from food.
- Dehydration preserves food, decreases its weight and bulk for transport, and provides convenience in food preparation.
- Food is prepared for drying by being sorted for quality, sliced, and pretreated.
- Pretreatment by sulfiting, sulfuring, or blanching reduces flavor loss, enzymatic browning, and deterioration during storage.
- Air temperatures that are too high can cause casehardening, while lack of air circulation prevents complete dehydration.
- Dehydration at home can be done by the sun, in an oven or room, or in a dehydrator.
- A dehydrator produces the best home–dried food because it provides a sanitary and consistent environment.
- Dried food should be stored in airtight containers to prevent moisture from reentering the food.

CHECK YOUR FACTS

1. List three reasons for drying food.
2. Explain the process of rehydration.
3. Why does food need to be pretreated before drying?
4. Name one disadvantage of sulfiting.
5. Name three advantages of sulfuring.
6. What is the purpose of blanching?
7. Why is steaming vegetables preferable to water blanching before dehydration?
8. What are three disadvantages of syrup blanching fruit?
9. List three advantages of sun drying.
10. What are three advantages of dehydrofreezing?
11. Why is dried food sometimes called a nutritional powerhouse?
12. Explain how dried food should be stored.

CRITICAL THINKING AND PROBLEM SOLVING

1. Since dried food must normally be kept in tightly closed containers, why would wheat left in tombs in Egypt 3000 years ago still be edible?
2. Why do backpackers frequently take dried food with them?
3. A recipe for dried beans says to soak them overnight before cooking. What would happen if you cook them without the overnight soaking?
4. What are the advantages and disadvantages of slicing food before drying it?
5. What is the main purpose of pretreating vegetables before dehydration? Fruit?
6. Why shouldn't fruit be steamed prior to drying?
7. Why do some fruits not need pretreating before dehydration?
8. Explain why raisins and prunes are dark in color, while the grapes and plums from which they are made are not.
9. Since drying temperatures are not high enough to kill bacteria, why is dehydrating an effective way to preserve food?
10. Explain why dehydrators produce the best quality home–dried food.

CHAPTER

19

Canning

This chapter will help you . . .

- Identify equipment used in home and commercial canning.
- Describe hot–pack and cold–pack methods of preparing food for canning.
- Explain the two methods of processing home–canned food.
- Compare heat transfer by conduction and by convection in canning.
- Discuss the similarities and differences in regular retort canning and aseptic canning.
- Review the properties of C. *botulinum* that make botulism poisoning a problem in improperly canned food.

Terms to Remember

agitation retorts
aseptic canning
cold–pack
cold point
hot–pack
pouch canning
pressure processing
raw–pack
retort canning
retorts
water–bath processing

In earlier chapters, you learned that fermentation and dehydration are methods of preserving food. Both of these processes have been used for centuries. However, other methods of food preservation have been and are still being developed to slow down or stop food spoilage. This chapter will discuss the method of preserving food known as canning.

Canning is one of the primary ways of preserving food today. During canning, food is processed and sterilized by being heated to a temperature that kills most bacteria present.

The temperatures needed to kill bacteria vary. High–acid foods, such as pickles or tomatoes, can be processed at lower temperatures than low–acid foods. The acid environment prevents the growth of many of the most troublesome microorganisms. Low–acid foods, such as green beans or corn, must be heated to temperatures above 140°C. This ensures that all harmful bacteria and their spores have been destroyed.

Because canned food is in a sealed container, it cannot be recontaminated and therefore spoil. This means that canned food has a long shelf life.

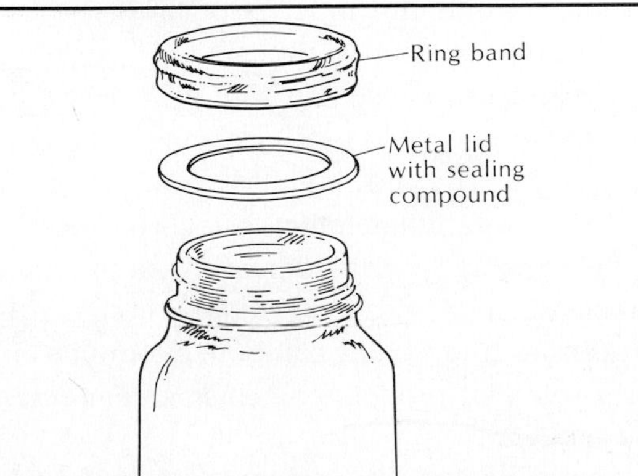

A metal lid with sealing compound and a ring band are used to create an airtight environment in the canning jar.

Pickles are a high–acid food and can be processed at a lower temperature than a low–acid food.

The Discovery of Canning

The ability to preserve food has been crucial to many military victories throughout history. When Napoleon was Emperor of France in the early 1800s, he marched his armies long distances from their source of supplies. Because he needed a means of preserving food until it reached the troops, he offered a prize to anyone who could solve the problem. A Frenchman named Nicolas Appert won the 12,000–franc prize for his technique of heating food in a sealed container. His work initiated the era of food canning.

It took fifty years before anyone could explain why canning worked. Louis Pasteur's work with microorganisms showed that the high temperatures used in canning killed the bacteria responsible for food spoilage.

The canning jar will seal only if the top of the jar is smooth and free from chips.

The handles on the rack in the canning kettle allow you to safely remove the canned food from the kettle.

HOME CANNING

A variety of foods can be canned at home. However, the most popular home-canned foods are fruits and vegetables. Successful home canning depends on having the necessary equipment, choosing the best method for packing the food, and using the correct processing method for the food being canned.

• EQUIPMENT

The equipment used in home canning is very important. Successful canning depends on creating a sealed airtight environment for the food. Containers (usually glass jars), lids, ring bands, and a canner are used to create the correct environment.

Canning jars are made of tempered glass, which can withstand high temperature and rough treatment. The top surface of the jars needs to be smooth and free from chips or scratches so the jars can be sealed. Wide-mouth jars are the most popular shape because they are easy to fill.

A canning jar is sealed with a flat metal lid that has a thin rim of sealing compound on the underside. The lid is held in place by a threaded ring band, which screws on the top of the canning jar. During heating, air in the jar is driven out. As the food in the jar cools after processing, the sealing compound forms an airtight seal that prevents organisms from entering the jar.

Some food can be processed in a canning kettle. The kettle contains a rack on which several jars can be placed. The rack allows water to circulate under and around the jars.

For other food, it is necessary to use a pressure canner for processing. It also has a rack for the jars. The lid of the pressure canner has a steam pressure gauge and a safety valve. The lid also has rubber rings that seal the canner so that no air or steam can escape while the canner is being used. When the lid is on and the canner is sealed, air is forced out of the canner and steam is created under pressure.

• PACKING FOOD

One method used to pack food to be canned is the **raw–pack** method. In this method, uncooked food is placed in a container that is then filled with boiling water or juice and closed with a lid and a ring band. This method is also called the **cold–pack** method. Raw–pack is usually recommended for food of relatively low density that may fall apart when cooked. Food tends to hold its shape better and is firmer when processed by the raw–pack method.

The second method used in packing food for canning is the **hot–pack** method. The food is heated in syrup, water, or juice to at least 77°C. While hot, it is packed into a container and closed with a lid and a ring band. Hot–pack is used for food that can be precooked slightly to allow a closer pack. For example, precooked spinach takes less space than raw spinach. Fruit canned without any sweetening is usually processed with the hot–pack method.

• PROCESSING METHODS

Food packed by either the raw–pack or hot–pack method is then processed. Processing canned food is necessary to kill harmful microorganisms and seal the canning containers. Food to be canned must be processed according to a reliable canning guide. Canning guides tell the best method of packing a particular food, what processing method is needed, and how long the food should be processed.

Cold–packed food is covered with boiling water or juice before the jar is closed with a lid and a ring band.

The juice from canned fruit contains the water–soluble vitamins and minerals lost from the fruit during processing.

NUTRITION AND YOU

The Nutritional Value of Canned Food

In general, the nutritional value of canned food is less than the nutritional value of fresh food. This is because of the high temperatures used in canning. Any nutrient that is affected by heat will deteriorate during the canning process. However, some nutrients, such as carbohydrate and fat, are not affected by the heat used in canning.

Vitamin C and thiamin are most affected by heat. Therefore they are not usually found in canned foods, especially those processed in a pressure canner. The one exception is tomatoes. Because tomatoes are a high–acid food, they can be processed at low temperatures. As a result, canned tomatoes retain more vitamin C than other canned vegetables.

The biggest difference in canned and fresh food is in the concentration of water–soluble vitamins and minerals. Water–soluble nutrients are lost when they dissolve into the liquid in canned food. If the canning liquid is used when a food is prepared or served, the vitamins and minerals will not go to waste.

One factor that affects the nutritional value of canned food is the material in which it is packed. For example, fruit that is packed in fruit juice is more nutritious than fruit packed in a heavy sugar syrup. Tuna canned in water has fewer kilocalories than tuna packed in oil.

Although canned goods do have a long shelf life, nutrients are lost in storage. The higher the storage temperature, the more nutrients are lost. Light can also destroy some nutrients, such as riboflavin. Storing food packed in glass containers in the dark will help prevent the loss of light–sensitive nutrients.

Which of these jars of peaches took longer to process?

The amount of time necessary to process a given sample of food depends on several factors. Longer heating times are required for:

- Large containers, rather than small ones.
- Food that is in large, rather than small, pieces.
- Glass, rather than metal, containers.

For example, processing small tins of tomato juice will not take as long as processing large jars of whole tomatoes.

Water–bath processing involves heating the containers of food in boiling water in a canning kettle. The kettle needs to be deep enough so that the containers are covered and there is 5–10 cm of space above the containers to allow the water to boil freely.

Tomatoes are processed in a water bath in a canning kettle.

Low-acid foods, such as green beans or corn, must be processed in a pressure canner.

Processing Times

Food	Pack	Jar Size	Processing Time	Processing Method
Lima beans	hot	0.47 L 0.94 L	40 minutes 50 minutes	pressure canner
Corn, kernels	hot	0.47 L 0.94 L	55 minutes 85 minutes	pressure canner
Peas, green	hot	0.47 L 0.94 L	40 minutes 40 minutes	pressure canner
Cherries	hot	0.47 L 0.94 L	10 minutes 15 minutes	water-bath
Peaches, halves	hot cold	0.47 L 0.94 L 0.47 L 0.94 L	20 minutes 25 minutes 25 minutes 30 minutes	water-bath
Tomatoes, whole	hot	0.47 L 0.94 L	35 minutes 45 minutes	water-bath

Commercial canning is done in huge pressure canners called retorts.

Canned foods have a long shelf life and maintain their quality for at least two years.

The containers must be processed until the temperature of the food at the coolest spot is approximately 88°C. A water bath can be used safely only with high–acid foods, such as fruit, tomatoes, and pickles.

The **pressure processing** method of canning heats containers of food under pressure in a pressure canner. The temperature reached in the pressure canner is greater than the normal boiling point of water at atmospheric pressure. The higher temperature helps kill the bacteria in low–acid foods, such as green beans or corn. If there is any question about the acid level of a food, pressure processing should be used.

COMMERCIAL CANNING

The commercial canning industry began in Philadelphia in 1874 with the development of commercial canners. Today, commercial canning of food is a major industry, which provides safe food for consumers.

Pressure processing is the type of canning carried out by commercial food processors. It is generally called **retort canning.** This is because the huge pressure canners used commercially are called **retorts.**

Commercial retort canning is carried out in large pressurized cookers. Food processed in this way is considered commercially sterile. This does not mean all microorganisms have been destroyed. However, all toxin–forming organisms that could cause illness and those that could cause spoilage under usual storage conditions have been eliminated.

Most canned food sold commercially today has a long shelf life. Although commercially canned food can be stored for long periods of time, it loses quality if kept over two years.

• HEAT TRANSFER

In retort canning, heat energy is transferred from the heat source to the food being sterilized. The transfer of heat is by conduction and convection.

As you know, conduction involves passing energy from particle to particle through molecular collisions. The molecules of the warmer substance transmit some of their energy to the molecules of the cooler substance until all molecules are the same temperature.

You will recall that the second method of heat transfer is convection. This is heat transfer by the motion of fluids or air. In a retort canner, conduction causes the liquid near the bottom of the container to become hot first. The heat causes the molecules to spread, expanding the liquid, which makes it less dense. Because it is now lighter than the cooler liquid above it, the hot liquid rises. The cooler liquid then sinks to the bottom where it is heated in turn. This continues until all the liquid in the container reaches the same temperature.

During canning, conduction occurs in solids and liquids, while convection occurs only in liquids or food packed in liquids. Therefore heat is transferred by both conduction and convection in liquids. However, heat is usually transferred only by conduction in solid food.

Convection occurs in juice and in the liquid around loosely packed food, such as peas or corn. Because convection does not occur equally well in all food, some commercial canners have **agitation retorts.** These are canners that can mechanically increase the movement of the food to shorten processing time.

To find out whether a can of food has been heated sufficiently, canners check the **cold point.** This is the point in the food that is the last to reach the temperature considered safe for killing microorganisms in that food. In a can heated only by conduction, the cold point is at the center of the can. This is because heat is evenly transferred from the outside into the center of the can by the collision of molecules. In a can heated by both conduction and convection, the cold point is slightly below the center of the can. This occurs because the movement of the fluid from the bottom to the top of the can leaves a spot slightly below the center that is the last to heat. The time it takes the cold point to reach the required temperature determines the overall processing temperature and time.

• ASEPTIC CANNING

Aseptic canning (ay–SEP–tik) is a method in which food is first sterilized by heat and then placed in sterilized containers. The main advantage of this process is speed. The food can

Heat Transfer

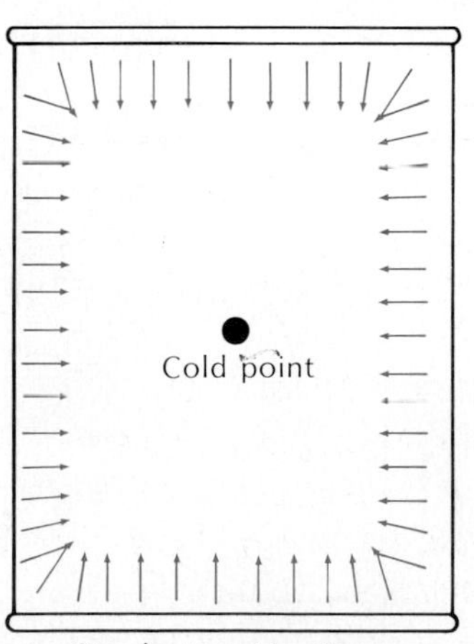

Conduction Heating

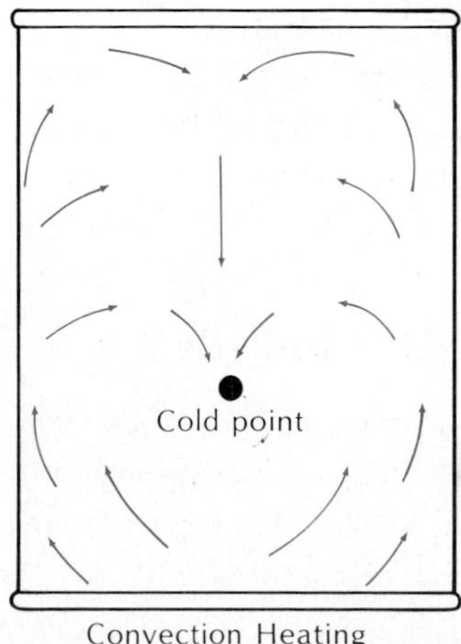

Convection Heating

The cold point in a can is the last place to heat.

Pouch Canning

Pouch canning is a method of preserving food that is gaining in popularity. This process is like retort canning except that flexible packages are used instead of cans or jars. Such containers usually weigh less and take up less space than more rigid containers. For these reasons, they are preferred by both manufacturers and grocers. Consumers appreciate pouches because they are easy to open and then throw away. Spaghetti precooked in a sauce is one example of a pouch canned food.

The use of a thin, flexible pouch allows more rapid heat penetration than occurs through cans. This means processing times are shorter, which produces a higher quality product while using less energy.

Retort pouches have been used in Europe for many years. They are also used by the United States military services. The federal government has established durability standards to ensure the safety of any pouches sold in the United States.

Pouch canning produces a high quality product because the processing time is short.

be sterilized in seconds and then placed in the container with a minimal loss of flavor or nutritional value. This is in sharp contrast to the traditional method of canning.

For example, milk canned by the traditional method is heated so long that the sugars in the milk react, causing a change in color and flavor. In contrast, aseptically canned milk has a flavor and nutritional value more similar to fresh milk.

One common example of aseptically packaged food is the individual packages of coffee cream found in many restaurants. The juice industry uses aseptic processing in marketing small flexible paperboard foil containers of juice.

When food is aseptically canned, it is heated very quickly in a plate– or tubular–shaped heat exchanger until it is sterile. The sterile food is then cooled quickly to protect its quality. Finally, the cooled sterile sample is added to sterile containers. This takes place in a sterile filling zone.

The only disadvantage of the aseptic method is that total control of the sanitary conditions must be maintained during processing. Special equipment is needed to ensure this total control.

Aseptic canning is fast, so food has a minimal loss of flavor or nutrients.

Not only is aseptic packaging faster than other canning methods, it is also less expensive. Although the technology necessary for aseptic canning has existed since World War II, the procedure has become widespread only during the 1980s. As mechanized processing becomes more streamlined, aseptic canning is increasingly popular.

BOTULISM POISONING

When canning is not done properly, problems can arise. The most dangerous is an outbreak of botulism. As you know, botulism is the most serious form of food poisoning known. It is caused by a toxin produced by the bacteria called *Clostridium botulinum*. Scientists think that 250 mL of this purified poison would be enough to kill all the people on earth.

Most cases of botulism occur because of improperly home–canned food. C. *botulinum* seldom survives the procedures used in commercial canning. When contaminated food is eaten without being boiled or heated to at least 80°C for 10 minutes, severe illness or even death will occur.

• PROPERTIES OF *C. BOTULINUM*

C. *botulinum* is a rod–shaped bacteria that lives in soil all over the world. Like many similar microorganisms, this bacteria is able to form spores. These spores tend to be very resistant to adverse conditions. They resist chemical treatment, heat, and other environmental changes that would destroy active cells. The result is that C. *botulinum* spores can exist indefinitely.

Sometimes the process used in canning food is not sufficient to destroy the spores. During storage, the spores germinate in the food to produce new bacteria. The bacteria actively grow in the food, and the toxin is produced.

Using the wrong processing method for green beans can allow the growth of C. *botulinum*.

Because canned food is sealed, an anaerobic environment is created where C. *botulinum* can grow.

C. *botulinum* grow anaerobically, that is, when there is no air present in the environment. When food is heated during canning, the air is driven out and then the container is sealed. Therefore canned food is an ideal place for C. *botulinum* to grow.

Air is also removed as food is heated. Therefore the interior of leftover food can be an anaerobic environment. If the leftovers are stored at room temperature, C. *botulinum* spores that survived being heated can grow and produce toxin. The absence of air prevents the growth of many organisms that can cause food to spoil, but it is perfect for the growth of C. *botulinum*.

In Chapter 5, you learned that one factor affecting the growth of C. *botulinum* is the acidity of the food. Acid foods, such as tomatoes, fruit, pickled red cabbage, sauerkraut, and berries, can be safely canned at boiling temperatures in a water bath. This is because the acidity of the food prevents the bacteria from growing. Food that has a pH above 4.6 requires pressure processing in canning. Examples of these foods are peas, corn, lima beans, meat, fish, poultry, spinach, asparagus, beets, and pumpkin.

Pressure processing these foods is needed to kill C. *botulinum* and its spores.

• AVOIDING BOTULISM

In some food, the growth of C. *botulinum* produces a foul, rancid odor. In other food that is just as toxic, little if any change in odor and appearance occurs. Therefore all food, cooked or canned, that shows any signs of spoilage should be discarded.

Sometimes the lid or end of a container of canned food bulges, showing signs of a buildup of pressure in the container. Since pressure buildup is a sign of microorganism activity, these canned foods should not be used.

Never use any product whose can is damaged or bulging.

EXPERIMENT 19–1

Environment and Food Preservation

In canning, as well as in other methods of food preservation, steps are taken to stop the growth of bacteria so food can be stored without spoiling. There are a number of factors that determine whether a given environment will promote the growth of microorganisms. This experiment will illustrate some of the factors that have an impact on bacterial growth.

PROCEDURE

1. Obtain 200 mL chicken broth, and put it in a 250 mL beaker.
2. Heat the broth–filled beaker on a medium–high setting. Boil the broth for 5 minutes. Remove the broth from the heat, and cool for at least 5 minutes or until the beaker is cool enough to handle safely.
3. Fill a large saucepan with tap water. Bring the water to a boil.
4. Place six empty 50 mL beakers in the boiling water for 5 minutes to sterilize. Remove each beaker with tongs, drain, and cool.
5. Fill each of the beakers one–half full of chicken broth.
6. Use masking tape to label the beakers A, B, C, D, E, and F. Also label with your name and class period.
7. Add the following substances to the specified beakers and stir. Use a clean stirring rod in each beaker.

   Beaker A—add 5 mL sugar.
   Beaker B—add 2.5 mL salt.
   Beaker C—add 5 mL salt.
   Beaker D—add 5 mL water.
   Beaker E—add 5 mL lemon juice.
   Beaker F—add nothing.
8. Place the beakers in the area indicated by your teacher.
9. On the sixth day, observe each beaker sample for color, general appearance, and odor. Do not taste the broth. Record your observations in your data table.
10. If any mold has appeared on your broth, use tweezers to transfer a small sample of the mold from the beaker to a microscope slide. Try not to crush the mold as you transfer it. Examine the mold under a microscope. Include drawings of the appearance of the mold in your laboratory report.

QUESTIONS

1. Which sample differed most from the others?
2. Which samples were most similar in their properties?
3. Which beakers contained mold? Why do you suppose mold grew in those beakers and not the others?
4. How do you think your results would have differed if you had refrigerated the samples?

SAMPLE DATA TABLE

Beaker	Color	Appearance	Odor
A			
B			
C			
D			
E			
F			

EXPERIMENT 19–2

Evaluating Canned Peas

You will recall that young vegetables contain mostly sugar, which turns to starch as the vegetables age, or mature. Young immature peas are sweet and tender, while mature peas have a tough starchiness. Since young peas are more desirable, the most important factor in evaluating or grading peas is maturity.

There are several ways to evaluate canned peas. One method involves placing peas in a salt solution. The young tender peas will float, while the mature peas sink because of the density of the starch they contain. Another way to check the maturity of peas is to observe the liquid, or brine, in which the peas are packed. The starch in mature peas dissolves into the brine, causing it to be cloudy, rather than clear.

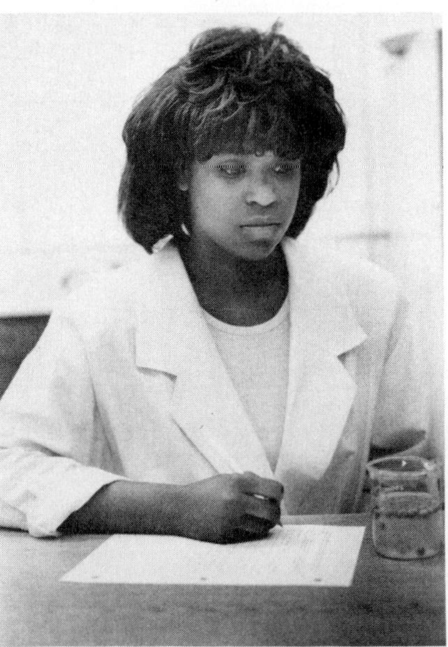

Finally, mature peas often have skins that are split and broken, while young peas are apt to have smooth unbroken skins. This experiment will give you the opportunity to evaluate various brands of canned peas.

PROCEDURE

1. Count 50 peas from the source indicated by your teacher.
2. Pour 200 mL brine solution provided by your teacher into a 250 mL beaker.
3. Add the peas to the brine solution, and observe for 30–60 seconds. Count how many peas sink to the bottom. If nearly all the peas sink, count how many remain floating and subtract from 50. Record this information in your data table.
4. Remove the peas from the brine solution, and place them on a paper towel. Count how many peas in your sample have broken skins. Record this information in your data table.
5. Note the appearance of the brine in the can from which you obtained the peas, and record it in your data table.
6. Obtain unit cost information for your brand of peas from your teacher, and write it in your data table.
7. Write your information on the chalkboard. In your data table, copy the information about the other brands of peas.

EXPERIMENT 19–2

QUESTIONS

1. Which brand of peas had the largest number of peas that sank? The smallest number?
2. Which brand of peas had the largest number of peas with split skins? The smallest number?
3. Was there any relationship between the number of peas that sank and the number that had broken skins?
4. Was there any relationship between the number of peas that sank and the cloudiness of the brine from which they came?
5. Which brand of peas seemed to be of the highest quality?
6. Were the peas with the highest unit cost the ones of the highest quality?

SAMPLE DATA TABLE

Pea Brand	Number That Sank	Number With Broken Skins	Appearance of Brine	Unit Cost

TO SUM UP

- The tempered glass jars usually used in home canning are sealed with a lid held in place by a ring band.
- Canning kettles are used for water bath processing of high–acid food, while pressure canners are needed for pressure processing of low–acid food.
- Food to be canned is packed into containers by either the hot–pack or cold–pack method.
- Processing canned food kills microorganisms and seals the food in an airtight environment.
- Commercial canning is called retort canning because it takes place in huge pressure canners called retorts.
- In retort canning, heat can be transferred by conduction and convection.
- Aseptic canning is fast, economical, and produces canned food with a minimal loss of flavor or nutritional value.
- C. *botulinum* grows anaerobically and produces spores that are resistant to heat and chemicals, making improperly home-canned food an ideal place for the bacteria to grow and produce toxin.

CHECK YOUR FACTS

1. Why does canned food have a long shelf life?
2. Name four pieces of equipment needed in home canning.
3. What is the most popular kind of jar for home canning? Why?
4. Why do canning kettles and pressure canners have racks on which the jars are placed?
5. What is the difference in the hot– and cold–pack methods of packing food for canning?
6. Why should a reliable canning guide be used in home canning?
7. What kind of food can be canned using water–bath processing?
8. Why is pressure processing needed to can low–acid food?
9. Why is commercial canning called retort canning?
10. What does it mean if a food is "commercially sterile"?
11. List two advantages and one disadvantage of aseptic canning.
12. What procedures should be used in canning to destroy C. *botulinum*?

CRITICAL THINKING AND PROBLEM SOLVING

1. Imagine that the apple tree in your back yard has produced too many apples for you to eat. You'd like to can applesauce, but you have no canning equipment. What factors would you consider in deciding if it was worth canning the applesauce?
2. Assume you decided to can the applesauce discussed in the first question. Locate a reliable canning guide, and explain how the applesauce should be packed, what processing method should be used, and how long the applesauce should be processed.
3. What would happen if a jar used for canning had a chipped top?
4. Which will take longer to process, a 227 g can of sliced peaches or a 454 g can of sliced peaches? Why?
5. Which will take longer to process, a 227 g can of peas or a 227 g can of sweet potatoes? Why?
6. Why is botulism generally associated with canned food?
7. Give examples of foods processed by water–bath processing, pressure processing, pouch canning, and aseptic canning. Do not repeat examples used in the chapter.

CHAPTER

20

New Techniques of Food Preservation

This chapter will help you . . .

- Examine the factors needed for successful freezing of food.
- Explain the role of sublimation in freeze drying.
- Identify examples of food that can successfully be freeze–dried and tell how they should be stored.
- Describe the process of food irradiation and its effect on food being irradiated.
- Define the units used to measure the amount of radiation used during irradiation.
- Discuss the effect the Delaney Anti–Cancer Clause has had on the irradiated food industry.
- List properties of containers needed for commercial food packaging.
- Identify factors related to the successful use of controlled–atmosphere packaging.

Terms to Remember

controlled–atmosphere packaging (CAP)
Delaney Anti–Cancer Clause
electromagnetic spectrum
electromagnetic waves
flash frozen
freeze drying
gray
immersion freezing
indirect–contact freezing
irradiation
krad
lyophilization
radiation
radiation absorbed dose (rad)

This chapter will look at some of the newer techniques for food preservation. These techniques depend on the technology of the twentieth century. Some of them were perfected in the process of preparing food for the astronauts.

FREEZING FOOD

One popular method of food preservation developed in the twentieth century is freezing. Frozen food can be preserved and stored for extended periods of time. Frozen food is convenient for consumers. It can be prepared quickly with very little effort. Indeed, eating habits changed in the 1950s with the advent of TV dinners.

While some microorganisms are killed by freezing, most are simply unable to grow at such low temperatures. Therefore frozen food that is allowed to thaw and warm to room temperature provides a medium in which bacteria can multiply quickly. The bacteria can cause spoilage or food poisoning.

The widespread use of frozen foods reflects how convenient they are for consumers.

Properly preparing food for home freezing helps maintain the food's quality and prevent freezer burn.

As you know, enzyme action is also slowed by freezing. However, to ensure that vegetables retain their fresh flavor, they are blanched before freezing to denature the enzymes.

The best temperature for freezing food is −18°C. When food is frozen at home, it is necessary to select a container or a freezer wrap that will not allow air to get to the food. A tight seal is needed to prevent freezer burn and to maintain food quality.

Most food has a maximum storage time. Therefore it is important to label and date frozen food. Food can then be used before its quality starts to deteriorate.

• SELECTING FOOD FOR FREEZING

Some foods freeze better than others. Selecting products that freeze well is necessary for successful freezing. Certain food products undergo negative changes in flavor or texture when frozen. For example:

- Fresh basil and chives can become bitter.
- Artificial vanilla will often develop an unpleasant flavor.
- Black pepper often becomes bitter.
- Uncooked garlic becomes stronger.
- Egg custard can separate and leak liquid.
- Grapes, pears, and apples may become mushy.
- Salad vegetables usually lose their shape and get watery.
- Hard–cooked eggs become tough and leathery.

• COMMERCIAL FREEZING

Food that is commercially frozen undergoes only limited changes in color, texture, size, and flavor. The rapid freezing process and low temperatures used commercially help preserve the quality of the frozen food.

There are three basic methods used in commercial freezing. The most common and oldest method is freezing in air, which is also the method used in home freezing. **Indirect–contact freezing** is carried out by placing food on belts or trays. The food is chilled rapidly by a refrigerant circulating through a cold wall. This is the method used by most of the major frozen vegetable processors. **Immersion freezing** is a method that uses nontoxic refrigerants. The food is immersed directly in the refrigerant to cause quick freezing. The refrigerant must not change the color, taste, or odor of the food dipped in it. This technique is used for commercially freezing seafood, such as fish and shrimp, and many fruits.

The packaging used for commercially frozen food is designed to prevent water vapor from leaking in or out of the package. Since food expands as much as 10 percent when it freezes, tough yet flexible packages are required. Most frozen food packages are opaque because

An egg custard generally does not freeze well because it will separate and leak liquid.

How frozen food is packaged affects its quality.

many foods lose flavor when they are exposed to light.

The supermarket industry places great emphasis on frozen food. Special freezer trucks are required to transport frozen food. However, transporting and storing frozen food requires a great deal of energy. If energy costs rise, other methods of preserving food may become more popular than freezing.

FREEZE DRYING

Freeze drying is a commercial process that combines freezing and drying. A frozen product is treated to remove the solvent from dispersed or dissolved solids. In most food, this means removing water. The technical name for freeze drying is **lyophilization** (lye–ahf–uh–luh–ZAY–shun).

In freeze drying, it is important to use high–quality food. Depending on what is being processed, the food sample may be raw or cooked.

• SUBLIMATION

During freeze drying, water sublimes. You will remember that sublimation means changing from the solid to the gaseous state without becoming a liquid. While ice can sublime at normal atmospheric pressure, the rate of sublimation under these conditions is rather slow. However, if the air pressure over ice is lowered, the ice will sublime at a more rapid rate.

Freeze drying takes place in a special chamber in which the pressure is maintained at a low level. The food samples are **flash frozen,** which means they are frozen very quickly. They are then kept at temperatures below freezing. The low pressure accelerates the rate at which ice crystals in the food become water vapor. The vapor is drawn off by low–temperature condenser plates until 99 percent of the moisture has been removed from the food.

When food is freeze–dried, sublimation occurs first on the surface. It continues as ice from inside the sample changes to water vapor. By the time the ice at the very center has sublimed, the food will contain as little as 1 percent of its original moisture. Since the food was

Commercial freezing methods cause only limited changes in the quality of the food that is frozen.

Freeze–dried food can only be produced commercially.

Freeze–dried food is lightweight, so it is often used by campers and backpackers.

Freeze–dried food has a long shelf life if properly packaged.

frozen and rigid during the freeze–drying process, the final product looks something like a sponge. All the places in the food that once held water or ice crystals are empty.

The conditions under which freeze drying occurs must be monitored very carefully. Manufacturers want to maximize the rate of sublimation without allowing the temperature to rise so that the ice melts.

Freeze drying is a highly technical and expensive process. It cannot be done at home because of the complex equipment involved. The companies that produce freeze–dried food have highly specialized computer–operated facilities, which constantly check the many variables that affect the final product.

• USE AND STORAGE

Freeze–dried food, like other dried food, is very lightweight. This makes shipping and handling it easier, as well as making it a highly desirable food supply for campers and backpackers.

Freeze drying is used to dehydrate many beverages, such as coffee and juices. It also works well with mushrooms; fresh fruit, such as strawberries; diced chicken; and some seafood, such as shrimp.

Freeze–dried food is reconstituted before being eaten. If stored properly, freeze–dried food has a better taste, appearance, and texture and a higher nutritional value after reconstitution than food dried by evaporation.

Food that has been freeze–dried can be stored for months or even years if it has been properly packaged. Since a freeze–dried food will reconstitute quickly under normal conditions, it must be protected from moisture in the air.

The freeze–drying process has several uses in addition to preparing food for home consumption or use by hikers. Flavors, cultured microorganisms, enzymes, and specialty chemicals are all freeze–dried. They are then sold to food processors, as well as to chemical, biotechnical, and pharmaceutical companies.

The Electromagnetic Spectrum

You learned in Chapter 4 that there are several kinds of energy. **Radiation** is the transfer of energy through space in the form of waves. These waves are called **electromagnetic waves.**

Not all electromagnetic waves have the same properties. Some of the waves have more energy than others, although they all travel at the same speed. The differences in energy are reflected in the length of the waves. Radio waves, which are low–energy waves, may have a wavelength as great as 10,000 m. At the other extreme, gamma rays, which are very high–energy waves, have a wavelength of only about .0000000001 (1×10^{-10}) m.

The waves are arranged in order of wavelength in the **electromagnetic spectrum.** The electromagnetic spectrum shows the continuous range of radiation, which varies from very low–energy radio waves to extremely high–energy gamma rays. The various portions of the electromagnetic spectrum are:

- Radio waves.
- Infrared rays.
- Visible light.
- Ultraviolet rays.
- X–rays.
- Gamma rays.

Several portions of the electromagnetic spectrum relate to food processing and preservation.

The shortest radio waves are called microwaves. Microwaves are used to cook food in microwave ovens. Microwaves can penetrate food to a depth of 5–7.6 cm.

Energy in the infrared region of the electromagnetic spectrum is heat energy. Heat energy is absorbed only at the surface of the food. Infrared lamps are used in restaurants to keep food warm.

Ultraviolet rays create enough energy to kill living cells. Therefore ultraviolet rays are sometimes used in food processing plants to destroy bacteria and preserve food. Ultraviolet rays are present in sunlight. They enable your body to convert the vitamin D precursor in the blood into vitamin D.

Gamma rays are used in the method of food preservation called **irradiation.** Irradiation means exposure to radiation. During irradiation, gamma rays and high–speed electrons, called beta rays, pass through food samples. Rather than cooking the food, the gamma rays destroy the living organisms in the food that would cause it to spoil.

The electromagnetic spectrum shows the range of radiation ordered by wavelength.

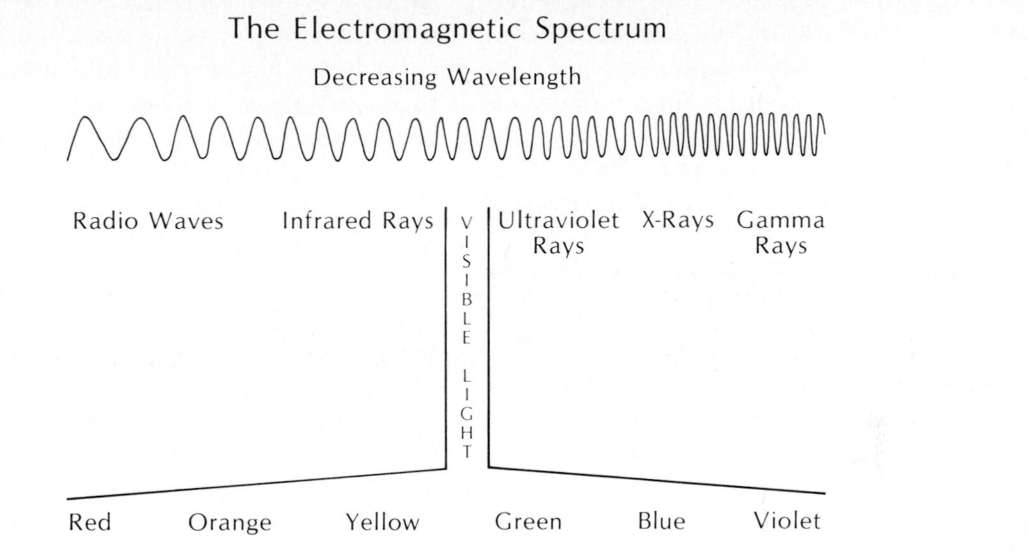

IRRADIATION

Irradiation is one of the newest methods of food preservation. Food to be irradiated is carried on a conveyor belt into a metal–plated room to the source of the gamma and beta rays. It is irradiated for a specified amount of time, then continues on the conveyor belt out of the radiation room.

Irradiated food undergoes very little change in flavor, odor, color, or nutritional value. Careful testing has shown that food treated this way does not retain or give off radiation. Most scientists feel food is perfectly safe to eat immediately after being irradiated.

Irradiation is called cold food preservation because the temperature of the food increases only slightly during the process. This is an important advantage of irradiation, since many nutrients are heat–sensitive and may be destroyed by other preservation methods. However, high doses of radiation do cause partial destruction of some amino acids, vitamins A, C, B_6, B_{12}, and E as well as niacin and thiamin.

• AMOUNTS OF RADIATION

The amount of radiation to which a food is exposed during processing can be described using various units of measure. One common unit is called a **radiation absorbed dose (rad).** A rad measures the amount of radiation energy absorbed by living tissue. Another unit, the **gray,** is equal to 100 rads. One thousand rads is called a **krad** (KAY-rad).

The preservation effect of irradiation depends on the amount of radiation to which the food sample is exposed. A low dose of 100 krads will give a longer shelf life to food such as fresh berries, which normally spoil in a matter of days. On the other hand, doses of 1000 krads are needed to sterilize food so that C. *botulism* spores are destroyed.

• REGULATION OF IRRADIATION

The concept of irradiation has been understood since the 1890s. However, experimentation with food irradiation did not begin until the early 1950s. In the United States, irradiation is regulated by the Food and Drug Administration (FDA).

In 1958, the United States Congress classified irradiation as a food additive. This means it must meet the requirements of the **Delaney Anti–Cancer Clause.** The Delaney Clause is a clause in the Food Additive Amendment to the Food, Drug, and Cosmetic Act. It says that a substance shown to cause cancer in humans or animals may not be added to food in any amount. Therefore irradiation cannot be added to a food if the irradiated food will cause cancer. Although no irradiated food has ever been shown to cause cancer, the FDA approves food for irradiation on a one–by–one basis. This approval is given only after irradiation of the food is shown to have no harmful effects.

Irradiation has been carefully studied in this country. The FDA has more reports of irradiation testing than of any other method of food preservation. The World Health Organization has reported that food subjected to up to 1000 krads of radiation is safe for human consumption.

Some people still have concerns about the safety of irradiated food. People opposed to food irradiation are worried about the dangers of radiation and of increasing the number of locations throughout the country where radiation takes place. Those in favor of irradiated food claim that irradiation centers would be less dangerous than the average x–ray laboratory in a hospital.

Irradiation preserves food by killing microorganisms that cause spoilage.

Uses of Irradiation

Irradiation is used to preserve a wide variety of foods. Spices have been routinely subjected to 1000 krads of radiation since July 1983. Irradiation of fresh fruits and vegetables has been done since 1986. Irradiation of potatoes and onions with 3–15 krads to inhibit sprouting has been approved since the 1960s.

Manufacturers in many countries use radiation during pasteurization of milk. In addition, radiation is being used on poultry products to control *Salmonella* contamination.

Irradiation is also used in a method of food preservation called radiation sterilization. Food to be sterilized is first blanched to inactivate the enzymes that are present. The food is then irradiated with very high levels of radiation, which kill all forms of microorganisms. Food that has been sterilized in this way has a shelf life of up to several years as long as the package remains sealed. Meat has a shelf life of up to seven years when stored in a sealed pouch after radiation sterilization.

This symbol tells you a product has been irradiated.

PACKAGING FOOD

How food is packaged is almost as important as the process used to preserve it. A faulty package can allow contamination of food by living organisms or promote the growth of organisms that are present. Dehydrated food can rehydrate and spoil if poor packaging lets the food come in contact with moisture.

• CONTAINERS

There are many common containers used to package food—cans, glass jars, rigid plastic containers, and plastic bags. All types of food containers need certain properties to be suited for commercial packaging. They must:

- Be nontoxic.
- Provide sanitary protection.
- Resist the normal bumping that occurs in a supermarket.
- Open easily.
- Reseal or pour well.
- Be attractive.
- Be relatively inexpensive.

A wide variety of containers are used to package food today.

Some containers are opaque because they contain food that needs to be protected from light. Other containers must provide protection from odors. Some containers are heat–resistant so that the foods they contain can be heated in them.

• CONTROLLED–ATMOSPHERE PACKAGING

One packaging technique the food industry has used to lengthen shelf life is **controlled–atmosphere packaging,** sometimes called **CAP.** This process alters the gaseous environment surrounding a food product. Generally, when this process is used, the air inside a package is replaced with a mixture of nonreactive gases. These gases do not readily react or combine with other elements or compounds.

The exact combination of gases is precisely tailored to suit the specific food product. The gas mixture that is best for packaging fresh meat may be totally wrong for packaging baked goods. Every type of food packaged this way is evaluated by the packer, the food company, and the gas supplier. They determine the combination of gases that will best maintain the quality of the product.

CAP has been used in Europe longer than in the United States, where its potential is only now being realized. Food processors have learned that there are four technical requirements for successful utilization of CAP.

- The gas mixture used must match the food being packaged.
- Quality machines capable of mixing gases precisely are needed.
- The bacteriological cleanliness of the packaging room, machines, and workers must be controlled during packaging.
- The CAP machine must create a tight seal, which will keep the atmosphere inside the container constant.

Special combinations of gases are used in CAP to lengthen the shelf life of food products.

CAP *and* Meat

It is generally believed that the meat industry would benefit most from using CAP. Packaged pork chops, chicken thighs, and other large family packs of meat products will maintain their quality much longer when stored in controlled–atmosphere packages. In addition to lasting longer without spoiling, meat looks fresher longer and is more sanitary if CAP is used.

Chicken remains fresh longest if packaged in 100 percent carbon dioxide. Beef, on the other hand, seems to do best in a mixture of nitrogen, carbon dioxide, and oxygen. The oxygen preserves the meat's redness, the carbon dioxide suppresses the growth of microorganisms, and the nitrogen helps to maintain the balance of the other two gases.

NUTRITION AND YOU

Food in Space

As space travel by humans began in the 1960s, keeping the astronauts well nourished was a major concern. At that time, no one was certain that humans could eat in the absence of gravity. Many scientists suspected that weightless food would be hard to swallow and would collect in the throat.

Early experiments showed that eating in space was fairly easy. However, because crumbs were a serious problem, the food taken on the first space flights was consumed through straws. Since the astronauts couldn't see or smell the food, they found they had little desire to eat. Over the years, however, a great variety of foods have been developed that are suitable for consumption not only in space but on earth as well.

All food taken into space today must meet certain requirements. The food must have a shelf life of six months at a temperature of 37.7°C. Since storage is limited, food products taken into space must be compact and lightweight to add as little weight as possible during liftoff. As a result, most of the food, including beverages, is dehydrated.

A typical food compartment in space could contain pouched or canned food, such as applesauce, chocolate pudding, or turkey and gravy. Irradiated bread and meat products, such as ham or corned beef, might be included. Also available could be freeze-dried strawberries and sliced bananas that would require just a squirt of water to make a delicious dessert. Snacks might include cookies, peanut butter, granola bars, or candy.

Today, astronauts do not suffer from a limited diet while in space. This means they are more apt to eat regularly and enjoy their meals. The nutritional value in the food they eat helps keep them well nourished and healthy.

Recent developments in food preservation and packaging provide well-balanced meals for the astronauts.

EXPERIMENT 20–1

Effect of Light on Flavor

To choose an appropriate packaging method for a food requires knowing the properties of the food, the microorganisms (if any) that affect the food, and how the food changes as its quality deteriorates. As you know, over time, fat oxidizes to become rancid, causing undesirable flavors and odors. These flavors sometimes develop in high–fat foods, such as peanut butter, potato chips, or crackers. How these foods are packaged can affect whether they become rancid, since both light and oxygen accelerate oxidation and rancidity. In this experiment, you will study the effect of light on the flavor of potato chips stored in different environments for a specified period of time.

PROCEDURE

1. Wrap a clean 400 mL beaker in aluminum foil. Tape the foil in place so that no light will enter the beaker after a final piece of foil is placed over the top.
2. Place fresh potato chips in the beaker wrapped in foil and in a second clean beaker without foil. Cover the first beaker with foil and the second beaker with plastic wrap.
3. Label the beakers with your name and class period. Place them in the location specified by your teacher.
4. Taste potato chips from each beaker every other day for two weeks. Rate their flavor on a 5–point scale:
   1—Strongly dislike the flavor.
   2—Slightly dislike the flavor.
   3—Neither like nor dislike the flavor.
   4—Like the flavor.
   5—REALLY like the flavor.

   Record your ratings for each treatment in your data table.
5. Make a graph of your data on the flavor of the potato chips versus the storage time. The y–axis, on the side of the chart, should be the flavor score. The x–axis, along the bottom of the chart, should be the time in days. Plot data for both samples on the same graph.

EXPERIMENT 20–1

QUESTIONS

1. As shown on your graph, when did the flavor of the chips in each sample begin to deteriorate?
2. Why did wrapping the beaker in aluminum foil preserve the flavor of the stored potato chips?
3. Why do you suppose the flavor of the chips in the covered container eventually began to deteriorate?
4. In what type of containers are the potato chips you purchase in the store sold? Why?

SAMPLE DATA TABLE

Day	Rating of Chips Exposed to Light	Rating of Chips Protected From Light
1		
3		
5		
7		
9		
11		
13		
15		

EXPERIMENT 20–2

Comparison of Orange Juices

The method used to preserve a food can affect the properties and quality of the food. In this experiment, you will use your knowledge of sensory evaluation to compare samples of fresh, frozen, freeze–dried, aseptically processed, and pouch canned orange juices.

PROCEDURE

1. Compare the samples provided by your teacher as to color, mouthfeel, and taste. Enter the information in your data table.
2. Your teacher will provide information on unit cost and the preservation method of each sample. Enter the information in your data table.

QUESTIONS

1. Which sample looked most like fresh orange juice?
2. Which sample "felt" most like fresh orange juice?
3. Which sample had the best taste?
4. Did the juice with the highest unit cost have the best taste?
5. Which juice would you buy on a day–to–day basis? Why?
6. Which juice would you take camping? Why?

SAMPLE DATA TABLE

Sample	Color	Mouthfeel	Taste	Unit Cost	Preservation Method

REVIEW

TO SUM UP

- The packaging selected for home and commercial freezing affects the quality of the frozen food.
- Freeze drying takes place in a special chamber in which the water in a frozen food is removed by sublimation.
- Freeze–dried food is lightweight, has a long shelf life, and is reconstituted before being eaten.
- Irradiation is a cold preservation method that involves passing gamma and beta rays through a food sample.
- The radiation used in irradiation is measured in rads, grays, and krads.
- Irradiation is regulated by the FDA, which approves food for irradiation only when it is shown that the irradiated food does not cause cancer.
- Containers for packaging food commercially should be nontoxic, sanitary, durable, easy to use, attractive, and economical.
- Controlled–atmosphere packaging involves altering the gaseous environment around a food.

CHECK YOUR FACTS

1. How should food be prepared for freezing?
2. Describe the process of sublimation and how it affects the appearance of a freeze–dried food.
3. What is a major disadvantage of freeze drying food?
4. Name three nonfood substances that are often freeze–dried.
5. What happens when gamma and beta rays pass through food?
6. Describe the requirements of the Delaney Anti–Cancer Clause.
7. What is the purpose of irradiating potatoes and onions?
8. Why is irradiation used with poultry products?
9. Why is proper packaging of a food thought to be almost as important as the method used for its preservation?
10. Which part of the food industry probably will benefit most from using CAP?

CRITICAL THINKING AND PROBLEM SOLVING

1. Explain the similarities and differences between freeze drying and dehydrofreezing (see Chapter 18).
2. Why is a very low pressure maintained during freeze drying?
3. Why is irradiated food safe to eat immediately after irradiation?
4. How has the Delaney Anti–Cancer Clause affected the use of irradiation as a means of food preservation?
5. Potato plants are grown by planting the eyes cut from potatoes. Would it be a good idea to plant the eyes of irradiated potatoes? Why or why not?
6. Choose a food product, and develop a new way of packaging that food. Describe the advantages and disadvantages of your proposed packaging.
7. Why is dehydrated food taken on space flights?
8. Plan a day's menu for a 30–mile weekend backpacking trip.

CHAPTER

21

Additives

This chapter will help you . . .

- Identify agencies involved in regulating food additives.
- Discuss the various purposes food additives serve.
- Describe properties of a desirable food preservative.
- Explain why additives used as antioxidants are added to food.
- Differentiate between natural and artificial additives.
- Identify kinds of sweeteners used in food processing.
- Name several nutrients that are used as food additives.
- Discuss the advantages and disadvantages of using food additives.

Terms to Remember

contaminants
enrichment
food additive
goiter
nutrification
restoration
stabilizer

It is almost impossible to go a day without eating a food that contains additives. As you know, an additive is a substance added in small amounts to something else to improve, strengthen, or otherwise alter it. A **food additive** is any substance added intentionally to food to improve appearance, flavor, texture, nutritional value, or storage properties. This chapter will discuss why and how additives are used.

REGULATING ADDITIVES

Additives are important in the production of safe and nutritious food. Therefore their use is regulated by the government. On the international level, the Food and Agriculture Organization (FAO) and the World Health Organization (WHO) are involved. In the United States, the Food and Drug Administration (FDA) regulates additives.

You will recall from Chapter 17 that the FDA has compiled the GRAS list. It is a list of ingredients that are Generally Recognized As Safe. The GRAS list includes over 600 substances, such as spices, natural seasonings, and flavorings, considered safe for human consumption. Items on the ingredient GRAS list are not considered additives.

The FDA severely restricts the use of food additives. It tests all food additives that are not on the GRAS list to ensure their safety. It has imposed a 100–fold margin of safety in the use of food additives. This means that a food

*CONTAINS LESS THAN 2% OF THE U.S. RDA OF THESE NUTRIENTS.
**PREPARED ACCORDING TO THE BASIC RECIPE—BACK OF PACKAGE.
CONTAINS: POTATO FLAKES, MONOGLYCERIDES, NATURAL AND ARTIFICIAL FLAVOR, SODIUM BISULFITE (TO MAINTAIN COLOR), CALCIUM STEAROYL LACTYLATE, BHA AND BHT (TO PROTECT FLAVOR), SODIUM ACID PYROPHOSPHATE, CITRIC ACID.

The use of food additives is regulated by the government.

Saccharin and the GRAS List

There have been instances when substances on the GRAS list have been removed because further testing proved there was at least some risk involved in their use. Saccharin, a calorie–free sweetener, was popular because it is 300 times as sweet as sugar.

Saccharin was removed from the GRAS list because extensive testing showed it could produce cancer in laboratory animals. Under the Delaney Anti–Cancer Clause, it would normally have been taken off the market. Because saccharin was so popular with diabetics who could not eat sugar, special legislation was passed by Congress to allow its continued use.

The FDA has published guidelines for the use of saccharin. It is now one of 2000 food additives that can be considered safe as long as they are used only in specific amounts.

Additives serve many purposes in this cake mix.

The wording on these containers indicates whether they contain natural or artificial grape flavoring.

sample can contain only 1/100 of the amount of an additive found to be safe in testing with laboratory animals.

The FDA also administers the Delaney Anti–Cancer Clause. As you learned in the last chapter, the Delaney Clause says that a substance shown to cause cancer in humans or animals may not be added to food in any amount.

Ingredient Labeling

The FDA requires manufacturers to list all ingredients in a food on its label. Labeling helps consumers make informed choices. Shoppers are able to look at what ingredients and additives are in a food product before deciding whether to buy it.

The FDA has strict rules about how additives are labeled and identified. Thus consumers who wish to do so can choose products containing only natural food flavors and colors. Other products may contain artificial additives. These are also called synthetic additives. They are substances made in a chemical laboratory that do not normally occur naturally in food.

For example, the phrase "raspberry yogurt" on a label tells consumers that the product contains only natural raspberry flavor. However, if the label says "raspberry–flavored yogurt," the product may contain natural raspberry flavor plus other natural flavorings. Finally, if the label reads "artificially–flavored raspberry yogurt," the yogurt contains either all artificial flavorings or a combination of artificial and natural flavorings.

USING ADDITIVES

Additives are used to preserve food. They also enhance color, flavor, nutritional value, and texture. Additives can prevent food from drying, foaming, hardening, or oxidizing. They also act as buffering, enriching, sweetening, stabilizing, or curing agents.

Food additives have many accepted uses. However, they may not be placed in food to deceive the consumer or to decrease the nutritional value of a food. They are not to be used to conceal damage, spoilage, or low quality. According to the law, additives may not be used to trick consumers.

• PRESERVATIVES

One of the main uses of food additives is as preservatives. Many foods are produced far from where they are consumed. The only way the food can be safely transported over great distances is by using preservatives to prevent deterioration and spoilage. Preservatives are used by manufacturers who are looking for ways to extend the shelf life of their products. In addition, there is an ever–increasing demand for food around the world. It is becoming more and more important to preserve all the food that is produced.

Preservatives are usually chemicals used to prevent bacterial growth that would cause spoilage. Preservatives need to be nontoxic and economical. They should not affect the flavor, color, or texture of the food.

Commonly used chemicals are sodium nitrite, sorbic acid, sodium bisulfite, and sodium nitrate. Sometimes preservatives serve more than one purpose. For example, sodium nitrate is used in cured meats, fish, and some poultry products to protect against botulism. Natural substances, including salt, organic acids (such as acetic acid in vinegar), sugar, and spices, can be used as preservatives but are not classified as additives.

• ANTIOXIDANTS

Oxidation is a natural process that takes place in food. In Chapter 8, you learned that oxidation is a chemical change in which a substance

Sodium nitrate is a preservative also used to cure meats, such as hot dogs and cold cuts.

The sulfur used in drying this fruit serves as an antioxidant.

Natural Additives

Natural additives are normal components of natural food products. These additives come from a food or a specific part of a plant. They are separated out for their particular properties. For example, casein, the main protein in milk, is used as a thickening agent in many milk products.

One important natural additive is alginate (AL–jin–ayt), which comes from kelp, a form of seaweed. The kelp is chemically changed to form the alginate that acts as a thickening agent or foam stabilizer in ice cream, cheese, candy, and yogurt.

Gums are natural substances that are taken from bushes, trees, and seaweed. They are used as thickening agents and stabilizers in ice cream, frozen puddings, salad dressings, and cottage cheese. They also help prevent the formation of sugar crystals. Two commonly used gums are gum arabic and guar gum carrageenin.

Vitamin E, or tocopherol, is both a nutrient and an antioxidant. It helps prevent oil from becoming rancid. Vitamin E is present normally in whole wheat, rice germ, and vegetable oils.

Ascorbic acid, more commonly known as vitamin C, is used as an antioxidant, nutrient, and color stabilizer in many foods. Ascorbic acid helps maintain the red color in cured meats. In addition, as you know from your fruit leather experiment, it prevents color change and preserves flavor in fruit. Ascorbic acid is present naturally in all citrus fruits, as well as in many other foods. Because it is easily destroyed by heat and light, it is often added to food after processing.

Citric acid is a natural additive present in all citrus fruits. It is used both to lower pH and as a flavoring because it has a tart taste.

Beta carotene, the vitamin A precursor, is present in many foods and is a natural additive in others. It is used as both a coloring agent and a nutrient. One of its more common uses is as a coloring agent in margarine.

Beta carotene is a natural additive used as a coloring agent in margarine.

loses electrons. In food science, oxidation usually involves the reaction of a food with oxygen. When oxidation occurs, vitamins and lipids can break down and changes occur in pigments and flavor.

Antioxidants are substances used to slow down or prevent oxidation. They are able to retard rancidity in fat and minimize the breakdown of vitamins. Antioxidants include the salt water used to keep apple slices from browning and the sulfur used in preparing dried fruit. Vitamin E, ascorbic acid, and lecithin can also be used as antioxidants.

• STABILIZERS

Food additives can also be used as aids in processing and preparing food. A **stabilizer** is a substance that can keep a compound, mixture, or solution from changing its form or chemical nature. Also called thickeners, stabilizers are used to prevent crystals from forming, stabilize foam, or reduce stickiness in products such as icing.

Stabilizers are often made from natural starches. They can also be proteins, such as pectin, casein, sodium caseinate, or gelatin. Stabilizers and thickeners are apt to be natural additives, while additives used for other purposes are often artificial.

The thickeners and stabilizers used in ice cream help prevent the formation of large crystals so that the ice cream won't feel grainy. The stabilizers added to peanut butter prevent the fat from separating from the protein. This gives the peanut butter a more appealing consistency.

• BUFFERS

In earlier chapters, you learned the importance of pH in the preparation and preservation of food. To maintain a desired pH, buffers are added to some foods. As you know, a buffer is a substance that helps maintain the relative balance of hydrogen and hydroxide ions. Citric acid, sodium citrate, and lactic acid are food additives that serve as buffers. In addition, bases, such as sodium bicarbonate and sodium hydroxide, are also buffers.

Alginate, a stabilizer and thickening agent, is made from kelp.

Stabilizers in peanut butter prevent the fat from separating from the protein.

• COLORS

Some additives are used to make food more appetizing to consumers. Appearance plays a large part in which food buyers select. Therefore manufacturers use many FDA–approved food colors to enhance the appearance of their products. For example, almost all soft drinks, cheeses, ice cream, jams, and jellies have coloring added.

Coloring is added to almost all jams and jellies.

Some colors are made from food. However, almost half of the colors commonly used are substances created in laboratories. These are called synthetic food colors.

Any synthetic food color is identified by number. For example, FD&C Red No. 40 is used in many foods, drugs, and cosmetics. In the past, synthetic food colors were often made from coal tar. Many people believed coal tar colors were harmful to health. Therefore the synthetic food colors now in use are *not* made from coal tar. The use of food colors is under constant review by the FDA.

• FLAVORS

Many substances are added to food to enhance flavor. For example, plain gelatin is not very appetizing, so flavoring is added to make it more appealing. There are about 2000 natural and synthetic flavors available. Flavors involve the largest number of food additives.

Flavorings are usually artificial. The demand for flavorings is so high that there are not

Flavoring is added to plain gelatin to make it more appetizing.

There are many natural sweeteners that add flavor to food.

enough natural flavorings available. The amount of grape–flavored products made in the United States is about five times the natural grape flavor available from the production of Concord grapes. Therefore a synthetic Concord grape flavor is used for most products.

• SWEETENERS

Sugar and other sweeteners are used more often than any other flavor enhancer. They make the taste or smell of food more pleasing to the consumer. Table sugar, brown sugar, maple syrup, molasses, and honey are natural sweeteners, which add flavor to food.

Sorbitol (SORE–buh–tahl) is a sugar alcohol very similar to natural sugar. However, it is only half as sweet as sucrose and does not metabolize as well. It is widely used by people who are dieting or who are diabetic. Sorbitol is used in "sugarless" gum because it does not cause as many dental cavities as sucrose or other sugars. However, it does contain as many calories as sucrose.

Sugarless gum and candy are made from sorbitol, which does not cause as many dental cavities as sucrose.

Saccharin is an artificial sweetener made from petroleum products, which is 300 times as sweet as sucrose. Saccharin has a bitter aftertaste if used in any great amount. It has been available for many years but its use is strictly regulated by the FDA.

Aspartame (AS–pur–taym) is a newer synthetic sweetener approved by the FDA. It has a clean, sweet taste with no aftertaste. Aspartame is made of the amino acids aspartic acid and phenylalanine. While it is not a problem under the Delaney Clause, there is some concern about the use of aspartame. This is because the amino acid combination involved is one that would normally be consumed in only very small amounts. Therefore the long–term effects of using aspartame are not known.

ADDITIVE PROS AND CONS

Most people feel that food products available in this country are of a better quality than they would be if additives were not used. Most additives are included by manufacturers for some constructive purpose. For example, ethylenediamine tetraacetic acid (EDTA) (ETH–uh–leen–DY–uh–meen TET–ruh–uh–SEE–tik) is an additive used to chemically trap metal ions. The metal ions enter food during processing when food is passed between large metal rollers or through other metal machinery. By removing the metal, the EDTA helps prevent rancidity and color changes that would occur because of the tiny pieces of metal.

A small percentage of additives are present because of mistakes made during food processing. These are called unintentional additives, or **contaminants.** These additives may have negative effects on food products.

As you know, one type of contaminant is residue of pesticides used in growing the food. These chemicals, used to kill pests and insects, can be harmful to humans if they remain on

NUTRITION AND YOU

Nutritional Additives

Some additives have been included in food for their nutritional value. The number of foods that have nutritional additives is increasing steadily. In the United States, the use of nutritional additives is regulated by the federal government.

As you know, fortification means adding nutrients to a food. The nutrients that are added are those not normally found in the food. The first time a food was fortified was in 1924 when iodine was added to table salt to prevent **goiter** (GOY–tur). Goiter is an enlargement of the thyroid gland because of a lack of iodine. Iodized salt has almost eliminated goiter as a health problem in this country.

Milk has been fortified with vitamin D since the 1930s to help prevent rickets, a childhood disease affecting bone growth. Vitamin A is added to margarine and vitamin C to many soft drinks. Diseases such as rickets and scurvy almost never occur because of the widespread use of fortification.

Sometimes, nutrients are lost in processing food. They are readded in the process called **restoration.** Restoration reestablishes the original nutritive value of the product. Vitamin C is added to canned citrus juice during restoration.

Enrichment also involves adding nutrients originally lost in processing. It is similar to restoration except, in enrichment, more nutrients can be added than were originally found in the unprocessed food. Enrichment is used with cereal products because many natural vitamins and minerals are lost during processing. Thiamin, niacin, riboflavin, iron, calcium, and vitamin D are the nutrients often used in enrichment. While enriched flour is common in the United States, England, and Canada, its use is forbidden in France.

Finally, nutrients can be added in a process called **nutrification.** This involves adding nutrients to a snack food with a low nutrient/calorie ratio so that the food can take the place of a nutritionally balanced meal. Breakfast bars are a food advertised as being able to provide all the nutrients needed in a meal.

food. While the FDA monitors residues, it is unable to check every sample of every product before it reaches consumers. Fortunately, most of the residue is on the outside of fresh produce. Careful washing before eating will remove most of the pesticide.

Salt was the first food to be fortified.

EDTA is a chemical additive that removes metal ions that enter food during processing.

To many people, food additives are a controversial topic. These people feel that the food industry adds ingredients that are nutritionally worthless and harmful to health. They fear the possible toxic effects of food additives. They are concerned with the allergic reactions food additives can cause in allergy–prone people. Opponents of food additives are concerned that the long–term effects of additives on the body are not known. They evaluate the risks and benefits of additives and believe the risks outweigh the benefits.

Informed consumers need to be aware of what additives are present in the food they buy and eat. Anyone who has a question or concern about a specific food additive can obtain information from the FDA or local government agencies.

Wise consumers take time to read food labels.

EXPERIMENT 21–1

Pudding Mixes and Additives

In this experiment, you will observe the effect of additives on vanilla pudding.

PROCEDURE

1. Follow the variation assigned by your teacher.
   a. **Variation 1.** Prepare a vanilla pudding mix according to the instructions on the package.
   b. **Variation 2.** Prepare a vanilla pudding mix. Add 80 g sugar to the dry mix before adding liquid.
   c. **Variation 3.** Prepare a vanilla pudding mix, substituting lemon juice for the liquid called for in the recipe. Use one–third as much lemon juice as you would have used of the other liquid.
2. List the ingredients on the pudding label in your laboratory report, and explain the purpose of each ingredient. You can do this while your pudding is cooking.
3. Place a glass plate over the line–spread test sheet provided by your teacher. Place a hollow cylinder in the center, and fill with the hot cooked pudding. Count the lines covered at each of 4 points around the circle, and average your results. In your data table, record this result for the variation you made.
4. Cool the rest of the pudding to room temperature by placing the container of pudding in a pan of cold water.
5. Repeat the line–spread test described in step 3 with the cool pudding.
6. Label two paper soufflé cups with your name, variation number, and class period. Fill the cups with the pudding mixture, and cover each with plastic wrap. Refrigerate one and freeze the other until the next class period.
7. Thaw the frozen pudding sample. Examine the thawed and refrigerated samples for retrogradation and syneresis. Record your observations in your data table.
8. Write your data on the chalkboard. In your data table, copy the information for the other variations.

EXPERIMENT 21–1

QUESTIONS

1. In what ways were the puddings different?
2. Which variation would you choose if you had to prepare a pudding the night before for a pie filling needed the next day? Why?
3. Explain the change that occurred when lemon juice was added.
4. Explain the change that occurred when sugar was added.
5. What changes occurred when the pudding was stored refrigerated?
6. What changes occurred when the pudding was frozen and thawed?
7. How do you feel the additives influenced the behavior of the pudding as compared with the starches in Experiment 7–2?

SAMPLE DATA TABLE

Variation	Line–spread Average		Appearance Refrigerated Sample	Appearance Frozen Sample
	Hot	Cold		
1				
2				
3				

EXPERIMENT 21–2

Effects of Minerals on Protein

Tofu, a basic part of the diet of Southeast Asians, is a protein product made of soybean curd. It is often used as a meat substitute in the United States. In this experiment, you will compare the effects of the mineral salts calcium sulfate and magnesium sulfate on the characteristics of tofu.

PROCEDURE

1. Mass 140 g dry soybeans. Wash the beans thoroughly, and place them in a 1 L beaker containing 500 mL water. Label the beaker with your name and class period. Let the beans soak overnight in the location specified by your teacher.
2. The next day, drain the beans and rinse them twice with tap water.
3. Place the rinsed beans in a blender with 250 mL water, and liquify.
4. Place 1 L water in a saucepan, and bring to a boil.
5. Add the liquified mixture to the water. This mixture is called soymilk.
6. Separate the residue of skins from the soymilk by straining the mixture through six layers of cheesecloth into a kettle.
7. Boil the soymilk over medium–high heat for 3 minutes or until a foam forms. Turn off the heat, and remove the kettle from the stove.
8. Follow the variation as directed by your teacher.
   a. **Variation 1.** Slowly stir the mixture as you add 4.5 g magnesium sulfate.
   b. **Variation 2.** Slowly stir the mixture as you add 2.9 g calcium sulfate.
9. Wait 10 minutes until the soymilk has curdled, forming tofu curds. Place the mixture in fresh cheesecloth in a clean kettle. Rinse and squeeze the curds.
10. Mass a clean dry 400 mL beaker labeled with your name, class period, and the variation used. Record the mass in your data table.

EXPERIMENT 21–2

11. Allow the curds to drain for 2–3 hours. Put the curds into the labeled beaker, cover with cold water, and store overnight in a refrigerator.
12. The next day, drain the curds and mass the beaker and tofu curds. Record the mass in your data table. Calculate the mass of the curds.
13. Write the mass of your curds on the chalkboard. In your data table, copy the mass of the curds of the other variation.
14. Cut the tofu into 1–cm cubes.
15. In a frying pan, melt 15 mL margarine over medium heat. Add one–half the tofu cubes and fry for 5–10 minutes or until the tofu is slightly golden brown in color.
16. Place the fried and plain tofu samples, labeled with the variation used, in the location indicated by your teacher.
17. Sample the tofu prepared according to both variations. Evaluate for tenderness, texture, and flavor.

QUESTIONS

1. How does the mass of the curds compare with the original mass of beans used? Did the variations differ? Why or why not?
2. Which tofu is the toughest? Which texture and flavor do you prefer?
3. Which tofu has the greater nutritive value? Why?

SAMPLE DATA TABLE

Variation	Mass of Empty Beaker	Mass of Beaker and Curds	Mass of Curds	Tenderness of Tofu		Texture of Tofu		Flavor of Tofu	
				Plain	Fried	Plain	Fried	Plain	Fried
1									
2									

REVIEW

TO SUM UP

- A food additive is a substance added intentionally to food to improve appearance, flavor, texture, nutritional value, or storage properties.
- The use of food additives is regulated by the FDA in the United States and by the FAO and WHO on the international level.
- Food additives used as preservatives help extend the shelf life of food products and prevent spoilage when food is transported long distances.
- Antioxidants prevent the breakdown of fat and vitamins that occurs when a food combines with oxygen.
- Additives can be used to improve the color and flavor of food.
- Nutritional value can be added to food through fortification, restoration, enrichment, or nutrification.
- Although additives are included in food for constructive purposes, some people feel that additives are nutritionally worthless and harmful to health.

CHECK YOUR FACTS

1. What is a food additive?
2. State four reasons for using food additives.
3. How does the Delaney Clause affect the use of food additives?
4. Why can saccharin be sold when it causes cancer in laboratory animals?
5. Explain what is meant by a 100–fold margin of safety.
6. What are required characteristics of food preservatives?
7. What is the purpose of using sodium nitrate as an additive?
8. What is an antioxidant?
9. What is the purpose of a stabilizer?
10. What is the difference between natural and artificial additives?
11. List three examples of natural food additives.
12. Why are food colorings used?
13. Why are artificial flavors used so frequently in food products?
14. What does it mean to fortify foods?
15. Why is EDTA added to food?

CRITICAL THINKING AND PROBLEM SOLVING

1. A proposed new food additive is found to cause undesirable side effects when 100 mg or more is used per serving. How much would the FDA allow in a serving of the food?
2. How would vanilla ice cream and artificially–flavored vanilla ice cream differ?
3. Why are stabilizers added to ice cream?
4. Why is it best not to use large amounts of saccharin or aspartame?
5. Why is iodine added to salt and vitamin D to milk?
6. Explain the similarities and differences among fortification, restoration, enrichment, and nutrification.
7. Why could the use of nutrified food products lead to unhealthy eating habits?
8. Give examples of five beverages fortified with vitamin C.
9. Read the labels of ten food items. List the additives named on the labels and give the purpose of each additive.

The food processing industry preserved fresh food so that consumers can enjoy flavorful meals and snacks.

UNIT 5

Institution Administration
ADMISSION
Admission requirements include a bachelor's degree
a "B" average on all upper division or graduate
previously completed. The following courses are
as undergraduate prerequisites:
Chemistry (including Biochemistry)
Human Physiology
Microbiology
Elementary Nutrition
Upper Level Nutrition
Food Preparation, Food Science
and/or Food Technology
Microbiology
Elementary Nutrition
and/or Business
FINANCIAL AID
of applicants.

Food Science and You

Unit 5 provides information that will help you develop your own food science experiment. The unit also offers a brief overview of career possibilities in food science.

Chapter 22 explains that the process of developing an experiment begins with careful consideration of what you want to discover. As you read the chapter, you will find guidelines on researching information, as well as actually developing an experiment. Finally, you will learn how to report and interpret data in a meaningful way.

In Chapter 23, you will survey the wide variety of food science careers that are open to you. The full range of possibilities—from research positions to careers in food and nutrition to jobs in the food service industry—are described for you.

CHAPTERS

CHAPTER

22

Developing Experiments in Food Science

This chapter will help you . . .

- Describe ways of choosing a topic for a food science research project.
- Identify resources that can be used to gather information for a research topic.
- Select a hypothesis and title for a food science experiment.
- Propose variables for a food science experiment.
- Develop a procedure for a food science experiment.
- Explain the importance of accurate supply and equipment lists for a food science experiment.

Terms to Remember

hypothesis variables

Throughout this course, you have learned about many topics important to food scientists. You have conducted experiments that explained and reinforced the material you read. However, food scientists do more than simply absorb information presented to them. Food scientists, like other scientists, need to be able to look up information about a topic of interest. They must also be capable of designing experiments to test their theories and increase their understanding.

In this chapter, you will have a chance to pursue a topic of special interest to you. You will learn how to investigate a topic and design an experiment related to it.

CHOOSING A TOPIC

Doing a research project in any subject involves picking a topic that is of interest to you. That way you will not become bored with the topic before you are finished studying it.

There are a number of ways to begin looking for a topic about food science. Review the subjects you have studied this year to find out whether there was a topic you wanted to know more about. Take a walk through your local supermarket to see whether there are any food products that you would like to learn more about. Are there products missing from the shelves that you think ought to be there? If these approaches do not suggest a project topic, scan newspapers and magazines for articles related to food.

RESEARCHING YOUR TOPIC

A scientist exploring a new field begins by reviewing the literature that already exists about the subject matter of interest. A trip to your school or local library is a good way to begin.

Exploring the supermarket may give you ideas for a food science experiment topic.

Background reading is the starting point for a research project.

Check the *Reader's Guide to Periodical Literature* for recent magazine articles on your topic. If the library has a computerized data base, ask for help in searching for magazine references about your subject. Journals such as FDA *Consumer, Food Technology, Food Engineering, Journal of Food Science,* or *Journal of the American Dietetic Association* may be of help to you.

These journals can help you learn about current topics in food science research.

Text or reference books may also contain useful information. The card catalog or computerized book list may yield sources you can review. Your teacher will provide you with a bibliography of sources that were useful in writing this text. The bibliography will also serve as an example of how to compile your own bibliography of the sources you use for your project.

Take notes as you review articles and books. Then you will have useful information available when you begin to develop an experiment on your topic. You will also use your notes in writing a paper on your topic.

In addition to reading about your topic, talk to people who might be able to give you helpful information. Home economics and science teachers are important resources easily available to you. If a university is located nearby, professors there may be able to help you. Your community may have a food company that produces a product related to your topic. If you contact the company, someone may be able to provide useful information.

Interviewing a person in the food industry may give you useful information for your research project.

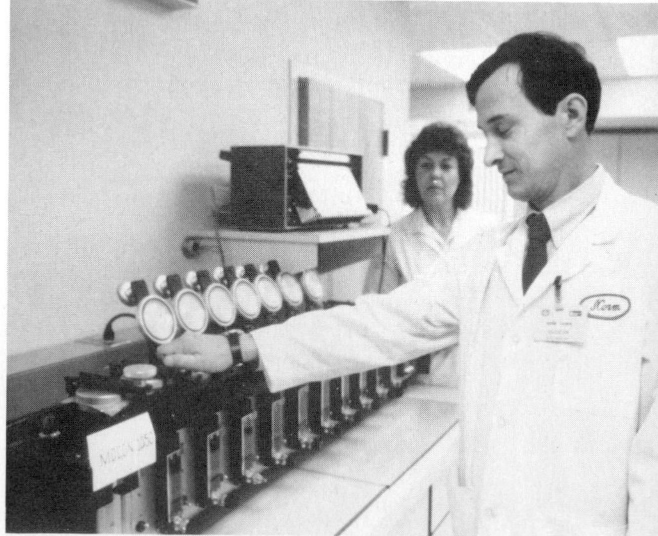

Scientific research is crucial to the discovery of new knowledge in the field of nutrition.

NUTRITION AND YOU

Nutrition Research

Nutrition is the branch of science concerned with nourishing the body. Scholars have been trying to understand the human body and its nutritional needs for thousands of years. Hippocrates, who lived from 460–377 B.C., was a famous Greek often called the father of medicine. He said, "Children produce more heat and need more food than adults." He further observed, "Persons who are naturally very fat are apt to die earlier than those who are slender." Clearly, how much food the body needs and how that food affects the body were topics of interest even in ancient times.

One of the first recorded experiments relating to nutrition was carried out in France by Antoine Lavoisier (1743–1794). Lavoisier designed an experiment to test the theory that respiration, or breathing, is a measurable chemical process. He studied guinea pigs and then his laboratory assistant. Lavoisier measured the oxygen consumed, the heat lost, and the carbon dioxide produced by each of his subjects. From his data, he concluded that respiration was a combustion process chemically similar to reactions in which a substance actually burned.

Lavoisier then designed experiments to measure how much oxygen each subject consumed while fasting and resting compared with how much oxygen was consumed when the subject was exercising. He found that oxygen consumption increased during periods of exercise. His data also showed that the amount of heat produced by both animals and humans was proportional to oxygen consumption. While Lavoisier's work has been refined by other researchers, his basic concepts were proven correct.

In the 1800s, experiments were conducted to prove that certain nutrients are essential to the health of both animals and humans. Magendie (1783–1855), another French scientist, carried out experiments designed to show that diet is related to health. He fed dogs a diet of distilled water combined with either butter, olive oil, sugar, or gum arabic. The dogs died when fed these restricted diets. Magendie concluded that protein is necessary for life.

These experiments may seem simple and the concepts they tested obvious. However, they were the beginning of the science of nutrition. Currently, complex nutritional experiments are being conducted throughout the world.

The United States Department of Agriculture and Department of Health and Human Services both allocate millions of dollars annually to nutrition research. Experiments cover a wide range of nutrition concerns. For people to be well nourished, nutrition must be understood on a molecular level as well as in terms of the body as a whole.

There is still much to be learned about nutrition. People who choose a career in nutrition research face interesting challenges. These range from determining the specific nutritional needs of a particular individual to finding ways to meet the nutritional requirements of an entire nation.

NARROWING THE FOCUS

After you have acquired a basic understanding of your topic, it is time to begin to narrow the focus. Concentrate on one area you want to study in depth. As you explore it, give some thought to developing an experiment related to the topic. Since you have only limited time to study the subject and carry out your experiment, it is important to settle on a topic that can be dealt with in the time available.

As you make your final decision about your experiment topic, remember that time is not the only limiting factor. It is also important to consider the resources available to you. How available are the ingredients you will need? For example, don't plan an experiment that uses kiwi fruit if it is unavailable when you will be doing your experiment. The space and equipment available in your food science classroom are factors you must also keep in mind.

DEVELOPING AN EXPERIMENT

When you have completed your background research, you are ready to design your experiment. An experiment contains several important parts.

• THE HYPOTHESIS

The first step in developing an experiment is to state its purpose. A **hypothesis** (hy–POTH–uh–sis) is a proposed solution to a scientific problem. It is a theory or explanation that accounts for a set of facts and that can be tested by further investigation. What hypothesis or theory are you trying to prove? What questions do you want to answer? What new product would you like to produce? Unless you know the point of your experiment, it is unlikely that you will develop a procedure that will lead to meaningful results.

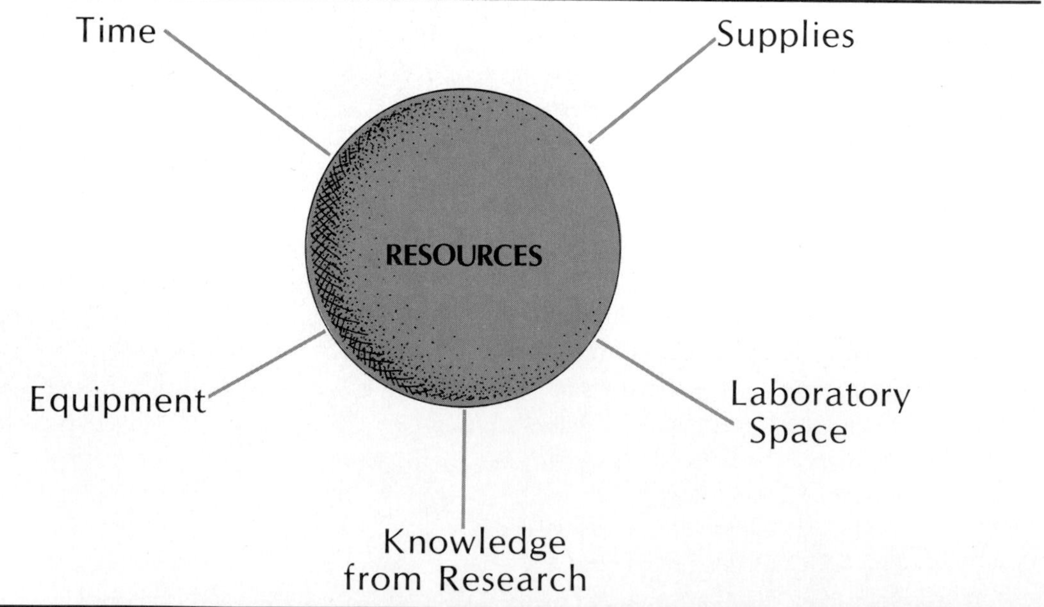

One step in developing a food science experiment is to consider your resources and how you can best use them.

The hypothesis of an experiment is a proposed solution to the questions you want answered.

• THE TITLE

Once you have settled on a purpose, the next step is to select a title for your experiment. The title should give another person an idea of what the experiment is trying to show or prove. Suppose you are going to compare the whipping quality of regular whipping cream and UHT whipping cream. A descriptive title would be "Comparing Whipping Quality of Whipping Creams."

• THE PROCEDURE

Once you have identified your purpose and decided on a title for your experiment, it is time to develop a procedure. To do this, you must decide how many **variables** you are going to consider. A variable is a factor being tested in an experiment. Only one variable can be tested effectively at a time, although several can be tested in one experiment.

In selecting variables, be sure to keep the number small. Otherwise, there will be so many possible explanations for what happens that you will be unable to decide what caused your final results. In the whipping cream example, you might compare two different brands of each type of whipping cream. Since it is the whipping cream itself you want to test, you need to make sure that all other factors are controlled. All the samples should be at the same temperature when whipped, thus controlling the temperature variable. The same size bowl made of the same material and the same type of beater should be used to avoid affecting the results.

It is best to perform an experiment several times to determine if the results will be consistent. When your class performs an experiment, it is possible to post the results and

Limiting the variables tested in your experiment helps you better interpret the results you obtain.

compare similarities or differences. However, if you or you and a partner are the only ones carrying out the experiment, you need several trials to see how the results compare. If the results are consistent, you will be able to draw valid conclusions from them.

• THE DATA TABLE

It is important to design a data table so you can record your results in an organized manner. For example, you might list the brand names of the four whipping creams in a column on the left of the data table. You could report the time needed to whip each cream to firm peaks during three different trials in columns to the right of the names.

Suppose you planned to test the stability of each of the whipped cream samples. You could place a measured amount of each product in a funnel over a graduated cylinder for a specified period of time. The milliliters of drainage from the cream could then be reported in additional columns in the data table. Such a data table might look like the Sample Data Table shown below.

The data table should organize the data obtained in the experiment.

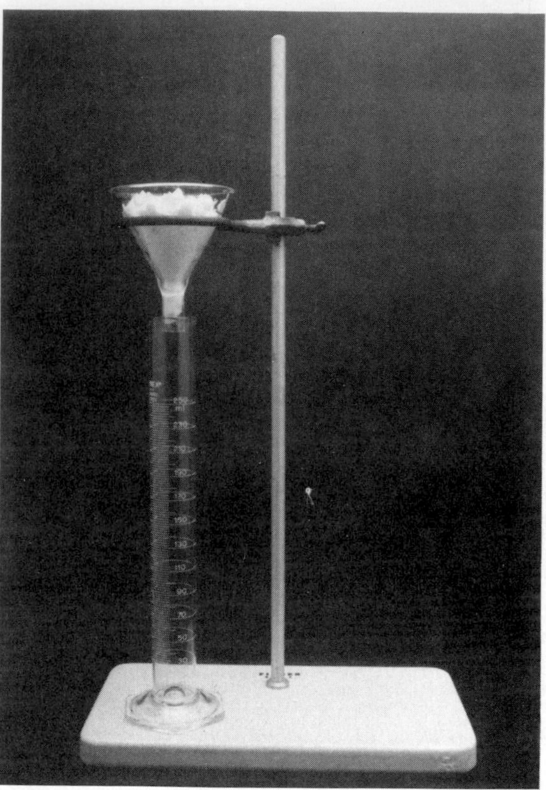

Sample Data Table

Brand of Cream	Time to Form Firm Peaks			Drainage After 10 Minutes		
	Trial 1	Trial 2	Trial 3	Trial 1	Trial 2	Trial 3

• SUPPLIES AND EQUIPMENT

You need to develop a list of the supplies you will be using to perform your experiment in class. For the experiment discussed above, you would decide which brands of whipping cream you wanted to test. You would list how much you need of each brand so the supplies could be purchased. Whether your teacher buys the supplies or you do, an accurate shopping list is needed.

You also need to identify what equipment you would use. The whipping cream experiment would require a small glass bowl, an electric mixer, a 100 mL graduated cylinder, and a funnel. Since you cannot be whipping more than one sample of cream at a time, you can wash the bowl and mixer between whipping the creams. However, you would need enough graduated cylinders and funnels to place each sample of freshly whipped cream into a funnel without waiting.

Having accurate supply and equipment lists helps you be more efficient when conducting your experiment. You can get the supplies and equipment out before starting the experiment. You will be able to work effectively because you will not have to stop to find missing supplies or equipment.

• WRITING THE EXPERIMENT

Before actually carrying out the experiment, you need to write it in the format used throughout the year. You should include the title, a paragraph explaining the purpose of the experiment, a step–by–step procedure, a data table, and any questions you hope to answer as a result of doing the experiment. Once you have completed the write–up and have your materials, you can proceed with performing the experiment.

You can work most efficiently when you gather all the equipment needed before beginning an experiment.

Your experiment needs to be written up in the experiment format before being conducted.

HISTORY OF AN EXPERIMENT

Experiment 22–1 is the last experiment outlined in detail for you in this textbook. It is an experiment to help you determine factors that influence whether or not corn pops.

Background reading on this topic indicated that one of the most important factors in whether corn pops is its water content. The pressure that builds up inside the kernel of corn as the water is heated is what causes the corn to explode, or "pop."

An experiment was designed to compare the percentage of kernels of corn that popped in three samples. The first is fresh popping corn that has not been altered in any way. The second sample is popping corn that has been heated in a food dehydrator overnight to drive off some of the water. The third sample is corn that has been punctured so the water will escape, rather than build up pressure, as it is heated.

To be as certain as possible that these will be the only variables involved in the experiment, all the corn will come from the same original sample of fresh popping corn. The same number of kernels will be put into the popper during each trial of the experiment. The same popper will be used for all samples. All the corn will be popped the same length of time.

The data table was designed to allow this information to be reported in a clear, easy–to–read format. The questions are to help you reach conclusions about what makes popcorn pop and, based on this information, to decide the best way to store unpopped popping corn. Now, even though you know more than usual about how Experiment 22–1 is supposed to turn out, try popping some corn!

What factors affect whether or not popcorn pops?

EXPERIMENT 22–1

Properties of Popping Corn

If you have ever popped popcorn, you know that after the popping stops, there are often some unpopped kernels of corn in the bottom of the popper. In this experiment, you will try to determine what factors influence whether corn pops.

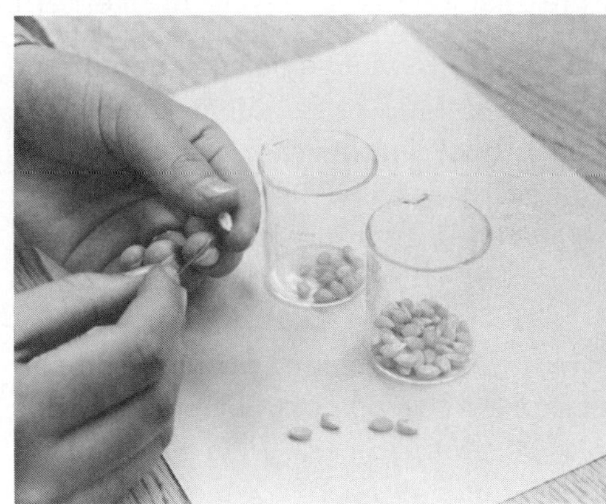

PROCEDURE

1. On the day before the experiment, help puncture kernels of corn with a needle. In addition, your teacher will place corn in the food dehydrator to dry overnight.
2. Follow the variation assigned by your teacher.
   a. **Variation 1**. Count out 100 kernels of fresh popcorn.
   b. **Variation 2**. Count out 100 kernels of the popcorn that has been dried.
   c. **Variation 3**. Count out 100 kernels of the popcorn that has been punctured with a needle.
3. When it is your turn to use the popper, pop your kernels of corn for 2 minutes. Count the number of unpopped kernels remaining after popping ceases.
4. Write your results in your data table and on the chalkboard. In your data table, copy the results from the other variations.

QUESTIONS

1. Which variation had the largest percentage of unpopped kernels? Why did this occur?
2. Which variation had the smallest percentage of unpopped kernels? Why did this occur?
3. What is the best way to store popcorn to preserve its "popability" as long as possible?

SAMPLE DATA TABLE

Variation	Number of Unpopped Kernels	Percent Unpopped Kernels
1		
2		
3		

EXPERIMENT 22–2

A Taste of Taste Testing

This experiment is to be an intermediate step between following instructions and designing a completely original experiment. Therefore the instructions for this experiment will be general, rather than detailed. It will be up to you to design the exact procedure you will follow.

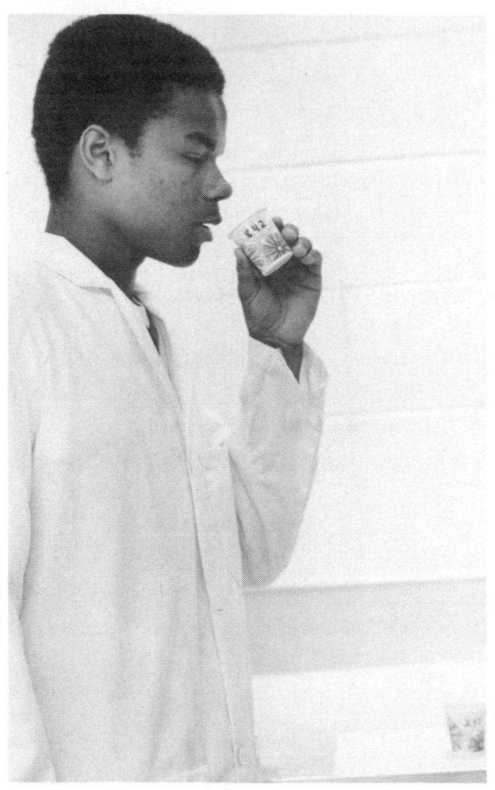

Many people who drink cola products say they have a preference for one product. However, how many people can actually distinguish their choice from the other colas? Given a choice between their product and another cola, how many will actually select their cola as the one they like best? In this experiment, you will use your knowledge of sensory testing to design and carry out a taste–testing experiment involving colas.

There are various ways taste–testing experiments can be done. In one format, tasters are given three randomly labeled samples and asked to select the one that is different from the other two. Another format involves giving tasters two samples and asking them to select the one they prefer. If the sense of sight can be eliminated, tasters can be given a cola product and a lemon–lime product and asked to select the "cola" they prefer.

In designing this experiment, remember what you learned earlier about nonpreferential labeling of samples. Eliminate as many variables as possible to make your results meaningful.

After you have written your procedure, designed your data table, and prepared questions, submit your proposed experiment to your teacher for approval. Once you have that approval, you can proceed with your cola taste test.

TO SUM UP

- A topic chosen for a research project should be of interest so the researcher does not get bored before the project is done.
- The card catalog, a computer search, or the *Reader's Guide to Periodical Literature* can lead to books and magazine articles that contain information on a particular subject.
- The focus of a research project must be narrowed so it can be finished in the time available.
- The hypothesis of an experiment is a proposed solution to a scientific problem.
- The variables in an experiment are the factors being tested.
- Several trials of an experiment are run to be sure results are consistent so valid conclusions can be drawn.
- A data table is used to record experiment results in an organized manner.

CHECK YOUR FACTS

1. What is the first step in researching a topic?
2. Name three journals that might be useful in doing a food science project.
3. What can you do to collect information on a topic besides read about it?
4. What factors must you consider in planning a food science experiment?
5. What is the first step in designing an experiment?
6. Why is selecting a title an important step?
7. Why is it necessary to limit the number of variables in an experiment?
8. Why should you design a data table for your experiment?
9. Why are accurate supply and equipment lists needed before doing an experiment?
10. What are the parts of an experiment included in an experiment write–up?

CRITICAL THINKING AND PROBLEM SOLVING

1. Why is narrowing the focus necessary for a research project?
2. Why would it be important to use the same type bowl for every sample in the whipping cream experiment?
3. Why is it necessary to repeat an experiment several times?
4. What other pieces of equipment not mentioned in the text would be useful in the whipping cream experiment?
5. What steps were taken to limit the number of variables in the popcorn experiment?
6. How do you think popping corn differs from corn that is consumed fresh?
7. What variables beyond your control might influence the popcorn experiment?

Careers

This chapter will help you . . .

- Evaluate whether a career in food science or related fields would be right for you.
- Identify career areas open to people with college degrees in food science and technology.
- List careers available to people with college degrees in home economics or a related field.
- Discuss the duties of a dietitian and the settings in which a dietitian might work.
- Differentiate between commercial and noncommercial establishments in the food service industry.
- Compare and contrast entry–level and higher–level jobs in the food service industry.

Terms to Remember

entry–level jobs
higher–level jobs
internship

As you may have concluded from the broad range of topics studied this year, food science has many branches. As a result, the career opportunities related to food science are almost endless. Exact job titles, descriptions, and responsibilities may vary with time and location. However, there is a good chance that a career in food science may be right for you. In this final chapter, you will be introduced to careers in the main areas of food science. You can get further career information by writing one or more of the agencies listed below.

Sources of Information About Careers in Food Science

American Bakers Association
Suite 300
1111 14th Street, NW
Washington, D.C. 20009
Booklet: "The Baking Industry: Career Dimensions"

American Culinary Federation
Educational Institute
P.O. Box 3466
St. Augustine, Florida 32084
Pamphlets: "National Apprenticeship Training Program for Cooks"
"National Certification Program for Chefs and Cooks"

American Dietetic Association
430 N. Michigan Avenue
Chicago, Illinois 60611
Pamphlet: "The Registered Dietitian, Your Nutrition Expert"

American Home Economics Association
2010 Massachusetts Avenue, NW
Washington, D.C. 20036
Careers Packet: "The Opportunity of a Lifetime"

Food Marketing Institute
Communications Department
1750 K Street, NW
Washington, D.C. 20006

Home Economists in Business
Tower Suite 505
310 Maple Avenue West
Vienna, Virginia 22180

The Institute of Food Technologists
221 North LaSalle Street
Chicago, Illinois 60601
Pamphlet: "The World's Largest Industry"

Office of Public Information
Food and Nutrition Service
U.S. Department of Agriculture
3010 Park Center Drive
Alexandria, Virginia 22302
Pamphlet: "Careers in the Food and Nutrition Service"

Many food science careers require a college degree.

FOOD SCIENCE CAREER AREAS

College graduates who majored in food science and technology are often called food scientists or food technologists. They apply science and engineering to food:

- Production.
- Packaging.
- Distribution.
- Preservation.
- Evaluation.
- Utilization.

The food scientist's goal is to ensure an adequate, acceptable, and safe food supply, both at home and on a world–wide basis. This means creating and using energy–efficient systems for the development, processing, and marketing of food products.

There are many career areas open to people with degrees in food science and technology.

Food scientists are involved in all aspects of producing food products for sale to consumers.

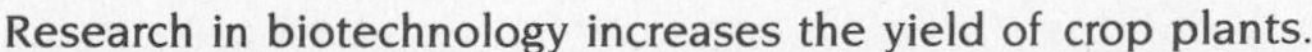

Research in biotechnology increases the yield of crop plants.

These include work in:

- Biotechnology (improving yields of plants and animals).
- Quality control.
- Product development.
- Processing.
- Technical sales.
- Research.

A food scientist may work for companies that produce food products that are dried, canned, frozen, pickled, smoked, irradiated, freeze–dried, fermented, refrigerated, or baked.

Food scientists work to find less costly food substitutes that are tasty, appealing, and nutritious. For example, soybeans can be added to ground beef in making hamburgers. Such hamburgers are hard to tell from all–beef burgers, but they cost less to produce.

The space program employs food scientists. They experiment with food products to decide which ones can be taken into space and how they should be packaged.

Food scientists are responsible for the processing plants found on large fishing vessels. They ensure that the fish caught maintain the highest possible quality, even though the ship may remain at sea for many weeks at a time. Harvesting machines for food produced on

Can you tell which burger contains soybeans?

land and the immediate steps needed for processing this food have been developed by food scientists.

Safety testing of food to ensure that no harmful bacteria or other contaminants are present is done by food scientists. They may work for individual manufacturers in quality control or as inspectors for the government.

The area of food science and technology is both complex and diverse. While the exact activities of those working in this field will surely change as time goes by, their work will continue to be important in producing an adequate, safe, and nutritious food supply.

FOOD AND NUTRITION

Careers in food and nutrition cover a wide variety of opportunities. A college degree in home economics or a related field is needed for these careers, which include:

- Food editor of a magazine.
- Home economist for a chain of supermarkets.
- Demonstrator or sales representative for a food company or equipment manufacturer.
- County or state Cooperative Extension Service agent.
- Dietitian.

By earning a degree in food and nutrition, a person acquires a knowledge of:

- The science of human nutrition.
- The chemical and physical nature of food.
- The maintenance of food quality during preservation and preparation.
- The lifetime relationship between food consumption and health.

The relationship between nutrition and lifelong health is still not completely understood,

Food scientists can be found in many places, such as on this commercial fishing boat.

but knowledge of it is constantly increasing.

Further study for an advanced degree (a degree beyond a four–year college degree) in food and nutrition qualifies a person to do food or nutrition research or to be a college teacher. Which of these or other jobs is right for any one person depends on personality type and special interests.

Besides providing careers that are diverse, challenging, and exciting, studying food and nutrition allows people to apply science to daily life. All people are affected by the food they eat. Athletes, for example, may spend a great deal of time studying the effects of diet on athletic performance.

Home economists are important in promoting new food products.

Careers in food and nutrition are often related to health services.

One example of a career that draws on science in everyday life is the work done by those who decide what food will be served on airline flights. These people determine what food will retain an appetizing appearance, as well as remain nutritious and safe to eat, while being held for a period of time at a given temperature in an airplane's galley.

• DIETITIAN

A specialized career that combines food and nutrition with food management is that of a dietitian. Some dietitians work as part of medical teams in hospitals to help patients recover and maintain their health. They teach people suffering from ulcers or diabetes how to control their conditions through proper eating habits.

Other dietitians supervise the feeding of large groups of people in schools or industries.

Some dietitians are trained to teach people how to manage their resources so they can obtain the most nutritious food. These dietitians may work in city health departments or with special programs for elderly or poor people.

Dietitians must acquire a strong academic background in the chemical and biological aspects of food, how food functions to maintain health, and the social sciences related to culture and economics. They participate in an **internship**, a time of supervised practical training, or other professional experience in preparation for becoming a dietitian. Most dietitians need good communication skills, since they spend much of their time working with people.

NUTRITION AND YOU

Careers in Nutrition

A variety of people study nutrition while in college. Teachers of physical education, health, home economics, and some areas of science receive training in nutrition. Medical doctors, dentists, and nurses also study nutrition and its importance to the body as part of their professional training.

Many careers in the area of nutrition are involved with education. Some private food companies employ nutritionists to promote nutrition education. Two of the largest private organizations that provide nutrition education are the National Livestock and Meat Board and the National Dairy Council.

Nutrition and how it relates to health are subjects of national interest. Many television and radio networks air programs relating to nutrition. It is important, however, to note the credentials of any person on television or radio who gives information on nutrition. Sometimes people who are not adequately trained promote concepts that are not based on correct nutrition information or on scientific research. Such people may make sensational claims based on their emotions or personal experiences rather than on experiment data.

People interested in a career in nutrition must be committed to getting a scientific education and then educating others. Nutritionists communicate basic information about the importance of food choices to health. They stress that wise food choices made as a part of a person's daily routine are the best way to be and stay nutritionally healthy.

THE FOOD SERVICE INDUSTRY

The food service industry is usually divided into two parts—commercial and noncommercial. Jobs in commercial food service are found with full–service restaurants, fast–food chains, or buffet–style restaurants. Noncommercial jobs are found in public schools, universities, hospitals, retirement and nursing homes, prisons, airlines, and industrial plants.

• ENTRY–LEVEL JOBS

The food service industry has many **entry–level jobs**, jobs for which no experience or advance training is needed. These are the jobs that many students hold, such as counter worker, waiter or waitress, assistant cook or baker, or dishwashing machine operator. The worker does about the same duties every day. Work routines in some establishments are divided into work stations, such as hot food, cold food, frying, baking, service, and sanitation. Depending on the location, a worker may need to obtain a food handler's license.

Schools, prisons, hospitals, and nursing homes are examples of the noncommercial food service industry.

Entry–level jobs in food service are often available at fast–food restaurants.

One step up from entry–level jobs are jobs that require some training. This training may be taken at a vocational school or at a school that specializes in food service training. Positions that usually require training include cook, chef, baker, or pie maker.

• HIGHER–LEVEL JOBS

Higher–level jobs in this industry are held by those who hold college degrees in food systems management or hotel and restaurant management. These people have training in all areas of food service, including planning, purchasing, production, and service. They are educated to hire, train, and motivate workers. They have learned to plan and control financial resources to serve nutritious, safe, and appealing meals at a cost consumers can afford.

Food service managers use their education in planning meals for summer camps, cruise ships, retirement centers, or restaurants. Others function as caterers or food brokers, agents who buy or sell food for others.

There are countless opportunities for employment in the food service industry. For those willing to work hard, there is the possibility for advancement. Because of the trend toward eating meals away from home, the food service industry should continue to grow and provide employment for many workers.

A person with a degree in food systems management might manage a restaurant like this.

TO SUM UP

- Because of the various branches of food science, there are many career opportunities in this field.
- Food scientists and food technologists have college degrees and work to apply science and engineering to various aspects of food production and processing.
- A wide variety of careers are available to those with a college degree in home economics or a related field.
- A dietitian combines food and nutrition with food management to help people in a variety of settings eat healthy diets.
- Opportunities in the food service industry fall into two areas—commercial and non-commercial.
- The amount of education and training people have affects whether they are qualified for an entry–level job or a higher–level job in the food service industry.

CHECK YOUR FACTS

1. What is the focus of careers in food science and technology?
2. Name three areas in which food scientists may work.
3. Why does the space program employ food scientists?
4. Name three job opportunities in food and nutrition.
5. What are the responsibilities of dietitians?
6. Name three locations where dietitians might work.
7. In what types of places do commercial food service employees work?
8. What types of positions do entry–level workers in the food service industry hold?
9. What sort of work is performed by holders of college degrees in food systems management?

CRITICAL THINKING AND PROBLEM SOLVING

1. How are food scientists helping expand the world food supply?
2. As an airline dietitian, what factors would you consider when planning in–flight menus?
3. Why would a hotel use the services of a food broker?
4. Read the want–ads section of a local or regional newspaper. Identify three entry–level and three higher–level positions available in the food service industry. Are you qualified for any of the jobs? If not, what would you have to do to become qualified?
5. Find three newspaper or magazine articles dealing with food science. Identify a job related to the subject of each article.
6. Research a food science career of interest to you. Use a minimum of three sources, including at least one person whom you interview about the job you are studying.

GLOSSARY

absolute zero. The temperature at which all molecular motion ceases and matter possesses no heat energy; −273°C. (4)

acid. A substance that ionizes in water to produce hydrogen ions (H^+). (5)

acidosis (as–ih–DOE–sis). A condition in which blood pH is 7.2 or lower. (5)

actin (AK–tin). A fibrous protein found in muscle. (9)

activation energy. The energy required to start a chemical or biological reaction. (12)

active site. The part of an enzyme molecule that attaches to the substrate; the enzyme surface where the chemical reaction takes place. (12)

additive. A substance added in small amounts to something else to improve, strengthen, or alter it. (17)

adenosine diphosphate (ADP) (uh–DEN–uh–seen dy–FOS–fayt). A compound used in forming ATP. (11)

adenosine triphosphate (ATP) (uh–DEN–uh–seen try–FOS–fayt). The carrier of energy in living cells. (11)

adipose tissue (ADD–uh–pohs). Fat cells. (8)

adulterated (uh–DULL–tuh–ray–tud). Made impure by the addition of improper ingredients. (17)

advanced degree. A degree beyond a four–year college degree. (23)

aerate (AIR–ayt). To add air or gas to a substance. (8)

aerobic. Requiring air or oxygen. (15)

aggregate (AG–ruh–git). A group or dense cluster of ions or molecules. (13)

agitation. Stirring or beating. (7)

agitation retort. A commercial pressure canner that can mechanically increase the movement of food being canned to shorten processing time. (19)

air pressure. The force that air exerts as it presses on the earth. (6)

albumin (al–BYOO–mun). Egg white; also, a protein found in egg white and milk. (9)

alcohol. An organic compound that contains a hydroxyl group (–OH). (7)

alginate (AL–jin–ayt). A natural additive made from the seaweed called kelp, which acts as a stabilizer or thickener. (21)

alkalosis (al–kuh–LO–sis). A condition involving too much base in the blood and body fluids. (5)

amine group (uh–MEEN). A combination of an atom of nitrogen with two atoms of hydrogen ($-NH_2$) found in amino acids. (9)

amino acid (uh–MEE–no). An organic acid containing an amine group, which chains with other amino acids to form protein. (9)

ammonia. An organic compound whose formula is NH_3; a waste product of protein metabolism. (11)

amphoteric (am–fuh–TER–ik). Able to react either as an acid or a base. (9)

amylopectin (am–uh–lo–PEK–tin). A starch molecule with a branched structure, which is found in potato and tapioca. (7)

amylose (AM–uh–lohs). A starch molecule with a linear structure, which is found in rice and wheat. (7)

anabolism (uh–NAB–uh–liz–um). The chemical processes involved when molecules combine to build larger molecules. (11)

anaerobic. Not requiring the presence of air or oxygen. (15)

anaerobic respiration. The first step in the breakdown of glucose, which occurs in the absence of oxygen; also called fermentation. (15)

anemia (uh–NEE–mee–uh). A deficiency disease caused by lack of iron. (10)

anorexia nervosa (an–uh–REX–ee–uh ner–VO–suh). An eating disorder characterized by self starvation resulting in the intake of fewer kilocalories than needed for a healthy body. (4)

anthocyanin (an–thoh–SIGH–uh–nin). A water-soluble plant pigment sensitive to pH changes. (5)

antibody. A protein that helps the body fight disease. (9)

antioxidant. A substance used to prevent oxidation. (8)

artificial additives. Substances added to food, which do not normally occur in it, that are made in a chemical laboratory. (21)

aseptic canning (ay–SEP–tik). A method of canning in which food is first sterilized and then placed in sterile containers, thus shortening processing time. (19)

aspartame (AS–pur–taym). An artificial sweetener made from amino acids. (21)

atherosclerosis (ath–uh–ro–skluh–RO–sis). A heart disease caused by the buildup of plaque along the inner walls of the arteries; often called hardening of the arteries. (8)

atom. The smallest particle of an element that keeps the chemical properties of the element. (3)

atomic mass. The sum of the mass of the protons and neutrons in the nucleus of an atom. (5)

atomic number. The number of protons in the nucleus of an atom. (5)

bacteria. Single–cell organisms that cause food spoilage. (5)

baking powder. A chemical leavening agent that contains baking soda, dry acid, and starch or other filler. (14)

baking soda. The compound sodium bicarbonate ($NaHCO_3$), which is used as a leavening agent in baked goods. (14)

balance. A scientific instrument that determines the mass of materials. (1)

basal metabolic rate. The rate at which energy is used by a body at rest after a 12–hour fast. (11)

basal metabolism. The amount of energy needed by a body at rest to maintain the automatic activities that support life. (11)

base. A substance that ionizes in water to produce hydroxide ions (OH^-). (5)

beaker. A laboratory container with a wide mouth; used for holding solids or liquids. (1)

beriberi (ber–ee–BER–ee). A disease of the nervous system caused by lack of thiamin. (10)

beta rays. High speed electrons used in food irradiation. (20)

biotin (BY–uh–tin). A B vitamin. (10)

blanch. To briefly immerse food in boiling water to inactivate enzymes. (12)

boil. To cause vapor bubbles to form within a liquid. (3)

boiling point. The temperature at which the vapor pressure of a liquid equals the pressure over the liquid. (6)

botulism (BOCH–uh–liz–um). Poisoning caused by the toxin of C. *botulinum*; the most serious form of food poisoning. (5)

bound water. Water that is tightly held by the various chemical groups in food molecules so it cannot be easily separated from the food. (6)

brine. A water–and–salt mixture containing large amounts of salt. (15)

brine pickling. A method in which the food being pickled is fermented in a brine solution for several weeks. (15)

buffer. A substance that helps maintain the relative balance of hydrogen and hydroxide ions in a solution. (5)

bulimia (byoo–LIM–ee–uh). An eating disorder characterized by gorging on food, then purging the body by vomiting or using laxatives. (4)

buret (byur–ET). A long thin glass cylinder calibrated to 0.1 mL; used to transfer very precise amounts of liquid. (1)

calibrate (KAL–uh–brayt). To check, adjust, or standardize the marks on a measuring instrument. (1)

calorie. The heat required to raise the temperature of 1 g of water 1°C. (4)

Calorie. A kilocalorie, or 1000 calories. (4)

caramelization (kar–uh–mul–uh–ZAY–shun). A browning reaction in sugar requiring high temperatures and either low or high pH. (7)

carbohydrate (kar–bo–HY–drayt). An essential nutrient that provides the body with energy; an organic molecule made of carbon, hydrogen, and oxygen, which can be a sugar, starch, or plant fiber. (1,7)

carboxyl group (kar–BAHK–sul). A group found in all organic acids consisting of a carbon bonded to an oxygen and a hydroxyl group (–COOH). (8)

carotene (KAIR–uh–teen). An orange plant pigment that can be changed into vitamin A. (10)

carrageenin (kair–uh–GEE–nun). A vegetable gum that is used to stabilize the milk protein casein in evaporated milk. (16)

caseharden. To form a hard outer layer on drying food, which traps moisture in the food. (18)

casein (KAY–seen). One of the two main proteins found in milk. (9)

catabolism (kuh–TAB–uh–liz–um). A chemical reaction in which large molecules break down into smaller molecules, releasing energy. (11)

catalyst (KAT–ul–ist). A substance that helps a chemical reaction occur without being destroyed in the process. (12)

cell respiration. A complex process in which glucose molecules are broken down in a cell. (15)

cellulose (SELL–yuh–lohs). A plant polysaccharide composed of a form of glucose that is not digestible by humans. (7)

Celsius (SELL–see–us). The metric temperature scale. (1)

centi–. A prefix used in the metric system to mean 1/100, or 0.01. (1)

chalaza (kuh–LAY–zuh). A ropelike structure in an egg that keeps the egg yolk centered. (9)

chemical bond. The force that holds the atoms in a molecule together. (3)

chemical change. A process in which substances become new and different substances. (3)

chemical reaction. A process in which properties of substances change as new substances with different properties are formed. (3)

chlorophyll (KLOR–uh–fill). The green pigment present in plants, which allows the process of photosynthesis to occur. (7)

cholecalciferol (ko–luh–kal–SIFF–uh–rawl). The active form of vitamin D. (10)

cholesterol (kuh–LESS–tuh–rawl). A fatty alcohol made from glucose or saturated fatty acids. (8)

clamp. A device attached to a ring stand to support pieces of equipment, such as test tubes, thermometers, or burets. (1)

Clostridium botulinum (klahs–TRID–ee–um boch–uh–LIN–um). The bacteria that causes botulism, the most serious form of food poisoning known. (5)

Clostridium perfringens (klahs–TRID–ee–um pur–FRIN–jens). A bacteria that causes food intoxication. (17)

coagulation (ko–ag–yuh–LAY–shun). To change a liquid into a soft semisolid or solid mass. (9)

coenzyme. A heat–stable organic molecule that must be loosely associated with an enzyme for the enzyme to function. (12)

cold–blooded. Having a body temperature that varies with the surroundings. (11)

cold–pack. A canning method in which uncooked food is placed in a container that is then filled with boiling water or juice, closed with a lid and a ring band, and processed; also called raw–pack. (19)

cold point. The location in a container of food being canned that is the last to reach the temperature considered safe for killing microorganisms in that food. (19)

collagen (KAHL–uh–jun). A fibrous protein found in connective tissue. (9)

colloid (KAHL–oyd). A particle in a colloidal dispersion. (6)

colloidal dispersion (kuh–LOYD–ul dis–PUR–zhun). A homogeneous mixture that is not a true solution because of the relatively large size of the solute particles. (6)

complete protein. A protein that contains all eight essential amino acids. (9)

complex carbohydrate. Another term for polysaccharides—starches and fibers. (7)

compound. A pure substance made up of two or more elements chemically attached together. (3)

concentration. A measure of the amount of a substance in a given unit of volume. (5)

condensation. The change of a gas to a liquid. (3)

condensed milk. Canned milk in which 50 percent of the water has been removed and sugar has been added. (16)

conduction (kun–DUK–shun). The transfer of heat energy from particle to particle through molecular collisions. (4)

contaminant. An additive present because of mistakes during food processing; also called an unintentional additive. (21)

continuous phase. A liquid in which droplets of an immiscible liquid are dispersed in an emulsion. (13)

control. The standard in an experiment with which other samples are compared. (10)

controlled–atmosphere packaging (CAP). A way of packaging food that alters the gaseous environment surrounding the food product. (20)

convection (kun–VEK–shun). The transfer of heat energy by the motion of fluids or gases. (4)

covalent bond (ko–VAY–lunt). A chemical bond formed when atoms share electrons. (3)

covalent compound (ko–VAY–lunt). A compound in which electrons are shared; also called a molecular compound. (3)

cracking. The breakdown of fats by repeated heating. (8)

cream. Milk that is extra rich in emulsified fat droplets. (16)

creaming. The process in which fat droplets associate in clusters and rise to float on the top of milk. (16)

cross contamination. Transferring of bacteria from one food to another. (17)

crystal (KRIS–tul). A solid in which the particles are arranged in a regular repeating pattern. (3)

culture. A controlled bacterial population or a colony of microorganisms; also called a starter. (16)

cultured milk. Any milk product fermented to produce a desired flavor or texture; also called fermented milk. (16)

curd. The solid formed by the coagulation of milk; used to make cheese. (12)

data (DAYT–uh). Recorded observations and measurements. (1)

deficiency disease. A disease caused by a lack of a specific nutrient. (10)

dehydration (dee–hy–DRAY–shun). The loss of water from a substance. (7)

dehydrator. An appliance that provides a steady supply of circulated heated air to dry food. (18)

dehydrofreezing. A method of food preservation that combines drying and freezing. (18)

Delaney Anti–Cancer Clause. A clause in the Food Additive Amendment to the United States Food, Drug, and Cosmetic Act that says that a substance shown to cause cancer in humans or animals may not be added to food in any amount. (20)

denaturation (dee–nay–chur–AY–shun). A change in the shape of a protein molecule that does not break its covalent bonds. (9)

density. The mass per unit volume of a substance. (6)

dentin layer. The hard dense layer of a tooth that is beneath the enamel. (10)

deoxyribonucleic acid (dee–ahk–see–ry–bo–noo–KLAY–ik). The compound that controls the type of cells that are produced. (10)

diabetes (dy–uh–BEE–tis). A disease in which the body does not regulate blood glucose level normally. (7)

dietitian. A specialist in food and nutrition and food management. (23)

digestion. The chemical processes of breaking down food and releasing nutrients in a form suitable for absorption. (5)

disaccharide (dy–SAK–uh–ride). A sugar made from two monosaccharides bonded together. (7)

dispersed phase. The substance existing in droplet form in an emulsion. (13)

double–acting baking powder. A leavening agent containing two acids, one that reacts with cold liquid and one that reacts with heat. (14)

double bond. A covalent bond in which each atom donates two electrons to form the bond. (8)

dried milk. Milk in which the water has been removed, leaving milk solids. (16)

elastin (ih–LAS–tin). A fibrous protein found in connective tissue. (9)

electromagnetic spectrum. The continuous range of radiation arranged in the order of wavelength. (20)

electromagnetic waves. Waves that transfer energy through space. (20)

electron. A subatomic particle with a negative electrical charge. (3)

electronegative. Tending to attract the shared electrons in a molecule and become negatively charged. (6)

element. The simplest type of pure substance from which all other materials are formed. (3)

emulsifier (ih–MUL–suh–fy–ur). A substance that coats the droplets of one immiscible liquid so it can remain mixed in another immiscible liquid; also called an emulsifying agent. (6)

emulsifying agent. A substance that coats the droplets of one immiscible liquid so it can remain mixed in another immiscible liquid; also called an emulsifier. (6)

emulsion (ih–MUL–shun). A mixture of two liquids whose droplets do not normally blend with each other. (6)

enamel. The outer layer of a tooth. (10)

end point. The point at which neutralization occurs; same as equivalence point. (5)

energy. The ability to do work. (4)

energy levels. Regions of space outside the nucleus of an atom in which electrons move. (3)

enrichment. The addition of nutrients that were lost in processing to a food at levels that can be greater than the original nutritional value of the food. (21)

entry–level job. A position for which no experience or training is needed. (23)

enzymatic browning (en–zuh–MAT–ik). The discoloration of fruits and vegetables caused by enzymes. (12)

enzyme (EN–zime). A protein that controls chemical activity in living organisms. (1)

equation. A written description of a chemical reaction using symbols and formulas. (3)

equivalence point. The point at which neutralization occurs; same as end point. (5)

Erlenmeyer flask (UR–lun–my–ur). A cone–shaped laboratory container with a narrow neck and a broad, flat bottom. (1)

essential amino acid. An amino acid that must be included in the diet because it cannot be manufactured by the body. (9)

ethylenediamine tetraacetic acid (EDTA) (ETH–uh–leen–DY–uh–meen TET–ruh–uh–SEE–tik). An additive used to chemically trap metal ions. (21)

evaporated milk. Canned whole milk that has been heated to remove 60 percent of its water. (16)

evaporation (ih–vap–uh–RAY–shun). Vaporization that takes place at the surface of a liquid. (6)

fasting. Consuming nothing but fluids, usually water. (11)

fat. An essential nutrient that provides the body with energy; a saturated lipid compound that is solid at room temperature. (1,8)

fat–soluble vitamin. A vitamin that will dissolve in fat but not in water and can be stored in the body. (10)

fatty acid. An organic acid made of a carbon chain with attached hydrogens and a carboxyl group at the end. (8)

fermentation (fur–men–TAY–shun). A chemical reaction that splits complex organic compounds into relatively simpler substances. (14)

fermented milk. Any milk product cultured to produce a desired flavor or texture; also called cultured milk. (16)

fiber. Carbohydrate that provides strength and support to the cell walls of plants. (7)

fibrous protein. Protein molecules that are rope-like and very strong, which serve as connective tissue. (9)

flash frozen. Frozen very quickly. (20)

flavor. The distinctive taste that comes from a food's unique blend of appearance, odor, mouthfeel, and sound. (2)

foam. A product formed when a liquid is whipped, trapping air in the liquid. (9)

folacin (FAWL–uh–sin). A B vitamin. (10)

food additive. A substance added intentionally to food to improve appearance, flavor, texture, nutritional value, or storage properties. (21)

food infection. A type of foodborne illness caused by pathogenic organisms or animal parasites that enter the body with food. (17)

food intoxication. A type of foodborne illness caused by chemical or bacterial toxins. (17)

food science. The study of the production, processing, preparation, evaluation, and utilization of food. (1)

foodborne illness. An illness caused by eating food that has been contaminated with pathogenic microorganisms, toxins produced by microorganisms, animal parasites or their eggs, or toxic chemicals. (17)

formula. A combination of chemical symbols used to represent the elements and the ratio of elements present in a molecule of a compound. (3)

fortification. The addition of a nutrient to a food. (16)

free water. Water found in food that readily separates from the food when it is sliced, diced, or dried out. (6)

freeze drying. A food preservation method in which a frozen food is processed to remove the solvent from dispersed or dissolved solids. (20)

freezing. The change of a liquid to a solid. (3)

freezing point. The temperature at which a substance changes from the liquid state to a solid. (8)

fresh–pack pickling. A method in which the food being pickled is placed in a brine for a few hours, drained, and immersed in a boiling mixture of vinegar and spices. (15)

fructose (FROOK–tohs). A simple sugar, a monosaccharide, found in fruits and the sap of trees. (7)

galactose (guh–LAK–tohs). A simple sugar, a monosaccharide, not found free in nature but formed from the hydrolysis of lactose. (7)

gamma rays. High–energy electromagnetic waves used in food irradiation. (20)

garnish. A decorative arrangement added to food or drink. (2)

gas. Matter with no definite shape or volume. (3)

gastric juice. One of the main digestive juices in the stomach. (5)

gel. A solid thickened starch mixture. (7)

gelatinization (ju–lat–un–uh–ZAY–shun). The absorption of water by starch molecules, causing them to swell and soften. (7)

globular protein (GLAHB–yuh–lur). A protein molecule that has a rounded shape like a ball of steel wool. (9)

glucose (GLOO–kohs). The basic sugar unit around which all other carbohydrates are built; often called blood sugar. (7)

gluten (GLOO–tun). An elastic, stretchy protein found in wheat, which gives baked products their shape and structure. (9)

glycerol (GLISS–uh–rawl). A three–carbon organic alcohol, which combines with fatty acids to form triglycerides. (8)

glycogen (GLY–kuh–jun). The form in which carbohydrates are stored in the body. (7)

goiter (GOY–tur). An enlargement of the thyroid gland because of a lack of iodine. (21)

graduated cylinder. A tall cylindrical container used for accurately measuring the volume of a liquid. (1)

gram. The basic unit of mass in the metric system. (1)

GRAS list. A list of over 600 ingredients generally recognized as safe in food. (17)

gray. A unit of measure of radiation equal to 100 rads. (20)

gum. A natural substance taken from bushes, trees, and seaweed, which is used as an additive. (21)

half–and–half. A milk product with at least 10 percent milk fat. (16)

hard water. Water that contains dissolved calcium or magnesium ions. (6)

heat of fusion. The energy required to change 1 g of a substance from the solid phase to the liquid phase. (6)

heat of vaporization. The amount of heat needed to change 1 g of a substance from the liquid phase to the gas phase. (6)

hemicellulose (hem–ee–SELL–yuh–lohs). A carbohydrate plant fiber. (7)

heterogeneous mixture (het–uh–ruh–JEE–nee–us). A combination of substances in which the individual substances can be recognized by sight. These mixtures are not uniform in makeup or properties. (3)

high–density lipoprotein (HDL). A lipoprotein that carries cholesterol from other parts of the body to the liver for disposal; also referred to as an alpha lipoprotein. (8)

high–quality protein. A protein that contains all the essential amino acids in amounts proportional to the body's need for them. (9)

higher–level job. A position for which a college degree is needed. (23)

histidine (HISS–tuh–deen). An amino acid essential for infants. (9)

homeostasis (ho–mee–oh–STAY–sis). The process through which the body regulates itself to maintain normal conditions and a relatively constant internal environment. (7)

homogeneous mixture (ho–muh–JEE–nee–us). A combination of substances that is the same in every part of a sample. The components cannot be recognized by sight. (3)

homogenization (ho–mahj–un–ih–ZAY–shun). A process that reduces the fat globules in milk to a smaller and approximately equal size. (13)

hormone. A chemical messenger, which affects a specific organ or tissue and brings forth a specific response. (7)

hot–pack. A canning method in which food has been heated in syrup, water, or juice to at least 77°C, packed while hot in a container, and closed with a lid and a ring band. (19)

hydrogen bond. An attraction occurring in polar compounds in which a hydrogen atom of one molecule is attracted to the negative end of another molecule. (6)

hydrogenation (hy–druh–juh–NAY–shun). The process of adding hydrogen to unsaturated fat to make it more solid and resistant to chemical change. (8)

hydrolysis (hy–DRAHL–uh–sis). Splitting a compound into smaller parts by the addition of water. (7)

hydroxide ion (hy–DRAHK–side). A negative ion formed from hydrogen and oxygen (OH^-). (5)

hydroxyl group (hy–DRAHX–sil). A combination of hydrogen and oxygen, which is written –OH. (7)

hyperglycemia (hy–pur–gly–SEE–mee–uh). An abnormally high blood glucose level. (7)

hypoglycemia (hy–po–gly–SEE–mee–uh). An abnormally low blood glucose level. (7)

hypothesis (hy–POTH–uh–sis). A proposed solution to a scientific problem; a theory or explanation that accounts for a set of facts and that can be tested by further investigation. (22)

immersion freezing. A method of commercial freezing in which the food to be frozen is immersed in a nontoxic refrigerant. (20)

immiscible (ih–MISS–uh–bul). Incapable of mixing or blending. (6)

incomplete protein. A protein that lacks one or more of the essential amino acids. (9)

incubation period (in–kyuh–BAY–shun). The time needed for the development of bacterial growth and fermentation. (16)

indicator. An organic dye that shows a color change when mixed with an acid or a base. (5)

indigenous microorganisms (in–DIJ–uh–nus). Microorganisms found naturally on a particular food. (15)

indirect–contact freezing. A method of commercial freezing in which food is placed on belts or trays and chilled rapidly by a refrigerant circulating through a cold wall. (20)

inert. A substance that does not readily react or combine with other elements or compounds. (20)

inoculation (ih–nahk–yuh–LAY–shun). Implanting microorganisms in another substance. (16)

insoluble (in–SAHL–yuh–bul). Incapable of dissolving. (1)

insulin. A hormone secreted by the pancreas that regulates the level of glucose in the blood. (7)

interfering agent. A substance added to a sugar solution to interfere with the size or rate of crystal growth. (7)

internship. A time of supervised practical training. (23)

inversion. The hydrolysis of sucrose. (7)

invert sugar. The mixture of fructose and glucose formed from the hydrolysis of sucrose. (7)

invertase (in–VUR–tase). An enzyme used in the hydrolysis of sucrose; also called sucrase. (7)

ion (EYE–ahn). An electrically charged particle formed when an atom gains or loses electrons. (3)

ionic bond. A chemical bond formed by the transfer of electrons from one atom to another. (3)

ionic compound. A substance formed when metals and nonmetals bond by transferring electrons; also called a salt. (3)

ionization (eye–ahn–ih–ZAY–shun). The process of forming ions. (5)

iron ring. A device attached to a ring stand to hold beakers or flasks. (1)

irradiation. Exposure to radiation; in food preservation, the passage of gamma and beta rays through food to destroy the living organisms that would cause the food to spoil. (20)

isoleucine (eye–suh–LOO–seen). One of the essential amino acids. (9)

joule (JOOL). The metric unit of heat flow equal to 0.239 cal. (4)

keratin (KER–uh–tun). A fibrous protein. (9)

ketone. An organic compound formed during the metabolism of protein. (11)

kilo– (KEY–low). A prefix used in the metric system to mean 1000. (1)

kilocalorie. A unit of 1000 calories used in measuring food energy. (4)

knead. To mix and work a dough into a mass by folding over, pressing, and squeezing. (7)

krad (KAY–rad). A unit of measure of radiation energy equal to 1000 rads. (20)

label. A display of written, printed, or graphic matter on a container. (17)

lactase (LAK–tase). An enzyme used in the hydrolysis of lactose. (7)

lactic acid. A waste product formed when glucose is not completely metabolized. (11)

lactose (LAK–tohs). A disaccharide found in milk. (7)

lactose intolerance. The inability of some people to digest milk because of the absence of lactase in the intestines. (16)

latent heat. The heat required to create a phase change without a change in temperature. (4)

leavening agent. A substance that helps baked products lighten or rise. (5)

lecithin (LESS–uh–thin). A phospholipid; used as an emulsifier in mayonnaise. (13)

leucine (LOO–seen). An essential amino acid. (9)

linoleic acid (lin–oh–LEE–ik). A polyunsaturated fatty acid. (8)

linolenic acid (lin–oh–LEN–ik). A polyunsaturated fatty acid. (8)

lipid (LIP–id). A family of chemical compounds, which include fats and oils. (8)

lipoprotein (lip–oh–PRO–teen). A cluster of lipids associated with protein, which serves as a transport vehicle for lipids in the blood. (8)

liquid. Matter with no definite shape but with a definite volume. (3)

liter (LEET–ur). A basic unit of volume in the metric system. (1)

low–density lipoprotein (LDL). A lipoprotein that transports cholesterol from the liver to other tissues; also referred to as a beta lipoprotein. (8)

low–fat milk. Fluid milk that contains from 0.5–2 percent milk fat. (16)

lyophilization (lye–ahf–uh–luh–ZAY–shun). The technical name for freeze drying, a food preservation method in which a frozen food is processed to remove the solvent from dispersed or dissolved solids. (20)

lysine (LYE–seen). An essential amino acid. (9)

macromolecule (mak–ro–MAHL–uh–kyool). A large molecule containing many atoms. (9)

major minerals. Minerals needed by the body in amounts of 0.1 g or more a day. (10)

maltose (MAWL–tohs). A sugar, a disaccharide, found in cereal and sprouting grain. (7)

mass. A measure of the amount of matter in a sample; also, to measure the amount of matter in a sample. (1)

mass percent. A method to express the concentration of solutions. (13)

matter. Anything that has mass and takes up space. (3)

mechanical energy. The energy of motion. (4)

medium. A substance through which something is transmitted or carried. (6)

megadose. An excessively large amount. (10)

melting. The process in which a solid changes to a liquid. (3)

melting point. The temperature at which a substance changes from a solid to a liquid. (6)

membrane (MEM–brayn). A thin layer of tissue covering surfaces or separating regions, structures, or organs in animals and plants. (11)

meniscus (muh–NIS–kus). The bottom of the curve formed by liquid in a narrow container such as a graduated cylinder or buret. (1)

metabolic rate (met–uh–BAHL–ik). The speed at which the chemical process of metabolism takes place. (11)

metabolism (muh–TAB–uh–liz–um). The chemical and physical processes occurring within the living cells of the body. (6)

metallic element. An element that is shiny, conducts heat and electricity, and can be drawn or pounded into various shapes. (3)

meter (MEET–ur). A basic unit of length in the metric system. (1)

methionine (muh–THIGH–uh–neen). An essential amino acid. (9)

metric system. The standard system of measurement used by scientists. (1)

micelle (my–SELL). An aggregation, or group, of molecules, often found in colloidal systems. (16)

microbes (MY–krohbs). Another name for microorganisms. (15)

microorganisms (my–kro–OR–gun–iz–ums). Animals and plants that cannot be seen by the human eye but can be studied through a microscope. (15)

microwaves. Invisible waves of energy used in cooking food in a microwave oven. (4)

milk solids. The protein, carbohydrate, fat, vitamins, and minerals dissolved in the liquid portion of milk. (16)

milli–. A prefix used in the metric system to mean $1/1000$, or 0.001. (1)

mineral. An essential nutrient; an inorganic element needed by the body. (1,10)

mixture. Matter made up of two or more substances combined in varying amounts but which are not chemically combined. (3)

molar solution. A solution in which a specific number of moles of solute is dissolved in 1 L of solution. (5)

molarity (mo–LAR–uh–tee). The number of moles of a substance in a liter of solution. (5)

mold. An organism that grows on organic matter giving it a fuzzy appearance; causes food spoilage. (5)

mole. The amount of a substance in grams equal to the atomic mass of the substance. (5)

molecular compound (muh–LEK–yuh–lur). A compound composed of molecules held together by covalent bonds; also called a covalent compound. (3)

molecule (MAHL–ih–kyool). A particle made up of two or more atoms held together by forces between the atoms. (3)

monosaccharide (mahn–oh–SAK–uh–ride). A single sugar, such as glucose, fructose, or galactose. (7)

monosodium glutamate (mahn–uh–SO–dee–um GLOOT–uh–mayt). A chemical that enhances flavors in food. (2)

mouthfeel. The scientific term that describes how a food feels in the mouth. (2)

myosin (MY–uh–sin). A fibrous protein found in muscle. (9)

natural additive. A substance that is a normal component of natural food products, which is added to food. (21)

neutral. A water solution that contains an equal number of hydrogen and hydroxide ions. (5)

neutralization (noo–trul–uh–ZAY–shun). A chemical reaction of an acid and a base to produce water and a salt. (5)

neutron (NOO–trahn). A subatomic particle with no electrical charge. (3)

niacin (NY–uh–sin). A major B vitamin. (10)

nonmetallic element. An element with a dull surface that conducts heat and electricity poorly, is brittle, and breaks easily. (3)

nucleus (NOO–klee–us). The dense core of an atom. (3)

nutrient. A substance found in food that is needed for life and growth. (1)

nutrient agar (AY–gar). A gelatinlike substance used as a base for bacterial growth. (17)

nutrient dense. A food that provides a relatively high quantity of one or more nutrients with a relatively low number of kilocalories. (14)

nutrification. The process of adding nutrients to a snack food with a low nutrient/calorie ratio so the food can take the place of a nutritionally balanced meal. (21)

nutrition. The scientific understanding of how food is used by the body. (1)

obese. A condition of excessive body fat. (4)

oil. An unsaturated lipid compound that is liquid at room temperature. (8)

oleic acid (oh–LEE–ik). A monounsaturated fat. (8)

organic acid. An organic compound that contains a carboxyl (–COOH) group. (8)

organic compound. A compound that contains the element carbon. (3)

osmosis (ahs–MO–sis). The movement of fluid across a semipermeable cell membrane so there is an equal concentration of solute on both sides of the membrane. (11)

osteomalacia (ahs–tee–oh–muh–LAY–shuh). The vitamin D deficiency disease in adults. (10)

osteoporosis (ahs–tee–oh–pore–OH–sis). A condition caused by lack of calcium, which results in thinner, less dense, and fragile bones. (10)

oxidation (ahk–suh–DAY–shun). A chemical change in which a substance loses electrons. (8)

pantothenic acid (pan–tuh–THEH–nik). A B vitamin. (10)

papain (puh–PAY–in). A dry powder containing enzymes, which is used to tenderize meat. (12)

parasite. An organism that grows and feeds on another organism. (17)

paste. A thickened starch mixture. (7)

pasteurization. A heat treatment used to destroy bacteria and other microorganisms in beverages such as milk and wine. (15)

pathogenic (path–uh–JEN–ik). Capable of causing disease. (17)

pectin. A carbohydrate plant fiber. (7)

pellagra (puh–LAY–gruh). A disease caused by a lack of niacin. (10)

peptide bond. A bond between two amino acids. (9)

periodic table. A chemical chart showing the known elements in order of their atomic number. (5)

permanently hard water. Water in which metal ions are present as sulfates. (6)

pesticide. A chemical used to kill insects and rodents. (17)

Petri dish (PEA–tree). A shallow glass or plastic laboratory dish with a loose–fitting cover. (1)

pH scale. A measurement of the relative number of hydrogen and hydroxide ions in a solution. (5)

phase. A state in which matter can exist—solid, liquid, or gas. (3)

phase change. The physical change of matter from one state to another. (3)

phenylalanine (fen–ul–AL–uh–neen). An essential amino acid. (9)

phospholipid. An organic compound similar to a triglyceride but that has a phosphorus–containing acid in place of one of the fatty acids. (12)

photosynthesis (foe–toe–SIN–thuh–sis). The process in which plants use the sun's energy to convert carbon dioxide and water into carbohydrate and oxygen. (7)

physical change. A process in which properties of a substance are altered but the identity of the substance does not change. (3)

plaque (PLAK). A mound of lipid material mixed with calcium and smooth muscle cells, which is deposited in the artery walls in and around the heart. (8)

polar covalent bond. A covalent bond in which electrons are shared unequally. (6)

polar molecule. A molecule that contains covalent bonds and has a division of charge so it has one slightly positive end and one slightly negative end. (6)

polymer (PAHL–uh–mur). A large molecule formed when small molecules of the same kind join together to form chains. (7)

polymerization (pahl–uh–mur–uh–ZAY–shun). The process of forming a polymer by linking small molecules of the same kind into chains to form a new substance. (7)

polypeptide. A protein molecule formed of many amino acids bonded together in peptide chains. (9)

polysaccharide (pahl–ee–SAK–uh–ride). A compound made from ten or more monosaccharides chemically linked together. (7)

pouch canning. A canning method in which flexible packages are used instead of cans or jars. (19)

precipitate (prih–SIP–uh–tayt). To cause a solid substance to be separated from a solution. (16)

precursor (pri–KUR–sur). A compound that can be converted to a vitamin in the body. (10)

pressure. A force that acts over a certain area. (6)

pressure processing. A method of processing canned food in which containers are heated in a pressure canner to kill harmful microorganisms. (19)

product. The elements or compounds formed during a chemical reaction. (3)

property. A feature or characteristic that helps identify a substance. (3)

protein. An essential nutrient that allows the body to grow and to heal after injury; a large complex organic compound made up of chains of amino acids. (1,9)

proton. A subatomic particle with a positive electrical charge. (3)

protoplasm (PRO–tuh–plaz–um). A colloidal substance of water, protein, lipid, carbohydrate, and inorganic salts, which is the main component of animal and plant cells. (11)

provitamin. A compound that can be converted to a vitamin by the body. (10)

pure substance. Matter made up of only one kind of material. (3)

puree (pyoo–RAY). To mash food through a strainer or food mill. (12)

quick breads. Bread products that do not need time to rise; usually made with baking powder or baking soda. (14)

radiation (ray–dee–AY–shun). The transfer of energy through space in the form of waves. (20)

radiation absorbed dose (rad). The unit that measures the amount of radiation energy absorbed by living tissue. (20)

rancid (RAN–sid). Having an unpleasant flavor, which develops during the oxidation of fat. (8)

raw milk. Milk that is unpasteurized. (16)

raw–pack. A canning method in which uncooked food is placed in a container that is then filled with boiling water or juice, closed with a lid and ring band, and processed; also called cold–pack. (19)

reactant (ree–AK–tunt). An element or compound present at the start of a chemical reaction. (3)

Recommended Dietary Allowances (RDA). Levels of protein, vitamins, and minerals suggested for good health. (1)

reconstitution (ree–kahn–stih–TOO–shun). Restoring to a former condition by adding water; also called rehydration. (18)

rehydration. (ree–hy–DRAY–shun). Replacing water previously removed in dehydration; also called reconstitution. (18)

residual. The matter remaining after a chemical or physical process; also called a residue. (17)

residue. The matter remaining after a chemical or physical process; also called a residual. (17)

restoration. The process of adding nutrients that were lost in processing to a food until it reaches its original nutritional value. (21)

retinol (RET–un–awl). The active form of vitamin A in food. (10)

retort. A huge pressure canner used commercially. (19)

retort canning. A commercial canning method that uses huge pressure canners called retorts. (19)

retrogradation (reh–tro–gray–DAY–shun). The ability of a starch to thicken as it cools. (7)

riboflavin (RY–bo–flay–vin). A major B vitamin, also called vitamin B_2. (10)

rickets. The vitamin D deficiency disease in children. (10)

ring stand. A device used with iron rings or clamps to hold equipment. (1)

saccharide (SAK–uh–ride). A sugar. (7)

saccharin. An artificial calorie–free sweetener. (21)

Salmonella (sal–muh–NEL–uh). A pathogenic bacteria found in raw food. (17)

salmonellosis (sal–muh–nel–OH–sis). The most common food infection; caused by *Salmonella* bacteria. (17)

salt. A compound formed when metallic and nonmetallic elements form ionic bonds. (3)

saturated fat. A fat in which all the bonds between the carbon atoms are single bonds so the molecule contains the maximum number of hydrogen atoms. (8)

saturated solution. A solution that contains all the solute it can possibly hold at a specific temperature. (13)

scurvy. A disease caused by a lack of vitamin C. (10)

semipermeable (sem–ee–PUR–me–uh–bul). Allowing varying amounts of certain substances to pass through, as with a membrane. (11)

sensory characteristics. The qualities of a food identified by the senses, such as appearance, odor, taste, mouthfeel, and sound. (2)

sensory evaluation. The scientific testing of food using the human senses of sight, smell, taste, touch, and hearing. (2)

sensory evaluation panel. A group of people who evaluate food samples. (2)

serum protein. Another name for whey protein, one of the main proteins found in milk. (16)

shelf life. The amount of time a food product can be safely stored before deteriorating. (16)

simple carbohydrate. Another term for a monosaccharide or a disaccharide. (7)

single–acting baking powder. A leavening agent that releases carbon dioxide as soon as liquid is added to it. (14)

single bond. A covalent bond in which each atom donates one electron to form the bond. (8)

skim milk. Fluid milk that has had all the fat removed. (16)

smoking point. The temperature at which a fat produces smoke. (8)

soft water. Water that does not contain metal ions. (6)

sol. A fluid thickened starch mixture. (7)

solid. Matter with a definite shape and a definite volume. (3)

solidification point. The temperature at which a melted fat regains its original firmness. (8)

solubility (sahl–yuh–BILL–uh–tee). The maximum amount of solute that can be dissolved in a definite amount of solvent at a specific temperature. (6)

soluble. Able to be dissolved. (6)

solute (SAHL–yoot). The substance that is dissolved in a solution. (6)

solution. A homogeneous mixture in which one substance is dissolved in another. (3)

solvent (SAHL–vunt). The substance that dissolves another substance to form a solution. (6)

sorbitol (SORE–buh–tahl). A sugar alcohol that is only half as sweet as sucrose and does not metabolize as well. (21)

specific heat. The energy needed to raise the temperature of 1 g of a substance 1°C. (4)

spore. A microorganism in a dormant, resting, or inactive state. (17)

stabilizer. A substance that can keep a compound, mixture, or solution from changing its form or chemical nature. (21)

standard atmospheric pressure. The pressure of the air at sea level on a clear day. (6)

Staphylococcus aureus (STAF–uh–lo–kahk–us OR–ee–us). A bacteria that causes a food intoxication. (17)

starch. A carbohydrate made from ten or more monosaccharides chemically chained together. (7)

starter. A controlled bacterial population; also called a culture. (16)

steam blanching. Placing food in a perforated basket over boiling water. (18)

subatomic particle. A small part of an atom, such as a proton, neutron, or electron. (3)

sublimation (sub–luh–MAY–shun). A process in which molecules change from the solid phase of matter directly into the gas phase. (6)

subscript. A small number written next to and slightly below a chemical symbol to indicate how many atoms of an element are found in a molecule. (3)

substrate. The substance with which an enzyme reacts. (12)

sucrase (SOO–krase). An enzyme used in the hydrolysis of sucrose; also called invertase. (7)

sucrose (SOO–krohs). Table sugar, a disaccharide from sugar cane or sugar beets. (7)

sugar. A sweet crystalline carbohydrate. (7)

sulfiting. A pretreatment method in which food is soaked in a sodium bisulfite or sodium metabisulfite solution prior to dehydration. (18)

sulfuring. A pretreatment method in which food is exposed to fumes from burning sulfur prior to dehydration. (18)

supersaturated (SOO–pur–SACH–uh–ray–tud). Containing more dissolved solute at a given temperature than is normal. (7)

superscript. A small letter, number, or symbol written above and to the side of another. (5)

surface tension. A property of liquids in which the molecules at the surface of the liquid move closer together, causing the liquid to behave as if it had a skin; occurs because the molecules at the surface are attracted toward the other molecules within the liquid. (13)

symbol. A one– or two–letter abbreviation used to represent the name of a chemical element. (3)

syneresis (suh–NEHR–uh–sis). The leakage or separation of fluids from a starch paste or other gel. (7)

syrup blanching. A pretreatment method in which food is soaked in a hot solution of sugar, corn syrup, and water prior to dehydration. (18)

taste blind. Unable to distinguish between the flavors of some foods. (2)

taste buds. Sensory organs located on various parts of the tongue, which are involved in identifying flavors. (2)

temperature. A measure of molecular motion. (4)

temporarily hard water. Water in which metal ions are present as dissolved bicarbonates. (6)

test tube. A laboratory container used to hold a small quantity of solid or liquid. (1)

test tube brush. A brush used for washing out test tubes or other narrow pieces of equipment. (1)

test tube rack. A device to support several test tubes. (1)

thermometer. An instrument used to determine the temperature of substances. (1)

thiamin (THIGH–uh–min). A major B vitamin, also called vitamin B_1. (10)

threonine (THREE–uh–neen). An essential amino acid. (9)

titration (ty–TRAY–shun). A way to find the concentration of one substance by using a known amount and concentration of another substance. (5)

tocopherol (toe–KAHF–uh–rawl). Vitamin E. (10)

toxin (TAHK–sin). A poisonous substance that has a protein structure. (9)

trace minerals. Minerals needed by the body in amounts of 0.01 g or less each day. (10)

translucent (tranz–LOO–sunt). Partly transparent. (15)

Trichinella spiralis (trih–kuh–NEL–uh spuh–RAL–is). A parasite found in raw pork. (17)

triglycerides (try–GLISS–uh–rides). A major class of food lipids; compounds made up of glycerol and three fatty acids. (8)

tryptophan (TRIP–tuh–fan). An essential amino acid. (9)

Tyndall effect. The ability to see the path of light as it passes through a colloidal dispersion. (13)

UHT milk. Milk that has been pasteurized at ultra–high temperatures for a short period of time to kill bacteria and to increase shelf life. (16)

unsaturated fat. A fat that has a double bond between carbon atoms, thus lacking the maximum number of hydrogen atoms. (8)

unsaturated solution. A solution that contains less solute that it can possibly hold at a given temperature. (13)

valine (VA–leen). An essential amino acid. (9)

vaporization (vay–pur–ih–ZAY–shun). The process in which a liquid changes to a gas. (3)

variable. A factor being tested in an experiment. (22)

viscosity (vis–KAHS–uh–tee). The thickness of a substance; the resistance to flow. (7)

vitamin. An essential nutrient; a complex organic substance vital to life that is needed in very small amounts. (1,10)

volatile (VALL–uh–till). Easily evaporated. (2)

volume. The amount of space material occupies. (1)

voluntary activity. Physical actions and movements for which energy is needed. (11)

warm–blooded. Maintaining a relatively constant internal body temperature. (11)

water. An essential nutrient. (1)

water–bath processing. A method of processing canned food in which containers of food are covered with boiling water and heated to kill harmful microorganisms. (19)

water displacement. A method of measuring the volume of an irregular object by finding out how much water it takes the place of. (3)

water–soluble vitamin. A vitamin that will dissolve in water and so is stored in the body in small amounts, if at all. (10)

weight. The gravitational attraction between an object and the earth. (1)

whey. One of the two main proteins found in milk. (16)

whole milk. Fluid milk that contains a minimum of 3.5 percent milk fat. (16)

yeast. A one–celled plant that causes food spoilage; also works as a leavening agent through the fermentation process. (5,14)

yield arrow. The arrow in a chemical equation that shows that a chemical reaction takes place. (3)

INDEX

CREDITS

American Heart Association: 140
American Institute of Baking: 233
Bolle, Frank: 16, 44, 53, 67, 73, 75, 103, 113, 116, 162, 197, 239, 258
California Raisin Advisory Board: 295
Centers for Disease Control, Atlanta, GA: 279, 280
Coffee Development Group/ICO Promotion Fund: 42
Custom Medical Stock Photo: 164, 167
Gangloff, Bob: 23, 25, 26, 37, 42, 52, 54, 56, 57, 58, 60, 69, 70, 71, 72, 81, 82, 85, 87, 88, 99, 102, 105, 106, 114, 116, 119, 124, 125, 140, 147, 148, 149, 152, 163, 170, 179, 180, 182, 197, 198, 199, 200, 203, 213, 215, 216, 218, 219, 243, 256, 264, 275, 281, 296, 305, 311, 314, 325, 356
Garvin, Ann: 12, 15, 18, 19, 24, 27, 28, 32, 33, 35, 36, 37, 39, 41, 43, 49, 50, 51, 55, 59, 60, 71, 72, 73, 83, 84, 87, 90, 91, 96, 101, 104, 106, 113, 114, 115, 119, 120, 121, 122, 125, 132, 133, 134, 135, 136, 137, 139, 148, 149, 150, 151, 153, 154, 161, 163, 164, 168, 169, 170, 186, 193, 194, 198, 202, 203, 204, 205, 211, 212, 215, 217, 218, 220, 225, 226, 227, 228, 229, 230, 232, 239, 240, 241, 242, 244, 245, 246, 247, 249, 255, 256, 257, 259, 262, 263, 264, 265, 266, 267, 272, 275, 276, 279, 280, 283, 285, 292, 293, 294, 295, 296, 297, 298, 305, 306, 307, 308, 309, 312, 313, 314, 320, 321, 323, 326, 327, 328, 335, 336, 337, 338, 339, 340, 341, 343, 349, 350, 357, 358, 359, 360, 367
Goeller, Jonne: 31, 45, 46, 62, 64, 77, 78, 92, 94, 108, 110, 126, 142, 144, 156, 158, 172, 174, 188, 190, 206, 208, 221, 222, 235, 236, 251, 252, 268, 270, 287, 288, 300, 302, 315, 316, 330, 332, 344, 346, 361, 362
Illinois Farm Bureau: 16, 278, 367
Impact Communications: 15, 19, 20, 21, 22, 29, 38, 49, 67, 88, 100, 106, 117, 138, 165, 166, 168, 169, 170, 179, 181, 182, 184, 185, 186, 200, 217, 241, 243, 255, 258, 259, 260, 265, 276, 277, 281, 282, 306, 310, 312, 320, 323, 343, 353, 354, 366, 369, 371, 372
National Aeronautics and Space Administration: 329
National Food Processors Association: 18, 284, 310, 343, 349
Oregon Freeze Dry: 322, 354, 366
Sabella, John and Associates: 368
Southern Illinois University Medical Center: 91
United States Department of Agriculture: 283
Walters, Gary and Associates: Cover, 2-3
Wine Institute: 248